slow wine

A YEAR IN THE LIFE OF ITALY'S VINEYARDS AND WINES

Slow Food Editore

slow wine 2015

A YEAR IN THE LIFE OF ITALY'S VINEYARDS AND WINES

Italian edition: Slow Wine 2015, Storie di vita, vigne, vini in Italia

Editors: Giancarlo Gariglio, Fabio Giavedoni

Deputy editors: Paolo Camozzi, Jonathan Gebser, Davide Panzieri, Fabio Pracchia

Editorial assistants: Alice Pierdomenico, Martina Terruzzi

Chief contributors: Francesco Abate, Davide Acerra, Richard Baudains, Alessia Benini, Francesca Bidasio degli Imberti, Gian Paolo Ciancabilla, Savio Del Bianco, Alessandra Etzo, Andrea Fontana, Stefano Ferrari, Fausto Ferroni, Vito Lacerenza, Maria Grazia Melegari, Francesco Muci, Luciano Pignataro, Francesco Quercetti, Diego Soracco, Fabio Turchetti, Maurizio Valeriani, Valentina Vercelli, Simone Zoli

Contributors: Marina Alaimo, Andrea Aldrighetti, Alberto Alfano, Maurizio Amoroso, Adriano Anglani, Stefano Asaro, Artemio Assiri, Bruno Bacci, Emidio Bachetti, Alessandro Barletta, Gabriele Bartalena, Salvatore Basta, Paolo Battimelli, Claudia Beccato, Marco Bechi, Annarita Beltrame, Nino Bentivegna, Anna Berghella, Lorenzo Berlendis, Michele Bertero, Carlo Bertilaccio, Silvia Bigarella, Margherita Bisoglio, Ludovica Bo, Carla Bocchio, Ivan Bon, Giulia Bonetti, Giulio Bonola, Simona Bonsignore, Valerio Borgianelli Spina, Paolo Bortolazzi, Ermanno Bosco Orsi, Nicola Bove, Marco Braganti, Massimo Brucato, Sebastian Burgos, Chiara Cafuri, Marco Cagnetta, Marco Callegari, Tommaso Calosci, Alberto Capasso, Giorgio Cariaggi, Luca Carletto, Giulio Carli, Pasquale Carlo, Matteo Carlucci, Sara Carnati, Nadia Castellaccio, Carlo Catani, Sofia Cavassa, Paolo Cesarini, Alessandro Cesca, Fabio Ceste, Roberto Checchetto, Valter Chiabolotti, Lucia Cioffi, Marco Cipolla, Maria Cobo, Paride Cocchi, Pierluigi Cocchini, Enzo Codogno, Filippo Colombo, Lorenzo Colombo, Sara Contu, Francesco Costa, Corinne Cremonini, Giovanni Cucchiara, Claudia Culot, Barbara D'Agapiti, Mario D'Alesio, Alice Deboli, Marco Dell'Era, Elisa De Nardo, Annamaria D'Eusanio, Emanuele De Vittoris, Massimo Di Cintio, Gianni Di Mattia, Giulio Di Sabato, Livio Di Sante, Alessandra Disnan, Sonia Donati, Alberto Farinasso, Luigi Fenoglio, Paolo Ferrarini, Lapo Ferrini, Daniela Filippi, Piero Fiorentini, Alessandro Foggi, Fabio Franzini, Mario Freda, Fabio Fusina, Andrea Gaggero, Sonia Gambino, Pietro Garibbo, Roberto Gazzola, Francesco Ghiglione, Andrea Ghisolfi, Federico Giovannone, Francesca Gori, Martina Graglia, Danilo Gramegna, Davide Grimaldi, Mauro Guastapaglia, Matteo Guidorizzi, Susan Hedblad, Karin Huber, Sandra Ianni, Marcello Ingrassia, Barbara Iuan, Francesco Paolo Lauriola, Gianpiero Laviano, Sante Laviola, Francesco Lazzarino, Riccardo Liopi, Francesca Litta, Cristiana Locci, Patrizia Loiola, Silvio Magni, Carmelo Maiorca, Benedetta Malvisi, Andrea Manfrin, Michele Marangio, Filippo Marchi, Michele Marchi, Lanfranco Mariotti, Sara Marte, Franco Martino, Mino Martucci, Mirco Masera, Daniele Massa, Patrizio Mastrocola, Silvano Mattedi, Lorenzo Marziali, Pierluca Masciocchi Monica Mastino, Valentina Masuelli, Giacomo Mazzavillani, Tommaso Mazzocca, Paolo Mazzola, Marco Meistro, Alberto Meneghel, Teresa Mincione,

Marco Minetto, Andrea Montanaro, Francesca Monticone, Francesco Motta, Gaia Muci, Pierfrancesco Multari, Nicola Nebbia, Giovanni Norese, Paolo Nozza, Gianmarco Nulli Gennari, Isabel Oberlin, Gabriel Olivieri, Daniele Parri, Giovanni Pastorino, Marco Peluso, Gianluca Pepe, Alice Pettenò, Peppino Placentino, Giorgio Picco, Adriana Pieroni, David Pieroni, Alessandra Piubello, Sonia Politi, Giuseppe Pollio, Antonio Previdi, Salvatore Pulimeno, Enrico Radicchi, Giancarlo Rafele, Elena Righini, Sara Rocutto, Giancarlo Rolandi, Daniele Romanin, Claudio Romano, Stefano Ronconi, Adriano Rossi, Francesco Rossi, Camilla Rostin, Andrea Russo, Giancarlo Russo, Susan Russo, Luisa Sala, Mauro Scarato, Maria Teresa Scarpato, Marco Schiavello, Vincenzo Scivetti, Perla Scotto, Gregorio Sergi, Eugenio Signoroni, Maurizio Silvestri, Giorgia Soriano, Benedetto Squicciarini, Maurizio Stagnitto, Enrico Tacchi, Riccardo Taliano, Salvatore Taronno, Stefano Tonanni, Lello Tornatore, Giulia Tramis, Silvia Tropea Montagnosi, Verena Unterholzner, Franco Utili, Andrea Vannelli, Federico Varazi, Laura Vescul, Riccardo Vendrame, Stefania Verna, Teodoro Viola, Alessandra Virno, Michele Vitali, Massimo Volpari, Andrea Zoccheddu, Andrea Zucchetti, Chiara Zucchetti

Italian editing: Tiziano Gaia, Bianca Minerdo, Valentina Vercelli

Translation editor: John Irving

Translation: John Irving, Carla Ranicki

Art director: Fabio Cremonesi

Graphics: Francesco Perona

Maps: Touring Editore

Printed December 2014
by G. Canale & C. SpA, Borgaro Torinese (Turin) ITALY

Slow Food Editore srl © 2014
All rights reserved under copyright law

Slow Food® Editore srl
Via della Mendicità Istruita, 45 - 12042 Bra (Cn)
Tel. 0172 419611 - Fax 0172 411218

Website: www.slowine.it - www.slowfood.it

Editor in chief: Marco Bolasco

Managing editor: Chiara Cauda

ISBN 978-888499-370-0

SWITZERLAND

AUSTRIA

SLOVENIA

FRANCE

VALLE D'AOSTA

PIEDMONT

LOMBARDY

ALTO ADIGE

TRENTINO

FRIULI
VENEZIA
GIULIA

VENETO

LIGURIA

EMILIA-ROMAGNA

TUSCANY

MARCHE

UMBRIA

LAZIO

ABRUZZO

MOLISE

CAMPANIA

PUGLIA

BASILICATA

SARDINIA

CALABRIA

SICILY

Contents

Introduction

The last five years have gone by in a flash—for us at *Slow Wine* and for you, the reader. Two phenomena in particular have marked this period, one relating to farming, the other to sales. Let's begin with the first. In 2010 the guide listed 450 wineries that were already organic or in the process of being converted to organics. In the 2015 edition the number has risen to 590, almost one cellar out of every three reviewed. An incredible increase that has affected the whole Italian peninsula. Even zones previously dubious about adopting sustainable practices, especially in Northern Italy, are now embracing them with conviction and enthusiasm. The phenomenon has made winegrowers change their perspective and they have now switched their attention from cellar to vineyard, the real protagonist of the "green revolution," once and for all. We have see this in the course of our winery tours: in 2011 when we asked producers to show us their vine rows first and their barrels and vats after, they would look at us with an air almost of bemusement. Now it's they who remind us with expressions that seem to say, "Let's get out into the vineyards! What are we waiting for?" And we often find them waiting at the door holding a pair of wellington boots for us ... The second phenomenon regards the increased weight of exports on winery balance sheets. In 2010 Italy was exporting fewer than four billion euros' worth of wine, now the figure has increased by 35% and is well in excess of five billion (*source*: Istat). For upscale wineries, the increase is even higher. The two phenomena described are intertwined: true, the desire for clean farming is born of producers' needs, but it can't be denied either that the trend has been partly induced by international customers no longer prepared to to take a winemaker's word for the naturalness of his or her products. In other words, our producers grasped the change that was taking place; they cottoned on to it and acted accordingly and promptly. *Carpe diem*? They seized the moment, not the day. And we have done the same. Five years ago Slow Food detected that the wine world was going in a new direction and needed a voice to extol the efforts being made by winegrowers. We followed our conviction and broke with the past—our own past—to create a guide with a single credo: "good, clean and fair." In the last few years we have grown slowly but surely, and the 2015 edition has added a new string to its bow which the attentive reader will have noted on the cover of the book. We are referring to the collaboration we have entered into with Fisar, the Italian Federation of Sommelier and Restaurateurs, which has adopted *Slow Wine 2015* as an official text for its members. The partnership heralds the birth of the largest community of wine lovers in Italy and will act as a driving force for the cultural promotion of Italian wine worldwide. As the American poet Walt Whitman wrote, "That the powerful play goes on, and you may contribute a verse." That's how we feel about the last five years in your company.

Giancarlo Gariglio and Fabio Giavedoni

Friulano & friends

Identity Card

Name

FRIULANO
former Tocai

Place of birth
Friuli Venezia Giulia - Italy

Year of birth
In 2008 the Tocai wine changes its name to "Friulano"

Distinguishing marks
A fine and delicate white wine, elegant, balanced and with a rich structure

Sipping
Friuli Venezia Giulia

ersa REGIONE AUTONOMA FRIULI VENEZIA GIULIA
Agenzia regionale per lo sviluppo rurale

with funds from:

MINISTERO DELLE POLITICHE
AGRICOLE ALIMENTARI
E FORESTALI

Ferrarelle *spa*

is a 100% Italian company, owned by LGR Holding SpA, which bottles Ferrarelle, Vitasnella, Boario, Natia and Santagata mineral waters and is the exclusive distributor in Italy for Evian.

It employs around 350 people and has three strategic units: the sales, marketing and commercial offices in Milan; Darfo Boario Terme (Brescia), home to the Boario and Vitas springs; the administrative and operational headquarters in Riardo (Caserta), also home to the Parco Sorgenti where the Fondo Ambiente Italiano protecting Ferrarelle, Santagata and Natia springs and open the public thanks to the company's cooperation with Fondo Ambiente Italiano*. On the international market, it operates in over 50 countries thanks to exports of Ferrarelle, the first and only mineral water certified as having natural effervescence, and still Natia, where it has gained a foothold in particular in delicatessens, top hotels and restaurants. Ferrarelle SpA ensures its consumers products of excellence thanks to high standards in terms of quality and safety and measures that respect and safeguard the environment: it carries out 615 analytical tests right along the water production chain from the source to the bottle; it has a photovoltaic system including 5000 solar panels producing 1 MW and modern bottling lines that have permitted a reduction in the quantity of packaging material; it recycles more than 90% of discarded production materials.

88 hectares of land in its Parco Sorgenti in Riardo have been given over to organic cultivation for the production of extra virgin olive oil, four varieties of honey and four kinds of artisan durum-wheat pasta, produced and marketed by the farming company Masseria delle Sorgenti Ferrarelle Srl.

The company also works in partnership with the most important Italian institutions in the world of art, culture and science: Teatro alla Scala, Fondo Ambiente Italiano and Fondazione Telethon.

* Usually referred to in English as the Italian National Trust.

Ferrarelle S.p.A. Via Ripamonti, 101 - 20141 Milano **Ph.** +39 02574608
export@ferrarelle.it
ferrarelle.com
Follow us

LEARN TO DRINK ITALIANO

How to read the guide

Winery:

◎⟋ snail
symbol awarded to a winery that we particularly like for the way it interprets Slow Food values (sensory perceptions, territory, environment, identity) and also offers good value for money.

▌ bottle
symbol awarded to wineries whose bottles presented excellent average quality at our tastings.

€ coin
symbol awarded to wineries whose bottles are good value for money.

Wines:

slow wine SLOW WINE
bottles of outstanding sensory quality, capable of condensing in the glass territory-related values such as history and identity, as well as offering good value for money.

Great Wine
the finest bottles from the sensory point of view.

Everyday Wine
bottles that offer excellent value for money with a retail price of €10 or under.

Welcome:
⬮ pot
A cellar which, either on the premises or in the immediate vicinity, offers food and refreshments.

⌐o key
A cellar which, either on the premises or in the immediate vicinity, offers hospitality.

Promotion:

10% discount
this symbol denotes wineries that offer a 10% discount on purchases to customers who present a copy of *Slow Wine* 2015. The promotion is valid for one year from January 2015 to January 2016.

ac

acres of land, owned or leased, managed and cultivated directly by the winery.

bt

total number of bottles produced by the winery.

○ white wine

⊙ rosé wine

● red wine

General abbreviations:

Cl. ....Classico (Classic)

Et. ....Etichetta (Label)

M. ....Method

        (e.g., M. Cl. = Metodo Classico/Classic Method)

P.R. ....Peduncolo Rosso (Red Bunchstem)

Rip. ....Ripasso

Ris. ....Riserva (Reserve)

Sel. ....Selezione (Selection)

Sup. ......Superiore (Superior)

V.T. ....Vendemmia Tardiva (Late Harvest)

**Geographical abbreviations
(names of DOCs and DOCGs):**

A.A. ....Alto Adige

C.B. ....Colli Bolognesi

COF ......Colli Orientali del Friuli

C.P. ....Colli Piacentini

O.P. ....Oltrepò Pavese

FERTILIZERS

PLANT PROTECTION

WEED CONTROL

YEASTS

GRAPES

CERTIFICATION

The data in the box on viticultural and enological practices were supplied directly by the wineries during our visits.

Glossary

FERTILIZERS

Organic-minerals
Obtained from the blending or reaction of one or more organic fertilizers with one or more parts of simple mineral fertilizer or compound, organo-minerals are halfway between organic fertilizers, with respect to which they have more nutritional elements, and mineral fertilizers, with respect to which they are more efficient. Nitrogen and phosphorus must come at least in part from organic fertilizers, while potassium and the remaining parts of nitrogen and phosphorus must derive from the mineral part.

Minerals
Fertilizers obtained from mineral compounds. Most of these products are made by the extractive and chemical industries, hence mineral fertilizers are largely known as chemical fertilizers. Since they do not contain carbon, they are defined by their principal component. Hence, phosphorus, nitrogen, potassium fertilizers and so on.

Manure
Manure is fundamental in any type of agriculture. It is an organic fertilizer which permits improvements to the physical and chemical characteristics of the soil. From the physical point of view, it acts as a soil improver, enriching the mechanical properties of the soil. From the chemical point of view, it provides precious substances for the fertility of the soil. The characteristics of a manure vary according to the animal it comes from.

Compost
Compost is made from the decomposition of a mixture of organic substances, residues from pruning, left-over food, manure and sewage. Fundamental agents are oxygen and the balance between the chemical agents present in the matter as it transforms. The action of micro and macro-organisms takes place in special conditions and tends to form a dark, damp mass of matter that is valuable for agriculture. Its use with the addition of organic substance improves the structure of the soil and the availability of nutritional elements. As an organic activator, compost also improves the biodiversity of micro-flora in the soil.

Biodynamic preparations
Agricultural actions designed to improve the physical and chemical peculiarities of the soil and vegetation in biodynamic vineyard management. There are basically two types of preparation: sprays and composts, both used in precisely defined quantities. The two main sprays are: 500, or horn manure, which develops the humus in the soil, and 501, or horn silica, which aids photosynthesis. Compost preparations are used to enrich the organic substances to be spread over the soil. Compost made with precisely defined vegetable and animal elements is a precious fertilizer.

Green manure
An agronomic practice whereby specific crops are ploughed under the soil to maintain and improve its fertility. Its many results include: increase in the amount of organic matter in the soil; suppression of soil erosion; preservation of the soil's nitrogen component. Especially important are leguminous green manures, which fix atmospheric nitrogen into the soil.

PLANT PROTECTION

Used to protect plants from the attack of parasites and pathogens, to control the development of weeds and ensure high quality standards for agricultural produce. They may be natural or synthetic and may be marketed only in sealed, tamper-proof wrappers or packages with labels authorized by the Italian Health Ministry bearing the name of the commercial formula and trademark, if any. Other compulsory information includes the primary activity or action performed by the active substance, denominated according to ISO classification, on the target (insecticide, fungicide, weed killer) and the type of formulation (dilutable, powder, emulsionable) with which the product is presented.

Chemicals
This group comprises all products made synthetically.

Copper and sulphur
The most common fungicides, copper against downy mildew, sulphur against powdery mildew. Sulphur presents risks of phytotoxicity in young shoots, especially with high summer temperatures. It may interfere with the fermentation process, especially in the case of early-ripening white grapes. The prolonged use of copper determines a sizeable increase in its levels in the soil, creating ecotoxicological problems for the environment.

Organics
Organic substances, such as milk, infusions and tisanes, are used in organic and biodynamic farming. Their action must be coordinated with a series of other interventions, mostly preventive, disciplined by the agricultural management system adopted.

WEED CONTROL

Weed control is an integral part of vineyard soil management and is designed to prevent weeds from entering into competition with the vine and jeopardizing its development. Chemical weeding is carried out with synthetic products which act by contact (on the visible part of the plant), by transfer (systemic products which attack root and plant) or by residual action (over time they prevent the seed from germinating). Although it damages organic substances in the soil, chemical weeding is now becoming simpler and more effective, safer for the plant and more respectful of the environment. Mechanical weeding uses mechanical actions, such as mowing, to remove weeds. This practice ensures total respect for the environment and is part of organic and biodynamic vineyard management.

YEASTS

Yeasts are responsible for fermentation, the process by which sugar in must is transformed into alcohol (ethanol) and carbon dioxide. Yeasts, known as native or wild or ambient yeasts, are to be found in the bloom of the skins of grapes. Improvements in cellar techniques have made it possible to select strains of yeast capable of responding to the special needs of each producer or to aid native yeasts if they encounter obstacles in this delicate and fundamental phase in the vinification process. On the basis of these requirements, each producer may choose to carry on the fermentation with native yeasts, hence only those of his or her own grapes, or with selected yeasts, when fermentation is performed with yeast strains brought in from the outside. Activating yeasts also exist. These are used with particularly lazy musts or in the case of a stuck fermentation.

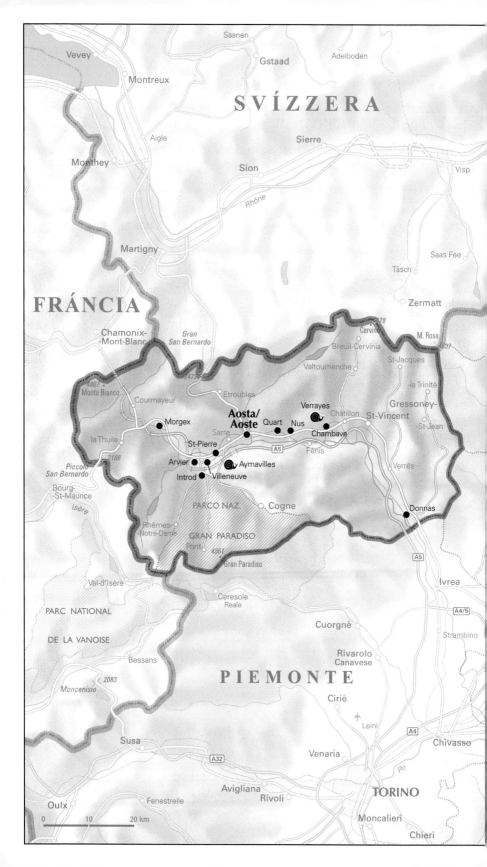

VALLE D'AOSTA

A region with just 1,200 acres of vineyard normally wouldn't even appear in a guide like ours, but this fortunately isn't the case of the Val d'Aosta. Such a low area might almost appear marginal in the overall national panorama, yet the Val d'Aosta is playing more and more in the top flight, sometimes turning in first-rate performances. Such encouraging results have their roots in the past, chiefly in the protection schemes implemented by the regional authority, which funded the cooperative system in the darkest years of Italian winemaking. The late 1950s and 1960s – when only a few winemakers felt they could count on their vines to make a decent living and were tempted to abandon their tough work in the mountains to look for jobs in the city – saw the birth of Cave di Morgex, Cave des Onze Communes, Crotta di Vegneron, Caves Coopératives de Donnas, and CoEnfer. Those were pioneering years when huge efforts were made but monetary rewards were few. Another decisive impulse for the growth of the regional winemaking movement came from the work of the Institut Agricole Régional, which promoted grape varieties with huge potential such as fumin or petite arvine. Then, at the end of the 1980s, we saw the Viticulteur Encaveur association stage an outright revolution. This increasingly numerous group of small producers put themselves on the line by starting to bottle the fruits of their labors in the vineyards directly. It's thanks to the likes of Costantino Charrère, Renato Anselmet and Vincent Grosjean, pioneering independent winemakers, that we can confidently affirm that some of the most interesting whites in Italy are now made in the Val d'Aosta. Red wine, which accounts for the majority of regional production, used to be slightly inferior in terms of quality, but it too is now starting to play a leading role. Special credit for this must go to the native grape fumin, a hard variety to work with both in the vineyard and in the cellar but with enormous potential which has begun to be exploited only recently. Other native varieties such as petit rouge, and international ones such as syrah and pinot noir are also performing increasingly impressively. These are just some of the reasons why we love this region, crossed by the Dora Baltea, where every vine row has been snatched from the rocks and viticulture appears as a mosaic of so many different vineyards, often cultivated as if they were kitchen gardens.

snails 🐌

16	LES CRÊTES
17	LA VRILLE

bottles 🍾

16	LO TRIOLET
17	ANSELMET

AYMAVILLES (AO)

Les Crêtes

Località Villetos, 50
tel. 0165 902274
www.lescretes.it
info@lescretes.it

INTROD (AO)

Lo Triolet

Frazione Junod, 4
tel. 0165 95437
www.lotriolet.vievini.it
lotriolet@vievini.it

---

62 ac - 220,000 bt | **10% discount**

12 ac - 45,000 bt

❝ The years go by but Costantino Charrère continues to be one of the most influential characters on the Italian wine scene. An untiring champion of winemaking in the Val d'Aosta and prove with the facts that, even in a far flung region like this, it's still possible to farm supremely well and produce wines of extraordinary caliber. ❞

PEOPLE - Work on the extension of the cellar and the addition a wonderful new tasting room will soon be terminated. Costantino is helped by his two daughters Elena and Eleonora and his wife Imelda.

VINEYARDS - With a set of vineyards of this importance, magnificently symbolized by the celebrated Coteau La Tour cru, experiments are possible but have to be carried out gradually. This is why the switch to organics and sustainable practices has been only partial to date, but we believe that Costantino Charrère's tenacity will ultimately win through over harsh soil and weather conditions.

WINES - The wines submitted for tasting were on top form. Our favorite was **Valle d'Aosta Petite Arvine 2013** Great Wine (O 27,000 bt), steel-fermented with hints of petrol and lemon zest on the nose and a tangy, almost salty palate of assertive acidity and good supporting alcohol. Just a rung down but very good nonetheless is **Valle d'Aosta Chardonnay 2013** (O 24,000 bt), which offers delicately tropical hints and a delicious, bright palate. On a par is the cask-aged **Valle d'Aosta Fumin 2011** (● 6,500 bt) with its nose of soil and roots and a finish redolent of cocoa powder. The charismatic **Valle d'Aosta Syrah Coteau La Tour 2012** (● 6,000 bt) is sure to age well, but we weren't entirely enamored of the toasty, warm style of **Valle d'Aosta Chardonnay Cuvée Bois 2012** (O 6,000 bt).

PEOPLE - Marco Martin is one of the most talented viticulturalists in the Val d'Aosta. After working with his parents, he took over the reins of the winery in 1993, and has since imposed his ideas, progressively increasing the quality level of the different typologies produced. The new tasting room soon to be annexed to the b&b will put the crown on an entrepreneurial vision aimed at promoting the local area.

VINEYARDS - The pinot grigio plots – of which Lo Triolet is a benchmark not only for the valley but for the rest of Italy too – are mostly in the commune of Introd, at an altitude of almost 3,000 feet. Marco tells us that his grapes ripen perfectly thanks to the position and the optimal microclimate up there.

WINES - Proof of the high quality of this year's range is **Valle d'Aosta Gewürztraminer 2013** (O 4,000 bt), which impressed us with its explosion of aromas on the nose, well-structured palate and clean, mineral finish. **Valle d'Aosta Muscat Petit Grain 2013** (O 3,000 bt) is long with lovely note of spring flowers. **Valle d'Aosta Pinot Noir 2013** (● 5,000 bt) is a bright and breezy red. **Valle d'Aosta Gamay 2013** (● 6,000 bt) is symmetrical and richly fruity. **Valle d'Aosta Pinot Gris 2013** (O 11,000 bt), one of the best of its kind in Italy, once more shows off great class and substance.

> **slow wine** **VALLE D'AOSTA FUMIN 2012** (● 4,000 bt) Who would have expected a white wine expert like Marco to come up with such a wonderful red? It's super-aromatic, elegant and juicy – quite a surprise! Well done!

FERTILIZERS natural manure	**FERTILIZERS** natural manure
PLANT PROTECTION chemical, copper and sulphur	**PLANT PROTECTION** chemical, copper and sulphur
WEED CONTROL chemical, mechanical	**WEED CONTROL** chemical, mechanical
YEASTS selected	**YEASTS** selected
GRAPES 30% bought in	**GRAPES** 20% bought in
CERTIFICATION none	**CERTIFICATION** none

VERRAYES (AO)

La Vrille 🐌

Hameau du Grandzon, 1
tel. 0166 543018
www.lavrille-agritourisme.com
lavrille@gmail.com

3.7 ac - 12,000 bt

66 Making great wine, like running a great restaurant, is a penchant of the soul. Hervé Deguillame and is wife Luciana Neyroz evidently possess that penchant. At their place they have wines with *goût de terroir*, clean agriculture and primary ingredients of the highest quality 99

PEOPLE - La Vrille is a cellar, an osteria and an inn, all rolled into one. Everything is as you'd like it to be, nothing is out of place. It's well worth a visit for an unforgettable experience.

VINEYARDS - In the vineyard everything is done by hand and no mechanization is involved at all. It's very hard work indeed, and the decision to give up chemical weed control makes it harder still for Hervé. A distinctive feature of the La Vrille vineyards is their very old wines, a fact which strongly characterizes the wines.

WINES - **Valle d'Aosta Chambave Muscat 2012** (○ 3,900 bt) has notes of bergamot and lemon zest on the nose and evident, edgy acidity on the palate, but without bitterness on the finish. **Valle d'Aosta Cornalin 2012** (● 1,100 bt) is well judged with a good amount of body. **Valle d'Aosta Gamay 2012** (● 700 bt), characterized by hints of white pepper, is always a joy to drink, while **Valle d'Aosta Chambave 2011** (● petit rouge, vuillermin; 1,800 bt) is a nicely balanced easy-drinker.

slow wine VALLE D'AOSTA CHAMBAVE MUSCAT FLÉTRI 2012 (○ 1,250 bt) A sweet wine of rare beauty and purity on the nose is made with grapes raisined for almost 90 days. With its bouquet of citrus fruit and palate poised between salt and acidity, it's one of the most convincing in its category in Italy.

FERTILIZERS natural manure	
PLANT PROTECTION copper and sulphur	
WEED CONTROL mechanical	
YEASTS selected	
GRAPES 100% estate-grown	
CERTIFICATION none	

VILLENEUVE (AO)

Anselmet

Frazione Vereytaz, 30
tel. 0165 95419
www.maisonanselmet.it
info@maisonanselmet.it

25 ac - 70,000 bt | **10% discount**

PEOPLE - Giorgio Anselmet is a producer who brims over with ideas and, despite his age of fifty, has the curiosity and restlessness of a teenager. He's also an outstandingly gifted vigneron with important experience at Iar in Aosta and La Crotta in Vegneron under his belt. In 1990s he began working with his father Renato, who set up the business in 1975. Now his wife Bruna Cavagnet, has joined the team too.

VINEYARDS - Anselmet owns vineyards in different positions, most of them at St. Pierre, though the 46 parcels extend as far as Chambave, at altitudes that vary from 2,000 to 3,000 feet. Giorgio cultivates all the classic grape varieties of the valley, including French ones, as well as riesling and viognier. Particularly impressive are the vineyards at Torrette, some of which are very old with low bush-trained vines.

WINES - In the cellar Giorgio uses wood masterfully to achieve structure and complexity. At the top of the category **Valle d'Aosta Chardonnay Élevé en Fût de Chêne 2013** Great Wine (○ 4,000 bt) is deep, subtly oaky and salty. The more straightforward, approachable **Valle d'Aosta Chardonnay 2013** (○ 3,000 bt) is terrific too. The excellent **Valle d'Aosta Petit Arvine Élevé en Fût de Chêne 2013** (○ 1,400 bt) is juicy and mineral with exotic fruit. We were struck by the extraordinary elegance, depth, structure and creaminess of **Valle d'Aosta Syrah Henri Élevé en Fût de Chêne 2012** (● 4,000 bt), made the Côtes du Rhône way with syrah and a soupçon of viognier. **Valle d'Aosta Torrette Sup. 2012** (● 15,000 bt) has density and creaminess and is enlivened by a solid salty, mineral finish. **Le Prisionier 2010** (● petit rouge, cornalin, fumin, mayolet; 1,200 bt), made with raisined grapes from the old vineyard, is complex and earthy.

FERTILIZERS manure pellets	
PLANT PROTECTION chemical, copper and sulphur	
WEED CONTROL chemical, mechanical	
YEASTS selected	
GRAPES 15% bought in	
CERTIFICATION none	

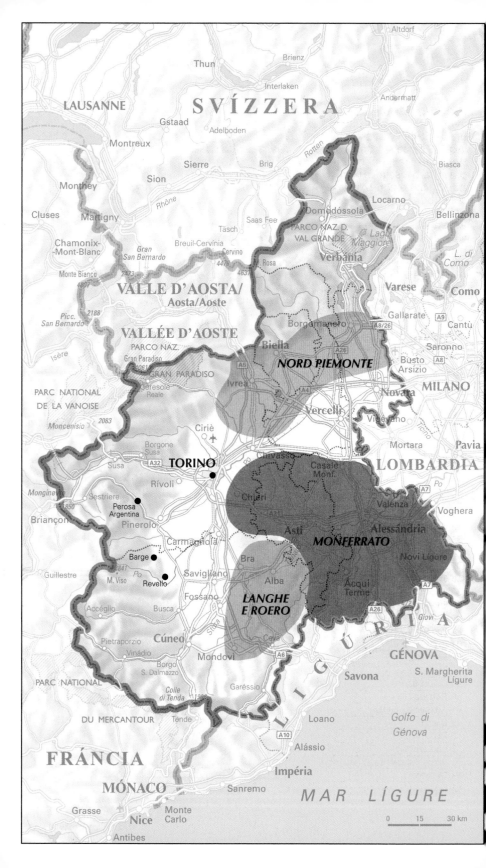

PIEDMONT

Habemus Unesco! After a series of delays and a few puffs of black and gray smoke, the big news for the region this year is the long awaited recognition of the "Wine Landscapes of the Langhe-Roero and Monferrato" as a UNESCO World Heritage Site. We are of course delighted and we hope that concern for the landscape and sustainability will grow apace with the great quality of wine, partly a consequence of a sequence of growing years that have favored, alternately, nebbiolo, barbera, dolcetto and the many other grape varieties of this splendid region. As far as Barolo is concerned, 2010 will be remembered not only as a superlative vintage, with racy, solid, stylish, deep wines, but also as a year of sensational success on overseas markets, especially in the USA. 2011 was a warmer vintage but nonetheless spawned excellent Barbarescos and, even more so, Barberas. Moscato d'Asti continues to perform well, despite the odd warning signal (it may be that they're making too much of the stuff), as does Roero Arneis, which was produced in huge quantities in 2013, arguably too huge (with the subsequent recourse to cellar techniques to make the wines richer). Northern Piedmont and the province of Alessandria once more turned out good, sometimes very good wines. Last but not least, we are happy to announce that two women winemakers were awarded the Snail symbol this year: Chiara Boschis and Nicoletta Bocca.

snails 🐌

21	LE PIANE
23	ANTICHI VIGNETI DI CANTALUPO
26	SERAFINO RIVELLA
27	ROAGNA - I PAGLIERI
28	GIACOMO BREZZA & FIGLI
29	E. PIRA & FIGLI - CHIARA BOSCHIS
30	GIUSEPPE RINALDI
30	G.D. VAJRA
31	CASCINA CA' ROSSA
32	BROVIA
33	CAVALLOTTO FRATELLI
34	CASCINA CORTE
35	PECCHENINO
35	SAN FEREOLO
36	ANNA MARIA ABBONA
37	ELIO ALTARE - CASCINA NUOVA
39	CONTERNO FANTINO
40	ELIO GRASSO
41	PIERO BUSSO
42	SOTTIMANO
42	ELVIO COGNO
46	CA' DEL BAIO
46	FIORENZO NADA
47	ALESSANDRIA FRATELLI
49	DACAPO
50	IULI
52	LUIGI SPERTINO
52	VIGNETI MASSA
54	CARUSSIN
55	CASTELLO DI TASSAROLO

bottles 🍷

22	NERVI
23	FAVARO - LE CHIUSURE
25	GIGI BIANCO
26	GAJA
27	BORGOGNO & FIGLI
29	BARTOLO MASCARELLO
31	MALVIRÀ
33	VIETTI
34	CA' VIOLA
36	LA SPINETTA
41	CASTELLO DI NEIVE
43	MOSSIO FRATELLI
43	CASA DI E. MIRAFIORE
44	ETTORE GERMANO
45	GIOVANNI ROSSO
47	G.B. BURLOTTO
53	LA RAIA
54	MARCHESI ALFIERI
55	LA COLOMBERA

coins €

21	PRODUTTORI NEBBIOLO DI CAREMA
25	MARCO E VITTORIO ADRIANO
37	BRANDINI
39	GIACOMO FENOCCHIO
40	GIOVANNI ALMONDO
49	L'ARMANGIA
51	BORGO MARAGLIANO
53	LA GIRONDA

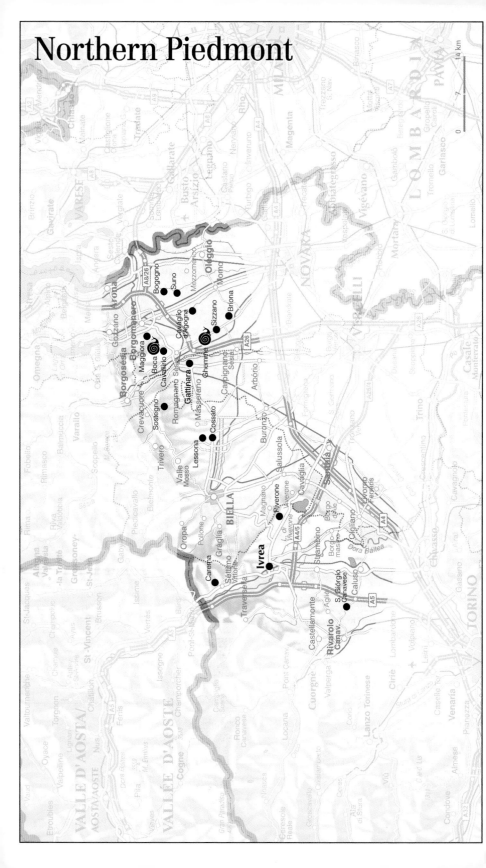

Le Piane

Piazza Matteotti 2,
tel. 348 3354185
www.bocapiane.com
info@bocapiane.com

21 ac - 45,000 bt

❝ Another step forward for the Swiss enthusiast Christoph Künzli, who came to live in Boca in the 1990s. After dedicating himself to rescuing the historical and wine heritage of this small DOC, he is now working with Turin University to develop an experimental vineyard to save malvasia di Boca and other grapes ❞

PEOPLE - The team in the vineyard is growing. Now it consists of four hard-working employees coordinated by Nicola del Boca.

VINEYARDS - The hillside vineyard in Traversagna has been contour-plowed to extend it by about 5,000 yards. Besides the boca vine rows for the project mentioned above, it also grows nebbiolo, vespolina and croatina, mostly from mass selections of *maggiorina*-trained vines. The vineyard is in a very good, south-facing position and offers a unique view over the Novara area, from which it receives good air circulation (though never icy thanks to the sheltering presence of Monte Fenera). The soil is acid and lean with porphyry of volcanic origin.

WINES - **Colline Novaresi Piane 2011** (● 7,000 bt) contains 90% croatina grapes and has acquired a well-defined identity thanks to a better interpretation of the grape: fleshy and fragrant, it impresses with its solid mid-palate, rhythm, sappiness and mature tannins. **Mimmo 2011** (● nebbiolo, croatina, vespolina; 11,000 bt), Boca's twin brother, has crisp fruit and hints of blossom; it's elegant, symmetrical and sensual. **La Maggiorina 2013** (● 20,000 bt), a blend of all the grapes, is always a good advert for the cellar. A novelty this year is a passito still without a name (○ erbaluce; 400 bt) from the 2011 harvest.

> **slow wine** **BOCA 2010** (● 9,000 bt) Once more a great wine, it has a nose of blood oranges and subtle spices, and follows through dynamically in a filigree of sinuosity, pleasurableness and succulence.

FERTILIZERS natural manure, green manure, humus
PLANT PROTECTION chemical, copper and sulphur, organic
WEED CONTROL mechanical
YEASTS native
GRAPES 15% bought in
CERTIFICATION none

Produttori Nebbiolo di €
Carema

Via Nazionale, 32
tel. 0125 811160
www.caremadoc.it
cantinaproduttori@caremadoc.it

42 ac - 60,000 bt

PEOPLE - A historic cooperative wine cellar that was set up in 1960 and now boasts 63 members, most of whom elderly part-time vinedressers. The history and fame of Carema's wine go back centuries, but to guarantee itself a future it needs to plan ahead for a generational turnover. This is why the cooperative, whose president is Viviano Gassino, would like to take over and revive a number of abandoned vineyards.

VINEYARDS - Carema is a village-cum-vineyard in which vines grow everywhere between the houses and the rocks. It's famous for its "topiary" architectures, which consist of pergolas supported by huge *pilun* (stone and cement columns) resting on a myriad of stone terraces to create heat tanks, fundamental for the ripening of the picotener nebbiolo clone and of the few neyret grapes left. The vines are situated at altitudes that vary from 1,150 to 2,300 feet and the sparse loose, mineral soil among the rocks is morainal in origin.

WINES - Enologist Maurizio Forgia, who has been working here since 2009, has reintroduced long macerations of up to 30 days in large barrels to Carema. This year's range of supple, austere yet enjoyable was splendid and typical Alpine. **Canavese Rosso Parè 2012** (● 3,400 bt) is a minor Carema with a youthful gait, flavor that chafes at the bit, and a minerality that explodes and lines the palate. **Carema Ris. 2010** (● 16,500 bt) is magnetic for the low-key elegance of its bouquet and the weightless energy of its mouthfeel, with lean but biting fiber and strong mineral character. **Canavese Rosato Tournet 2013** (⊙ 2,500 bt) is good, too.

> **slow wine** **CAREMA 2011** (● 30,000 bt) Notes of fruit and jam, articulacy and a good mid-palate, juice and flavor, character and tenacity – a wine that allows the facts to speak for themselves to demonstrate the quality potential of this unique and extraordinary terroir.

FERTILIZERS mineral, natural manure
PLANT PROTECTION chemical, copper and sulphur
WEED CONTROL chemical, mechanical
YEASTS selected
GRAPES 100% estate-grown
CERTIFICATION none

GATTINARA (VC)

Nervi

Corso Vercelli, 117
tel. 0163 833228
www.nervicantine.it
info@nervicantine.it

GATTINARA (VC)

Giancarlo Travaglini

Via delle Vigne, 36
tel. 0163 833588
www.travaglinigattarra.it
info@travaglinigattarra.it

---

40 ac - 120,000 bt

114 ac - 265,000 bt

PEOPLE - Nervi, founded in the early 20th century, is one of Gattinara's historic cellars. After years of financial problems that eroded its prestige, in 2011 it was taken over by four Norwegian partners, among whom Eling Astrup holds the majority interest. Erling, who has been an admirer of Nervi's wines ever since his student years in Milan, intends to respect tradition.

VINEYARDS - The new management has kept on enologist Enrico Fileppo, who has been at Nervi for 30 years, and agronomist Daniele Gilberti. The pretty vineyards include parcels on the best growing land round Gattinara: the splendid natural amphitheater of Molsino, for example, or the renowned Valferana cru, which adds finesse and minerality to the wines.

WINES - The stupendous **Gattinara Molsino 2008** (● 4,000 bt) is juicy and tangy with lovely notes of herbs and blossom and has a long life ahead of it. This year's novelty is **M. Cl. Brut Jefferson 1787** (☉ nebbiolo, uva rara; 1,300 bt), a soft approachable rosé which matures for nine months on the lees. It's named for the American president who passed through in 1787 and praised the local wines as "fizzy, sweet and astringent." **Rosa 2013** (☉ nebbiolo, uva rara; 32,500 bt), made with the drawing-off method, is a simple, immediate rosé with residual sugar that makes it very enjoyable as an aperitif.

> **slow wine** **GATTINARA 2008** (● 29,000 bt) Daint and very, very tangy with delicately spicy notes. A red as old as this and as pleasurable as this at a price like this is a rarity on the Italian wine scene.

PEOPLE - This historic cellar, founded in 1985 by Giancarlo Travaglini and now run by his daughter Cinzia with her husband Massimo Collauto, is a symbol of the denomination. Giancarlo, who has always believed in this terroir and worked it in earnest, deserves credit for letting the world know about the wines of Gattinara. Cinzia's collaborators include enologist Sergio Molino and agronomist Flavio Bera.

VINEYARDS - In the 1960s, Giancarlo Travaglini was the first local winemaker to replace the traditional maggiorino training system, which ensured more quantity and quality, with the Guyot. The vineyards stand at altitudes of 950-1,380 feet and rest on rocky soils rich in porphyry and granite. They stretch over the most important crus: Molsino, Lurghe, Valferana, Ronchi, Permolone, Ucineglio and Sas dei Mariani.

WINES - "We're a traditional cellar but we make wine innovatively," says Cinzia Travaglini. "We use mainly oak barrels and ferment for 15-18 days." **Gattinara Tre Vigne 2009** (● 23,000 bt) is a nice assemblage of grapes from three historic parcels posed between finesse and enjoyability. **Gattinara Ris. 2009** (● 33,000 bt) is tannic and will need time to express itself to the full, whereas **Coste della Sesia Nebbiolo 2012** (● 17,000 bt) comes from a fortunate vintage and offers clear-cut aromas and a well-focused tangy and fresh-tasting palate. **Sogno 2010** (● nebbiolo; 4,000 bt) is made with slightly raisined grapes but preserves freshness despite its weightiness.

> **slow wine** **GATTINARA 2010** (● 180,000 bt) Elegant and terroir-based with decadent notes that amalgamate well with freshness and linearity. The price is very reasonable for a wine of this quality.

FERTILIZERS organic-mineral, natural manure
PLANT PROTECTION chemical, copper and sulphur
WEED CONTROL chemical, mechanical
YEASTS selected
GRAPES 15% bought in, wine bought in
CERTIFICATION none

FERTILIZERS organic-mineral, natural manure
PLANT PROTECTION chemical, copper and sulphur
WEED CONTROL chemical, mechanical
YEASTS selected
GRAPES 100% estate-grown
CERTIFICATION none

Antichi Vigneti di Cantalupo

Via Michelangelo Buonarroti, 5
tel. 0163 840041
www.cantalupo.net
info@cantalupo.net

82 ac - 180,000 bt

66 Alberto Arlunno, who has been managing the winery since the 1980s, descends from a family that has lived in Ghemme since the 16th century. He is the true steward of the denomination and the rebirth of local viticulture 99

PEOPLE - We thoroughly recommend a visit to the winery's lovely cellar. Not only because Arlunno is an inexhaustible mine of information about the history and wine of the area, but also because its possible to buy old vintages of his Ghemme there.

VINEYARDS - Eighty acres of vineyard are scattered over various parcels in some of the most celebrated and best crus in the Ghemme hills, such as Carelle and Breclemae. Terraces have had to be built to cope with the steep slope of the four-acre vineyard above the cellar. The local soil is very unusual, rich as it is in stones and minerals from different geological eras.

WINES - Alberto and his consultant enologist Donato Lanati make elegant, very mineral wines with a sense of place. We were particularly impressed by **Ghemme Cantalupo Anno Primo 2008** (● 15,000 bt). mature, sappy, elegant, bright – a champion in its category. **Ghemme Collis Breclemae 2007** (● 10,000 bt) is full-bodied, velvety and tangy. **Colline Novaresi Agamium 2009** (● 15,000 bt) is a monovarietal nebbiolo with plenty of ripe fruit and a burly palate with soft tannins. **Colline Novaresi Nebbiolo Il Mimo 2013** (☉ 70.000 bt) is an approachable, drinkable wine with enjoyable residual sweetness.

> **slow wine** **GHEMME COLLIS CARELLAE 2008** (● 1,500 bt) A stunning red of extraordinary complexity, a consequence of the unique local soil. Its incredible *goût de terroir* make it ideal for anyone keen to discover the denomination's potential.

FERTILIZERS organic-mineral, natural manure
PLANT PROTECTION chemical, copper and sulphur
WEED CONTROL chemical, mechanical
YEASTS selected
GRAPES 100% estate-grown
CERTIFICATION none

Favaro - Le Chiusure

Strada Chiusure, 1 B
tel. 0125 72606
www.cantinafavaro.it
info@cantinafavaro.it

8.5 ac - 18,000 bt

PEOPLE - A good winery run by a capable close family. Camillo Favaro directs operations in the cellar and on the sales side, while the driving force is his father Benito, who set up the business in 1992, an indefatigable worker out in the vineyard. Completing the team are Camillo's sister, Elena, and her husband Claudio, who farm the red grape vineyards, their brother Nicola Favaro, forever out in the fields, and their mother Rosanna.

VINEYARDS - The Favaro vineyards are near Ivrea, on the so-called "Serra," an incredible and imposing 25-mile sequence of hills of morainal origin. The soil is composed of pebbles, debris from various geological eras, clay and silt. The erbaluce vineyard of Le Chiusure grows round the cellar itself and is as neatly kept as a domestic garden. It was the first to be planted and its vines are trained with the so-called *pergola trentina* system, a variation of the arbor model.

WINES - Camillo has shown once again exactly how his terroir should be interpreted. **Erbaluce di Caluso 13 mesi 2012** (○ 1,220 bt), 50% barrique-fermented and 50% cement-fermented, is improving all the time; it's compact on the nose with oaky, mineral notes and a moderate degree of butteriness. The new **Ros 2012** (● 300 bt) is a monovarietal nebbiolo with deft blossomy and fruity tones and a gutsy, well-articulated palate. **Rossomeraviglia 2012** (● syrah; 300 bt) bowled us over with its steeliness, and the excellent **Freisa F2 2012** (● 750 bt) seduces with grip, weight and elegant tannins.

> **slow wine** **ERBALUCE DI CALUSO LE CHIUSURE 2013** (○ 11,500 bt) We were amazed once again by this white wine and its crystalline hints of fruit and herbs. It engulfs the palate with an energy that leaves the drinker astonished but, above all, satisfied. The palate is markedly acid but also juicy, distinctly salty and long.

FERTILIZERS natural manure, none
PLANT PROTECTION chemical, copper and sulphur
WEED CONTROL mechanical
YEASTS selected
GRAPES 100% estate-grown
CERTIFICATION none

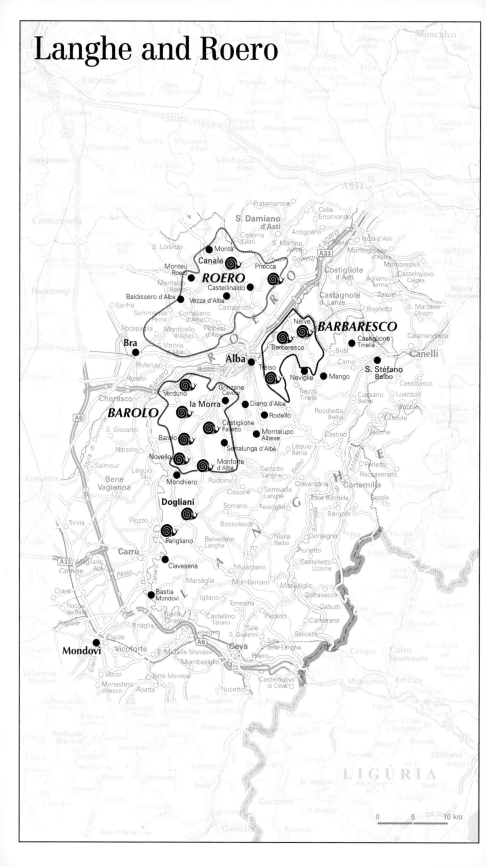
Langhe and Roero

Marco e Vittorio Adriano €

Frazione San Rocco Seno d'Elvio, 13 A
tel. 0173 362294
www.adrianovini.it
info@adrianovini.it

57 ac - 140,000 bt `10% discount`

PEOPLE - Go and see the Adriano brothers in the enchanting valley of San Rocco Seno d'Elvio and you'll see exactly why at least one part of the Langhe district thoroughly deserves to be a UNESCO world heritage site: steep hills here, rolling hills there, well-kept vineyards interspersed with woodland and, lower down, hazelnut groves in a landscape dotted with just a handful of buildings. Marco and Vittorio promote the area in a number of ways, first and foremost through their wines.

VINEYARDS - We were guided round the hills of San Rocco by Vittorio Adriano, who knows everything about this land that he loves. In the hollow known as Rocca dei sette fratelli, it's possible to observe the stratification of the soil and its classic Langhe limestone marls. The Adriano brothers have abandoned weed control not only in their vineyards but also in their hazelnut groves, which cover an area of 20 acres. They also own important vineyards at Neive.

WINES - **Barbaresco Basarin 2011** (● 25,000 bt) has fresh, zesty fruit on the nose and a palate full of verve and sweet tannins. **Barbaresco Sanadaive 2011** (● 15,000 bt) is simple and immediate with ripe fruit and great drinkability. Also quaffable is **Barbera d'Alba Sup. 2012** (● 12,000 bt), which has classic cherry notes on the nose, followed by freshness, brio and sweet fruit. **Ardì 2013** (○ moscato; 8,000 bt) is a dry, very enjoyable version of Moscato. **Moscato d'Asti 2013** (○ 30,000 bt) offers scents of exotic fruit, mild sweetness on the palate and a clean, fruity finish.

slow wine BARBARESCO BASARIN RIS. 2009 (● 5,000 bt) A wine that displays fine symmetry between the sweetness of the fruit, tannic texture and acidity, plus a well-rounded, juicy finish. Quality at a very reasonable price: don't miss it.

FERTILIZERS manure pellets
PLANT PROTECTION chemical, copper and sulphur
WEED CONTROL mechanical
YEASTS selected
GRAPES 100% estate-grown
CERTIFICATION none

Gigi Bianco

Via Torino, 63
tel. 0173 635137 - 339 2225840
www.gigibianco.it
aziendagigibianco@libero.it

6 ac - 18,000 bt

PEOPLE - This small family cellar produces exceptional Langhe wine and is situated under the village's medieval tower. Susanna Bianco, her mother Maria Vittoria, who's an enologist, and her partner Salvatore run the whole show: work in the vineyards, vinification and sales (95% direct, knocking on doors in Barbaresco). You'll be welcomed with contagious good humor in the tasting room, which is full of mementoes of Susanna's charismatic dad Gigi.

VINEYARDS - The Ovello and Pora crus are the core of the cellar's properties. The first grows barbera, planted in 1977 and 1983, and nebbiolos of different ages: young (2011), medium-young (2004), planted by Gigi), and old (1968), planted by grandfather Alfredo Bianco. In the second grow nebbiolo and dolcetto, planted in 1961. Angelo and Sergio Lembo, friends and member growers of the Cantina Produttori, help out with work in the country. The vineyards are managed rationally with a relatively non-interventionist approach.

WINES - Cleanness, expressivity, elegance and land-rootedness make Gigi Bianco's wines a Langhe must. Filtration and fining are banned and sulfur is used, in small amounts, only in crushing and bottling. The drinkability of the wines is high and, released on the market after bottle-aging, they are of very high quality. Waiting for Pora, we enjoyed the grapey, charismatic **Langhe Nebbiolo 2012** (● 1,300 bt). **Langhe Nebbiolo 2010** (● 2.500 bt) is more complex. Excellent too are **Barbera d'Alba 2011** (● 3,000 bt), which is juicy and powerful, and **Dolcetto d'Alba 2013** (● 1,800 bt), which is forthright and fruity.

slow wine BARBARESCO OVELLO 2011 (● 6,000 bt) A sensational red by virtue of an exceptional, balanced nose and a long palate. Eminently quaffable with a very strong sense of place.

FERTILIZERS none
PLANT PROTECTION chemical, copper and sulphur
WEED CONTROL mechanical
YEASTS native
GRAPES 100% estate-grown
CERTIFICATION none

Gaja

Via Torino, 18
tel. 0173 635158
info@gaja.com

---

227 ac - 350,000 bt

PEOPLE - Gaja is more than just a farm (arguably one of the most progressive in terms of vineyard management), it's also a status symbol, a brand and a way of being. Nothing is left to chance: painstaking attention to detail at every stage in production, reflection and action constitute the backbone of the company's philosophy. The close-knit Gaja family (in recent years the ever active Angelo has been flanked by his daughters Rossana and Gaia) are a symbol of Barbaresco worldwide.

VINEYARDS - It takes care for the vineyard and the soil to produce great wines. The company's vineyards – 28 parcels across Barbaresco, Treiso, La Morra and Serralunga – are naturally grassed. Experiments are being made on the sowing of cereals and international consultants are studying the possible use of bioindicator plants. The use of copper has been largely replaced by resistance inducers to give the vines equilibrium.

WINES - Meticulous care in the cellar (supervised by Guido Rivella with Sandro Albarello, a youngster from Barbaresco, under his wing) combined with the very best grapes from the harvest ensures faultless wines. **Barbaresco 2011** Great Wine (● 50,000 bt) is fruity and very soft with just the right amount of tannins. The three crus, from single vineyards in the Barbaresco DOCG zone, are made with 95% nebbiolo and 5% barbera: **Langhe Nebbiolo Costa Russi 2011** (● 12,000 bt) is the readiest of the three; **Langhe Nebbiolo Sorì Tildin 2011** (● 12,000 bt) has structure and depth; **Langhe Nebbiolo Sorì San Lorenzo 2011** (● 12,000 bt) is the most complex. From the Barolo area, La Morra to be precise, comes the stylish **Langhe Nebbiolo Conteisa 2010** (● 15,000 bt), while from Serralunga comes the long, firm **Langhe Nebbiolo Sperss 2010** (● 24,000 bt).

FERTILIZERS natural manure, compost
PLANT PROTECTION copper and sulphur
WEED CONTROL mechanical
YEASTS na
GRAPES 100% estate-grown
CERTIFICATION na

Serafino Rivella

Località Montestefano, 6
tel. 0173 635182

---

5 ac - 11,500 bt

❝ It's always a thrill to meet Teobaldo and Maria. Their kindness, frankness and straight talking come from deep knowledge of their land and its characteristics ❞

PEOPLE - Teobaldo Rivella and his wife Maria Musso run this gorgeous little cellar in Barbaresco and make wines that, year by year, are a perfect mirror of the terroir and its diversity.

VINEYARDS - Even on dismal days, Teobaldo's Montestefano is a sight to behold: the steep slopes, the old vines (the whole vineyard, nebbiolo and dolcetto, was planted in 1963), the insects and the flora (no chemicals here, thank you very much), and the care devoted to pruning and every other farming task make it a veritable jewel, a source of inspiration for other vinedressers. The position and the drainage are perfect.

WINES - The new development in recent years has been the addition of two bottle storage cellars adjacent to the barrel room. Macerations are long and spontaneous and aging takes place in large barrels (one of which old and dark with a chestnut bottom) and in the bottle in conditions of impeccable hygiene – tradition at its best. **Dolcetto d'Alba 2013** (● 3,000 bt) is one of those wines you'd never stop drinking and enjoying, what with its fresh, scented fruity notes, depth and quaffability. Just two wines – but what wines!

> slow wine **BARBARESCO MONTESTEFANO 2010** (● 8,500 bt) Left to rest a year as always, this is, in our view, a true masterpiece. Still austere but deep with nuanced aromas, solid, punchy and lingering on the plate, it ends with gorgeous hints of blossom.

FERTILIZERS manure pellets, natural manure
PLANT PROTECTION copper and sulphur
WEED CONTROL mechanical
YEASTS native
GRAPES 100% estate-grown
CERTIFICATION none

BARBARESCO (CN)

Roagna - I Paglieri 🐌

Località Paglieri, 9
tel. 0173 635109
www.roagna.com
info@roagna.com

BAROLO (CN)

Borgogno & Figli 🍾

Via Gioberti, 1
tel. 0173 56108
www.borgogno.com
info@borgogno.com

---

30 ac - 60,000 bt

42 ac - 130,000 bt | 10% discount |

---

66 Roagna is an indestructible fortress of traditional nebbiolo – inimitable in style, exceptionally long-lasting, exquisite – but also the steward of an increasingly rare farming model, which sees nature not as a servant but as an ally when it comes to safeguarding biodiversity and a legacy of old vineyards of inestimable value 99

PEOPLE - Luca Roagna represents the fifth generation of his family and is ably assisted by his father Alfredo.

VINEYARDS - "I identify a lot with the call of the wild," says Luca as he takes us round the grassed vine rows of Pira, his splendid monopole cru under the new cellar at Castiglione Falletto. Chemicals are banned completely, as are mowing and topping, while only young vines are thinned out. At Roagna the concept of *vieilles vignes* is taken very seriously: the Pira Vecchie Vigne selection, for example, is made with grapes from extraordinary vines planted in 1936, whereas the 1945 vines aren't considered old at all.

WINES - The wines are born and age in wood vats with long submerged-cap macerations. **Barbaresco Pajé Vecchie Vigne 2009** (● 2,000 bt) has a succulent, fleshy palate that enwraps its snappy tannins. From the top of the hill, the best part, hails from **Barbaresco Crichet Pajé 2005** Great Wine (● 1,600 bt), a wine of infinite beauty, deep, very long … pure emotion! The most elegant is the deft but assertive **Barbaresco Asili Vecchie Vigne 2009** (● 1,430 bt). Exuberant, ebullient and energetic, **Barbaresco Montefico Vecchie Vigne 2009** (● 1,500 bt) is made with grapes from the oldest vineyard, planted in 1920. The spicy, earthy **Barolo Pira 2009** (● 7,790 bt) is a classy introduction to **Barolo Pira Vecchie Vigne 2009** (● 1,480 bt), a solid, very deep wine of inebriating linearity that concentrates the essence of Barolo in the glass. And what a glass!

PEOPLE - This historic Barolo winery continues to move at a fast pace. Since it was taken over in 2008 by the Farinetti family, a revolution has taken place. The main building has been restored to its former glory, erasing the architectural disasters of the 1960s. In the cellar, cement vats have reappeared, selected yeasts and weed control have been abandoned and three new crus have been launched. All this thanks to the work of Andrea Farinetti, 25.

VINEYARDS - The minor revolution in the vineyard has involved the elimination of chemical weedkillers and fertilizers and more painstaking work has been done especially on so-called "minor" grapes: dolcetto, barbera and freisa. At least three vineyards command absolute prestige: Cannubi, Fossati and Liste. Thanks to the consultancy of Alberto Grasso, these three pearls have been fully valorized from the agronomic point of view.

WINES - We were spellbound by **Barolo Cannubi 2009** Great Wine (● 6,000 bt), an austere red with hints of tobacco and leather on the nose and warm mouthfeel, very well crafted, long and linear despite the poor growing year – excellent! Only a rung below it are the other two crus, barrel-aged according to tradition: **Barolo Liste 2009** (● 6,000 bt) is earthy and acid and tangy; **Barolo Fossati 2009** (● 6,000 bt) has riper fruit than past versions. Partly thanks to the favorable vintage, **Langhe Nebbiolo No Name 2010** (● 18,000 bt) is magnificent, and is proving more and more to have been something of a brainwave. For Barolo beginners, it could be the right wine to start with. We welcome warmly the terroir-based **Langhe Freisa 2012** (● 4,500 bt), a grape that deserves to be better valorized. **Dolcetto d'Alba 2013** (● 10,000 bt) is enjoyable.

FERTILIZERS none
PLANT PROTECTION copper and sulphur
WEED CONTROL mechanical
YEASTS native
GRAPES 100% estate-grown
CERTIFICATION none

FERTILIZERS natural manure
PLANT PROTECTION chemical, copper and sulphur
WEED CONTROL mechanical
YEASTS native
GRAPES 100% estate-grown
CERTIFICATION none

BAROLO (CN)

Damilano

Via Roma, 31
tel. 0173 56105
www.cantinedamilano.it
info@damilanog.com

130 ac - 320,000 bt

PEOPLE - This large Langa wine company is run by Guido and brothers Mario and Paolo Damilano, who diversify their investments to operate in other product sectors. They have an attractive store in the center of Barolo and their cellar is situated at the foot of the village. Here mostly large barrels are used to age heavyweight local wines. The consultant enologist is Beppe Caviola.

VINEYARDS - An important new development this year was the scaling down of the company's vineyards – especially in the Asti area where the acreage was cut from 170 to 130 – under the supervision of agronomist Gian Piero Romana. In the most prestigious vineyard, I Cannubi, the Damilanos own about 25 acres of land, and other parcels produce the grapes for Barolo Lecinquevigne. They also rent vineyards at Vezza d'Alba, in the Roero district, for their Arneis, and they adopt a conventional viticultural approach.

WINES - **Barolo Cannubi 2010** Great Wine (● 45,000 bt) has elegant aromas with beautifully delicate tannins on the palate and a lingering finish. It's fair to say that this label never fluffs a vintage and is rapidly becoming a Langa classic. **Barolo Lecinquevigne 2010** (● 60,000 bt) has a classic bouquet of rose petals with a hint of wild strawberry and a nicely juicy, weighty palate and composed tannins. Dedicated to Guido's late sister Margherita, **Langhe Nebbiolo Marghe 2012** (● 70,000 bt) has excellent freshness, brio and delicious fruity flesh. **Barbera d'Asti 2012** (● 70,000 bt) has very typical acidity and suggestions of damp soil. **Dolcetto d'Alba 2013** (● 10,000 bt) offers notes of red berries, hints of grass and a bitterish finish, while **Langhe Arneis 2013** (○ 30,000 bt) releases typical notes of apples and pears.

FERTILIZERS	manure pellets
PLANT PROTECTION	chemical, copper and sulphur
WEED CONTROL	chemical, mechanical
YEASTS	selected
GRAPES	100% estate-grown
CERTIFICATION	none

BAROLO (CN)

Giacomo Brezza & Figli

Via Lomondo, 4
tel. 0173 560921
www.brezza.it
brezza@brezza.it

38 ac - 90,000 bt

66 Enzo Brezza is following the organic road with the earnestness, belief and understated passion that have always distinguished this impressive Barolo winery. Besides selling top class wines at reasonable prices, the place gives foreign tourists a positive image of our country as a whole 99

PEOPLE - As of this year. in the cellars that house the large barrels, native yeasts are used even for the limited production of Arneis.

VINEYARDS - Vineyards covered with a special mix of grasses to keep the soil healthy and fertile, increasingly light machinery (quad bikes, for example) to prevent it from compacting, prestigious plots with ideal soil and climate conditions, with more clay at Castellero and sand at Cannubi and the pretty Sarmassa cru – these are the factors that allow Brezza to create land-rooted wines with respect for the balance of nature.

WINES - The Barolos are impeccably traditional in style, the fruit of long macerations at low temperatures. The company's cutting-edge wine **Barolo Sarmassa 2010** (● 8,500 bt) is very stylish but is also packed with telluric power, rich in sweet juice and filled with very fine tannins. **Barolo Cannubi 2010** (● 9,400 bt) is still a little backward but is sure to give great satisfaction in the course of time by virtue of its understated blossomy hints and customary elegance. The exemplary **Barolo 2010** (● 12,400 bt) conflates typicality and graceful tannins, earthiness and plenty of juice. **Langhe Nebbiolo 2013** (● 9,300 bt) is approachable and drinkable, while **Barbera d'Alba 2012** (● 7,000 bt) is elegant and full of verve.

slow wine BAROLO CASTELLERO 2010 (● 5,500 bt) The most compact and structured of the crus, is packed with beautifully ripe fruit. Lip-smacking and land-rooted.

FERTILIZERS	natural manure
PLANT PROTECTION	copper and sulphur
WEED CONTROL	mechanical
YEASTS	native
GRAPES	100% estate-grown
CERTIFICATION	converting to organics

E. Pira & Figli
Chiara Boschis 🐌⤳

Via Vittorio Veneto,1
tel. 0173 56247
www.pira-chiaraboschis.com
info@pira-chiaraboschis.com

21 ac - 35,000 bt   **10% discount**

❝ Chiara Boschis has always made great wines, but now she also wants to change the Langa hills with eco-sustainability schemes and projects to rescue old mountain villages through farming and pastoralism. She's a woman of indomitable spirit ❞

PEOPLE - Solar, positive, passionate and volitive. That's Chiara Boschis and that's how she's been ever since we met her a few yeas ago when she was making her first steps in the Langa wine world. Those were the days when the few women making wine were viewed with diffidence.

VINEYARDS - The Cannubi parcel, like all the winery's other vineyards, received organic certification this year. It's a sight to be seen with its steep slopes, limestone soil with traces of sand and optimal air circulation. The new acquisition in the Conterni district, now part of the Mosconi cru, is a fine vineyard, too. Other parcels at Barolo and Serralunga (Gabutti and Baudana) traditionally produce grapes for Barolo Via Nuova.

WINES - Barbera d'Alba 2012 (● 5,000 bt) has plump fruity pulp and bundles of brio with classic hints of plum and cherry. **Langhe Nebbiolo 2012 (●** 2,500 bt) is a good introduction to the world of Barolo with its blossom and tempting succulence. **Barolo Cannubi 2010 (●** 4,000 bt) is as elegant as ever with notes of fruit on the nose and palate, lively flesh, fine sweet tannins and lingering finish. Our favorite in this star-studded range was the **Barolo Mosconi 2010** Great Wine (● 4,000 bt) whose compact tannins leave sensations of beautifully ripe fruit, remarkable depth and a long finish. **Barolo Via Nuova 2010 (●** 7,000 bt) has great energy, succulence and sweet tannins. **Dolcetto d'Alba 2013 (●** 4,000 bt) is a joy to drink.

FERTILIZERS natural manure, green manure	
PLANT PROTECTION copper and sulphur	
WEED CONTROL mechanical	
YEASTS selected	
GRAPES 100% estate-grown	
CERTIFICATION organic	

Bartolo Mascarello 🍾

Via Roma, 15
tel. 0173 56125

13.5 ac - 33,000 bt

PEOPLE - Bartolo Mascarello occupies a special place in the history of Langa winemaking: his self-designed labels, his manifestoes, his untiring battle to protect the purest essence of Barolo, and, above all, his wines constitute an inestimable heritage. His daughter Maria Teresa has made a brilliant job of carrying on where her father left off; proud and true to traditions (her family's and that of Barolo), she runs this legendary cellar with the selfsame rigor.

VINEYARDS - Cannubi, San Lorenzo and Ruè at Barolo, Rocche dell'Annunziata at La Morra – all top-notch vineyards that come together in the same Barolo. Maria Teresa hasn't let fame go to her head and keeps her feet firmly on the ground: her decision to practice sustainable agriculture without espousing one school or another, is hers and hers alone, taken without any commercial motive whatsoever. Not that she'd need one.

WINES - "Normal," is how Maria Teresa describes her approach to the wine cellar. Today as ever nothing is done or added to the wines that might obfuscate their purest expression of the terroir. The wines are cement-fermented (barring the Barolo, which is fermented in wood vats) and aged in barrels. We were bowled over yet again by **Barolo 2010** Great Wine (● 17,000 bt), with its overwhelming floweriness, burly but refined palate, close-knit and fresh tannins, rare quaffability and elegance. **Dolcetto d'Alba 2013 (●** 5,000 bt) is typical and deft, and punchy with it. **Barbera d'Alba 2012 (●** 5,000 bt) is supple and succulent. The scent-drenched **Langhe Nebbiolo 2012 (●** 2,500 bt) is a wine of aerial lightness and sweet tannins. **Langhe Freisa 2012 (●** 2,000 bt) is nice and earthy with a delightful, lightly sparkling palate.

FERTILIZERS organic-mineral	
PLANT PROTECTION copper and sulphur	
WEED CONTROL mechanical	
YEASTS selected	
GRAPES 100% estate-grown	
CERTIFICATION none	

Giuseppe Rinaldi

Via Monforte, 3
tel. 0173 56156

16 ac - 38,000 bt

❝ A century-old history, a charismatic character like Beppe "Citrico" Rinaldi, a cultivated, perceptive winemaker and a tenacious defender of classic Barolo and a unique, nonpareil company style, immune to fashion and ready to take on time … Despite all this, the Rinaldi legend is still accessible for common mortals (stocks permitting). Not forgetting that the viticulture is exemplary too ❞

PEOPLE - Beppe has been helped by his young daughters Marta and Carlotta for some years now.

VINEYARDS - The vineyards are situated in historically proven growing areas – Cannubi San Lorenzo, Ravera, Brunate and Le Coste – from which Beppe used to produce two labels that we have learned to love (earlier still they provided the grapes for a classic Barolo and a Brunate Riserva). Without going along with predefined currents, sustainable viticulture has been practiced here for years. Recently the soft pruning techniques preached by "Preparatori d'Uva" have been adopted.

WINES - Since it is no longer possible to write the names of two vineyards on the label, this year we find **Barolo Brunate 2010** (● 7,000 bt) with 15% Le Coste (which the law permits): deep and enfolding, it's a tad edgier than usual on the nose. The other three crus end up in **Barolo Tre Tine 2010** (● 9.000 bt) whose complicated, earthy nose preludes a linear palate of marked acidity. The exceptional **Langhe Nebbiolo 2012** (● 7,000 bt) is blossomy and pure, racy and flavorsome. The delicious **Barbera d'Alba 2013** (● 8,000 bt), justly classic, juicy and acid, and the highly palatable **Dolcetto d'Alba 2013** (● 3.700 bt) are worthy representatives of their respective typologies. A rare bird in the Langa zone is the scented bright, fruity **Rosae 2013** (● ruché, 2.500 bt), which has much more understated aromas than comparable wines in the Monferrato.

FERTILIZERS natural manure	
PLANT PROTECTION copper and sulphur	
WEED CONTROL mechanical	
YEASTS native	
GRAPES 100% estate-grown	
CERTIFICATION none	

BAROLO (CN)

G.D. Vajra

Via delle Viole, 25
tel. 0173 56257
www.gdvajra.it
info@gdvajra.it

148 ac - 350,000 bt

❝ This family is continuing in its endeavors to achieve excellence and offer Barolo lovers wines that speak only one language, that of the terroir they're born in ❞

PEOPLE - Milena and Aldo Vaira set out in the mid 1980s. Now their whole family takes an active part in the business, their three children Francesca, Giuseppe and Isidoro first and foremost.

VINEYARDS - For the last few years, besides farming the historic crus of Bricco delle Viole, Fossati, Ravera and Coste di Vergne between Barolo and Novello, the family has also managed the Baudana cellar and its vineyards at Serralunga offering as a "dowry" the magnificent Cerretta cru, which they interpret with their considerable knowhow.

WINES - The range of bottles presented this year was mind-boggling with a number of wines worthy of our various symbols. In the end, we plumped for **Barolo Ravera 2010** Great Wine (● 8,000 bt), which has delicious hints of violet and raspberry tart, and a flavorful, deep, suitably tannic palate. The magnificent **Barolo Bricco delle Viole 2010** (● 16.000 bt) is elegant and vertical. **Barolo Baudana Cerretta 2010** (● 4,000 bt) is, for us, the best version produced to date. And what can we say about **Barolo Albe 2010** (● 50,000 bt)? Just that you won't find a better wine at this price anywhere in Italy. Last of the reds is the unique, unusual **Langhe Freisa Kyè 2011** (● 7,000 bt), a monument to a grape that's slowly disappearing. Last but not least, the splendidly mineral **Langhe Riesling Pètracine 2013** (○ 10,000 bt) should be bought now and buried in the cellar.

FERTILIZERS natural manure, green manure	
PLANT PROTECTION copper and sulphur	
WEED CONTROL chemical, mechanical	
YEASTS selected	
GRAPES 100% estate-grown	
CERTIFICATION none	

CANALE (CN)

Cascina Ca' Rossa 🐌

Località Cascina Ca' Rossa, 56
tel. 0173 98348
www.cascinacarossa.com
angelo.ferrio@gmail.com

32 ac - 80,000 bt

❝ 'I was born in the country and I'll die in the country.' So speaks Angelo Ferrio, a farmer who's proud of his roots and has always moved in the same direction, farming the land and, in recent years, adopting organic methods ❞

PEOPLE - Angelo is now flanked by his son Stefano, 22, who seems to take after his father. Go and visit this splendid family and breathe in the atmosphere, at once old-fashioned and modern, in their pretty red farmhouse.

VINEYARDS - The vineyards of the Roero hills are notoriously steep and, with soil composed mainly of sand, hard to work. This is the case of Mompissano, where Angelo grows nebbiolo and barbera. Audinaggio is an almost vertical wall that looks impossible to cultivate. Other vineyards grow arneis and barbera. As of this year, the seal of organic certification will appear on the bottles.

WINES - **Roero Arneis Merica 2013** (○ 25,000 bt) possesses all the brightness of the vintage and suitably ripe fruit with a finish full of verve. The very drinkable **Barbera d'Alba Mulassa 2012** (● 5,000 bt) matures in large barrels and is succulent and sappy, fleshy and fresh. The inviting **Langhe Nebbiolo 2012** (● 15,000 bt) has measured sweet tannins. **Langhe Nebbiolo 2013** (● 18,000 bt) has also been released; it's elegant with plenty of juice and a graceful floral finish. **Roero Audinaggio 2012** (● 4,000 bt), made from vines planted over 60 years ago, has stylish aromas and, on the palate, shows none of the adverse effects of cask-aging.

slow wine **ROERO MOMPISSANO 2011** (● 6,000 bt) Aged 30 months in wood barrels, a wine of rich ripe fruit, full, succulent flesh and a lip-smacking finish. The best version ever.

FERTILIZERS natural manure
PLANT PROTECTION copper and sulphur
WEED CONTROL mechanical
YEASTS selected, native
GRAPES 100% estate-grown
CERTIFICATION organic

CANALE (CN)

Malvirà 🍾

Località Canova
Case Sparse, 144
tel. 0173 978145
www.malvira.com
malvira@malvira.com

104 ac - 300,000 bt **10% discount**

PEOPLE - It's always the same old story; you get to Malvirà, owned and run by brothers Massimo and Roberto Damonte, and you think: "If only it were a few miles further down the road, it would be a world superstar." Not that it isn't justly famous where it is; its top level wines, in fact, from the Arneises (we don't know many producers who know how to age it so well) to the Roeros, are terroir-based and built to last.

VINEYARDS - The process of conversion to organics is already underway at Malvirà. Knowing how serious the Damonte brothers are and how much they love their land, we have to say we were expecting it. Another welcome piece of news is a Barolo made with grapes from La Morra, in the Boiolo subzone. This year Renesio, the splendid cru for which Arneis may or may not be named, was, if possible, even lovelier than usual, bathed first by rain and then by sunshine. And the same goes for Trinità.

WINES - It's always hard to choose among Malvirà's Nebbiolos. The most forward seems to be **Roero Renesio Ris. 2010** (● 11,000 bt), blossomy and juicy with a nice sweet finish. **Roero Mombeltramo Ris. 2010** (● 8,000 bt) has more weight with close-knit sweet tannins, excellent length and depth. **Barolo 2010** (● 3.700 bt) makes an impressive debut; it has floral aromas, discreet body and plenty of verve on the palate. We were impressed by both Arneises: **Roero Arneis Trinità 2012** (○ 20,000 bt) has reasonably mature fruit, brio and a note of pear on the finish; **Roero Arneis Saglietto 2012** (○ 11,000 bt), half-fermented in wood, offers a note of aniseed on the nose and an agreeably bitterish finish.

slow wine **ROERO TRINITÀ 2010** (● 20,000 bt) A wine that opens with clear-cut red berry fruit aromas and follows up with weight and length. A good leson in the potential of the Roero district.

FERTILIZERS humus
PLANT PROTECTION copper and sulphur
WEED CONTROL mechanical
YEASTS selected
GRAPES 100% estate-grown
CERTIFICATION converting to organics

CANALE (CN)

Marco Porello

Corso Alba, 71
tel. 0173 979324
www.porellovini.it
marcoporello@porellovini.it

CASTIGLIONE FALLETTO (CN)

Brovia

Frazione Garbelletto
Via Alba-Barolo, 54
tel. 0173 62852
www.brovia.net
info@brovia.net

42 ac - 130,000 bt

PEOPLE - Marco Porello is the owner and driving force of this small family winery that began bottling under his grandfather for a number of customers in Turin. As in many other cases, at the time the farm used to grow fruit and raise a few cattle, but today it produces only traditional Roero wines, including an agreeable Favorita.

VINEYARDS - Porello's vineyards are farmed mainly by Marco's mother Enza with a few trusted collaborators. They are situated mostly at Vezza d'Alba and Canale in areas where the soil is very sandy. Recently the cellar also bought 5 acres of vineyard at Guarene. Planted with nebbiolo and barbera grapes, they will be productive at the end of the year. The viticulture is conventional but weed control is now being phased out and plans are underway to switch to organics.

WINES - Roero Torretta 2011 (● 6.000 bt), aged in barrels and mid-size casks, is well-developed and mature with nice fruity flesh, tanginess and an intriguing finish of sour cherry. **Nebbiolo d'Alba 2012** (● 16,000 bt), made partly with grapes earmarked for Torretta, which wasn't produced in this vintage, has fruit and verve with well-poised tannins and a hint of grass on the finish. **Barbera d'Alba Filatura 2012** (● 4,200 bt) has all the freshness typical of the grape, fairly fruity flesh and a pleasantly bitter finish. **Barbera d'Alba Mommiano 2013** (● 12,000 bt) is fresh-tasting and vivacious, fruity and drinkable. We were really taken by the Roero Arneis Camestrì 2013 Everyday Wine (○ 35,000 bt), produced with a very short maceration on the skins, with its sweet fruit and body. **Roero Arneis 2013** (○ 20,000 bt) is typical.

40 ac - 60,000 bt

❝ Virtuous viticulture managed with scrupulousness and passion, wines of great stylistic rigor and exceptional quality, openness to dialogue and simplicity – these are the keys to the success of this magnificent winery, which never ceases to amaze us with its humanity and the quality of its wines ❞

PEOPLE - Cristina and Elena Brovia (who lost their father Giacinto, a Langa legend, this year) and Alex Sanchez, Elena's husband, make up the management team at this magnificent cellar.

VINEYARDS - It's our belief that, initial difficulties notwithstanding, the switch to organics is a natural consequence for Brovia, especially in view of Cristina and Elena's love of the land and their eagerness to take care of its health. The company's crus – from the burly Villero to the refined Rocche and Brea di Serralunga – are at the top of their class. They grow in the old parts of the vineyards, which have an average age of 40 years.

WINES - Barolo Rocche dei Brovia 2010 (● 5,000 bt) comes close to perfection with the exceptional finesse of its tannins, its combination of depth and fluency, its length, its zest and its leisureliness. If anything, **Barolo Villero 2010** Great Wine (● 5,000 bt) is even better: albeit still a little stiff, almost austere, it's nonetheless very assertive on the palate, and its finish is interminable. **Barolo Brea Vigna Ca' Mia 2010** (● 5,000 bt) has all the sweet fruit typical of Serralunga and tight-knit, very juicy tannins followed by an encore of sweet fruit. The only fault of the excellent, thoroughly enjoyable **Barolo Garblet Suè 2010** (● 3,500 bt) is that it has such overwhelming elder brothers! **Barolo 2010** (● 13,000 bt) works well and constitutes a solid, elegant introduction to the world of Barolo. **Barbera d'Alba Sorì del Drago 2012** (● 7,000 bt) is typical and satisfying.

FERTILIZERS organic-mineral, natural manure	**FERTILIZERS** natural manure, green manure
PLANT PROTECTION chemical, copper and sulphur	**PLANT PROTECTION** copper and sulphur
WEED CONTROL mechanical	**WEED CONTROL** mechanical
YEASTS selected	**YEASTS** native
GRAPES 100% estate-grown	**GRAPES** 8% bought in
CERTIFICATION none	**CERTIFICATION** organic

Cavallotto Fratelli

Località Bricco Boschis
Strada Alba-Monforte, 40
tel. 0173 62814
www.cavallotto.com
info@cavallotto.com

---

57 ac - 100,000 bt

❝ A family which combines high-quality winemaking with respect for the environment, carrying on with intelligence and innovative spirit a tradition that makes the Langa hills unique the world over **❞**

PEOPLE - Brothers and sister Alfio, Giuseppe and Laura Cavallotto run their winery, one of the very best in Italy, with commitment and with total dedication. Their classic, deep wines have made the area's fortune.

VINEYARDS - The Cavalottos have taken yet another virtuous choice; after much thought and study, they have, in fact, decided to repudiate the use of copper for plant protection treatments. Last June the Bricco Boschis vineyard treated us to a magnificent spectacle with vines laden with leaves and a light breeze mitigating the heat and keeping molds and fungi at bay. The soil in the valley contains a fair amount of sand and the classic marl of the Langa.

WINES - Barolo Bricco Boschis Vigna San Giuseppe Ris. 2008 (● 13,300 bt) is agile and, at once, punchy and graceful, dense and subtle, though we did notice an uncharacteristic stiffness on the nose. **Barolo Vignolo Ris. 2008** (● 6,600 bt) has sweet, measured fruit, never aggressive tannins and a nicely log finish of freshly mown grass. **Barolo Bricco Boschis 2010** (● 24,500 bt) has notes of rose and licorice on the nose and a tangy, juicy palate with just the right amount of sweetness. **Langhe Nebbiolo 2011** (● 15,000 bt) has a classic floral bouquet and a fleshy, enjoyable palate. **Barbera d'Alba Vigna Cuculo 2011** (● 13,500 bt) is rich and full-bodied with refreshing acidity and juicy, succulent finish. **Dolcetto d'Alba Vigna Scot 2013** (● 13,000 bt) is clear-cut on both nose and palate and nicely supple.

FERTILIZERS green manure
PLANT PROTECTION copper and sulphur
WEED CONTROL mechanical
YEASTS native
GRAPES 100% estate-grown
CERTIFICATION organic

Vietti

Piazza Vittorio Veneto, 5
tel. 0173 62825
www.vietti.com
info@vietti.com

---

85 ac - 250,000 bt **10% discount**

PEOPLE - Stylistic rigor, class and classicism are the distinctive features of the wines of Vietti, one of the oldest and acclaimed maisons, and rightly so, of the Langa zone. Its strong point is its matchless arsenal of vineyards, accrued over decades by farsighted characters such as Mario Vietti and Alfredo Currado. Their philosophy of uncompromising quality is being carried forward today by Luca Currado, his wife Elena Penna, and his brother-in-law Mario Cordero.

VINEYARDS - Brunate, Rocche, Villero and Lazzarito are names that appear regularly on Vietti labels. The list could go on: Fiasco, Bricco Boschis, Liste, Bricco Viole, Fossati, Ravera and more besides. All the vineyards that combine to produce the grapes for the excellent Barolo Castiglione. Then there's the Scarrone barbera vineyard, 90 years old, which occupies a position that many another producer would have already given over to Barolo. Get the idea?

WINES - Every Vietti label is a guarantee of quality and, unfortunately, for reasons of space, we can't list them all here. **Barolo Ravera 2010** Great Wine (● 3,000 bt) is simply stunning. It has the lot ... solidity and guts, class and the purest of floral notes. It's only a Great Wine because the "Very Great Wine" category doesn't exist. Excellent too is **Barolo Brunate 2010** (● 3,000 bt), which is warmer, dark, dense and potent. **Barolo Lazzarito 2010** (● 3,000 bt) is as earthy as ever, this year with rare finesse and aerial character. **Barolo Rocche 2010** (● 3,000 bt) impresses for silky texture and depth. **Barbera d'Alba Scarrone Vigna Vecchia 2012** (● 3,500 bt; 38) has bulk and power. **Barbera d'Asti La Crena 2011** (● 6,500 bt) is as finely wrought as ever.

FERTILIZERS organic-mineral, manure pellets, natural manure, compost, green manure
PLANT PROTECTION chemical, copper and sulphur
WEED CONTROL mechanical
YEASTS selected
GRAPES 100% estate-grown
CERTIFICATION none

DOGLIANI (CN)

Cascina Corte

Borgata Valdiberti, 33
tel. 0173 743539
www.cascinacorte.it
info@cascinacorte.it

DOGLIANI (CN)

Ca' Viola

Borgata San Luigi, 11
tel. 0173 70547
www.caviola.com
info@caviola.com

12 ac - 25,000 bt

25 ac - 50,000 bt

66 Gentle intransigence, neither rigid nor over the top, born of the deep belief that respect for nature means respect for oneself and others, not only for the environment. This is how Sandro Barosi sees the hard work of the winemaker, living inside and with his vines and all that surrounds them 99

PEOPLE - His excellent, charismatic wines, which he's not unwilling to criticize, faithfully mirror Sandro and the terroir.

VINEYARDS - Care for the wine is Sandro's point of departure. His farmhouse, with a small b&b in the annex, is surrounded by vineyards (and trees, including fruit trees, some of which wild) in which he has never used chemicals. He simple employs lots of manual labor to grow healthy, ripe grapes from the classic local varieties, chiefly the underrated dolcetto, but also nebbiolo and barbera.

WINES - **Dogliani 2013** (● 7,000 bt) is the simplest version of the typology and has notable freshness and a lingering finish. **Langhe Nebbiolo 2012** (● 6,000 bt) has the solidity and compactness characteristic of the grape and a drinkability unusual for such a tannic wine. **Langhe Barbera 2012** (● 6.000 bt) stands out for its lively acidity, zest on the palate and succulent finish. Made with the drawing-off method and named for Sandro's firstborn, **Rosato Matilde 2013** (● dolcetto; 1.200 bt) is enjoyable and appropriately vivacious.

slow wine **DOGLIANI SUP. VIGNA PIROCHETTA 2012** (● 6,000 bt) A wine with the fruity notes typical of the grape, with hints of fresh cherry and plum, nicely dynamic with a solid suite of tannins.

PEOPLE - Spending the two hours of our visit in the company of Beppe Caviola is always a pleasure. He's an enologist of renown with consultancies all over Italy and with him it's possible to speak about the potential and problems of Italian viticulture. He opened this cellar in the early 1990s in the splendid Villa Bracco, where he also has his enology lab.

VINEYARDS - The cellar has two main terroirs. The first is at Montelupo, the Caviola family's village of origin, and grows dolcetto and barbera; the second, a more recent acquisition, is at Novello, a long-term lease on the prestigious Sottocastello cru where Beppe has been producing his Barolo since 2006. This year the dynamic young Matteo Toso started working at the cellar.

WINES - In his own cellar Caviola experiments with new techniques and makes wine the way he likes it to be, without compromise. **Barolo Sottocastello 2009** Great Wine (● 6,500 bt) has shaken off some of the notes of sweet spices and cocoa that used to characterize it. Now the fruit is crystalline and wonderful, and the tannic texture's interesting too. One of the best 2009 Barolos. As always, **Barbera d'Alba Bric du Luv 2012** (● 6,000 bt) is excellent, one of the best wines in its category. The intriguing, varietal **Langhe Nebbiolo 2012** (● 2,000 bt), a magnificent advert for all lovers of the grape. And let's not forget dolcetto, the grape variety that made Caviola's name as an enologist; hence **Dolcetto d'Alba Barturot 2013** (● 8,000 bt), juicy and very fleshy, and **Dolcetto d'Alba Vilot 2013** (● 5,000 bt) simpler and drinkable. Cherry and strawberry distinguish **Barbera d'Alba Brichet 2013** (● 13,000 bt).

FERTILIZERS natural manure	**FERTILIZERS** manure pellets, natural manure
PLANT PROTECTION copper and sulphur	**PLANT PROTECTION** chemical, copper and sulphur
WEED CONTROL mechanical	**WEED CONTROL** chemical, mechanical
YEASTS native	**YEASTS** native
GRAPES 100% estate-grown	**GRAPES** 100% estate-grown
CERTIFICATION organic	**CERTIFICATION** none

DOGLIANI (CN)

Pecchenino

Borgata Valdiberti, 59
tel. 0173 70686
www.pecchenino.com
pecchenino@pecchenino.it

62 ac - 120,000 bt

66 Expending energy for one's own local area, not only for oneself and one's cellar, and seeking to valorize all its resources – this is the philosophy behind the work Attilio and Orlando Pecchenino do on a daily basis in and around Dogliani, producing wines that evoke a sense of place but are also a joy to drink 99

PEOPLE - The farmhouse restructured with traditional building materials is well worth a visit.

VINEYARDS - The vineyards are farmed as sustainably as possible and constant study and research work is carried out in collaboration with various scientific institutions: problems addressed include the fight against the vine moth and the modern scourge, *flavescence dorée*. Here agriculture isn't the slave of science and technology but vice versa, in a virtuous process rooted in the finest rural tradition. The winery has bought new plots in the Bussia and Ravera districts at Monforte.

WINES - A large number of bottles of the enjoyable, approachable **Dogliani San Luigi 2013** (● 80,000 bt) were produced. **Dogliani Bricco Botti 2011** (● 6,800 bt) comes close to perfection for typicality, drinkability and depth on the palate, and its juicy finish is irresistible. We were favorably impressed by **Langhe Pinot Nero 2012** (● 2,000 bt), at once varietal and very "Langa" in style. **Barolo San Giuseppe 2010** (● 5,800 bt), from the Le Coste cru, is commendably harmonious with measured sweet tannins and excellent texture. **Barolo Le Coste 2010** (● 5,700 bt) offers the nose floral aromas and unleashes all the typology's youthful impetuousness on the palate.

slow wine **Dogliani Sup. Sirì d'Jermu 2012** (● 22,000 bt) Albeit the product of a wet year, a wine that conserves plenty of fruity flesh, followed up by a lingering finish. A hymn to a magnificent grape and a magnificent terroir.

FERTILIZERS	compost, green manure, humus
PLANT PROTECTION	copper and sulphur
WEED CONTROL	mechanical
YEASTS	selected
GRAPES	100% estate-grown
CERTIFICATION	none

DOGLIANI (CN)

San Fereolo

Borgata Valdibà, 59
tel. 0173 742075
www.sanfereolo.com
info@sanfereolo.com

32 ac - 35,000 bt

66 From the moment she decided to make wine, Nicoletta Bocca married the philosophy of biodynamics, applying it rigorously and coherently in the vineyard and in life with great results both in her wines and in the vitality of her vines 99

PEOPLE - When you have the pleasure of spending a few hours with Nicoletta, you can see why she enjoys the esteem and consideration of so many of her colleagues and wine enthusiasts. Her coherent, courageous choices are an example for anyone intent upon pursuing quality in the broadest sense of the term, from vineyard to bottle.

VINEYARDS - A walk among biodynamically farmed vineyards is different from one among vineyards treated with chemicals. The throbbing life and the lushness of the vegetation, the flowers, the insects and even the vine diseases create a sensation of contagious vitality and energy.

WINES - There are self-styled natural wines that are flawed, imprecise and unpalatable. Then there are truly natural enjoyable wines, like those of San Fereolo. Starting from **Dogliani Valdibà 2013** (● 13,000 bt), which combines rich, sweet flesh with freshness to create irresistible drinking pleasure. **Langhe Bianco Coste di Riavolo 2010** (○ 3,000 bt), a successful assemblage of gewürztraminer and riesling, has concentrated, elegant aromas on the nose and a well-textured, impressively dense, bright palate. **Langhe Rosso Austri 2007** (● barbera; 7,000 bt) is fresh, fleshy and fruity.

slow wine **Dogliani Sup. San Fereolo 2008** (● 13,000 bt) Yet another demonstration of Dogliani's vocation for dolcetto. A deep, intense wine, still full of youthfulness and verve, with intact fruit and a lingering finish.

FERTILIZERS	biodynamic preparations, green manure
PLANT PROTECTION	copper and sulphur, organic
WEED CONTROL	mechanical
YEASTS	native
GRAPES	100% estate-grown
CERTIFICATION	organic

FARIGLIANO (CN)
Anna Maria Abbona

Frazione Moncucco, 21
tel. 0173 797228
www.annamariabbona.it
info@annamariabbona.it

30 ac - 75,000 bt

66 A winery whose absolute, unbending credo is to protect the landscape, the dolcetto grape and rural culture 99

PEOPLE - In 1989, spurred on by the tales of her grandfather, who had a cellar here in the 1940s and sold his wine to bottlers in Narzole, Anna Maria Abbona, helped by her husband Franco Schellino, gave up her work as a graphic artist and pulled on her wellingtons.

VINEYARDS - "Being from Moncucco used to be great once a year," recalls Anna Maria. "In the spring when we used to go down to Dogliani with a flask with a sample of our wine for the merchants contending the best batches in town." The vineyards, of which just over ten acres with vines planted 50-80 years ago, are all at her native Moncucco, apart from the ones growing nebbiolo for Barolo, which are in the hamlet of Manzoni di Monforte. Worthy of mention is the rescue work carried out on the old parcels of the village elders and the magnificent San Bernardo vineyard.

WINES - Under enologist Giorgio Barbero, the recipe in the cellar is simple: barrels for wines from old vineyards (Cadò and San Bernardo) and Langhe Nebbiolo, steel for Dolcettos from the youngest vines; six months of aging for Langhe and Sorì dij But, 22 for Maioli. **Langhe Dolcetto 2013** (● 14,000 bt) is a truly typical, reasonably-priced easy drinker. Più Dogliani Sorì dij But 2013 Everyday Wine (● 28,000 bt) is more complex but it too offers great value for money. **Dogliani Sup. San Bernardo 2011** (● 4,000 bt) has a lot of acidity and well-balanced tannins. The classic **Langhe Nebbiolo 2011** (● 6,000 bt) is a wine to be reckoned with and the vast range is rounded off by the bright and breezy **Rosà 2013** (⊙ nebbiolo; 3,300 bt) and the commendable **Barolo 2010** (● 3,300 bt).

FERTILIZERS organic-mineral	
PLANT PROTECTION chemical, copper and sulphur	
WEED CONTROL chemical, mechanical	
YEASTS selected	
GRAPES 100% estate-grown	
CERTIFICATION none	

GRINZANE CAVOUR (CN)
La Spinetta

Località Campé
Via Carzello, 1
tel. 0141 877396
www.la-spinetta.com
info@la-spinetta.com

247 ac - 450,000 bt

PEOPLE - It's astonishing to think that 20 years ago the Rivettis – brothers Giorgio, Bruno and Carlo, and sister Giovanna – still weren't producing Barolo and Barbaresco. Since then, they have asserted their brand, first in the Langa zone, then in the rest of Italy, and now also worldwide. By buying the right vineyards and estates and brands (the latest being Contratto), in that order, they have created a small empire founded on labor, dynamism and, above all, quality.

VINEYARDS - The secret of all this success has been the decision to select only great vineyards for the production of wines and to work them with respect for the environment, seeking to prolong the lives of the vines, especially in the principal crus. Weed control has been banned, as have chemical fertilizers. They also cultivate beautiful vineyards in the Asti area, given over chiefly to barbera and moscato (the latter, incidentally, being the grape that made the family's fortune).

WINES - The cellar produces a vast range of wines, so we've decided to focus on the Barolos and Barbarescos. The one that impressed us the most was **Barolo Vigneto Campé 2010** Great Wine (● 10,000 bt), which has heady notes of raspberry and a more laid-back palate than in the recent past with well-worked tannins and an excellent finish. We were won over by the maison's two debut wines, **Barbaresco Vigneto Bordini 2010** (● 10,000 bt) and **Barolo Vigneto Garretti 2010** (● 6,000 bt). The 2011s are all rich, potent, and complex. Here they are in our order of preference: **Barbaresco Vigneto Valeirano 2011** (● 7,000 bt), **Barbaresco Vigneto Starderi 2011** (● 14,000 bt) and, finally, **Barbaresco Vigneto Gallina 2011** (● 10,500 bt).

FERTILIZERS green manure, humus	
PLANT PROTECTION chemical, copper and sulphur	
WEED CONTROL mechanical	
YEASTS selected	
GRAPES 100% estate-grown	
CERTIFICATION none	

LA MORRA (CN)

Elio Altare
Cascina Nuova

Frazione Annunziata, 51
tel. 0173 50835
www.elioaltare.com
elioaltare@elioaltare.com

32 ac - 80,000 bt

❝ Traditional viticulture without chemicals as it was for decades. The soil is fertilized with natural manure and no herbicides or systemic products are used. The leader of the Barolo Boys never ceases to amaze with wines of pure class that speak the language of the Langa with elegance and precision ❞

PEOPLE - 'To make great wines you have to drink great wines.' The words sum up Elio Altare, a farmer of great experience, curious and combative, who never rests on his laurels. Elio can count on a competent team formed by his daughter Silvia, her partner Massimo Marengo, and other trusted collaborators.

VINEYARDS - Some of the vineyards, scattered between La Morra and Serralunga, are very old indeed and all enjoy fine health – proof of the effectiveness of the agronomic practices adopted. The latest news is that the winery has bought seven acres of vineyard in Monforte, outside the Barolo DOCG, which takes its total to 32.

WINES - A wine of great elegance with good juiciness and perfect symmetry, **Langhe Rosso Larigi 2012** (● barbera; 2,300 bt) is proof of Elio's ability to interpret the grape. **Langhe Rosso La Villa 2012** (● 2,300 bt) cleverly combines the fruit of Barbera with the structure of Nebbiolo to achieve great depth. Also admirable is **Langhe Rosso Giàrborina 2012** (● nebbiolo; 2,300 bt), which displays sweet, well-balanced tannins. **Barolo 2010** (● 12,000 bt) owes its enjoyable palate to the perfect symmetry of its components. **Barolo Arborina 2010** (● 8,000 bt) has inebriating floral fragrances and a juicy, harmonious palate. **Barolo Vigna Bricco Cerretta 2008** (● 6,000 bt) combines fruity, mineral notes on the nose with an irresistibly racy palate.

FERTILIZERS	natural manure
PLANT PROTECTION	copper and sulphur
WEED CONTROL	mechanical
YEASTS	native
GRAPES	100% estate-grown
CERTIFICATION	none

LA MORRA (CN)

Brandini

Frazione Brandini, 16
tel. 0173 50266
www.agricolabrandini.it
info@agricolabrandini.it

23.5 ac - 70,000 bt

PEOPLE - In just a few years, this cellar has made an undoubted step forward in quality. The wines have improved beyond all recognition partly thanks to the enological consultancy of Beppe Caviola, the farming methods have received organic certification, and this year a beautiful *agriturismo* has also been opened. The project is developing under the auspices of the Eataly business group, which has contributed to the growth achieved by Brandini over the last five months.

VINEYARDS - It isn't always easy to farm organically in the Langa zone, and 2014 was certainly a tough test for anyone trying to do so. All the more reason why we should applaud Brandini. The vineyards are almost all in the Brandini subzone, the part of La Morra that looks towards Cherasco and Santa Vittoria. The consultant agronomist is the gifted Alberto Grasso.

WINES - The cellar is run by the enthusiastic young Danila Chiotti. The range of wines submitted for tasting this year was arguably the best ever. The excellent **Barolo 2010** (● 30,000 bt), in which cherry and violet crown a zesty, flavorful palate. We were also intrigued by this year's white, **Langhe Bianco Le Coccinelle 2013** (○ arneis, viogner; 9,000 bt) which has an exotic nose and a rich salty mouthfeel. **Dolcetto d'Alba Filari Lunghi 2013** (● 5,000 bt) is enjoyably drinkable and very fruity.

slow wine **BAROLO RESA 56 2010** (● 4,500 bt) Named for the hailstorm that lowered the production of the vineyard whose grapes are earmarked for selection (*resa* means yield in Italian). An extremely elegant wine with a raspberry bouquet, a delicious, nicely acid palate, and a very long, deep finish. A land-rooted product of organic farming.

FERTILIZERS	manure pellets
PLANT PROTECTION	copper and sulphur
WEED CONTROL	mechanical
YEASTS	native
GRAPES	100% estate-grown
CERTIFICATION	organic

LA MORRA (CN)

Alessandro Veglio

Frazione Annunziata
Borgata Ciotto, 53
tel. 338 5699102
av@alessandroveglio.com

MONFORTE D'ALBA (CN)

Diego Conterno

Via Montà, 27
tel. 0173 789265
www.diegoconterno.it
info@diegoconterno.it

11 ac - 28,000 bt

PEOPLE - Yet another nice story to tell ... Though his parents had entirely different jobs, Alessandro Veglio, 30, decided to emulate his grandfather and become a winegrower. True, starting out these days is more complicated than it was 20 years ago, but Alessandro has strength of character and talent and receives a not insubstantial amount of support from his family and colleagues.

VINEYARDS - We fully endorse Alessandro's decision to stop using chemical weedkillers. This of course involves extra work but the guy knows what he's doing. We took a walk with him through the Gattera cru, a stone's throw from the famous Lebanon cedar at La Morra, and it was some experience, what with the lush grass and the vineyard that contains plants over 40 years age. The nebbiolo for the Langhe comes from the Roero area.

WINES - Veglio's style too is maturing with the years. His mentor was none other than Renato Corino, but he increasingly relies on his own sensibility. His excellent **Barolo Gattera 2010** (● 2,500 bt) is aged in different-sized casks and barrels and has flesh and substance, warmth from the favorably located vineyard and extraordinary drinkability. **Langhe Nebbiolo 2012** (● 5,000 bt) is delicately colored, blossomy and very Roero in style. The young and exuberant **Barbera d'Alba 2013** (● 7,500 bt) is a red that goes well with food. Drinking **Dolcetto d'Alba 2013** (● 4,500 bt) is like biting into a plum just plucked from the tree.

| slow wine | **BAROLO 2010** (● 7,000 bt) Readier to drink than the cru at the moment, with less biting tannins and intense flavor. Maybe that's why we enjoyed it and, given the price, would be prepared to recommend to anyone. |

18.5 ac - 40,000 bt

PEOPLE - A cellar founded in 2003 as an offshoot of Conterno-Fantino, which Diego Conterno left in 2000. In 2002 Diego bought the necessary land, planted the wines, built the cellar and released his debut wine in 2006 (he'd previously produced the 2003 Barolo and, in the new cellar, the 2005). For the last five years, he has been helped by his son Stefano.

VINEYARDS - The most important portion, which belongs to Diego's father, is the three-acre nebbiolo plot at Ginestra (in the three historic Vigna del Gris, Sorì Ginestra and Pajana parcels), which gives life to the cellar's only Barolo. The other vineyards, which grow nebbiolo, barbera and nascetta, are at Bricco Monguglielmo, in the Ferrione region where the cellar is, just outside the Barolo denomination. The oldest dolcetto and barbera grapes, planted 60 years ago, are at Bricco Rosso, in the Sant'Anna district.

WINES - On the basis of his past experience and his knowledge of the Monforte area, Diego has decided to bank on Barolo by valorizing a grand cru like Ginestra and in the near future will be able to use the name "Barolo del Comune di Monforte." His approach to heavyweight reds is classical, with long 20- to 30-day fermentations in steel vats and in new and second-use midsize casks for 24 months. The long- well-built **Barolo Ginestra 2010** (● 5,000 bt) is a pure thoroughbred. **Barolo Le Coste di Monforte 2010** `Great Wine` (● 3,000 bt) is fruity with superlative tannins. **Barolo 2010** (● 5,500 bt), made with grapes from San Pietro, Le Coste and Ginestra, has good length. **Nebbiolo d'Alba Baluma 2012** (● 6,500 bt) has a balsamic nose and an imperious palate. **Dolcetto d'Alba 2013** (● 6,000 bt) is fragrant, **Langhe Nascetta 2013** (○ 1,500 bt) is inviting.

FERTILIZERS natural manure	**FERTILIZERS** organic-mineral
PLANT PROTECTION chemical, copper and sulphur	**PLANT PROTECTION** chemical, copper and sulphur
WEED CONTROL mechanical	**WEED CONTROL** mechanical
YEASTS native	**YEASTS** selected
GRAPES 100% estate-grown	**GRAPES** 100% estate-grown
CERTIFICATION none	**CERTIFICATION** none

MONFORTE D'ALBA (CN)

Conterno Fantino ⊚

Via Ginestra, 1
tel. 0173 78204
www.conternofantino.it
info@conternofantino.it

---

67 ac - 150,000 bt

❝ Rigorous, coherent, virtuous viticulture backed by professionalism and competence in turning ripe, healthy grapes into top quality wines. This is what awaits you at this magnificent winery run by Claudio Conterno, Guido Fantino and his son Fabio ❞

PEOPLE - There isn't a single step in the productive process that isn't carefully analyzed to find optimal, eco-sustainable solutions to the various problems.

VINEYARDS - The vineyards are farmed organically with the collaboration of Gian Piero Romana. Their names are well known among enthusiasts: Ginestra (the Sorì parcel is 40 years old), Mosconi (with plantings dating to 1980 and 1999 and the use, following careful selection, of a special clone), Castelletto and Bussia. The properties are managed perfectly to produce wines, including an excellent Chardonnay, that express the depth and character of the terroir.

WINES - The Barolo 2010 performed brilliantly, especially **Barolo Sorì Ginestra 2010** (● 11,000 bt), refined and potent, already richly nuanced, mineral and very, very long. **Barolo Mosconi 2010** Great Wine (● 3,000 bt) is on a par and offers a sense of fullness and balance with earthy notes and fine sweet tannins, juicy but never bitter. **Barolo Vigna del Gris 2010** (● 6,500 bt) completes the trio with elegant floral notes and a racy palate with perfect symmetry between fruit and tannins. **Langhe Rosso Monprà 2011** (● 10,000 bt) weds nebbiolo and barbera (without cabernet sauvignon) and it's a happy marriage. **Barbera d'Alba Vignota 2012** (● 25,000 bt) is impeccable and typical, while **Langhe Nebbiolo Ginestrino 2012** (● 30,000 bt) is an easy drinker without being banal.

MONFORTE D'ALBA (CN)

Giacomo Fenocchio €

Località Bussia, 72
tel. 0173 78675
www.giacomofenocchio.com
claudio@giacomofenocchio.com

---

37 ac - 90,000 bt   `10% discount`

PEOPLE - Meeting Claudio Fenocchio was a pleasure again this year: for the spirit, by virtue of his cordiality, affability and frankness; for the eyes, as his cellar dominates most of the Bussia district and environs; for the palate, since his wines are good, well crafted, and traditional in the best sense of the term – plus they're reasonably priced!

VINEYARDS - Fenocchio has about 25 acres of vineyard in the celebrated Bussia subzone, of which six are given over to nebbiolo grapes for Barolo; at Cannubi di Barolo, there is one acre or so, at Villero di Castiglione Falletto a couple, all growing nebbiolo. Tasting the three vintages to come – 2011, 2012 and 2013 – we were able to appreciate the differences between these three magnificent vineyards.

WINES - The Barolos undergo long macerations, around 40 days in fact. **Barolo Villero 2010** (● 6,000 bt) has heady notes of undergrowth and ripe fruit on the palate with sweet tannins and huge depth. **Barolo Cannubi 2010** (● 3,200 bt) shines for aromatic finesse, elegant flavor and overall harmony. **Barolo Bussia 2010** (● 30,000 bt) has subtle blossomy notes on the nose, reasonably solid, mature tannins on the palate, and a spicy, leisurely finish. We liked the raciness and fruit of **Barbera d'Alba 2012** (● 20.000 bt), which works effectively despite the awkward growing year. **Dolcetto d'Alba 2013** (● 15,000 bt), finally, is fruity and quaffable.

slow wine **BAROLO BUSSIA RIS. 2008** (● 5,000 bt) All the verve and drinkability of the vintage without foregoing character and bite, not to mention a long, well-balanced finish. A unique red made with total respect for terroir and grape both.

FERTILIZERS compost, green manure	**FERTILIZERS** humus
PLANT PROTECTION copper and sulphur	**PLANT PROTECTION** chemical, copper and sulphur
WEED CONTROL mechanical	**WEED CONTROL** chemical, mechanical
YEASTS native	**YEASTS** selected
GRAPES 100% estate-grown	**GRAPES** 100% estate-grown
CERTIFICATION organic	**CERTIFICATION** none

Elio Grasso

Località Ginestra, 40
tel. 0173 78491
www.eliograsso.it
info@eliograsso.it

45 ac - 90,000 bt

66 A family that valorizes all the potential of a unique local area, respecting not only the environment but also the people who live in it and producing wines of the very highest standard 99

PEOPLE - Elio Grasso and his wife Marina can be content with what they have achieved and handed on to their gifted son Gianluca, assisted, in turn, by his wife Francesca. Their farmhouse in the Gavarini district is well worth a visit.

VINEYARDS - The vineyards are farmed with love and attention to every minor detail. They are covered with a mixture of grasses and treated by alternate rows with green manure every year. Thinning is drastic and Elio uses his expertise to ensure that the grapes are harvested only when perfectly ripe. The nebbiolo vineyards are in the Gavarini and Ginestra districts just below the farmhouse. All chemicals are banned and the viticulture practiced is sustainable.

WINES - We were won over by the stylish and apparently ready-to-drink **Barolo Gavarini Chiniera 2010** (● 12,000 bt), exceptionally deep, punchy, racy and taut. **Barolo Ginestra Casa Matè 2010** Great Wine (● 12,000 bt) is a young thoroughbred that's champing at the bit but will grow to gift huge satisfactions to anyone prepared to wait for it: dense and juicy, it has close-knit tannic texture. **Langhe Nebbiolo Gavarini 2013** (● 18,000 bt) provides an easy and enjoyable introduction to the world of the nebbiolo grape. **Barbera d'Alba Vigna Martina 2011** (● 20,000 bt) was an opportunity not to be missed for Elio and Gianluca: the product of a perfect vintage, it's so good no adjective would suffice to describe it. **Dolcetto d'Alba dei Grassi 2013** (● 20,000 bt) is typical, **Langhe Chardonnay Educato 2013** (○ 8,000 bt) is bright and breezy.

FERTILIZERS natural manure	
PLANT PROTECTION copper and sulphur	
WEED CONTROL mechanical	
YEASTS selected	
GRAPES 100% estate-grown	
CERTIFICATION none	

Giovanni Almondo

€

Via San Rocco, 26
tel. 0173 975256
www.giovannialmondo.com
almondo@giovannialmondo.com

37 ac - 105,000 bt

PEOPLE - It's hard to say what struck us most during our visit, whether the professionalism and scrupulous work that goes into every stage of the distribution chain, or the breathtaking beauty of the vineyards, or the huge value of the wines, Arneis in especial, or the centuries-old bond that ties the Almondo family – Domenico, his wife and his two keen sons Stefano and Federico – with the Roero district in general and Montà d'Alba in particular.

VINEYARDS - The Burigot vineyard is set among chestnut and acacia woods (there's also an Almondo honey). It's very steep and contains very old vines. Its grassed vine rows and thir very sand soil – you'd think you were walking on a beach – are an unforgettable spectacle. No less beautiful is Bricco delle Ciliegie, where the soil contains a larger component of limestone. The viticulture adopted is invariably virtuous.

WINES - Tangy and vaguely lemony, **Roero Arneis Vigne Sparse 2013** (○ 45,000 bt) is precise, fresh-tasting and distinctly land-rooted. **Langhe Bianco Sassi e Sabbia 2013** (○ riesling renano; 1.200 bt) is a huge success: made partly with grapes affected with botrytis, it's dry, it's taut, it's mineral, and it's well worth waiting for. The two Roeros are good, too: **Roero Bric Valdiana 2011** (● 4,000 bt) has bundles of juicy, deep fruit, while **Roero Giovanni Almondo Ris. 2011** (● 2,000 bt) is assertive with suggestions of peach and beautifully crafted tannins. **Barbera d'Alba Valbianchera 2012** (● 3,000 bt) is good.

> **slow wine** **ROERO ARNEIS BRICCO DELLE CILIEGIE 2013** (○ 40.000 bt) Forever living up to its reputation, this great white combines classic notes of pear with mineral scents. Full but lean body on the palate, good acidity and almost earthy finish. The best Arneis we've tasted this year.

FERTILIZERS organic-mineral, natural manure	
PLANT PROTECTION chemical, copper and sulphur	
WEED CONTROL mechanical	
YEASTS native	
GRAPES 100% estate-grown	
CERTIFICATION none	

Piero Busso

Via Albesani, 8
tel. 0173 67156
www.bussopiero.com
bussopiero@bussopiero.com

Castello di Neive

Corso Romano Scagliola, 205
tel. 0173 67171
www.castellodineive.it
info@castellodineive.it

---

24 ac - 45,000 bt

" A family of farmers whose wines have improved in quality year by year thanks to a virtuous approach to viticulture that protects an environment that many exploit without caring about the future **"**

PEOPLE - Piero Busso, his wife Lucia and their son Pier, now privy to all the secrets of winemaking are a veritable institution for all lovers of the great wines of Langa.

VINEYARDS - A joy for the eyes: that's the thought that came to mind among the steep vine rows – tended with almost maniacal care, and almost entirely by hand, by Piero and Pier – of the Borgese vineyard in the historic Albesani cru. We spared ourselves San Stefanetto because it's so steep it induces vertigo, though father and son love this vineyard no less than the others. The winery's properties also include a parcel in the excellent Gallina cru.

WINES - Wines are matured in wood barrels, traditionally with notable attention to hygiene in the cellar. In the range of Barbarescos presented, each bottle was better than the last. Deserving of special mention is **Barbaresco Gallina 2010** (● 3,000 bt), which we reviewed by mistake last year. It's an austere red of remarkable structure, deep and assertive, emblematic of the greatness of the nebbiolo grape. The magnificent **Barbaresco San Stunet 2011** (● 5,000 bt) has solid structure. **Barbaresco Mondino 2011** (● 5,500 bt) is simpler but precise and quaffable. **Barbera d'Alba Sup. San Stefanetto 2011** (● 2,500 bt), matured in wood casks, is spacious and full of verve, while **Barbera d'Alba Majano 2012** (● 6,500 bt) is racy.

> **slow wine** **BARBARESCO ALBESANI BORGESE 2011** (● 5,000 bt) Stylish and elegant with stupendous tannins. Deep, long and lingering, a hymn to the nebbiolo grape.

FERTILIZERS natural manure
PLANT PROTECTION copper and sulphur
WEED CONTROL mechanical
YEASTS native
GRAPES 100% estate-grown
CERTIFICATION none

---

67 ac - 160,000 bt

PEOPLE - This cellar, owned and run by the affable Italo Stupino, was first opened in 1964 in the splendid 18th-century palazzo of the Counts of Castelborgo right in the center of Neive. Two years ago it moved to a new, functional building but its aging paraphernalia, mostly wood barrels and casks, are still in the old palazzo. Since 1999 Italo has been joined by the gifted enologist and manager Claudio Roggero and young cellarman Andrea Ramello.

VINEYARDS - The cellar owns about 150 acres of land, 66 of which are vineyards, 50 hazelnut groves. In 1982 the clonal selection of the arneis grape was carried out here in collaboration with Turin University, which continues to participate in experimental work in the cellar and in the vineyards. Hence the use of sexual confusion traps for vine moths and at Santo Stefano, in a 15-acre monopole plot in the Albesani cru, a weather station monitored by the Horta project, this time coordinated by Piacenza University.

WINES - **Barbaresco Gallina 2011** Great Wine (● 3,500 bt) is the quintessence of the elegance of the nebbiolo grape in Neive; it has an aerial, citrusy nose, excellent grip and a subtle suite of flavors. **Dolcetto d'Alba Basarin 2012** (● 8,000 bt) is deep and articulate on the nose, compact yet lively, nicely juicy and flavorful. We were impressed by **Langhe Albarossa 2009** (● 2,500 bt) for its outstanding, well-fused, effectively dynamic mouthfeel. **Barbaresco Santo Stefano Ris. 2009** (● 3.500 bt) has a splendid nose of fruity jam and mid-palate bulk. **Barbaresco 2011** (● 60,000 bt) offers tertiary aromas on the nose and good drinkability. **Langhe Arneis Montebertotto 2013** (○ 36,000 bt) has a bouquet of crisp fruit and a palate that combines butteriness with acid thrust. **Barbaresco Santo Stefano 2011** (● 12,000 bt) releases mature aromas with hints of quinine and a muscular palate on which the tannins are still not fully resolved.

FERTILIZERS none
PLANT PROTECTION chemical, copper and sulphur
WEED CONTROL chemical, mechanical
YEASTS selected
GRAPES 100% estate-grown
CERTIFICATION none

Sottimano

Località Cottà, 21
tel. 0173 635186
www.sottimano.it
info@sottimano.it

45 ac - 85,000 bt

6 6 A true farming family, proud of their identity, confident and convinced of the decisions they have taken. But who keep a low profile despite their success. Attentive agriculture, wines of consistent quality, respect for the land 9 9

PEOPLE - For some years now, Rino Sottimano has been helped in vineyard and cellar by his son Andrea, while his wife Anna and daughter Elena take care of sales. A winery that stands out for quality and professionalism.

VINEYARDS - Rino and Andrea farm their vineyards between Neive and Treiso painstakingly and according to precise rules. They have never practiced weed control, they keep the soil under the vines soft to allow it to "breathe," and they don't use systemic products or botryticides. The Cottà vineyard below the cellar occupies part of the splendid valley of the same name. Other parcels are in the Pajorè district at Treiso and in the Currà, Fausoni and Basarin districts.

WINES - The standout among the Barbarescos, fruits of a warm growing year, is **Barbaresco Pajorè 2011** (● 5,000 bt), a combination on the nose of toastiness and rich ripe fruit, which enjoys an encore on the symmetrical, dynamic palate. **Barbaresco Cottà 2011** (● 10,000 bt) is characteristically full-bodied and weighty with measured tannins and a certain brightness on the finish. **Barbaresco Fausoni 2011** (● 4,800 bt) is subtler and suppler, with nice sprightliness and sweet fruit. With its raciness and typical blossomy notes, **Langhe Nebbiolo 2012** (● 22,000 bt) proves itself to be on a par with its "big brothers." **Dolcetto d'Alba Bric del Salto 2013** (● 22,000 bt) has compelling vinosity. **Maté 2013** (● brachetto; 5,000 bt) has the classic aromas of the grape variety.

FERTILIZERS	natural manure
PLANT PROTECTION	copper and sulphur
WEED CONTROL	mechanical
YEASTS	native
GRAPES	100% estate-grown
CERTIFICATION	none

Elvio Cogno

Via Ravera, 2
tel. 0173 744006
www.elviocogno.com
elviocogno@elviocogno.com

32 ac - 74,000 bt

6 6 Attention to detail, great sensitivity towards the environment and workplace conditions, outstanding wines, commitment and passion across the supply chain 9 9

PEOPLE - Nadia Cogno and Walter Fissore, who run this splendid hilltop winery, aren't ones to rest on their laurels. On the contrary, every year they come up with interesting novelties. They are assisted in their task by Daniele Gaia and Szymon Jachimowicz.

VINEYARDS - We took a walk among the vine rows around the 18th-century farmhouse when the vines were in full blossom. Healthy soil and spontaneous ground cover teeming with life – a spectacle of nature on a classic Langa terrain, where limestone predominates. A new parcel in the Pasinot district, under the castle of Novello, has been planted with nebbiolo. The average age of the vineyards is high and management is organic, de facto if not formally.

WINES - Hailstorms prevented the production of Barolo Vigna Elena, but Walter and Nadia have made up for that with a sumptuous version of **Barolo Ravera 2010** (● 13,000 bt) with a bouquet of meadow flowers and an energy-filled, very racy, lengthy, lingering finish. **Barolo Bricco Pernice 2009** Great Wine (● 4,000 bt), with its ample, generous fruity aromas and full-bodied, fleshy palate, was even better. **Barolo Cascina Nuova 2010** (● 20,000 bt) is arguably less deep but it has a graceful, blossomy bouquet and racy palate with beautifully calibrated sweet tannins; it's a wine well worth buying. This year the excellent **Langhe Nebbiolo Montegrilli 2013** (● 6,000 bt) replaces Langhe Rosso, while **Barbera d'Alba Bricco dei Merli 2012** (● 12,000 bt) is supple and sprightly. As always we were also impressed by **Langhe Nascetta Anas-cëtta 2013** (○ 16,000 bt).

FERTILIZERS	natural manure, green manure
PLANT PROTECTION	copper and sulphur
WEED CONTROL	mechanical
YEASTS	native
GRAPES	100% estate-grown
CERTIFICATION	none

Mossio Fratelli ▮

Via Montà, 12
tel. 0173 617149 - 338 4002835
www.mossio.com
mossio@mossio.com

25 ac - 50,000 bt | **10% discount** |

PEOPLE - In their old 16th-century farmhouse, nestling on a hillock that affords a breathtaking view over a landscape of vineyards and woods, streams and orchards, Remo and Valerio Mossio carry on the family business. The former oversees the vineyards and the cellar, the latter takes care of administrative affairs and visitors. They both do their jobs with a simplicity that adds even more value to their already excellent wines.

VINEYARDS - The Mossios own about 15 acres of vineyard, virtually in a single plot round the farmhouse. The south-facing Bricco Caramelli vineyard is over 60 years old and yields wines that are at once rich and fresh-tasting thanks to the notable altitude (1,300 feet). The Piano delli Perdoni vineyard, over 30 years old, enjoys an equally good position and very good air circulation. Viticulture is conventional, but without the use of systemic products.

WINES - Year after year Mossio comes up with impressive Dolcettos, clean, precise and typical, all of them good. Dolcetto d'Alba Piano delli Perdoni 2013 Everyday Wine (● 25,000 bt) has nuanced aromas of freshly mown grass with notes of red berries that play out an encore on the typical, well-balanced palate before giving way to a truly impressive finish of sweet almonds. **Dolcetto d'Alba Bricco Caramelli 2013** (● 5,000 bt) offers fruity notes to the nose and sweet, juicy fruit to the palate, braced by mature tannins and accompanied by excellent freshness. The remarkable and effective **Dolcetto d'Alba Sup. Gamus 2012** (● 2,800 bt) is wood-aged for a year and has delicious flesh. The excellent **Barbera d'Alba 2012** (● 4,500 bt) is typical, full of verve and very drinkable. **Langhe Nebbiolo 2010** (● 5,000 bt) has all the floweriness of the grape and mellow tannins.

FERTILIZERS manure pellets, natural manure	
PLANT PROTECTION copper and sulphur	
WEED CONTROL chemical, mechanical	
YEASTS native	
GRAPES 100% estate-grown	
CERTIFICATION none	

Casa di E. Mirafiore ▮

Via Alba, 15
tel. 0173 626117
www.mirafiore.it
info@mirafiore.it

50 ac - 100,000 bt

PEOPLE - Casa di E. Mirafiore is a very interesting project that's well worth talking about. Fontanafredda has revived the historic brand and given it a very precise style. The most important selections, made uncompromisingly using a hyper-traditional style (zero selected yeasts, barrel-aging, only the best grapes) for lovers of very land-rooted wines, under the Mirafiore label.

VINEYARDS - Fontanafredda's finest vineyards have been selected to make the wines of the brand. One such is the gorgeous Paiagallo cru, at the entrance to the village of Barolo, which enjoys a magnificent location on a dizzy slope. The formula applied in the vineyard, under the supervision of agronomist Alberto Grasso, is common to all the group's other wineries: no weedkillers and no chemical fertilizers.

WINES - The work being carried out by enologist Danilo Drocco is very rigorous, "extreme" even. And you can tell in the glass. The best of the bunch is **Barolo Paiagallo 2010** Great Wine (● 13,000 bt): aged in large oak barrels, it has hints of anchovy and raspberry on the nose and a forthright, juicy palate with perfectly harmonious tannins. If you're fans of the traditional barrel-matured barbera grape, this is the place to come and the right wine for you is **Barbera d'Alba Sup. 2011** (● 20,000 bt), which has a bouquet of ripe cherry and truffle and a suitably acid palate. **Dolcetto d'Alba 2013** (● 20,000 bt) is redolent of plum and a real joy to drink.

FERTILIZERS manure pellets	
PLANT PROTECTION chemical, copper and sulphur	
WEED CONTROL mechanical	
YEASTS native	
GRAPES 100% estate-grown	
CERTIFICATION none	

Ettore Germano

Località Cerretta, 1
tel. 0173 613528
www.germanoettore.com
germanoettore@germanoettore.com

Guido Porro

Via Alba, 1
tel. 0173 613306
www.guidoporro.com
guidoporro@guidoporro.com

---

37 ac - 80,000 bt

PEOPLE - Sergio Germano is known locally and among his colleagues as the "gentle giant," partly because of his size, partly on account of his great generosity and kindness. He's helped by his wife Elena, who runs a homely bed and breakfast. Sergio loves putting himself on the line and this explains how he has come up with awesome Metodo Classicos and a Riesling of rare goodness.

VINEYARDS - The cellar owns some very good vineyards at Serralunga. Especially worthy of mention are Lazzarito, Prapò, Cerretta and the newly acquired legendary Vigna Rionda. The Riesling vineyards, instead, are a long distance away in the commune of Cigliè near Mondovì at an altitude of 2,000 feet. The Maritime Alps are just a stone's throw away, hence sharp night-day temperature swings that are manna for the noble German grape.

WINES - It's hard not to be impressed by a range of wines like Sergio's. Let's start with our favorite, **Barolo Lazzarito Ris. 2008** Great Wine (● 3,000 bt), which has unique character: the bouquet starts with hints of violet, then veers towards raspberry tart, after which comes a sappy, salty palate with delicious tannins. **Barolo Prapò 2010** (● 6,000 bt) is robust and rich and rugged with all the class we associate with maison Germano. Still very youthful, **Barolo Cerretta 2010** (● 10,000 bt) is rigorously crafted. One of the most fortunate whites is **Langhe Riesling Hérzu 2012** (○ 10,000 bt). **Barbera d'Alba Sup. Vigna della Madre 2012** (● 10,000 bt) is as deliciously fruity and enjoyable as ever. Sergio also shows his handiness with whites in **Langhe Nascetta 2012** (○ 3.000 bt).

20 ac - 40,000 bt

PEOPLE - Guido Porro is anything but old, but he already boasts enviable winegrowing experience and can also still count on the precious help and in-depth knowledge of the terroir of his father Giovanni, not to mention the support of his wife Giovanna. In the recently extended cellar are the large barrels in which Guido's classic, beautifully crafted Barolos mature. He subsequently sells the wine at reasonable prices to a large number of loyal private customers.

VINEYARDS - We shared the thrill of a trip with Guido to the legendary, very steep Serralunga cru on the Vigna Rionda property. Here the lush three-year-old-vines grow in neat rows interspersed with herbs and flowers, Guido having given up weed control and, virtually, the use of pesticides. Another prestigious vineyard is Lazzairasco, where the vines have an average age of 50, the cellar's first along with the younger Santa Caterina.

WINES - Barolo Santa Caterina 2010 (● 5,000 bt) has adequate finesse and structure, irresistible fleshiness, length and a precise finish. **Barolo Seivì 2010** (● 3,000 bt) offers notes of black cherry and sweet tannins, good mouthfeel and suitably leisurely development. The nicely succulent **Langhe Nebbiolo Camilu 2013** (● 3,000 bt) will be at its best after another few months in the bottle. **Barbera d'Alba Vigna Santa Caterina 2013** (● 6,000 bt) and **Dolcetto d'Alba Vigna Pari 2013** (● 4,000 bt) are typical and enjoyable.

slow wine **Barolo Lazzairasco 2010** (● 11,000 bt) Unfiltered like all of Guido's wines and attractively bright in color. Still muted notes of dried flowers lead into a light yet punchy palate of great verve and balance. A masterpiece at a mind-boggling price.

FERTILIZERS natural manure	**FERTILIZERS** manure pellets
PLANT PROTECTION chemical, copper and sulphur	**PLANT PROTECTION** copper and sulphur
WEED CONTROL chemical, mechanical	**WEED CONTROL** mechanical
YEASTS selected	**YEASTS** native
GRAPES 100% estate-grown	**GRAPES** 100% estate-grown
CERTIFICATION none	**CERTIFICATION** none

Giovanni Rosso

Località Baudana, 6
tel. 0173 613340
www.giovannirosso.com
info@giovannirosso.com

Schiavenza

Via Mazzini, 4
tel. 0173 613115
www.schiavenza.com
schiavenza@schiavenza.com

---

37 ac - 110,000 bt

PEOPLE - Davide Rosso is unstoppable. He now has a new cellar just outside Serralunga, complete with large cement vats and wood tubs to mature noble red wines. With the help of trusty collaborators Andrea Delpiano and Armando Brigante, he launches one project after another. He believes as we do that Barolo and its terroir are worthy of a leading role on the international wine scene.

VINEYARDS - Davide's point of departure was his vineyards and he now owns first-rate properties: at Serralunga La Serra, a beautifully positioned two-acre plot with very sandy soil in the lower portion; at Cerretta, five acres of clayey soil that produce well-built, elegant wines; at Vigna Rionda, a world famous cru, another two-acre plot. Not far away, at Roddino, he also owns a lovely parcel of land surrounded by woods and given over to nebbiolo and barbera.

WINES - Still very, very young, **Barolo La Serra 2010** (● 4,500 bt) has faint suggestions of the wine's classic floral, earthy notes, a supple, solid palate, and perfectly mature fruit braced by a long, juicy finish. Our favorite in a superlative range is **Barolo Cerretta 2010** Great Wine (● 8,000 bt) has a refined bouquet and palate, where the delightful sweetness of the fruit surfaces with stylish, biting tannins. **Barolo Serralunga 2010** (● 40,000 bt) is on a par thanks to the precision of its fruity notes and symmetrical palate. **Langhe Nebbiolo 2012** (● 20,000 bt) has irresistible notes of violet and is wonderfully drinkable. **Barbera d'Alba Donna Margherita 2013** (● 40,000 bt) is living proof of just how enjoyable this typology can be.

---

22 ac - 40,000 bt

PEOPLE - Luciano Pira is at the helm of this lovely Serralunga winery, which he steers with application and skill. He's helped by his wife Maura and his brother-in-law Walter Anselma. It was the latter who was kind enough to meet us and take us round. The cellars house traditional large barrels and cement vats, the wines are faithful to the terroir and on sale at reasonable prices. Next door is the family trattoria where we warmly recommend you stay for a meal.

VINEYARDS - The vineyards are all in the commune of Serralunga and have names wine lovers know well: from Prapò to Cerretta to Brolio, with Cerrati and Meriame for the Barolo Serralunga. The viticultural approach has gotten gradually more attentive and sustainable, and we're pleased to announce that weed control and the use of chemical pesticides have been stopped altogether. Dolcetto and barbera are also grown to make wines that invariably sell like hotcakes.

WINES - The Barolos are good, in especial the two Riservas, the fruits of very fortunate vintages. **Barolo Brolio Ris. 2008** (● 4,000 bt) has suggestions of rose and tar followed by a solid, succulent palate and a pleasingly sweet finish. **Barolo Prapò 2010** (● 5,000 bt), still austere and stiff, offers a subtle note of licorice and a palate of power and depth. **Barolo Cerretta 2010** (● 4,000 bt) has a mixed bouquet of flowers, fruit and soil, a palate marked by solid but never raspy tannins, and a long, lingering finish. **Barolo Brolio 2010** (● 5,000 bt) is simpler with a juicy sweet of tannins, **Barolo del Comune di Serralunga 2010** (● 7,500 bt) is a very impressive assemblage.

> slow wine **BAROLO PRAPÒ RIS. 2008** (● 2,400 bt) The best of the bunch with great initial olfactory impact, solid structure and deep-reaching mouthfeel. A very traditional Barolo at a very attractive price for a Riserva.

FERTILIZERS natural manure
PLANT PROTECTION copper and sulphur
WEED CONTROL mechanical
YEASTS native
GRAPES 100% estate-grown
CERTIFICATION none

FERTILIZERS humus
PLANT PROTECTION copper and sulphur
WEED CONTROL mechanical
YEASTS native
GRAPES 100% estate-grown
CERTIFICATION none

Ca' del Baio

Via Ferrere, 33
tel. 0173 638219
www.cadelbaio.com
cadelbaio@cadelbaio.com

62 ac - 120,000 bt

66 Excellent land-rooted, value-for-money wines and rural culture in aid of a worthy project 99

PEOPLE - The Grasso family – parents Giulio and Luciana and their daughters Paola, Valentina and Federica – continue to delight us with magical wines that evoke the local area without tricks or shortcuts.

VINEYARDS - Giulio hasn't used systemic products for years and he only practices weed control in the early spring, after which he uses solely mechanical equipment. His beautiful Valgrande and Marcarini vineyards are round the farm, face from east to west, and grow on the classic local soil. Others are at Barbaresco in two prestigious crus, Asili and Pora. They also grow barbera and dolcetto and the white riesling and chardonnay grapes.

WINES - The magnificent **Barbaresco Asili 2011 (●** 11,000 bt) has irresistible floral aromas with mineral notes, at once punchy and well-rounded, juicy and very bright with a long finish. Just as good is **Barbaresco Pora 2010 (●** 2,500 bt), with its stylish nose, racy, solid palate and a finish redolent of undergrowth. **Barbaresco Marcarini 2011 (●** 14,000 bt) is beautifully aromatic and drinkable with hefty tannins, while **Barbaresco Valgrande 2011 (●** 14,000 bt), made with grapes from the younger vineyards, is still stiff but promises well with its sweet tannins and subtle floweriness. **Dolcetto d'Alba Lodoli 2013 (●** 13,000 bt) is typical and drinkable, **Langhe Riesling 2012 (○** 3.500 bt; 10 €) has good grip and acidity.

Fiorenzo Nada

Località Rombone
Via Ausario, 12-C
tel. 0173 638254
www.nada.it
nadafiorenzo@nada.it

21 ac - 45,000 bt

66 You have to have the good fortune to climb up to Rombone to understand why this winery has the Snail symbol: superb wines, painstaking farming and great sensitivity in every operation 99

PEOPLE - We were accompanied by Bruno's son Danilo who, after studying in other fields has decided to farm the land. This is a sign of the power of the Langa and its protagonists, as well as a virtuous continuity that we find heartening."

VINEYARDS - While we were walking in the vineyards, Danilo said, "We hope to switch to organics, in fact we're almost there." This is our hope too, as the cover-cropped vineyards are beautifully kept. Chemicals haven't been used here for years, the vines are old and the crus (Rombone e Manzola) are perfectly located. A small investment was made recently in two plots nearby.

WINES - The difference between Rombone and Manzola lies chiefly in the respective vineyards. The former has vines that are 51 years old, whereas the latter was planted 20 years ago and has soil with a higher percentage of sand. **Barbaresco Manzola 2010 (●** 6,600 bt) has floral aromas, elegant weight and perfectly balanced juice. **Langhe Rosso Seifile 2010 (●** barbera, nebbiolo; 3,000 bt), in which barbera predominates, is as splendid as ever, with plenty of acidity and tanginess and fruity elegance. **Langhe Nebbiolo 2012 (●** 10,000 bt) is magnificent to drink now and **Barbera d'Alba 2012 (●** 5,000 bt) and **Dolcetto d'Alba 2013 (●** 10,000 bt) are very enjoyable too.

> **slow wine** **BARBARESCO ROMBONE 2010 (●** 4,000 bt) is a real bomb of a wine. It offers hints of cocoa and coffee with an encore of ripe red berries. The palate is powerful with good, non-invasive tannins.

FERTILIZERS organic-mineral, manure pellets	**FERTILIZERS** natural manure
PLANT PROTECTION chemical	**PLANT PROTECTION** copper and sulphur
WEED CONTROL chemical, mechanical	**WEED CONTROL** mechanical
YEASTS selected	**YEASTS** native
GRAPES 100% estate-grown	**GRAPES** 100% estate-grown
CERTIFICATION none	**CERTIFICATION** none

VERDUNO (CN)
Alessandria Fratelli

Via Beato Valfrè, 59
tel. 0172 470113
www.fratellialessandria.it
info@fratellialessandria.it

35 ac - 80,000 bt `10% discount`

❝ A historic cellar that looks to the future through the young but experienced eyes of Vittore Alessandria: conscientious farming, fair prices, wines of absolute quality ❞

PEOPLE - The cellar is housed in a magnificent 18th-century palazzo in one of the loveliest villages in the Barolo DOCG, and the winery is certainly one of the most historic in the Langa district. It has been owned by the Alessandria family only since 1870. Vittore Alessandria, who represents the fifth generation of the family, is sensitive and conscientious, an advocate of innovation by small steps. Working alongside him in the vineyard and the cellar are his father Gian Battista and uncle Alessandro.

VINEYARDS - The vineyards are spread over two communes: there are three acres at Verduno in one of the most renowned Barolo crus, Monvigliero, where the splendid vines are up to 40 years old. Then there are the parcels of San Lorenzo, Pisapola, Neirane and Rocca, among others, and four acres at Monforte, one of which in the Gramolere cru, noted for the finesse of its grapes.

WINES - Wines of considerable elegance and sensibility. **Barolo Monvigliero 2010** (● 7,000 bt) is as graceful and airy on the nose as it is tangy and juicy on the palate. This year grapes from the San Lorenzo cru were rechanneled into **Barolo 2010** (● 15,000 bt), an inviting little gem of a wine with fruity and tertiary aromas, vertical and tonic without being austere or rigid. **Verduno Pelaverga Speziale 2013** (● 15,000 bt) bewitches with the finesse of its fruit and intriguing spiciness, its combination of flavor and acidity balancing the alcohol to create great drinkability. **Langhe Nebbiolo Prinsiot 2012** (● 10,000 bt) is solid and enjoyable.

`slow wine` **Barolo Gramolere 2010** (● 5,000 bt) Balsamic with notes of crisp apples and pears and a deep, flavorful palate. A minor Langa masterpiece.

FERTILIZERS mineral, manure pellets, green manure
PLANT PROTECTION chemical, copper and sulphur
WEED CONTROL mechanical
YEASTS native
GRAPES 100% estate-grown
CERTIFICATION none

VERDUNO (CN)
G.B. Burlotto

Via Vittorio Emanuele, 28
tel. 0172 470122
www.burlotto.com
burlotto@burlotto.com

37 ac - 80,000 bt

PEOPLE - At the Burlotto cellar, a historic institution for Verduno and Barolo both, you breathe an air of yesteryear. Not dust and cobwebs, mind you! No, here tradition is lived not as something to dwell upon but as a springboard for a unique, unmistakable winemaking style, at once pure and simple, rooted in the terroir. The show is directed by Fabio Alessandria, with his parents Giuseppe Alessandria and Marina Burlotto in the wings.

VINEYARDS - Verduno is the epicenter of the Burlotto vineyards. Its flagship cru is Monvigliero, too often overlooked today but remembered by local small farmers as one of the Langa's finest. Other Verduno vineyards include Neirane, Breri and Rocche dell'Olmo, and the Burlottos also own plots in the prestigious Cannubi district, near Barolo.

WINES - To begin with, the excellent **Verduno Pelaverga 2013** (● 20,000 bt), which is elegant and subtle with delicious peppery spiciness. Tangy with notes of gooseberry and nettle, **Langhe Sauvignon Veridies 2013** (○ 6,000 bt) has nothing to envy the best the typology has to offer. **Barolo Acclivi 2010** (● 4,500 bt), an assemblage of grapes from different Verduno vineyards, buttonholes you with its airy character, in which citrusy, spicy nuances are very much to the fore. **Barolo Cannubi 2010** (● 4,000 bt) is the most robust, well-built and overwhelming of the trio. The textbook **Langhe Nebbiolo 2012** (● 7,000 bt) is deliciously aromatic and Barolo-ish.

`slow wine` **Barolo Monvigliero 2013** (● 7,000 bt) Huge elegance and unique character. The wine's strong sense of place can be detected in its notes of aromatic herbs, graphite and berry fruits. It's living proof of how Monvigliero is up there among the grands crus of Barolo.

FERTILIZERS natural manure
PLANT PROTECTION chemical, copper and sulphur
WEED CONTROL chemical, mechanical
YEASTS selected
GRAPES 5% bought in
CERTIFICATION none

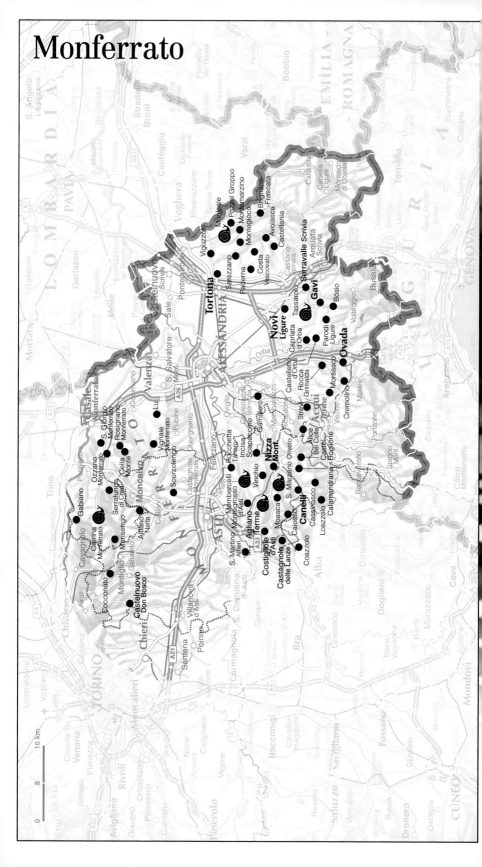

Monferrato

AGLIANO TERME (AT)

Dacapo

Strada Asti-Mare, 4
tel. 0141 964921
www.dacapo.it
info@dacapo.it

18 ac - 45,000 bt `10% discount`

❝ Dino Riccomagno and Paolo Dania have now received organic certification, another step forward in their pursuit of eco-sustainability. Again this year they presented a range of classic local wines ❞

PEOPLE - The oldest part of the farmhouse, surrounded by vineyards, dates to the 17th century. Since then it has undergone extensions and alterations.

VINEYARDS - Some of the company's vineyards occupy the hillsides to the rear of the farmhouse. The central section is planted with barbera, the upper with grignolino. The location is optimal and air circulation good. The pinot nero and ruchè plantings are at Castagnole Monferrato. The viticultural approach is organic with the use of green manure. As in many other areas of the Monferrato district, the grapes – especially barbera and pinot nero – are vulnerable to *flavescence dorée*.

WINES - The release of Metodo Classico 2010 has been delayed to wait for a more complex, nuanced version. **Barbera d'Asti Sup. Nizza Vigna Dacapo 2011 (●** 7,000 bt) is a red with intense sweet aromas of red berries and a fleshy palate with spicy notes and an earthy finish. **Barbera d'Asti Sup. Sanbastian 2012 (●** 19,000 bt) matures on steel and reveals lively, clear-cut fruit with tinges of fresh herbs and nice symmetry. **Piemonte Pinot Nero 2011 (●** 2,500 bt) offers notes of berries on the nose and rich palate with adequate acidity and a spicy lingering finish. The well-built **Ruchè di Castagnole Monferrato Majoli 2013 (●** 10,000 bt) expresses classic notes of rose petal with a precise aromatic finish. **Grignolino d'Asti 2013 (●** 2.000 bt) is floral, spicy and herby with juice and solid tannins.

FERTILIZERS	green manure
PLANT PROTECTION	copper and sulphur
WEED CONTROL	mechanical
YEASTS	selected
GRAPES	100% estate-grown
CERTIFICATION	organic

CANELLI (AT)

L'Armangia €

Regione San Giovanni, 122
tel. 0141 824947
www.armangia.it
armangiavini@libero.it

26 ac - 95,000 bt `10% discount`

PEOPLE - Competence, humility and a spirit of camaraderie – these are just some of the things we like about Canelli-based *vigneron* Ignazio Giovine, a source of inspiration and support for many colleagues in the area. His adventure in the wine world began in 1988, when he was a specialist in whites. Following the success of his first Barbera Titòn in 1995, he had to review his approach – nothing dramatic about this for a curious experimenter who relishes a challenge.

VINEYARDS - The vineyards are split up and scattered over seven different plots of land, bought over the years with commendable insight at Canelli, Moasca and San Marzano. Given these premises, Ignazio doesn't bank on single-vineyard wines. On the contrary, since he knows his vineyards like the backs of his hands, he prefers to compensate for the flaws and/or excesses of certain plots (in terms of weight, alcohol, aromas and so on) by assembling wines to achieve maximum balance and to reflect the vintage as faithfully as possible.

WINES - The steel-fermented **Barbera d'Asti Sopra Berruti 2013 (●** 15,000 bt) is full of verve, close-knit and packed with fruit, whereas the wood-fermented **Piemonte Chardonnay Robi&Robi 2012 (○** 2,300 bt) releases subtle toasty notes, which are followed by a dense palate with a stylish acid-savory backbone. At the top of its category as ever is **Moscato d'Asti Canelli 2013 (○** 7,000 bt), which is creamy and citrusy in style. **Piemonte Albarossa Macchiaferro 2011 (●** 2,700 bt) is concentrated with suggestions of iron and a burly, clinching palate. The complex **Monferrato Rosso Pacifico 2009 (●** 4,000 bt) is an assemblage of nebbiolo, freisa and albarossa with cabernet and merlot.

> **slow wine** BARBERA D'ASTI SUP. NIZZA TITÒN **2011 (●** 6,700 bt) A cask- and barrique-fermented red with velvety, dense, succulent pulp. The aromas are Barbera through and through. Sheer perfection!

FERTILIZERS	humus
PLANT PROTECTION	chemical, copper and sulphur
WEED CONTROL	chemical, mechanical
YEASTS	selected
GRAPES	100% estate-grown
CERTIFICATION	none

CANELLI (AT)

Contratto

Via Contratto, 56
tel. 0141 823349
www.contratto.it
info@contratto.it

CERRINA MONFERRATO (AL)

Iuli

Via Centrale, 27
tel. 0142 946657
www.iuli.it
cavimon@iuli.it

---

61 ac - 265.000 bt

PEOPLE - In 2014 the Contratto cellar effectively became part of a World Heritage Site, just like Canelli's other Metodo Classico "cathedrals." The aging tunnels hewn into the rock are spectacular, likely unique in Italy, and reminiscent of those at French champagne maisons. In 2011 the company was taken over by the Rivetti family who, like a latter-day King Midas, are totally overhauling the historic brand (which dates from 1867) to restore it to its early 20th-century glory.

VINEYARDS - Giorgio Rivetti realized that change had to start from the vineyards as soon as he set foot on the property. And that's what's happened, the company renting 60 acres at Montalto Pavese, with vineyards 30-50 years old at altitudes in excess of 1,300 feet. The rest of the grapes are bought in either through dedicated purchases or from Contratto's historic vinedressers.

WINES - The style is clear and precise: no dosages and only single vintages. The excellent **M. Cl. Brut Pas Dosé Blanc de Blancs 2010** (O chardonnay; 12,000 bt) has very complex aromas that range from flint to meadow flowers to iodine, an acid, biting palate (with residual sugar of just 3 g/lt of sugar), an elegant perlage and an inviting finish. The enticing, flavorsome **M. Cl. Extra Brut 2010** (O chardonnay, pinot noir; 90,000 bt), is matured 30 months on its yeasts without barrique-aging, again with residual sugars of just 3 g/lt). The nose is a triumph of peach and apricots and delicate yeasts, the palate is dry and saline. Last but not least, a house classic, **Asti M. Cl. De Miranda 2011** (O 6,000 bt).

---

42 ac - 50,000 bt

66 A small cooperative, authentic, nonconformist and healthily rebellious, that has valorized and stewards an area of Piedmont that is often forgotten about 99

PEOPLE - The heart and soul of the company is Fabrizio Iuli, a talented, gifted winemaker. Humble, serene and generous, he has clear ideas but is also open to dialogue, and is endowed with rare sensitivity and respect towards his land and everything that surrounds him. He is helped in this "adventure" of his by his wife Summer Wolf, his sister Cristina, brothers Dan and Gad Lerner, and the wife of the latter, Umberta.

VINEYARDS - The vines have always been cultivated organically, ever since the company was set up in 1998, but the real buzzword here is basically "common sense." Fabrizio regards himself as a *barberista* but also relishes a challenge. After years of experience with nebbiolo and pinot nero, he's now dedicating himself heart and soul to slarina, a rare native grape now on the verge of extinction.

WINES - The ability to manage the subtle *fil rouge* between *laissez-faire* and delicate manual interventions to help the must become a faithful mirror of its terroir are the sign of a great *vigneron*. Fabrizio's wines are stylistically precise with great expressive naturalness and aging ability. **Monferrato Rosso Nino 2012** (● pinot nero; 4,000 bt) is intense, robust and subtly spicy, consigning itself to the palate with grace and delicacy. **Monferrato Rosso Malidea 2010** (● 3,500 bt) is an excellent Nebbiolo, monovarietal as of this year.

> **slow wine** BARBERA DEL MONFERRATO SUP. BARABBA 2010 (● 5,000 bt) Made with grapes planted more than 70 years ago, a wine that shows no ill effects from barrique-aging – on the contrary. It expresses pure, intact, juicy fruit with a sprightly, racy palate and a taut, acid heart.

FERTILIZERS organic-mineral, green manure	FERTILIZERS none
PLANT PROTECTION chemical, copper and sulphur	PLANT PROTECTION copper and sulphur
WEED CONTROL chemical, mechanical	WEED CONTROL mechanical
YEASTS selected	YEASTS native
GRAPES 30% bought in	GRAPES 100% estate-grown
CERTIFICATION none	CERTIFICATION organic

Borgo Maragliano €

Regione San Sebastiano, 2
tel. 0144 87132
www.borgomaragliano.com
info@borgomaragliano.com

Cascina la Ghersa

Regione Chiarina, 2
tel. 0141 856 012
www.laghersa.it
info@laghersa.it

---

62 ac - 310,000 bt   `10% discount`

PEOPLE - We at *Slow Wine* have to consider ourselves fortunate; scouting the country for the guide, we come across splendid places and wonderful people. Take Borgo Maragliano and the husband-and-wife team of Carlo Galliano and Silvia Quirico, for example. Carlo and Silvia run their cellar with a steady hand, their sights always set on the production of quality wine. They rely on the precious help of Carlo's dad, Giuseppe Galliano, and their top wines are the Moscato and the Metodo Classicos.

VINEYARDS - A parcel on the ridge of the hill in front of the cellar (which has zero environmental impact) has been planted with a Riesling clone from a Rhineland winery which will soon give life to a Metodo Classico. Pinot nero, which performs well here, has been planted on the northern side, and in the best, sunniest positions grow chardonnay and moscato. Not far away, at Bistagno, are the traditional brachetto grapes and a new planting of chardonnay.

WINES - Chardonnay Brut (○ 68,000 bt), a long Metodo Charmat, is pleasantly fresh-tasting with delicate perlage. **M. Cl. Brut Blanc de Blancs Francesco Galliano 2011** (○ chardonnay; 14,000 bt) has complex aromas with a nuanced, very lively palate. **M. Cl. Brut Giuseppe Galliano 2010** (○ 21,000 bt) marries the sexy fruit of pinot nero with the elegance of chardonnay to produce wonderfully stylish mousse. **M. Cl. Brut Rosé Giovanni Galliano 2010** (○ 7,000 bt), a monovarietal pinot nero, has seductive creaminess, sweet fruit and acid brio. Moscato d'Asti La Caliera 2013 `Everyday Wine` (○ 131,000 bt) has its customary sweet notes, braced by refreshing citrus fruit. **Loazzolo 2010** (○ 3,360 bt), a wine of consummate class made with late-harvested grapes, has notes of exotic fruit and moss.

---

59 ac - 150,000 bt   `10% discount`

PEOPLE - Massimo Pastura represents the fourth generation of this family cellar, which he has been running since 1989. Pragmatic, enterprising and concrete, sells his wines on markets all over the world without betraying his own distinctive style. The challenge he faces from day to day is the valorization of his local area, which, in his opinion, still has a lot of unexpressed potential. He does so by seeking to get the best out of the finest single terroirs.

VINEYARDS - The arsenal of vineyards spread out over a number of different communes. The feathers in the cellar's cap are Vignassa, planted in 1925 and Le Cave, planted in 1996 by Massimo himself, after selecting the most suitable clones and rootstock. Massimo is also enamored of the five acres of timorasso and croatina at Sarezzano and the Poggio vineyard at Gavi. A tiny amount of grapes is also bought in from trusted vinedressers who, like Massimo, work without and use systemic products very prudentially.

WINES - La Ghersa adopts a classic style with long macerations for the Barbera selections, fermentations in cement vats and wood casks and careful use of barrels. **Barbera d'Asti Sup. Vignassa 2011** (● 5,000 bt) is characterized by close-knit minerality and the verve, compactness and bite of its body. **Barbera d'Asti Sup. Muascae 2011** (● 2,700 bt) is "reinforced" with raisined grapes to add depth without compromising elegance. The cellar's "warhorse" is the gutsy, fruity Barbera d'Asti Piagè 2013 `Everyday Wine` (● 55,000 bt), Excellent too is the rose version, **Piagè Rosé 2013** (◑ 15,000 bt). **Barbera d'Asti Sup. Camparò 2012** (● 40.000 bt) is solid and close-knit. The aromatic profile of **Colli Tortonesi Timorasso Timian 2011** (○ 2,200 bt) is marked by wild flowers with a streak of saltiness.

FERTILIZERS manure pellets, natural manure
PLANT PROTECTION chemical, copper and sulphur
WEED CONTROL chemical, mechanical
YEASTS selected
GRAPES 30% bought in
CERTIFICATION none

FERTILIZERS organic-mineral, natural manure
PLANT PROTECTION chemical, copper and sulphur
WEED CONTROL mechanical
YEASTS selected
GRAPES 6% bought in
CERTIFICATION none

MOMBERCELLI (AT)

Luigi Spertino

Strada Lea, 505
tel. 0141 959098
www.luigispertino.it
luigi.spertino@libero.it

MONLEALE (AL)

Vigneti Massa

Piazza Capsoni, 10
tel. 0131 80302
vignetimassa@libero.it

---

22 ac - 40,000 bt	10% discount

❝ Over the years this friendly farming family has not only practiced eco-friendly viticulture but also produced wines of the highest standard ❞

PEOPLE - Mauro Spertino and his father Luigi gave us a warm welcome when we visited. This time round we tasted a top-notch barbera-pinot nero blend that testifies to the prowess and skill of Mauro in the vinification of healthy, ripe grapes.

VINEYARDS - The Barbera selection is made with raisined grapes from the oldest vines in the La Mandorla distict. Here we were able to admire turfed vine rows awash with flowers where the high grass was about to be mown. All the operations are manual to avoid the soil from compacting and this translates into many more hours of work in the vineyard. The varieties cultivated are barbera, cortese and pinot nero, while the grignolino grapes come from the renowned Portacomaro growing area.

WINES - Barbera d'Asti Sup. Vigna La Mandorla 2012 (● 3,000 bt) is leaner with less residual sweetness than usual, but it does have nice body with a chirpy acidity that makes for excellent drinkability. **Barbera d'Asti 2012** (● 14,000 bt) has nice firm fruit on the nose and palate, where freshness and fruity flesh are beautifully symmetrical, and a juicy finish. An extra year's aging has benefited the truly interesting **Piemonte Cortese Vilet 2011** (○ 2,000 bt): macerated on the lees for 40 days, it's full of impact on both nose and palate, nuanced and pervasive.

> **slow wine** **GRIGNOLINO D'ASTI 2013** (● 16,500 bt) A red that's as wonderful as ever. It has precise classic notes of grass on the nose and punchiness on the palate. A true evergreen.

---

57 ac - 110,000 bt

❝ A maestro for many colleagues, a promoter of the local area, an independent vinedresser and a gifted winemaker. The many faces of one man: Walter Massa ❞

PEOPLE - Walter began dressing vines in the late 1970s and released his first bottles of Timorasso, a grape and wine he rediscovered and helped launch in the early 1990s.

VINEYARDS - This cellar owes its fortune to thoughtful and intelligent selection of the most suitable local vineyards for the different grape varieties, notably timorasso, complicated because it's susceptible to humidity, then the other classic Monferrato grapes such as barbera, freisa, croatina and moscato. The vineyards are situated at an altitude of 900 feet and the soils vary greatly with components ranging from pebbles to clay to limestone.

WINES - In protest against the red-tape of denominations, Walter Massa has abandoned them altogether. All the wines tasted were monovarietal timorassos. **Derthona 2012** (○ 40,000 bt) has a very personal style with a few sensory imprecisions due to its young age, but the palate is edgy and flavorsome with a very sprightly finish. **Derthona Sterpi 2012** (○ 4,000 bt) is unctuous and imposing with classic chalky notes. **Derthona Montecitorio 2012** (○ 4,000 bt), made with grapes from the coolest vineyard, is subtler and more mineral.

> **slow wine** **DERTHONA COSTA DEL VENTO 2012** (○ 6,000 bt) A wine of tremendous aromatic tone, redolent of chamomile, orange zest and lime. The palate is acidic and saline with a benzene finish. Weight and drinkability – two qualities that don't come together very often.

FERTILIZERS natural manure
PLANT PROTECTION copper and sulphur
WEED CONTROL mechanical
YEASTS native
GRAPES 100% estate-grown
CERTIFICATION none

FERTILIZERS organic-mineral, mineral, natural manure, compost, green manure
PLANT PROTECTION copper and sulphur
WEED CONTROL chemical, mechanical
YEASTS native
GRAPES 100% estate-grown
CERTIFICATION none

La Gironda €

Strada Bricco,12
tel. 0141 701013
www.lagironda.com
info@lagironda.com

La Raia

Strada di Monterotondo, 79
tel. 0143 743685
www.la-raia.it
info@la-raia.it

---

21 ac - 40,000 bt `10% discount`

PEOPLE - It's no secret for readers of our guide that we admire this cellar a lot, and for a variety of reasons: 1) huge value for money in view of the immense quality of the wines; 2) it practices very sustainable agriculture; 3) Susanna Galandrino is the standard-bearer of an entire terroir and fought with all her might to bring the Nizza DOCG into being. Three good reasons, among many others, to make a detour down this way.

VINEYARDS - As we said, here the vineyards are farmed carefully and rationally. Weedkillers are banned and, under the supervision of agronomist Piero Roseo, chemical treatments are limited to a bare minimum. Most of the vineyards encircle the cellar, but a large number, planted with nebbiolo grapes, are also to be found at Calamandrana on steep slopes at a considerable altitude.

WINES - The common denominators of the wines are cleanness and drinkability, landrootedness and craftsmanship. The specialty of the house is the barbera grape. The steel-fermented **Barbera d'Asti La Lippa 2013** (● 10,000 bt) is delicious, braced by supporting acidity. Made with grapes from an old vineyard with a low yield, the magnificent **Barbera d'Asti La Gena 2012** (● 8,000 bt) is concentrated and fruity, streaked with softness and flavor. Original and elegant, **Monferrato Rosso Soul 2010** (● nebbiolo; 1,000 bt). **Moscato d'Asti 2013** (○ 3,500 bt) and **Brachetto d'Aqui 2013** (● 3,500 bt) are both enjoyable.

| slow wine | LA BARBERA D'ASTI SUP. NIZZA LE NICCHIE **2011** (● 7,000 bt) A barrique- and tonneau-fermented wine in which the wood is set off by earthy tones that make it one of the finest in its category. |

---

104 ac - 120,000 bt `10% discount`

PEOPLE - The Rossi Cairo family project at La Raia is evolving all the time and, year after year, new bits are being added to it. Following the stable and the barn, vital for the biodynamic practices implemented, this year saw the creation of the Fondazione La Raia. The foundation's purpose is to place permanent works of art among the vineyards, hence to bind art, culture and land indissolubly.

VINEYARDS - The vineyards are immersed in an ecosystem of great beauty and charm. Last year they were extended by about 25 acres with the purchase of a neighboring estate. The grapes cultivated are almost all cortese, and the average age of the vineyards is about 28 years, with the exception of the one in which the grapes for Gavi Pisè are harvested, which is 70 years old.

WINES - The wines in this years range were once more linear, well crafted and dependable. Top of the list is the nice **Gavi Pisè 2012** (○ 15,000 bt), which starts a little stiff on the nose before opening out to reveal floral and fruity notes that supplement a palate replete with grip, flavor, juice, and length. We also liked **Gavi 2013** `Everyday Wine` (○ 80,000 bt) and its pleasing, well-defined aromas of fruit and wild flowers, tangy, refreshing, long palate, and enjoyable almond-edged finish. Notes of aromatic herbs and a mature blossomy tone characterize **Gavi Ris. 2012** (○ 7,000 bt), which follows up with a linear plate and something of a low-key finish. Wood-aging is very much to the fore in **Piemonte Barbera Largè 2010** (● 3,000 bt), which has toasty, spicy notes. Simple, pleasurable, and drinkable – that's **Piemonte Barbera 2013** (● 16,000 bt).

FERTILIZERS natural manure
PLANT PROTECTION copper and sulphur
WEED CONTROL mechanical
YEASTS selected
GRAPES 100% estate-grown
CERTIFICATION none

FERTILIZERS biodynamic preparations, green manure
PLANT PROTECTION copper and sulphur, organic
WEED CONTROL mechanical
YEASTS native
GRAPES 100% estate-grown
CERTIFICATION biodynamic, organic

SAN MARTINO ALFIERI (AT)

Marchesi Alfieri

Piazza Alfieri, 28
tel. 0141 976015
www.marchesialfieri.it
alfieri@marchesialfieri.it

SAN MARZANO OLIVETO (AT)

Carussin

Regione Mariano, 27
tel. 0141 831358
www.carussin.it
ferrobruna@inwind.it

---

52 ac - 100,000 bt | **10% discount**

PEOPLE - If you happen by this magnificent Monferrato winery, be sure to have a stroll through the beautifully kept park round the villa, part English-style lawns and landscaping, part ornamental Italian garden. Sisters Antonella, Emanuela and Giovanna San Martino have entrusted Mario Olivero with the management and he has been assisted for some years now by the young and enthusiastic Christian Carlevero. The lovely cellars date from 1703, as an engraved stone tablet attests.

VINEYARDS - The barbera vineyard that produces the grapes for Alfiera rests on limestone soils with traces of sand and clay. The farming is de facto organic and it was planted in 1937. Despite the odd gap, many of the old vines enjoy excellent health. Another small parcel a few miles away, a few rows of pinot nero, was planted as long ago as 1860, supposedly at the wish of Camillo Cavour. The vineyards account for only about 50 of the 350 acres of land owned by the farm.

WINES - The mind-blowing **Barbera d'Asti Sup. Alfiera 2011** (● 15,000) is a clever mix of ancient and modern, opulent yet vibrant, dripping with juice and concentrated, perfectly balanced. The precise, elegant, typical **Terre Alfieri 2011** (● nebbiolo; 2,600 bt) is blossomy on the nose, stylish on the palate, and very well-developed. **Piemonte Pinot Nero 2011** (● 3,000 bt) has a bouquet of berry fruits and a lush, powerful, pulpy, well-balanced palate. **Monferrato Rosso Sostegno 2012** (● barbera, pinot nero; 15,600 bt) is a simple red with juicy fruit and nice flesh. **Piemonte Grignolino 2013** (● 4,500 bt) is spicy and herby.

> **slow wine** **BARBERA D'ASTI LA TOTA 2012** (● 58,000 bt) As always, a jewel of drinkability and typicality, a veritable standard-bearer for the denomination.

---

37 ac - 80,000 bt | **10% discount**

❝ Donkeys, sheep, unkempt vines, the farm school and the coming and going of enthusiasts make Carussin a unique place, in some respects magical ❞

PEOPLE - Bruna Ferro, her husband Luigi and their children Luca and Matteo are a close bunch. They not only run the winery but also the "agribar" Grappolo contro Luppolo (Grapes v. Hops), which they opened a couple of years ago, where you can taste wines and craft beers in a laid-back atmosphere.

VINEYARDS - It's not organic certification or biodynamic practices that raise Carussin to icon status in the world of sustainable viticulture. Respect for the landscape, dialogue with plants, idea-sharing with other producers, coexistence with the fauna, the exaltation of biodiversity (viz. the recent purchase of a wood in the Langa hills near Asti) – these are the distinctive features of a vision of pure, authentic farming.

WINES - Don't expect esoteric features in the wine or characteristics drawn from schools of enological fanaticism. Just let yourself be won over by a style that privileges drinkability, varietal and geographical recognizability, the Asti tradition and personality. Aromatic, typical, happy, full of fun and drinkable, **Barbera d'Asti Asinoi 2013** (● 50,000 bt) is a successful portrait of the soul of Carussin. As is Barbera d'Asti Lia Vi 2013 Everyday Wine (● 15,000 bt), which is rich and tangy. Nizza Ferro Carlo was absent this year but there are still bottles from the 2007 vintage at the cellar. **Carica L'Asino 2013** (○ 3,500 bt), a tribute to this unusual grape, is a little husky. **Moscato Filari Corti 2013** (○ 5,000 bt), fermented only with native yeasts, is enjoyable.

FERTILIZERS organic-mineral, compost
PLANT PROTECTION chemical, copper and sulphur
WEED CONTROL chemical, mechanical
YEASTS selected
GRAPES 100% estate-grown
CERTIFICATION none

FERTILIZERS biodynamic preparations, green manure
PLANT PROTECTION copper and sulphur
WEED CONTROL mechanical
YEASTS native
GRAPES 25% bought in
CERTIFICATION organic

Castello di Tassarolo ☺

Località Alborina, 1
tel. 0143 342248
www.castelloditassarolo.it
info@castelloditassarolo.it

La Colombera

Frazione Vho
Strada Comunale per Vho, 7
tel. 0131 867795
www.lacolomberavini.it
info@lacolomberavini.it

---

42 ac - 120,000 bt | 10% discount

❝ Thanks to years of biodynamic farming, the results shine through, even in a difficult vintage like the last. The fact is that the wines resist adversity well and only very few of them suffering ❞

PEOPLE - It's always a pleasure to meet Massimiliana Spinola and Henry Finzi-Constantine, partners in life and in business, who have been running this wonderful winery for years. For them, their biodynamic and "naturalist" approach is not just a matter of cultivation techniques but also, and above all, a life choice. Sharing their work with them is enologist Vincenzo Munì.

VINEYARDS - Henry oversees the vineyard personally and uses biodynamic accumulation to prepare the manure. "It's the best soil nourishment possible," he says, "the missing link to improve the soil and give it more life."

WINES - We have doubts about the labels without added sulfites, but we liked the traditional ones a lot. **Gavi del Comune di Tassarolo Spinola 2013** (○ 40,000 bt) is dynamic and nuanced with crisp fruit, vegetal tinges, lean body and very good flavor. Gavi del Comune di Tassarolo Il Castello 2013 Everyday Wine (○ 40,000 bt) is enjoyable fruity, rounder and generous with a racy finish. Wood-aged **Gavi del Comune di Tassarolo Alborina 2012** (○ 6,000 bt) has spicy, Mediterranean tones. Without added sulfites and wood-aged briefly, **Gavi del Comune di Tassarolo Titouan 2013** (○ 3,000 bt) is a wine with aromas of sweet fruit, meat and officinal herbs. **Gavi Spinola Senza Solfiti 2013** (○ 20,000 bt) has notes of ripe apples and pears and citrus fruit. **Monferrato Rosso Cuvée 2013** (● barbera, cabernet sauvignon; 13,000 bt) is well crafted.

---

49 ac - 70,000 bt

PEOPLE - La Colombera was founded in 1937 by Elisa Semino's grandparents. Elisa is a young and enthusiastic winemaker with a degree in enology at Milan University. The present cellar is situated in the Vho hills, a few miles from the center of Tortona. It released its first label in 1998 and its first Timorasso in 2000. Elisa is flanked in the vineyard by her dad and Piercarlo, who also cultivates the famous peaches of Tortona.

VINEYARDS - Of the cellar's 50 or so acres of vineyard, 34 form a single plot. All have clayey soil with a sizable limestone component produced by the local Sant'Agata marl. Situated at an altitude of 885-1,020 feet, the vineyards were planted in 1997 and are Guyot-trained. The varieties cultivated are all local: first and foremost timorasso, then freisa, barbera, nibiô, and croatina. A new timorasso vineyard will become productive in two years' time.

WINES - Elisa's wines stand out year by year for their grace and elegance. She also sells very good bottled wine that's much admired locally and beyond. She told us 2012 was a good vintage for Timorasso and, having tasted the two labels presented, we have to say she's right. **Colli Tortonesi Timorasso Il Montino 2012** (○ 4,500 bt) is a paragon of elegance, brightness and balance. **Colli Tortonesi Cortese Bricco Bartolomeo 2013** (○ 9,000 bt) has character and a sense of place. Of the reds, **Colli Tortonesi Croatina La Romba 2012** (● 5,000 bt) is succulent with fruit and spices well to the fore.

> **slow wine** **COLLI TORTONESI TIMORASSO DERTHONA 2012** (○ 16,000 bt) Perfect tangy, fruity notes with faint hints of petrol and fantastic length.

FERTILIZERS biodynamic preparations, green manure
PLANT PROTECTION copper and sulphur, organic
WEED CONTROL mechanical
YEASTS native
GRAPES 100% estate-grown
CERTIFICATION organic

FERTILIZERS natural manure, green manure
PLANT PROTECTION copper and sulphur
WEED CONTROL mechanical
YEASTS selected
GRAPES 100% estate-grown
CERTIFICATION none

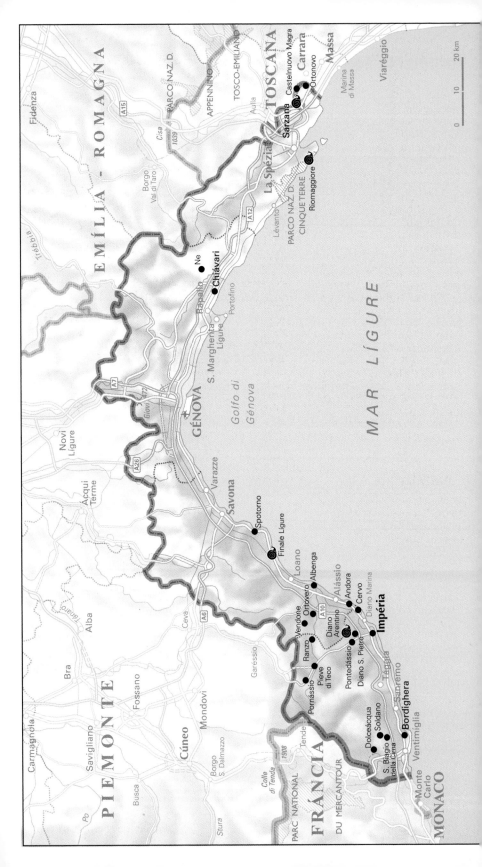

LIGURIA

Once again this year the region produced a lot of interesting wines, despite unfavorable climatic conditions that caused first outbreaks of coulure, then delayed the ripening of the grapes, which ultimately proved slightly over-acidic. In general, the wineries listed in the following pages stood out for their consistency, which translated into quality wines and a growing awareness of the need to bank on the specificity of their grape varieties and vineyards that is earning Liguria plaudits even beyond its borders. This is why it is important to stress the renewed attention to rossese di Dolceacqua, Liguria's principal red grape, which seems to have overcome its crisis of identity once and for all, thanks to the excellent work of producers who have captured all its potential and peculiarity. Browsing through ISTAT Agricultural Census data from 2010, rossese is grown on a total area of about 375 acres of land, of which 77% in the DOC; it is to be found almost exclusively in the province of Imperia, apart from a few acres that spill over into the province of Savona. Vermentino is much more common, especially in eastern Liguria, accounting for 23% of the region's vineyards, a total of 865 acres. Pigato, the most representative grape of western Liguria, occupies 494 acres of land. The three grapes – rossese, vermentino and pigato – account for 46% of the total amount of land planted with vines, about 3,800 acres, while 4-5% is dedicated to the cultivation of albarola, bosco, dolcetto and sangiovese. Then comes a long list of "minor" grape varieties, such as bianchetta genovese, lumassina, and ciliegiolo. Making wine in Liguria is a laborious business since most of the vines are cultivated on sometimes steep terraces on scattered hard-to-work plots. Space is tight and the conformation of the terrain draws an uncompromising landscape, with the sea besieging the whole of the southern part of the region, inland from which it is largely mountainous and, to a lesser extent, hilly. There are no other alternatives.

snails ☺↵

Maria Donata Bianchi ⊚⌇

Località Valcrosa
Via Merea
tel. 0183 498233
www.aziendaagricolabianchi.it
info@aziendaagricolabianchi.com

---

10 ac - 25,000 bt

❝ Emanuele Trevia is a fighter, one of the winemakers who have most contributed to the improvement of Ligurian whites. Open to technique but with an eye to tradition, he captures the specific character of the hills of Diano in his wine **❞**

PEOPLE - Then there are Emanuele's wife Donatella Bianchi who, after a long career as a lawyer, now runs the family *agriturismo*, and their daughter Marta, a young enologist who's currently picking up experience abroad.

VINEYARDS - In the valley once sacred to Diana goddess of the hunt are scattered a number of outlying villages all named Diano, from Diano Arentino to Diano Castello. Here mostly white grape varieties grow, Guyot-trained on calcareous-clay soil. The largest vineyard, which stands picturesquely on a hillside near the cellar, has vines that are 15 years old and faces eastwards. In other vineyards there are vermentino vines over 50 years old and red grape vines up to 20 years old.

WINES - The wines are blended to evidence symmetry and elegance, and have an excpetional capacity to combine land-rooted and stylistic expressiveness. The latest vintage has certainly lived up to our expectations. **Riviera Ligure di Ponente Vermentino 2013** (○ 15,000 bt) is low-key as opposed to loud, its fruity tones beefed up by a tangy, full palate, linear and taut with bright richness of flavor in a context of great harmony.

> **slow wine** RIVIERA LIGURE DI PONENTE PIGATO 2013 (○ 10,000 bt) This white is on better form than ever. Self-confident and penetrative, it's a refined combination of fruity tones and hints of thyme and sage. Textured flavor merges with full-bodied structure and a whiff of bitterish saltiness to soar into a long finish.

FERTILIZERS	natural manure, green manure
PLANT PROTECTION	copper and sulphur
WEED CONTROL	mechanical
YEASTS	selected
GRAPES	100% estate-grown
CERTIFICATION	none

Cascina delle Terre Rosse ⊚⌇

Via Manie, 3
tel. 0196 98782

---

14 ac - 24,000 bt

❝ Well-defined and packed with character, these wines mirror the man who makes them and are among the best produced in Liguria **❞**

PEOPLE - Baked by the sun and beaten by the wind, Valdimiro "Vladi" Galluzzo's face is like that of a landlubber sailing among the vines. After 40 years of hard work, he's still as enthusiastic as he was as a young man. Recently he has started listening to the advice of technicians Giuliano Noè and Gianni Forte, but he tends to end up doing his own thing. This is a fact familiar to his wife and sales manager Paola, who has had to put up with him all this time.

VINEYARDS - The vine rows are undersown with mustard, which acts as a cover-crop, and design diverse and perfect geometries. The scenic vineyard at Le Banche, on the Le Manie plateau, near the cellar and the woods, grows 20 to 30-year-old south-facing vines. At Monte younger vines look seawards from narrow rows on very steep slopes. The 40-year-old vines at Pietra Ligure grow in a similar setting.

WINES - **Le Banche 2013** (○ pigato, vermentino; 570 bt) banks on good texture, complexity and flavor. The intense and fruity **Riviera Ligure di Ponente Pigato 2013** (○ 9,700 bt) has above-average iodine brightness and chewy pulp. **Riviera Ligure di Ponente Vermentino 2013** (○ 5,200 bt) is enjoyable from beginning to end, while **Acerbina 2013** (○ lumassina; 1,600 bt) displays nice fruit and well-judged acidity. **Solitario 2012** (● granaccia, barbera, merlot; 520 bt) is as well crafted as ever.

> **slow wine** APOGEO 2013 (○ pigato; 3,100 bt) A white that won us over with its elegant varietal aromas. Dynamic and fragrant, it follows through into a juicy, smooth palate.

FERTILIZERS	green manure
PLANT PROTECTION	copper and sulphur
WEED CONTROL	mechanical
YEASTS	selected
GRAPES	100% estate-grown
CERTIFICATION	none

RIOMAGGIORE (SP)
Walter De Batté
Via Trarcantu, 25
tel. 0187 920127

SARZANA (SP)
Santa Caterina
Via Santa Caterina, 6
tel. 0187 629429
andrea.kihlgren@alice.it

12.5 ac - 12,000 bt

❝ Walter De Batté sometimes feels as if he were in exile, yet his Prima Terra winery is just few hundred yards from his native Cinque Terre, a terroir for which he has battled and with which he's head-over-heels in love ❞

PEOPLE - For some years now De Batté has been bottling his wines under the Prima Terra umbrella. Here he produces labels both from the La Spezia area and the Cinque Terre, and they all have a strong sense of place.

VINEYARDS - Walter has cherry-picked a number of vineyards outside the Cinque Terre National Park, of which one at Montenero at an altitude of 1,600 feet, where he has decided to grow two red grapes, granaccia and syrah. At Riomaggiore he still has a wonderful vineyard full of old perola-trained vines. He also has some very old parcels on very steep slopes in the Colli di Luni denomination.

WINES - This year's batch was rich by Walter's standards. The philosophy is clear: significant extractions with moderate macerations, just a few days for whites. Çericò 2010 (● grenache, alicante, syrah; 2,000 bt) is macerated for longer, for up to about 40 days in fact; highly scented, in the glass it slowly releases hints of truffle, moss and cherry, which lead into a rich, acid, tangy palate. **Harmoge 2011** (○ bosco, vermentino, albarola; 2,000 bt) undergoes brief maceration and has aromas that range from apricot to hay to coffee, followed by a perfectly symmetrical salty, acid, alcoholic palate. **Underwood 2011** (○ bosco; 2,000 bt) is named for the grape and conjures up sea spray and iodine. **Altrove 2011** (○ 1,500 bt), finally, is a blend of an incredible number of well-macerated varieties.

19 ac - 20,000 bt

❝ Andrea Kihlgren is a very sensitive guy, as you can tell from every detail of his work, from his care and attention in the vineyard to his relatively non-interventionist approach to vinification in the cellar ❞

PEOPLE - The ringing of the bells from the church of Santa Caterina mark the rhythm of work at the winery, where Andrea and his wife Alessandra have been practicing natural viticulture for more than 20 years.

VINEYARDS - The Ghiarètolo is made up of three contiguous plots of merlot vines with an average age of 20 years. The tocai grapes all come from a vineyard of over 15 years of age in the Giuncàro district. The vermentino grapes are to be found on the Santa Caterina estate, where the vines have an age of 15-25 years. Here there are also some new albarola vines taken from a native biotype discovered on the old property.

WINES - The 2013 harvest was poor and production had to be cut by half. Which is a real pity because the range presented was one of the best of the last few years. **Giuncàro 2013** (○ sauvigno blanc, tocai; 2,700 bt) is, quite simply, stupendous: on the nose it's complex with a prevalence of grassy, fruity hints and a smooth tangy and mineral palate with an energy that makes the finish go on and on. Also very good is **Colli di Luni Vermentino 2013** (○ 10,000 bt), which is pleasantly fresh with hints of citrus fruit on the nose. **Colli di Luni Vermentino Poggi Alti 2013** (○ 2,000 bt) has a concentrated nose of aromatic herbs and dried fruit. **Colli di Luni Albarola 2013** (○ 300 bt) is fresh and enjoyable. The exquisite **Passito 2011** (● 400 bt), made with canaiolo grapes, amazes with distinctive aromas of cocoa powder and Mediterranean scrub.

FERTILIZERS organic-mineral
PLANT PROTECTION copper and sulphur
WEED CONTROL chemical, mechanical
YEASTS selected, native
GRAPES 100% estate-grown
CERTIFICATION none

FERTILIZERS compost, biodynamic preparations, green manure
PLANT PROTECTION copper and sulphur, organic
WEED CONTROL mechanical
YEASTS native
GRAPES 100% estate-grown
CERTIFICATION none

LOMBARDY

Eagerly awaited, idealized, criticized and – why not? – dreamt of, Expo 2015, the universal exhibition that will put the city of Milan in the world limelight, will soon be upon us. What better opportunity for the Lombardy region as a whole to identify with the spirit and mission of the great event and open its doors to the international public. Wine and gastronomy plus landscape, hospitality and a cordial welcome – these are all vital elements in the promotional policies of the region's winegrowing districts, all very much on the mind of the many vinedressers and winemakers keen to play a key role in making the event a success. It would be superfluous to add that only a vision that sees beyond the event itself will allow Expo 2015 to go off with a bang. It won't be attendance figures and square yards of exhibition space that will determine its triumph or otherwise, but rather its ability to leave a mark, to penetrate the cultural fabric of people and future land development policies geared to an alternative idea of agriculture. The pages that follow serve – in this edition more than ever before – as a guide for the thousands of visitors who, between pavilions, manage to get out into the country among the vineyards and cellars to see for themselves the true face of wine and the stories and people and landscapes behind it. Proof of the great ferment the region has been experiencing over the last few years is the coming to the fore of small winegrowing zones in search of visibility and identity. The zones we have in mind are Terre Lariane, Monte Netto, Valcamonica and Botticino, rejuvenated by the advent of a new generation of farmers. As far as the classic zones are concerned, we note a growing pursuit of sustainable viticultural practices, despite climatic difficulties in some. Franciacorta leads the field by virtue of the commitment of major companies that are moving confidently towards organic wine production. Similar signs are also visible in the Lugana zone, which stood out for the very high quality of its wines this year. The picture is rosy in the Garda area too, where the Valtènesi DOC is particularly busy promoting Chiaretto. In Valtellina, management difficulties may be growing, but not so much as to contain the proliferation of new small cellars thanks to the courage of passionate young winemakers. Encouraging signals from the Oltrepò Pavese, an area riven by identity crises and political problems, were the institution of the Distretto del Vino di Qualità and the birth of groups and associations of young producers in parallel with the general improvement of the Cruasé project. The picture in Valcalepio, alas, is still cloudy from a technical and enological point of view, but we feel that the positive experience of Moscato di Scanzo will encourage the district to find a new identity by placing the priority on simpler, brighter wines.

Andrea Picchioni

CANNETO PAVESE (PV)

Frazione Camponoce, 8
tel. 0385 262139
www.picchioniandrea.it
picchioniandrea@libero.it

24.5 ac - 70,000 bt | 10% discount

❝ With determination, though maybe without realizing it, Andrea Picchioni has set off a little big revolution inside the variegated, in some respects fuzzy world of the wine of the Otrepò. He thoroughly deserves the symbol ❞

PEOPLE - Andrea runs his small winery working hand in glove with his enologist friend Beppe Zatti and with his ears open to the views of other local winegrowers. He is also helped by the whole family.

VINEYARDS - The vineyards of La Solinga, a fully-fledged Buttafuoco cru, overlook the cellar. Here croatina, barbera and uva rara grapes grow in perfect symbiosis with the local area, evidencing its suitability for winegrowing. Work in the vineyard is mostly performed by hand following exclusively and disinterestedly organic methods.

WINES - Though Andrea may have appeared as something of a spumante man over the last few years (witness his celebrated Metodo Classico Profilo, aged 12 years on the yeasts), his heart still lies with his reds. Buttafuoco Luogo della Cerasa 2013 Everyday Wine (● 10,800 bt), an assemblage of barbera, vespolina and croatina, is an extraordinary fusion of terroir, technical prowess and flavor. The more ambitious **Buttafuoco Bricco Riva Bianca 2010** (● 5,000 bt) is the barrel-matured version made with grapes from the oldest vineyard; to the nose it offers quinine nuances, to the palate body and juice. Andrea is good at making the most of simplicity, as may be seen in O.P. Bonarda Vivace Luogo dei Ronchi 2013 Everyday Wine (● 20,000 bt), which is vibrant, taut and eminently quaffable. **Rosso d'Asia 2010** (● 5,000 bt), a well-structured Croatina, is a joy to drink.

FERTILIZERS natural manure
PLANT PROTECTION copper and sulphur
WEED CONTROL mechanical
YEASTS native
GRAPES 100% estate-grown
CERTIFICATION organic

Nino Negri

CHIURO (SO)

Via Ghibellini, 3
tel. 0342 485211
www.ninonegri.it
negri@giv.it

89 ac - 800,000 bt | 10% discount

PEOPLE - Nino Negri is a symbol of the Valtellina, the oldest cellar and the one with the highest production figures. Founded in 1897 by a tradesman and hotelier from Aprica, it's now part of the Gruppo Italiano Vini. Since 1971 the managing enologist has been Casimiro Maule and Matteo Borserio oversees the farming side. It was Maule who geared the entire terroir towards quality by setting an example with impeccable enological style.

VINEYARDS - The company's 70 acres of vineyards are supplemented by another 320 belonging to about 250 associated vine dressers in all the Valtellina subzones. The grape harvest is followed by over 100 separate processes of vinification, which, after blending, give rise to about 20 labels with a nebbiolo base. The new plantings face from east to west and this favors grape ripening and reduces the risk of disease.

WINES - The quality of the labels submitted for tasting was very high indeed. **Sforzato della Valtellina 5 Stelle 2011** (● 30,000 bt) is as elegant as ever with a complex bouquet, albeit slightly held back by its young age. **Sforzato della Valtellina Carlo Negri 2011** Great Wine (● 30,000 bt) is simply outstanding, showing great finesse, freshness and a very long finish. The Valtellina Superiores stood out for their fresh flavor and drinkability. The best of the bunch is **Valtellina Sup. Sassella Le Tense 2011** (● 70,000 bt) with its nicely ripe fruit and firm acid backbone. **Valtellina Sup. Inferno Carlo Negri 2011** (● 30,000 bt) has well-calibrated wood. **Valtellina Sup. Grumello Sasso Rosso 2011** (● 15,000 bt) and **Valtellina Sup. Vigneto Fracia 2011** (● 13,000 bt) are both well-crafted.

FERTILIZERS manure pellets, natural manure, green manure
PLANT PROTECTION chemical, copper and sulphur
WEED CONTROL chemical, mechanical
YEASTS selected
GRAPES 70% bought in
CERTIFICATION none

Rainoldi

CHIURO (SO)

Via Stelvio, 128
tel. 0342 482225
www.rainoldi.com
rainoldi@rainoldi.com

24.5 ac - 180,000 bt `10% discount`

PEOPLE - Aldo Rainoldi holds the Valtellina banner high. His winery is an effective and successful model that combines impressive production figures (in proportion to the size of its properties), very high quality, and a philosophy bound to the promotion of local identity. Aldo is, in fact, the spokesperson for an established group of small-scale viticulturists. His canteen, on the state highway that leads up into the high valley, is open to everyone and well worth a visit.

VINEYARDS - The Rainoldi vineyards are rich and variegated, mostly made up of small parcels of land tended by small viticulturists who sell their grapes to the cellar. The winery also owns plots of its own, most of them contour-plowed to make them easier to farm. For some years now, Aldo has been the local spokesperson for the Simonit&Sirch agronomic protocol.

WINES - The range presented this year was exemplary. Technique, well-calibrated use of wood, exaltation of the terroir, and extreme cleanliness – these are the common denominators of the wines, from first to last. Of the many – arguably too many – labels produced, let's begin with **Sforzato di Valtellina Fruttaio Ca' Rizzieri 2010** (● 12,000 bt), which has raisiny notes blended with elegance and finesse, though it's still of course on the young side. One of the best of the range, **Sforzato di Valtellina 2010** (● 9,000 bt), theoretically the base version but actually much more than that. The real masterpiece, however, is the long, land-rooted **Valtellina Sup. Sassella Ris. 2009** `Great Wine` (● 20,000 bt). The excellent Valtellina **Sup. Grumello Ris. 2009** (● 3,000 bt) still has traces of wood and **Rosso di Valtellina 2012** (● 20,000 bt) is well-crafted.

FERTILIZERS organic-mineral, natural manure	
PLANT PROTECTION chemical, copper and sulphur	
WEED CONTROL mechanical	
YEASTS selected	
GRAPES 35% bought in, wine bought in	
CERTIFICATION none	

Togni Rebaioli

DARFO BOARIO TERME (BS)

Frazione Erbanno
Via Rossini, 19
tel. 0364 529706
www.togni-rebaioli.it
info@togni-rebaioli.it

8.5 ac - 12,000 bt

❝ Being a winemaker today in the Valcamonica might be considered a crazy way of making a living. Yet Enrico Togni does it every day, conscientiously. And doing so, he achieves great enological, symbolic and social satisfactions, for himself and for the whole area ❞

PEOPLE - Enrico attends to every aspect of his small concern, working naturally with great respect for the land. The help of his mother in the vineyard and in the wine cellar and the support of his wife Cinzia are fundamental.

VINEYARDS - The property has built up round the historic vineyards of Enrico's grandfather and grown with the acquisition or leasing of bordering parcels. The wines are terraced on steep slopes at an altitude of about 980 feet. According to position, all the new plantings are given over to nebbiolo or erbanno, an extremely disease-resistant variety typical of the area for which Enrico nourishes a strong passion.

WINES - 2011 was a problematic growing year in the Valcamonica, and Enrico had to give of his all to salvage what he could. His wines have always been not incredible exactly, but undoubtedly good, full of personality, capable of expressing the terroir in which they are born. **Merlot 2009** (● 2,000 bt) is a wine with delicious intact fruit, well modulated on the palate with massive character. A warm, soft Nebbiolo, **1703 2011** (● 1,300 bt) offers slightly overripe fruit accompanied by notes of spice and tobacco. **San Valentino 2012** (● 1,200 bt) is made with erbanno grapes fermented in steel vats and has a bright nose of blackberries followed by nice acidity and plenty of background flavor. **Barbera Vidur 2011** (● 1,500 bt) has a slight vinegray kink on the nose but follows up with a spacious, fruity palate.

FERTILIZERS none	
PLANT PROTECTION copper and sulphur	
WEED CONTROL mechanical	
YEASTS native	
GRAPES 100% estate-grown	
CERTIFICATION none	

PONTE IN VALTELLINA (SO)

Dirupi 🐌

Località Madonna di Campagna
tel. 0342 050667
www.dirupi.com
info@dirupi.com

11 ac - 26,600 bt

66 Winemaking fever and the arrival of new young faces among the dry stone walls are undoubtedly the outcome of the original, pioneering process set into motion by Davide Fasolini and Pierpaolo Di Franco, the faces of Dirupi 99

PEOPLE - After graduating in viticulture and enology in Milan, Birba and Faso, as they're nicknamed, returned to the Valtellina with the idea of saving a wine and natural heritage on the verge of extinction and the intent of making wine that they liked themselves. Mission accomplished!

VINEYARDS - If you visit the vineyards of Dirupi, remember to wear sensible shoes and pray you won't suffer from vertigo. As he clambers like a mountain goat among the drystone walls on the dizzying slopes, Faso talks of the many old clones present in the vineyards and of the winery's property: 11 acres rented from 18 proprietors in 18 different zones!

WINES - These wines are good precisely because they are land-rooted, clean and easily approachable. **Rosso di Valtellina Olé 2013** (● 9,000 bt) is steel-fermented and has good acidity and brightness, while **Valtellina Sup. Dirupi 2012** (● 14,000 bt) is made with grapes from all the vineyards that don't end up in Olé: it's a wine with plenty of ripe fruit to the fore and great brightness. **Sforzato di Valtellina Vino Sbagliato 2012** (● 1,100 bt) is somewhat atypical for the typology. "We wanted to make a Sforzato that was drinkable and bright," says Faso. The vineyard the grapes come from is the first of Dirupi's to be farmed organically.

slow wine **VALTELLINA SUP. RIS. 2011** (● 2,500 bt) Made with grapes from the Dossi Salati zone, where the soil adds great richness of flavor, this mineral, supple wine is a paragon of elegance and typicality. It's a key to understanding the Dirupi model.

FERTILIZERS none
PLANT PROTECTION chemical, copper and sulphur, organic
WEED CONTROL chemical, mechanical
YEASTS selected
GRAPES 100% estate-grown
CERTIFICATION none

POZZOLENGO (BS)

Tenuta Roveglia

Località Roveglia, 1
tel. 030 918663
www.tenutaroveglia.it
info@tenutaroveglia.it

173 ac - 550,000 bt

PEOPLE - The ongoing Lugana boom has been made possible by the commitment of wineries like this one, founded in the late 19th century and elevated by the Zweifel and Azzone families to its present high levels of production and quality. The delightful cellar, encircled by the vineyards at Pozzolengo, may be visited by reservation.

VINEYARDS - Paolo Fabiani holds the reins of the agronomic side of the business. Working in synergy with the owners, he manages a host of vineyards, mostly in a single plot round the cellar. The local soil has a high concentration of clays with many traces of limestone. Notwithstanding their massive area, the vineyards are farmed sustainably, with the onus on mechanization as opposed to chemicals.

WINES - Flavio Prà oversees cellar operations and it's thanks to him that the winery has developed year by year into one of the most commendable for quality in the whole Lugana zone. The entire range is very impressive indeed and, in our view, the most produced wine is the best of all. We are referring to Lugana Limne 2013 Everyday Wine (○ 400,000 bt), a good introduction for anyone approaching this particular terroir for the first time; it's well-crafted and its distinguishing features are softness and delicious saltiness. The taut, tangy, vibrant **Lugana Vigne di Catullo Ris. 2010** (○ 25,000 bt) is more ambitious. **Lugana V.T. Filo d'Arianna 2012** (○ 8,500 bt) is a highly personal interpretation of overripe turbiana grapes and, by virtue of its moreish fresh, slightly acidy flavor, it works. **Lugana Brut** (○ 8,000 bt) is good, too

FERTILIZERS natural manure
PLANT PROTECTION copper and sulphur
WEED CONTROL mechanical
YEASTS selected
GRAPES 100% estate-grown
CERTIFICATION none

Barone Pizzini

Va San Carlo, 14
tel. 030 9848311
www.baronepizzini.it
info@baronepizzini.it

Agnes

Via Campo del Monte, 1
tel. 0385 75206
www.fratelliagnes.it
info@fratelliagnes.it

---

116 ac - 282,000 bt `10% discount`

66 Barone Pizzini is both a condensate of research, innovation and land-rootedness, and a successful model for another clean, pragmatic and sustainable agriculture 99

PEOPLE - Silvano Brescianini is the seething, pulsing heart of Barone Pizzini. He deserves the credit for the visionary strategic choices that have raised the winery to where it is today.

VINEYARDS - Adamant advocates of responsible agriculture, Brescianini and his collaborators never stop trying to improve themselves. They combine sheer hard work in the vineyard with meticulous analysis of the grapes, hence wines differentiated by micro-parcels that seek to express the single terroirs with as much purity as possible and to recover an identity of their own.

WINES - The wine range is very broad, so in order to identify the thread that sews them together we've decided to begin with the two that impressed us the most: **Franciacorta Brut Animante** (○ 110,000 bt) is fleshy and rich without losing anything in terms of verve on the palate, and **Curtefranca Bianco Polzina 2013** (○ 26,000 bt), the cellar's base white. **Franciacorta Brut Rosé 2010** (⊙ 20,000 bt) is juicy and enjoyable, while **Franciacorta Satèn 2010** (○ 30,000 bt) makes the most of the favorable year with great drinkability. The feather in the cellar's cap continues to be **Franciacorta Dosaggio Zero Bagnadore Ris. 2008** (○ 10,000 bt), a wine built to last that expresses the character of the Roccolo vineyard.

slow wine **FRANCIACORTA NATURE 2010** (○ 20,000 bt) This wine is one of the outright best in its category. It's fragrant and lingering on the nose, rigorous and vertical on the palate. An excellent visiting card for the typology.

52 ac - 120,000 bt `10% discount`

66 Century-old vines, work in aid of local culture, candid wines and humility – these are the factors that make Agnes a pioneer in the Oltrepò craft revolution 99

PEOPLE - Sergio and Cristiano Agnes are the company's leading players. Their mission is to maintain local traditions, especially the culture of the croatina grape, preserving the old vine heritage at all costs.

VINEYARDS - Croatina, croatina and still more croatina! The century-old parcels actually contain a diversified variety of other local grapes, thus making the Agnes patrimony all the richer. The Loghetto vineyard (planted in 1906!) is proof of farming nous to the nth degree. As are the other vineyards, which have an average age of 60 years.

WINES - It's incredible how the Agnes family manage to turn out such an impressive, extraordinary range of wines from croatina di Rovescala grapes of different provenances and selections. **O.P. Bonarda Millennium 2009** (● 2,500 bt) has fruit, body and ripeness on the nose and great length. **Possessione del Console 2012** (● 6,000 bt) has more vegetal notes and a bright, fresh palate. The barrique-aged **Poculum 2011** (● 3,000 bt) is a coherent wine with toasty, sweet nuances. **Loghetto 2013** (● 1,500 bt) is the essence of lightness, body and drinkability bolstered by delightful prickle. O.P. Bonarda Vivace Cresta del Ghiffi 2013 Everyday Wine (● 13,000 bt) is deep and taut, as is **O.P. Bonarda Frizzante Campo del Monte 2013** (● 13,000 bt).

FERTILIZERS compost	**FERTILIZERS** green manure
PLANT PROTECTION copper and sulphur	**PLANT PROTECTION** copper and sulphur
WEED CONTROL mechanical	**WEED CONTROL** mechanical
YEASTS selected	**YEASTS** native
GRAPES 100% estate-grown	**GRAPES** 100% estate-grown
CERTIFICATION organic	**CERTIFICATION** none

Ca' Lojera

Frazione Rovizza
Via 1866, 19
tel. 045 7551901
www.calojera.com
info@calojera.com

44.5 ac - 100,000 bt

PEOPLE - Intelligence and sensitivity – these are the best words to describe the work of Ambra and Franco Tiraboschi, the owners of this, a farm that used to specialize in fruit and vegetables. In the past, the grapes were sold to a local wine cellar, but in 1991 they were left uncollected. Hence the decision to make wine in situ with the help of enologist Alberto Musatti. As fate would have it, Ca' Lojera now heads the denomination in terms of quality.

VINEYARDS - The turbiana vineyards are round the cellar, near the lake. They grow on white clay soil, which gives the wines minerality and longevity. The company also owns a 14th-century farmhouse, once the property of the local diocesan administration and the summer residence of the Bishop of Brescia, which the Tiraboschis have saved from ruin. This year they have also opened a new tasting room along side the excellent restaurant of their holiday farm.

WINES - "The 2013 vintage was a tough one for turbiana," says Ambra Tiraboschi. Maybe, but our tasting of the Luganas of Ca' Lojera showed once more that they're among the finest in their typology. **Lugana 2013** (○ 80,000 bt) has great balance and extraordinary drinkability. **Lugana Del Lupo Ris. 2011** (○ 6,000 bt), produced with botrytized grapes harvested in November, is long and complex. Worthy of a taste, finally, is the drawn-off Rosato Monte della **Guardia 2013** (◉ merlot, cabernet sauvignon; 15,000 bt), fruity and well-structured.

> **slow wine** **LUGANA SUP. 2012** (○ 6,000 bt) A well-structured, full-bodied Lugana that banks on linearity but, thanks to two years of barrel-aging, is also wonderfully drinkable.

FERTILIZERS mineral
PLANT PROTECTION copper and sulphur
WEED CONTROL mechanical
YEASTS selected
GRAPES 100% estate-grown
CERTIFICATION none

SONDRIO

Ar.Pe.Pe.

Via del Buon Consiglio, 4
tel. 0342 214120
www.arpepe.com
info@arpepe.com

---

32 ac - 70,000 bt   **10% discount**

❝ Ar.Pe.Pe. is an interesting, revolutionary phenomenon which joins together innovation and tradition in a perfect marriage. The aim is to promote the Valtellina in every aspect and a distinctive, visionary winemaking style ❞

PEOPLE - Isabella and Emanuele Pelizzatti are the heart and soul of the project. Theirs is a historic cellar that has evolved in original ways over the years. It's well worth a visit.

VINEYARDS - Emanuele farms his family's numerous vineyards with seriousness and dedication. You only have to walk, or rather climb, up the Buon Consiglio or Regina vineyards to understand the meticulous work behind Ar.Pe.Pe's great wines. From the agronomic point of view, the company is weathering huge management difficulties to gear itself to sustainable practices.

WINES - Given the right degree of aging, the company presented two exciting "grand reserves." **Valtellina Sup. Grumello Buon Consiglio Ris. 2005** (● 8,500 bt) is a rich wine with oxidative nuances alternating with fresh, acid vibrancy on the palate. The more elegant, outstandingly youthful **Valtellina Sup. Sassella Vigna Regina Ris. 2005** (● 5,000 bt) is a typical expression of its famous subzone. **Valtellina Sup. Grumello Rocca de Piro 2010** (● 11,000 bt) is spicy and slightly flawed by the wood, while **Valtellina Sup. Inferno Fiamme Antiche 2010** (● 5,300 bt) is balsamic and stylish. As always **Rosso di Valtellina 2012** (● 30,000 bt) is a good advert for the terroir.

> **slow wine** **VALTELLINA SUP. SASSELLA STELLA RETICA RIS. 2010** (● 24,000 bt) A crystalline, vertical, hearty, generous wine; an ideal compromise between structure, drinkability, sense of place, number of bottles and affordable price. Valtellina to the nth degree!

FERTILIZERS organic-mineral, manure pellets, natural manure
PLANT PROTECTION chemical, copper and sulphur
WEED CONTROL mechanical
YEASTS native
GRAPES 10% bought in
CERTIFICATION none

TEGLIO (SO)

Fay

Località San Giacomo di Teglio
Via Pila Caselli, 1
tel. 0342 786071
www.vinifay.it
info@vinifay.it

32 ac - 60,000 bt

❝ Marco Fay is the leader of the group of young winemakers who are bringing the Valtellina back to life. He puts his competence at the service of the entire area ❞

PEOPLE - Marco studied enology in San Michele all'Adige before picking up vital professional experience abroad. On returning home he rejuvenated his family's cellar.

VINEYARDS - Discovering the Valtellina with Marco is an exciting experience. Carterìa and Cà Moréi, the cellar's crus come from the best hillside vineyards at an altitude of 1,500-2,000 feet. The grapes for Sforzato Ronco del Picchio thrive above 2,000 feet, whereas those for Costa Bassa grow below 1,500 feet. All the cellar's vineyards, except for a couple of acres at Sassella, are in the Valgella subzone.

WINES - Fay's wines have strong identity and their quality is consistent. The impressive **Valtellina Sup. Valgella Carterìa 2011** (● 9,200 bt) is characterized by elegance, succulence and brightness. Excellent too is **Valtellina Sup. Costa Bassa 2011** (● 19,790 bt), a simple, drinkable wine and a perfect primer for anyone keen to understand what mountain nebbiolo is. **Valtellina Sup. Sassella Il Glicine 2011** (● 4,300 bt) is an approachable red with bundles of fruit, while **La Faya 2011** (● nebbiolo, merlot, syrah; 4,300 bt) is well-rounded and spicy. **Sforzato di Valtellina Ronco del Picchio 2010** (● 9,543 bt) still shows the signs of wood and will take time to develop.

slow wine **VALTELLINA SUP. VALGELLA CÀ MORÉI 2011** (● 9,200 bt) A label that tells the story of the work Marco and his dad Sandro have done to get the cry concept across. A wine with complex aromas, fragrant fruit and a long, lingering finish.

FERTILIZERS natural manure
PLANT PROTECTION chemical, copper and sulphur
WEED CONTROL chemical, mechanical
YEASTS selected
GRAPES 100% estate-grown
CERTIFICATION none

TORRICELLA VERZATE (PV)

Monsupello

Via San Lazzaro, 5
tel. 0383 896043
www.monsupello.it
monsupello@monsupello.it

130 ac - 230,000 bt

PEOPLE - Monsupello is a shining beacon in the Oltrepò zone and its owners, Pierangelo and Laura Boatti know it. It's they, helped by their mother Carla, who are carrying on all the good work of their late father, the visionary Torricella producer Carlo Boatti. The wines, especially the Metodo Classicos, owe their squeaky-clean quality to their multitalented technical director, the affable Marco Bertelegni.

VINEYARDS - The family owns numerous vineyards, which they have carefully selected and purchased over the years. A great deal of energy has been poured into work on the pinot nero grapes earmarked for the Metodo Classico, grown in the best positions on the coolest hillsides. The gorgeous Podere La Borla is plot given over to red grapes, especially barbera and croatina.

WINES - Marco told us that one of the company's aims is to slightly reduce its range, which currently consists of a host of labels in all the Oltrepò typologies. "This would allow us to focus even more on the Metodo Classico," he says. The extraordinary **M. Cl. Brut Pinot Nero 2009** (○ 10,000 bt) is precise and crystalline with vibrant acid backbone. Deserving of a special mention is the very rare, masterful M. Cl. Nature Carlo Boatti 2002, a limited selection produced to commemorate the founder of the cellar. We also recommend the effective varietal **Riesling 2013** (○ 10,000 bt) and the juicy, quaffable **O.P. Bonarda Frizzante Vaiolet 2013** (● 45,000 bt).

slow wine **M. Cl. NATURE** (○ 45,000 bt) A truly exceptional, value-for-money Metodo Classico, a "calling card" not only for the cellar itself but also for the entire terroir. Generous and pervasive and deep, it's full of grip and a joy to drink.

FERTILIZERS organic-mineral, manure pellets
PLANT PROTECTION chemical, copper and sulphur
WEED CONTROL chemical, mechanical
YEASTS selected
GRAPES 100% estate-grown
CERTIFICATION none

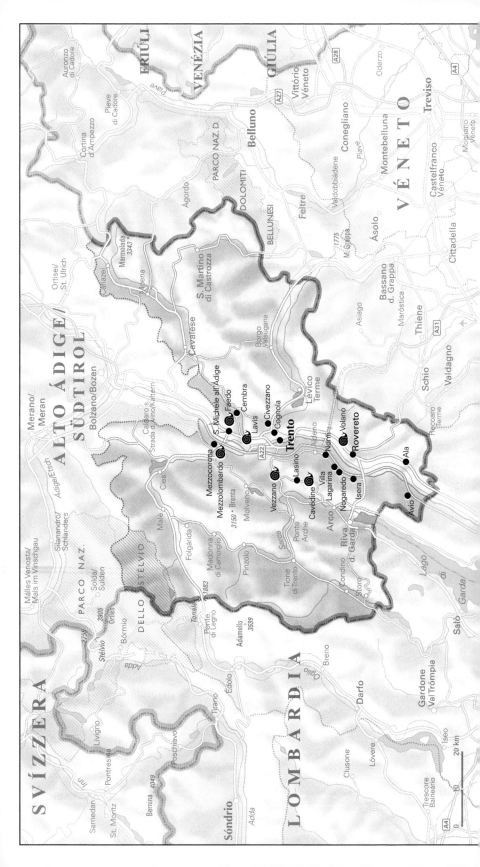

TRENTINO

Trentino is controversial territory, a land of a thousand nuances, a species of yin and yang, where positive aspects and negative live side by side. In a region in which wine cooperatives still predominate, we are obviously happy to see an exponential increase in the number of small wine cellars seeking to carve out a niche for themselves on the Italian wine scene. We are more and more convinced that identifying a symbolic wine for the Trentino region (Trentodoc? The missing Nosiola? The versatile Chardonnay? The omnipresent Pinot Grigio? The native Teroldego?) is a waste of time. Whereas it's not a waste of time to try to identify the peculiarities of each single zone, where what stands out is not what you cultivate but where. Take the Pressano zone, for example, which produces heavyweight wines at once elegant and rich with distinct aromas and full flavor: Incrocio Manzoni, Nosiola, Sauvignon … Then there's the Val di Cembra, whose porphyritic soils and particular microclimate are conducive to subtle, elegant wines, among which Müller Thurgau. Or the Valle dei Laghi, where the *ora del Garda*, the breeze from the lake and mild temperatures ensure optimal ripening of the grapes, especially nosiola, and create the ideal conditions for the production of the inimitable local treasure Vino Santo Trentino. Or, last but not least, think of the historic, prestigious Piana Rotaliana and its Teroldego. What emerged from our tastings was the recognizability of one terroir from another; pinpointing a typology capable of lording it over others in terms of quality was a secondary factor. Moving on to the Metodo Classicos, we recorded a constant increase in new and commendable labels. Not that all of them were under the Trento denomination, within which what often emerges (as we've argued for some time) is the style of the various cellars as opposed to the "feel" of the terroir. As expected, 2013 proved more favorable for white wines. In all, the vintage was odd, something of a yo-yo affair. It began with a delay in vine growth caused by low temperatures in the springtime, followed by a cool May with record rainfall, which raised concerns about the health of the grapes; *flavescence dorée* increased exponentially and mealy bug began to spread for the first time, though powdery mildew was less of a problem compared to previous years. Luckily, the summer was warm and served to ripen white grape varieties in particular. The red grape harvest was less fortunate on account of heavy rainfall in October. Despite everything, however, the year will be remembered as a good one. Indeed, according to data published by the Consorzio di Tutela dei Vini del Trentino, the regional protection consortium, wine production was up by 29% with respect to 2012.

snails ◐

70 POJER & SANDRI
70 VIGNAIOLO FANTI
71 MASO FURLI
71 FORADORI
72 REDONDEL
73 FRANCESCO POLI
73 EUGENIO ROSI

bottles ▮

72 FERRARI

FAEDO (TN)
Pojer & Sandri

Località Molini, 4
tel. 0461 650342
www.pojeresandri.it
info@pojeresandri.it

64 ac - 250,000 bt

66 Inventive, innovative – almost futuristic. These are just some of the qualities attributable to the two owners of the winery 99

PEOPLE - Mario Pojer, fresh from his enology studies, and Fiorentino Sandri, owner of a small vineyard, began their adventure in the wine world in 1975, a story of friendship, collaboration and success that has pushed viticulture in the Faedo hills and Cembra valley to the heights of quality.

VINEYARDS - The company's properties range from plots where the red varieties are grown in the Faedo hills at an altitude of 800 feet, to the ones where the pinot nero and chardonnay for the Metodo Classico, and the müller thurgau are grown in the Palai district at an altitude of 2,300 feet. The viticultural approach is attentive and brings out the best the land has to offer. An interesting experimental vineyard was recently planted on a piece of land recently reclaimed at Grumes, in the Cembra valley.

WINES - The company presented an interesting wide range of wines, suitable for every palate and every pocket. Pick of the crop is the ever elegant **Besler Biank 2010** Great Wine (Ο 5,500 0.5-lt bt), a perfect union of incrocio Manzoni, kerner and riesling, with bright, deep notes of ripe fruit and stone. **Filii 2013** (Ο 7,000 0.5 lt bt) is an intriguing blend of riesling and its "offspring," namely müller thurgau, kerner and incrocio Manzoni, which, thanks to an early harvest, is low proof but hugely complex nonetheless. The project to produce a wine from resistant grape varieties has finally come to fruition with **Zero Infinito 2013** (Ο solaris; 6,600 bt), a zero chemical-impact sparkling wine with a back palate. We also recommend the bright and breezy **Brut Rosé** (⊙ 9,700 bt).

FERTILIZERS natural manure, green manure	
PLANT PROTECTION copper and sulphur	
WEED CONTROL mechanical	
YEASTS selected	
GRAPES 100% estate-grown	
CERTIFICATION organic	

LAVIS (TN)
Vignaiolo Fanti

Località Pressano
Piazza G. N. della Croce, 3
tel. 0461 240809
www.vignaiolofanti.it
info@vignaiolofanti.it

11 ac - 17,000 bt

66 Alessandro Fanti wears a melancholic smile. As he speaks to you about the difficulties winemakers are enduring on account of what's happening in the Trentino wine world, you realize he's a member of that bizarre species, the pragmatic dreamers 99

PEOPLE - Listening to Alessandro as we walk among the vines, he has the expression of the kid who candidly told the schoolmistress his dream as a grown-up was not to walk on the moon but to be a farmer: "When I grow up I want to make wine!"

VINEYARDS - Alessandro feels a sense of "subjection" towards the vine. "In trying to impose myself I've made a lot of mistakes, so I've learned to let the vine lead me," he says. Interpreting the vineyard, understanding its needs, and assuming the risk of taking decisions are the duties of any sensible grape farmer. The vineyards are situated between Pressano, Sorni and Meano at altitudes of 300-600 meters.

WINES - The character and originality of the wines come from the terroir. Pressano shapes its into a singular style characterized by depth, creamy minerality and warmth. **Nosiola 2012** (Ο 4,000 bt) has elegant, buttery, bright aromas and a juicy, vibrant palate, and is sure to grow. **Pritianum 2012** (Ο chardonnay, incrocio Manzoni; 2,000 bt) is more harmonious and vivacious on the nose with good balance between the warmth and pungency of the two varieties on the palate. **Manzoni Bianco 2012** (Ο 3,500 bt) and **Isidor 2011** Great Wine (Ο incrocio Manzoni; 2,500 bt) have sensational power and richness of flavor: the first has fruitier aromas and tanginess, the second is subtly vegetal, with citrusy acidity and sometimes salty minerality maintaining a deep grip on the extremely rich, perfectly balanced palate.

FERTILIZERS biodynamic preparations	
PLANT PROTECTION copper and sulphur	
WEED CONTROL mechanical	
YEASTS selected	
GRAPES 100% estate-grown	
CERTIFICATION organic	

LAVIS (TN)

Maso Furli

Località Furli
Via Furli, 32
tel. 0461 240667
www.masofurli.it
masofurli@alice.it

10 ac - 15,000 bt

66 Listening to his silences and catching his gaze while he tastes his wines, you understand Marco Zanoni's sensibility and his ability as a winemaker 99

PEOPLE - Humble and authentic, Marco perpetually looks to the glass for confirmations or negations of his *modus operandi*. His parents were sharecroppers who managed to buy their *maso*, or farm, in the 1980s. In 1997 Marco stopped selling his grapes to the local wine cooperative to produce his own wines.

VINEYARDS - In the early days he was in awe of more famous colleagues and vowed to learn from their experience. He stopped using weedkillers in the vineyard and gradually converted to organics and biodynamics. The care and attention he dedicates to the wines conjure up the precision and meticulousness of a bespoke gentleman's tailor.

WINES - Awareness is increasing among wine makers in this wonderful growing area that they actually have a Pressano style all of their own: flavorsome, dense, tangy, potent whites, even though they are made with different varieties. It comes as no surprise therefore that **Trentino Chardonnay 2012** (○ 1,700 bt) is so deep, at once supple and zesty. **Trentino Sauvignon 2012** (○ 4,500 bt) is stiffer on the nose with a fuzzy, sometimes tart bouquet and a sappy palate. Though it comes from a severe growing year, **Rosso Furli 2010** (● 1,000 bt) performs well again; it's dark and balsamic with notes of blackcurrant syrup and a solid palate.

slow wine **MANZONI BIANCO 2011** (○ 1,500 bt) One of the region's most original and finest whites: piquant and vegetal with sweet peaches on the nose, it's glycerine-rich but vibrant on the palate.

FERTILIZERS biodynamic preparations, green manure
PLANT PROTECTION copper and sulphur
WEED CONTROL mechanical
YEASTS selected, native
GRAPES 100% estate-grown
CERTIFICATION organic

MEZZOLOMBARDO (TN)

Foradori

Via Damiano Chiesa, 1
tel. 0461 601046
www.elisabettaforadori.com
info@elisabettaforadori.com

29 ac - 160,000 bt

66 Elisabetta Foradori is a winemaker who loves her job. "I adore being among my vineyards, living in nature … it's my den." Watching her caress her vines, which she seems to know one by one, you realize that hers isn't rhetoric, it's the honest truth 99

PEOPLE - Elisabetta grew up in her family's winery and took over the reins when she was just 20. That was the beginning of a career that's evolving all the time.

VINEYARDS - Besides the historic vineyards round the wine cellar at Mezzolombardo, where she grows her teroldego, Elisabetta also owns a *maso*, or farm, in the Cognola district, where the nosiola and incrocio Manzoni vineyards are. She has been adopting a biodynamic approach for some time. It's the only way she has to develop her idea of wine as the fruit of the close dialogue between humankind and nature.

WINES - "For me, my wines are "alive" and perception of their beauty and wholesomeness runs on a knife-edge between what's comprehensible and what isn't." Some years ago Elisabetta began to make some of her wines in earthenware pitchers: in our view, the Sgarzon and Morei work, the Nosiola Fontanasanta less so. The excellent, wonderfully expressive **Teroldego Morei 2012** (● 10,000 bt) is light and elegant with salty, blood-rich suggestions on the nose. On the palate it has juiciness accompanied by long acid grip. **Teroldego Sgarzon 2012** (● 10,000 bt) needs more time in the glass but then, timidly, it releases pleasant fruity nuances that recur in the mouth, together with enfolding flavor.

slow wine **TEROLDEGO FORADORI 2012** (● 90,000 bt) A perfect Teroldego, characterized by great elegance and personality, with a rich, fruity nose and a well-rounded lingering palate. Woe betide anyone who dares to call it a "base wine."

FERTILIZERS compost, biodynamic preparations
PLANT PROTECTION copper and sulphur, organic
WEED CONTROL mechanical
YEASTS native
GRAPES 100% estate-grown
CERTIFICATION biodynamic, organic

MEZZOLOMBARDO (TN)

Redondel

Via Roma, 28
tel. 0461 601618
www.redondel.it
info@redondel.it

TRENTO (TN)

Ferrari

Via del Ponte di Ravina, 15
tel. 0461 972 311
www.cantineferrari.it
info@ferrarispumante.it

7.5 ac - 9,500 bt `10% discount`

66 Stubborn and patient, Paolo Zanini knows how to wait for his vines and his wines, letting them have all the time they need to give of the their best. Even if the world came to an end, he'd still be there waiting for the right moment 99

PEOPLE - It's often said that wines resemble the people who make them. Knowing Paolo, one might say that the opposite is true. It's he who's a lot like Teroldego! He may appear surly and curmudgeonly at first, but he doesn't take long to show his real character, which is generous, sincere and authentic.

VINEYARDS - Seven small parcels, vineyards that in the mind's eye of a child appear old, very old indeed: 25, 40, 80 years. For his fellow wine-growers, they're simply unkempt and wild with too much grass, too many leaves. Paolo, instead, who has a symbiotic relationship with his vines, reckons they're balanced and healthy, capable of giving grapes the characteristics that will subsequently be heightened in the cellar: hence concentration, mood, the flavor of the sand and the gravel and the pebbles of the Piana Rotaliana.

WINES - There are three versions of teroldego, one for each nuance this generous variety has to offer. Fruit dominates in Teroldego Rotaliano Rosato Assolto 2013 `Everyday Wine` (☉ 2,000 bt), which is refreshing and chewy, accompanied by suggestions of spices and dried fruit, dynamic and enjoyable with tempting flavor. **Teroldego Rotaliano Dannato 2010** (● 6,000 bt) stands out for its potency, with well-calibrated wood enriching dark, crisp fruit and offering blood-rich, earthy nuances with clear hints of walnut and honey, followed by a well-rounded, velvety finish. For a taste of the new vintage of Teroldego Beatome, we'll have to wait until Paolo is totally convinced that it has reached the right degree of maturity. In the meantime, we had a second taste of the excellent 2007, and were impressed by its perfect combination of elegancy, delicacy and structure.

300 ac - 4,410,000 bt `10% discount`

PEOPLE - A historic world-famous maison specialized in sparkling wines, Ferrari was formed over a century ago and is now a benchmark brand for lovers of the Metodo Classico. It was founded by Giulio Ferrari in 1902 and taken over by Bruno Lunelli in 1952. It's now managed by the latest generation of the Lunelli family: Camilla, in charge of communications, Marcello, the production manager, and Matteo, head of sales.

VINEYARDS - The grapes are all top quality and come from the company's vineyards, which are scattered across the hills round Trento. They are split up among eight masi, or farms, among which the famous Pianizza, where the chardonnay grapes earmarked for the Riserva del Fondatore are grown. Some of the grapes are also bought in from trusted growers, who comply with a rigid production protocol geared towards sustainable viticulture.

WINES - The Ferrari style is unmistakable and credit for this is due to Ruben Laurentis, the enologist and cellar manager who, for the last 30 years and more, has been creating wines of great personality, such as the extraordinary **Trento Brut Giulio Ferrari Riserva del Fondatore 2004** `Great Wine` (○ 39,000 bt), yet again a Metodo Classico among Italy's finest, a marriage of delicacy and character redolent of honey and dried fruit with vibrant, deep freshness. **Trento Extra Brut Perlé Nero 2008** (○ 28,000 bt) is compelling and elegant with considerable acid grip. Produced exclusively with chardonnay grapes, **Trento Brut Perlé 2008** (○ 440,000 bt) is an intriguing, tempting mix of softness and full flavor. Fragrant and thirst-quenching, **Trento Brut Maximum** (○ 640,000 bt) is excellent value for money.

FERTILIZERS none
PLANT PROTECTION copper and sulphur
WEED CONTROL mechanical
YEASTS native
GRAPES 100% estate-grown
CERTIFICATION organic

FERTILIZERS manure pellets, natural manure, biodynamic preparations, green manure
PLANT PROTECTION chemical, copper and sulphur
WEED CONTROL mechanical
YEASTS selected
GRAPES 70% bought in
CERTIFICATION none

VEZZANO (TN)

Francesco Poli

Frazione Santa Massenza
Via del Lago, 13
tel. 0461 340090
www.distilleriafrancesco.it
info@francescopoli.it

---

16 ac - 28,000 bt

66 Alessandro Poli manages his family's cellar and distillery with great passion and humility, virtues he has inherited from his dad, the indefatigable Francesco 99

PEOPLE - In this cellar in the heart of Santa Massenza one notes a genuine love for the job and a constant urge to find out more and to experiment. Alessandro farms organically, adding biodynamic practices here and there.

VINEYARDS - A spirit of enterprise and curiosity have led Alessandro to plant powdery mildew-resistant grape varieties on a plot above Vezzano at an altitude of 1,800 feet, an area in which others had failed to satisfy on account of the soil and weather conditions. In the Sottovi-Le Valete district grow nosiola, lagrein and cabernet, while the schiava and rebo vineyards are near the cellar.

WINES - The intriguing and unique **Massenza Belle sui Lieviti 2013** (O 1,600 bt), made with nosiola and peverella grapes, has delicate aromas, while the palate is wrapped in an exciting explosion of lemon and chewy fruit. The same wine is produced in a Charmat version. We were intrigued by **Naranis 2013** (O bronner, solaris; 1,500 bt), redolent of rock and dried fruit with fruity fleshiness in the mouth. Excellent and typical with it is **Massenza Rosso 2012** (● rebo; 2,500 bt).

> **slow wine** MAIANO 2012 (O 6,000 bt) A textbook Nosiola with elegant aromas of honey and hazelnut. The palate has well-rounded fruit and a dry finish of bitter almonds.

> **slow wine** VINO SANTO TRENTINO 2002 (O 4,800 bt) A "must have" in which acidity and sweetness fuse perfectly as a prelude to long, lingering suggestions of ripe apricots and dried fruits.

FERTILIZERS natural manure, biodynamic preparations, green manure
PLANT PROTECTION copper and sulphur
WEED CONTROL mechanical
YEASTS native
GRAPES 100% estate-grown
CERTIFICATION organic

VOLANO (TN)

Eugenio Rosi

Via Tavernelle, 3 B
tel. 0464 461375
tamaramar@virgilio.it

---

12 ac - 21,000 bt

66 The features that distinguish the work and the wines of Eugenio Rosi, one of Italy's foremost practitioners in the sector and an example to follow for all budding natural producers 99

PEOPLE - Rosi was born and bred among the vine rows of Vallagarina. Then he completed his studies and worked as an enologist for a number of great Trentino cellars. In 1999 he decided to start making wine in his own right and began cherry-picking vineyards to cultivate on his home turf.

VINEYARDS - His sparse vine rows grow on a number of plots faraway one from another. The white grapes are at Noriglio, marzemino thrives in the vineyard at Ziresi, and chardonnay enjoys the altitude, 2,500 feet, of Vallarsa. The other red grapes grow in the Rovereto hills. In all these places Eugenio applies a viticultural approach based on observation, study and natural interpretation of the vine's needs.

WINES - The wines grow up in the palazzo-cellar at Calliano. We say "grow up" because Eugenio pampers and educates them without intervening invasively and seeking to understand how they are evolving and what they are evolving into. He considers himself a craftsman and that's what he is, though we also see him as a master and a mentor. **Anisos 2011** (O 3,000 bt), made with macerated pinot bianco, nosiola and chardonnays, has deep minerality and a broad suite of flavors. The uber-elegant, silky **Cabernet Franc Dieci-Undici-Dodici** (● 1,000 bt) never falls short on austerity and typicality. The stockily built **Poiema 2011** (● 6,000 bt) is made with partly raisined marzemino grapes and has warmer fruit than in previous vintages.

> **slow wine** ESEGESI 2010 (● 8,000 bt). A classical refined, rigorous Bordeaux blend of cabernet and merlot that displays all the character and steel of the man who made it and the land it comes from.

FERTILIZERS natural manure, green manure
PLANT PROTECTION copper and sulphur
WEED CONTROL mechanical
YEASTS native
GRAPES 100% estate-grown
CERTIFICATION organic

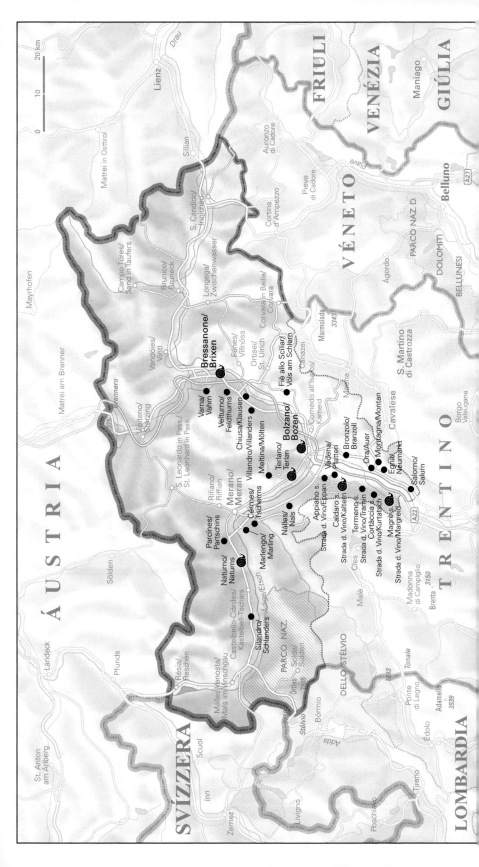

ALTO ADIGE

Viticulture in Alto Adige is growing vertically. You can tell simply by driving along the Adige and Isarco rivers, veritable north-south arteries of a denomination that boasts 13,000 acres of vineyard. In the course of time the rivers, like human beings and their farming activities, have sculpted the landscape. On the clayey, pebbly plains along their banks grow fruit trees, but soon as the land starts to rise, vines appear. It is the lie of the land, the composition of the soil and the climate that give this small winegrowing area its force and its energy, the granite mixed with clay and light sand, altitudes over 3,6000 feet and night-to-day temperature swings providing the grapes with their unique identity. Though accounting for just 1% of the total national area given over to vine growing it is a mere drop in the Italian wine ocean, Alto Adige viticulture has achieved levels of absolute elegance. More than that, it has established itself in the collective imagination as capable of ensuring quality products in every typology. Credit for this is due to the organization of the sector, geared to promoting the production of stylistically consistent wines.

It's our belief that this cohesive image should be taken as a model by other Italian regions, some of which still caught up in anachronistic and pointless local rivalries. Paradoxically, the region's capacity to produce wine of incredibly consistent quality is also the reason for the only criticism that we have to level. Namely that exaggerated technique masks the more personal traits of Alto Adige viticulture, clouding a potential for originality that is certainly high but which we would like to see more of. Pinot Bianco continues to rule the roost in Val d'Adige, as do Sylvaner and Riesling in Valle Isarco and Val Venosta. In other words, the picture appears somewhat static, formally unexceptionable but a tad short on exciting surprises. We know most Alto Adige producers share this impression and many of them, dynamically but pragmatically, are already looking for the right solutions. The theory may also be extended to the increasingly impressive production of native reds. We like the juiciness, the approachability on the palate and the fruitiness in the finest Schiavas, wines for the times that combine flavor with expressive delicacy. The same applies to the lagrein grape, which works better in airy, dynamic wines than in dark, concentrated ones, designed to age without a care for immediate, yet necessary, pleasure on the palate.

snails 🐌

77	NUSSERHOF - HEINRICH MAYR
77	KUENHOF - PETER PLIGER
78	MANINCOR
80	TENUTAE LAGEDER
80	UNTERORTL - CASTEL JUVAL
81	CANTINA TERLANO

bottles 🍾

76	CANTINA GIRLAN
79	CASTELFEDER
79	PETER DIPOLI
81	CANTINA TRAMIN

coins €

78	ERSTE + NEUE

Cantina Colterenzio

Località Cornaiano
Strada del Vino, 8
tel. 0471 664246
www.colterenzio.it
info@colterenzio.it

Cantina Girlan

Località Cornaiano
Via San Martino, 24
tel. 0471 662403
www.girlan.it
info@girlan.it

---

740 ac - 1,600,000 bt   **10% discount**

PEOPLE - Ever since it was founded in 1960, this prestigious cooperative has always been at the cutting edge and, thanks to the skill and vision of Luis Raifer, kellermeister in the 1980s and 1990s, it was one of the first to adopt a modern productive and marketing philosophy based on quality. Luis' worthy heir, his son Wolfgang Raifer, is now sales manager, working with enologist Martin Lemayer and president Hubert Dorfmann.

VINEYARDS - Care for the vineyards is a very serious business at Colterenzio and the cooperative's 300 members are attentively supervised in their vineyard management. The minimum goal is integrated farming, but a select quality team also cultivates their vines according to even more virtuous protocols. The core of the cooperatives properties is in the hills near Cornaiano and Colterenzio, among the sunniest in the whole region.

WINES - The two flagship wines were on top form this year: **A.A. Sauvignon Lafóa 2012** Great Wine (○ 22,000 bt) is solid and compact with the smooth texture and vibrant acid backbone, while **A.A. Cabernet Sauvignon Lafóa 2011** (● 5,000 bt) is deep, pervasive, earthy and very elegant. In the Cornell line, **A.A. Chardonnay Formigar 2012** (○ 15,000 bt) still shows faint traces of barrique-aging, but has body, juice and raciness. In the Praedium line, which brings out the qualities of broader single zones, the great classic **A.A. Pinot Bianco Weisshaus 2013** (○ 30,000 bt) is edgy and mineral, and the light, blossomy **A.A. Schiava Menzenhof 2013** (● 10,000 bt) is always a joy to drink. The Classic line is always very good, as the bright, fruity, exceptionally enjoyable **A.A. Chardonnay 2013** (○ 160,000 bt) demonstrates.

---

530 ac - 1,500,000 bt   **10% discount**

PEOPLE - Girlan has 200 members who cultivate 530 hectares of vineyard. They are small operators, but if enologist Gerhard Kofler is right when he says that "People with a small amount of land grow vines as a hobby, hence with greater care and passion," then they're likely a cut above the rest. The cooperative was formed in 1923, and extended and restructured its cellar in 2010. The president is Helmut Meraner and Oscar Lorandi is the manager.

VINEYARDS - At Cornaiano the morainal, glacial soil is relatively shallow and acid, while the Gschleier area is sandy with a warmer climate. At Mazzon the soils are calcareous and the temperatures are cooler. The schiava vineyard with pergola-trained, century-old vines is well worth a visit. Annual yields are; 6 tons for red wines, 10 tons for schiava and 8 tons for white wines.

WINES - "We were the first to make a top quality Schiava with Gschleier, while Fass N° 9 production began in 1961." All this care for the grape variety can be seen in the excellent **A.A. Schiava Fass N° 9 2013** Everyday Wine (● 85,000 bt); light and fruity it has a delicious, tangy palate and wonderful drinkability. **A.A. Pinot Nero Trattmann 2011** (● 20,000 bt) is one of the best examples of the typology in Italy; it's complex and elegant, its fruity notes perfectly amalgamated with wood and spices – just as a pinot nero should be. Moving on to the whites, **A.A. Gewürztraminer Flora 2013** (○ 10,000 bt) is attractively lively and juicy. Last but not least, **A.A. Gewürztraminer Pasithea Oro 2012** (○ 2,000 bt) is a wonderfully stylish passito.

> **slow wine** **A.A. Schiava Gschleier 2012** (● 14,000 bt) An exciting wine, already ready to drink and sure to improve in the course of time. It has ripe fruit, notes of spices and quinine, bundles of elegance and a charismatic personality.

FERTILIZERS mineral, natural manure, humus
PLANT PROTECTION chemical, copper and sulphur
WEED CONTROL mechanical
YEASTS selected, native
GRAPES 100% estate-grown
CERTIFICATION none

FERTILIZERS natural manure
PLANT PROTECTION copper and sulphur, organic
WEED CONTROL chemical, mechanical
YEASTS selected
GRAPES 100% estate-grown
CERTIFICATION none

BOLZANO/BOZEN

Nusserhof 🐌⌇
Heinrich Mayr

Via Josef Mayr-Nusser, 72
tel. 0471 978388

8.5 ac - 15,000 bt

66 Hemmed in between warehouses, railroads and the River Isarco, Nusserhof is an emblem of agricultural resistance against oppressive overbuilding and also against excessive red-tape and enological homogenization. Its subtly old-fashioned labels hark back to an era when chemicals had yet to appear in vineyards and wine was made with grapes alone 99

PEOPLE - Heinrich Mayr and his wife Elda, the charismatic owners, steward a winemaking tradition that dates back to 1778 with gentle tenacity.

VINEYARDS - Walking into Nusserhof is like entering another world. Here the agricultural approach, certified organic since the 1990s, is sensible and healthy. The lagrein, teroldego and blatterle vines grow on deep, warm alluvial soils, full of porphyric and dolomitic rock and the position of the vineyards, at the mouth of the Valle Isarco, ensures good air circulation. A few miles further north is the old vineyard of the schiava and other old grapes that go into the Elda.

WINES - B....... 2011 (○ 2,000 bt) is made with blatterle, an old native grape variety on the verge of extinction (it doesn't even appear among the authorized varieties, which is why it's not allowed to appear on the label either); a racy, graceful, laser-like wine with scents of lemon and alfalfa, and hefty acidity. The same red tape issues apply to **T....... 2011** (● 850 bt), a well-structured, deep monovarietal teroldego with a typical floral, spicy character. In its most traditional version **A.A. Lagrein Kretzer 2012** (○ 1,300 bt) is a robust, well-structured rosé with delicious fruity notes. **A.A. Lagrein Ris. 2009** (● 10,000 bt), which ages in large oak casks, has excellent mouthfeel and moderate proof. Edgy when young, it has great aging potential.

FERTILIZERS green manure	
PLANT PROTECTION copper and sulphur	
WEED CONTROL mechanical	
YEASTS native	
GRAPES 100% estate-grown	
CERTIFICATION organic	

BRESSANONE/BRIXEN (BZ)

Kuenhof 🐌⌇
Peter Pliger

Località Mara, 110
tel. 0472 850546
pliger.kuenhof@rolmail.net

16 ac - 35,000 bt   `10% discount`

66 An exemplary pioneering winery that drove the whole zone in the 1990s and is still a paragon for the quality of its wines and its virtuous, impeccable viticulture. This isn't Peter Pliger's aim but, rather, a side-effect of his humble vision of wine and man's role in creating it 99

PEOPLE - Peter took over the reins of a 13th-century *maso* (farm) that had been in his family for 200 years in the 1980s. After restoring the place and replanting the vines, he began making wine in 1990. The synergic presence of his wife Brigitte has been vital to the process.

VINEYARDS - High altitudes of 1,800-2,300 feet, soil rich in shale and quartz, a harsh climate with sharp day-night temperature swings, no chemical short-cuts but hours and hours of manual labor – these are all factors that contribute to the unique quality of the Pligers' wines. One of the family's outstanding achievements has been the rehabilitation of the magnificent, steeply terraced historic Lahner vineyard.

WINES - The 2013 growing year was a good one, giving the wines power, structure and supporting acidity. The impressive **A.A. Valle Isarco Sylvaner 2013** (○ 13,000 bt) is subtle and precise with clear-cut aromas of fruit and mountain herbs and a seductive palate that conflates succulence with delicate saltiness. **A.A. Valle Isarco Veltliner 2013** (○ 7,000 bt) sets off a certain warmth with fresh grassy tones, an intriguing smoky note and lively acidity on the finish. Sharp and flinty without being austere, **A.A. Valle Isarco Riesling Kaiton 2013** (○ 17,000 bt) is another masterpiece of equilibrium and character. **A.A. Valle Isarco Gewürztraminer 2013** (○ 3.000 bt) is well-developed, wholehearted and all-embracing.

FERTILIZERS natural manure	
PLANT PROTECTION copper and sulphur, organic	
WEED CONTROL mechanical	
YEASTS native	
GRAPES 100% estate-grown	
CERTIFICATION none	

CALDARO/KALTERN (BZ)

Erste + Neue

Via delle Cantine, 5
tel. 0471 963122
www.erste-neue.it
info@erste-neue.it

---

650 ac - 1,400,000 bt

PEOPLE - This old winery was founded in 1900 and subsequently merged with the wine cooperative in Caldaro. It has since reinvented itself by modernizing production and overhauling its image. The "+" in the logo conjures up the positive attitude of the team captained by president Manfred Schullian and enologist Gerhard Sanin, while the color blue evokes the aprons of Alto Adige artisans, hence symbolizing a bond with tradition and the land.

VINEYARDS - With about 430 members, Erste + Neue is now one of the most important wine cooperatives in the Alto Adige. Its vineyards are centered in Caldaro but extend to Termeno, Laives, Santa Maddalena and other communes, hence embrace vary different soils, positions and altitudes. The trick is to pinpoint the most suitable zones for each single grape variety, valorizing the finest with careful selections and meticulous viticulture.

WINES - Production is split into three lines: the Classic line features A.A. Pinot Bianco 2013 Everyday Wine (○ 30,000 bt), precise, subtle and racy; the Cru line is dominated by the great classic **A.A. Lago di Caldaro Cl. Sup. Leuchtenburg 2013** (● 55,000 bt), fruity, light and juicy and also reasonable priced, and **A.A. Sauvignon Stern 2013** (○ 45,000 bt), a typical expression of the grape, full of force and concentration but also grip and dynamism; and the Puntay line with its impressive **A.A. Gewürztraminer Puntay 2012** Great Wine (○ 10.000 bt), which has discreet aromas, solidity, softness and vibrant tangy backbone. **A.A. Lagrein Puntay Ris. 2011** (● 10,000 bt) has class and measure and **A.A. Lago di Caldaro Cl. Sup. Puntay 2013** (● 25,000 bt) is austere and sure to last.

CALDARO/KALTERN (BZ)

Manincor

San Giuseppe al Lago, 4
tel. 0471 960230
www.manincor.com
info@manincor.com

---

124 ac - 250,000 bt

66 'Biodynamics,' says owner Michael Goëss-Enzenberg, 'demands people doing their job conscientiously.' This is why Manincor is more than a business; it's a project-cum-workshop shared and carried forward by everyone who works there 99

PEOPLE - The man who made the project materialize was Helmut Zozin, who came to manage Manincor in 2008 after working as a cellarman in Caldaro.

VINEYARDS - Most of the vineyards surround the cellar, sloping down towards Lake Caldaro. One of these, the Kail parcel, was first planted in the 18th century and today grows very old pergola-trained schiava vines. Then there are the 24-acre Liebenaich estate in Terlano, which grows exclusively white grapes on soil rich in porphyry and quartz, and a few acres given over to pinot nero and petit manseng at Mazzon, overlooking Caldaro. The orchards, woods and fields round the vineyards are also farmed biodynamically.

WINES-A.A. Terlano Pinot Bianco Eichhorn **2013** (○ 12,000 bt), impresses with complexity and elegance, thrust and dynamism, and intense fruitiness. **A.A. Terlano Réserve della Contessa 2013** (○ pinot bianco, chardonnay, sauvignon; 45,000 bt) is also very fruity with a full palate and a touch of intense acidity and flavor. **Le Petit 2012** (○ 4,000 bt), made with petit manseng grapes, is well molded, bulky, almost unctuous and intensely fruity. Last but not least, **A.A. Pinot Nero Mason 2012** (● 15,500 bt) is one of the best in the region for its typology thanks to enormous elegance, fragrant fruity flesh and velvety tannic texture.

slow wine **A.A. Terlano Sauvignon 2012** (○ 3,000 bt) Uniquely expressive and compact, a wine of perfect harmony with pervasive, complex aromas and a rich, juicy palate, taut and deep by virtue of its gossamer saltiness.

FERTILIZERS organic-mineral, green manure, humus
PLANT PROTECTION chemical, copper and sulphur
WEED CONTROL mechanical
YEASTS selected
GRAPES 100% estate-grown
CERTIFICATION none

FERTILIZERS compost, biodynamic preparations, green manure
PLANT PROTECTION copper and sulphur
WEED CONTROL mechanical
YEASTS native
GRAPES 100% estate-grown
CERTIFICATION biodynamic, organic

EGNA/NEUMARKT (BZ)

Castelfeder

Via Portici, 11
tel. 0471 820420
www.castelfeder.it
info@castelfeder.it

136 ac - 450,000 bt

PEOPLE - Castelfeder is a dynamic family cellar with an international feel. It was founded in 1970 by Alfons Giovannet and is run today by his son Günther and grandsons Ivan and Ines, who oversee the technical side and sales respectively. In 2011 Ivan, who studied enology in Italy and Germany, also opened a small winery in the Moselle in partnership with a friend from university.

VINEYARDS - Castelfeder's vineyards are scattered over some of the best growing areas in the south of the region. Pinot nero, schiava, sauvignon and gewürztraminer grow on their clayey and calcareous soils, pinot grigio, pinot bianco, chardonnay and lagrein on the sandier ones. "Since my grandfather set up the business, our team of vine dressers has remained the same and we still draw up the contracts by hand," says Ivan.

WINES - "Relations with our growers is important," Ivan goes on. "I vinify the various grapes separately, then organize tastings to stimulate competition among them." The method seems to work as the average quality of the wines is very high. **A.A. Chardonnay Burgum Novum Ris. 2011** Great Wine (○ 9,000 bt) is a paragon of elegance and symmetry, full of flavor by virtue of textbook barrel-aging. Terrific too is **A.A. Pinot Bianco Tecum 2012** (○ 1,400 magnum), whose label bears the fun acronym: "niente di troppo," ie not too much: it ages in steel vats on its lees for a year and a half and is fresh and enjoyably drinkable. **A.A. Lagrein Burgum Novum Ris. 2011** (● 10,000 bt) is varietal, while **A.A. Pinot Nero Burgum Novum Ris. 2011** (● 12,000 bt) is all ripe fruit. **A.A. Schiava Breitbacher 2013** (● 15,000 bt) is crisp and concentrated.

FERTILIZERS none
PLANT PROTECTION chemical, copper and sulphur
WEED CONTROL chemical, mechanical
YEASTS selected
GRAPES 65% bought in
CERTIFICATION none

EGNA/NEUMARKT (BZ)

Peter Dipoli

Via Villa, 5-I
tel. 0471 813400
www.peterdipoli.com
vino@finewines.it

11.5 ac - 40,000 bt

PEOPLE - Energetic and impulsive and a proud advocate of his own ideas, Peter Dipoli is one of the characters of the Italian wine world. His wines, made with painstaking artisan care, are straightforward, blunt and matter-of-fact. Peter lives wine on many fronts: as a producer first and foremost but also as a distributor, consultant, talent scout and, with an untiring combative spirit, as a "lobbyist," always ready to defend the interests and identity of small *vignerons*. More than one young talent has emerged thanks to his intuition and support. In 1987 he crowned is dream of owning a winery of his own and he did so as always with very clear ideas: to produce great *vins de terroir*.

VINEYARDS - The breathtaking Voglar is at Penon, in the hamlet of Cortaccia, at an altitude of 1,600-2,000 meters. The sandy, pebbly soils are of dolomitic origin and are ideal for sauvignon, which by virtue of the altitude and east-northeast location matures slowly, conserving acidity without developing a grassy character. Iugum is made with grapes from a vineyard at Magrè with limestone and clay soils ideal for Bordeaux varieties.

WINES - **A.A. Merlot-Cabernet Iugum 2010** (● 7,000 bt), made prevalently with merlot grapes, fermented in wood vats and matured in barriques, is a structured wine, austere to the right degree with a classic, elegant dark fruity, earthy tone and evident minerality.

slow wine **A.A. Sauvignon Voglar 2012** (○ 24,000 bt) One of Italy's great Sauvignons, made with fully ripe grapes, barrel-fermented and released after at least a year's aging. A solid, well-structured wine, tangy, taut and long with a rugged character.

FERTILIZERS none
PLANT PROTECTION chemical, copper and sulphur
WEED CONTROL chemical, mechanical
YEASTS selected **GRAPES** 100% estate-grown
CERTIFICATION none

MAGRÈ/MARGREID (BZ)

Tenutae Lageder 🐌

Vicolo dei Conti, 9
tel. 0471 809 500
www.aloislageder.eu
info@aloislageder.eu

NATURNO/NATURNS (BZ)

Unterortl - Castel Juval 🐌

Località Stava/Staben
Juval 1 B
tel. 0473 667580
www.unterortl.it
familie.aurich@dnet.it

---

123 ac - 280,000 bt

❝ A wine merchant by trade, Alois Lageder listened to his head and his heart without turning his back on his past, and is now one of the greatest advocates of clean viticulture, implementing the precepts of biodynamics to make better wines while respecting the environment and consumers ❞

PEOPLE - The brilliant young Kellermeister Georg Meißner, who joined the company a couple of years ago after working as a researcher at the University of Geisenheim, is also a great believer in biodynamic viticulture.

VINEYARDS - The white grapes mature on the highest ridges overlooking Magrè, while the oldest vineyards, which grow the Bordeaux varieties used to make Löwengang, are lower down. The eponymous Chardonnay comes from a high-trained vineyard near the park of Hirschprunn. The other red grapes ripen on the steep terraces of Römigberg, a *maso* (farm) high up over Lake Caldaro.

WINES - First, yet another wonderful version of **A.A. Chardonnay Löwengang 2011** (45,500 bt), a wine with a classic feel that impresses more and more with its sumptuous elegance, masterful extracts and great tanginess. **A.A. Cabernet Sauvignon Cor Römigberg 2010** (● 9,360 bt) opens on the nose with stunningly crisp fruit and follows up with a well-knit, suavely elegant palate. **A.A. Lagrein Lindenburg 2010** (● 13,200 bt) is husky to the right degree with fleshy pulp and oodles of fruit. The pleasant **A.A. Pinot Bianco Haberle 2012** (○ 13,300 bt) is approachable and fragrant.

slow wine	**A.A. CABERNET LÖWENGANG 2010** (● 12,200 bt) A masterpiece of elegance and depth that stands out for its silky texture and the finest of vegetable notes that puts it up there with the great Bordeaux. One of Alto Adige's iconic wines.

9.5 ac - 32,000 bt

❝ As he walks cautiously but confidently through his vineyards, challenging the incessant wind, Martin Aurich looks like a mountaineer approaching a summit. Working here isn't the same as climbing K2, but the conditions do demand great skill and determination. It's a heroic feat just the same ❞

PEOPLE - The Unterortl belongs to Reinold Messner, famous for his mountaineering achievements, and is managed by husband and wife team Martin and Gisela Aurich.

VINEYARDS - Most of the vineyards extend across the slopes of the Juval at an altitude of 1,950-2,780 feet. Due to the gradient and the Föhn, the warm wind that blows all day without respite, manual interventions are constantly necessary. The dark gneissic soil gives the wine a great deal of minerality and the sharp day-night temperature swings allow the grapes to conserve all their aroma and acidity.

WINES - The novelty this year is **A.A. Riesling Sonnenberg 2013** (○ 1,400 bt), which has distinctive aromas of saffron and citrus fruit and compelling tanginess. **Juval Glimmer 2013** (○ 3,600 bt), made with müller thurgau and fraueler, an interesting native Val Venosta grape variety, has full, fleshy fruit and fresh, mineral drinkability. The fruity **A.A Valle Venosta Riesling 2013** (○ 5,000 bt) conjures up pear and mango, but is at once rugged and solid. We liked the balanced dynamism of **A.A. Valle Venosta Pinot Bianco 2013** (○ 6,900 bt).

slow wine	**A.A. VALLE VENOSTA RIESLING WINDBICHEL 2012** (○ 2,500 bt) Larger than life and seductive, direct and sharp with overwhelming minerality: a praiseworthy, highly personal interpretation of the typology.

FERTILIZERS compost, biodynamic preparations, green manure
PLANT PROTECTION copper and sulphur, organic
WEED CONTROL mechanical
YEASTS native
GRAPES 100% estate-grown
CERTIFICATION biodynamic, organic

FERTILIZERS organic-mineral, natural manure, compost
PLANT PROTECTION chemical, copper and sulphur, organic
WEED CONTROL mechanical
YEASTS selected
GRAPES 100% estate-grown
CERTIFICATION none

TERLANO/TERLAN (BZ)

Cantina Terlano

Via Colli d'Argento, 7
tel. 0471 257135
www.cantina-terlano.com
office@cantina-terlano.com

370 ac - 900,000 bt

❝ Cooperative viticulture at the highest levels. Terlano has written the history of this terroir with exceptional wines of incredible longevity, and continues to set its sights higher and higher with a concept of across-the-board quality rooted in virtuous work in the vineyard **❞**

PEOPLE - Founded in 1893 the winery is run today by Kellermeister Rudi Kofler, manager Klaus Andergassen and president Georg Höller who carry on the legacy of the celebrated winemaker Sebastian Stockinger,

VINEYARDS - About 100 members cultivate their vineyards with great pride under the supervision of agronomist Norbert Spitaler and following a virtuous protocol of sustainable practices. Reddish sandy soil of porphyritic origin, altitudes of 820-2,950 feet and a warm, dry, sunny climate make Terlano a unique terroir, famous for its full-bodied, deep, long-lasting white wines.

WINES - A.A. Terlano Pinot Bianco Vorberg Ris. 2011 (O 51,700 bt) is a great classic, dense, lingering and chalky against a backdrop of refined notes of tropical fruit, rock and salt. **A.A. Pinot Bianco Rarità 2002** (O 3,340 bt) has developed beautifully into a wine of soft, elegant composure. Terlano's ambition culminates with **A.A. Bianco Grande Cuvée 2011** `Great Wine` (O pinot bianco, chardonnay, sauvignon; 2,850 bt) rich, complex, well-structured and never heavy thanks to vibrant supporting acidity and minerality. **A.A. Terlano Nova Domus Ris. 2011** (O 21,100 bt), one of the best whites tasted this year, follows suit with greater approachability and energy. **A.A. Terlano 2013** (O 220,000 bt) is the most frivolous but forthright version, while A.A. Pinot Bianco 2013 `Everyday Wine` (O 110,000 bt) is juicy, lively and dynamic, and offers unbeatable value for money.

FERTILIZERS mineral, compost, biodynamic preparations
PLANT PROTECTION chemical, copper and sulphur, organic
WEED CONTROL mechanical
YEASTS selected
GRAPES 100% estate-grown
CERTIFICATION none

TERMENO/TRAMIN (BZ)

Cantina Tramin

Strada del Vino, 144
tel. 0471 096633
www.cantinatramin.it
info@cantinatramin.it

618 ac - 1,800,000 bt

PEOPLE - This historic wine cooperative, one of the most interesting in the region, is managed by the gifted enologist Willi Stürz. A few years ago work was completed on a new high-tech, functional cellar, complete with a point of sale where members go to chill out and chat over their own wine.

VINEYARDS - Willi and his team's direct and constant rapport with the members of the cooperative is fundamental. Great care and attention are devoted to sustainable farming and the 300 members are encouraged to abandon weed control, which is now only practiced in a small percentage of the vineyards. Some of the vineyards are organically farmed and are yielding good results.

WINES - Of the wines submitted for tasting, we thoroughly recommend **A.A. Gewürztraminer Nussbaumer 2013** (O 70,000 bt), the product of a cold growing year and less opulent than in the past with delicate aromas of exotic fruit and spices; having drunk old vintages of the wine, however, we can vouch for its longevity. The beautifully crafted **A.A. Gewürztraminer 2013** (O 300,000 bt) is elegant and deep, packed with fruit and wrapped in spices and dried flower. We also liked **A.A. Bianco Stoan 2013** (O chardonnay, sauvignon, pinot bianco, gewürztraminer; 40,000 bt), redolent of citrus fruit and pervasive with good acid grip. The "minor" blend, T Bianco 2013 `Everyday Wine` (O chardonnay, sauvignon, pinot bianco, riesling; 150,000 bt), is juicy and tangy and a pleasure to drink. **A.A. Pinot Bianco Moriz 2013** (O 45,000 bt) is flavorsome and crystalline, delicate and bright.

FERTILIZERS organic-mineral, mineral, natural manure, compost, biodynamic preparations, green manure
PLANT PROTECTION chemical, copper, sulphur, organic
WEED CONTROL mechanical
YEASTS selected, native
GRAPES 100% estate-grown
CERTIFICATION part of the vineyards certified biodynamic or organic

VENETO

With the 2013 grape harvest Veneto came top of the Italian regional wine production table once again, turning out about nine million hectoliters and showing a 12% increase with respect to the previous year. Especially over the last couple of decades, a group of producers (from small winegrowers to large companies) have supplemented these record figures with increasingly high quality. The region is a "macro-terroir," very complex and variegated, in which wines of world renown such as Amarone and Prosecco live side by side with historically consolidated denominations such as Soave and Valpolicella and the more low-profile Lessini Durello, Colli Euganei, Colli Berici, Bardolino, Custoza and Gambellara. It's in this latter cluster that we detect the liveliest innovation and experimentation, whereas the major denominations risk being more static. In eastern Veneto, Prosecco – with the two excellent DOCGs, Conegliano Valdobbiadene Superiore and Asolo and massive production in the DOC zone, which stretches over five provinces in Veneto and the entire Friuli region – prevails over other interesting areas, such as Piave with its raboso grapes, Montello with its Bordeaux blends and Lison Pramaggiore with its tai. As far as the quality of Prosecco is concerned (the guide only takes into account the historic Prosecco production zone in the province of Trevigiano), albeit tending towards high, it is by and large somewhat uniform. We were impressed this year by a lovely array of bottle-refermented Proseccos, a typology that's attracting the interest of a growing number of consumers. In the western part of the region, the two monoliths – Valpolicella and Soave – performed consistently, in some cases brilliantly, consolidating their results in terms of quality and expression of their vast and diversified terroirs. As usual, alas, there were few vintage Valpolicella and Valpolicella Ripasso labels to match the many Amarones. In the Lake Garda area, Bardolino and Custoza expressed themselves well as they continued in their ongoing pursuit of greater recognizability. Finally, this year the biggest novelties and surprises, in terms of quality and originality of expression, came from Lessini Durello Metodo Classico, Tai Rosso dei Colli Berici, and the solar, intense Bordeaux-style wines of the Colli Euganei, great and hugely enjoyable wines from zones slightly in the shade on the market – a singular travesty, this.

snails 🐌

85	LE FRAGHE
87	CORTE SANT'ALDA
88	MONTE DALL'ORA
89	VILLA BELLINI
91	LA BIANCARA
93	PRÀ
94	FONGARO
95	LEONILDO PIEROPAN
97	VIGNETO DUE SANTI
99	TESSÈRE
100	CASA COSTE PIANE
101	SILVANO FOLLADOR
101	SORELLE BRONCA

bottles 🍾

86	TENUTA SANT'ANTONIO
86	CAV. G.B. BERTANI
87	BRIGALDARA
88	SPERI
89	MONTE DEL FRÀ
92	GINI
95	SUAVIA
97	LA MONTECCHIA CONTE EMO CAPODILISTA
99	MALIBRAN

coins €

85	GIOVANNA TANTINI
91	DAMA DEL ROVERE
92	LE BATTISTELLE
93	DANIELE NARDELLO
94	MONTE TONDO
100	VALDELLÒVO

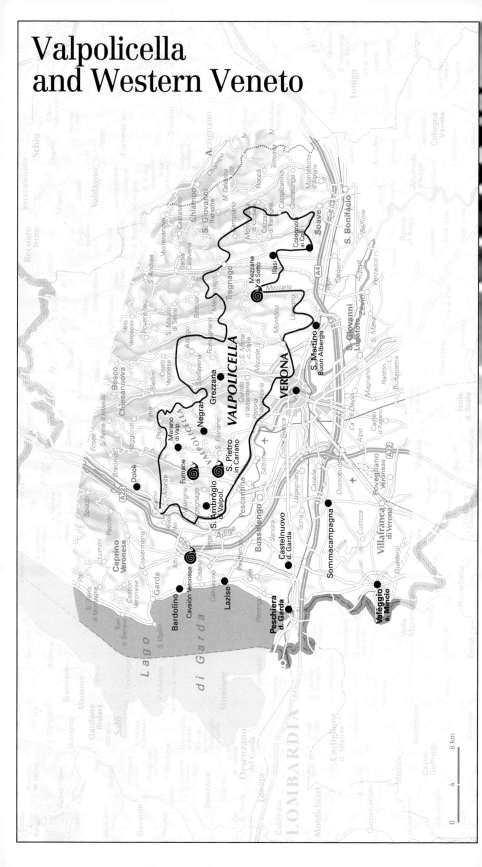

Valpolicella
and Western Veneto

CASTELNUOVO DEL GARDA (VR)

Giovanna Tantini €

Località I Mischi
Via Unità d'Italia 10
tel. 045 7575070
www.giovannatantini.it
info@giovannatantini.it

29 ac - 25,000 bt `10% discount`

PEOPLE - Giovanna Tantini is a determined producer who has developed this impressive winery in the space of just a few years. Step by step she has purchased vineyards, built the cellar and, more recently, launched an *agriturismo*, or holiday farm, by the shores of Lake Garda. Attilio Pagli and Laura Zuddas provide vital technical consultancy.

VINEYARDS - Walking among the vineyards, one breathes in the scents from the lake. This is why Giovanna has opted to cultivate the grape varieties most faithful to the identity of the terroir, which, thanks to the well-ventilated climate and the structure of the soils – limestone of glacial origin – produce fresh yet character-packed wines. She also grows a few international grape varieties. The vineyards are immaculately farmed using sustainable methods.

WINES - Right from the outset Giovanna has always been very clear about the characteristics she wants her Bardolino to have; namely the capacity to narrate the terroir in an original manner, banking on the capacity and evolutional potential that the corvina grape can express if it is interpreted properly. This is why she releases the wine a year later than the majority of others in the denomination. **Bardolino 2012 (●** 10,000 bt) possesses its customary well-developed and complex olfactory characteristics with strong notes of spice and tobacco. If anything, it's slightly subtler and less assertive than usual on the palate, though it does display good equilibrium and drinkability. Simple, approachable and linear, **Bardolino Chiaretto 2013 (⊙**7,000 bt) is a rigorous interpretation of the typology.

CAVAION VERONESE (VR)

Le Fraghe ✎

Località Colombare, 3
tel. 045 7236832
www.fraghe.it
info@fraghe.it

70 ac - 110,000 bt `10% discount`

❝ Matilde Poggi now has 30 grape harvests under her belt. She made her name making precisely the wines she wanted to make, with her own ideas and her own style, at the same time responsibly respecting her tradition, her land and her origins ❞

PEOPLE - The dynamic, determined Matilde runs a wine cellar with 70 acres of vineyard, nestling among which a pretty little holiday farm. She also happens to be president of the Federazione Italiana Vignaioli Indipendenti, the Italian Federation of Independent Winegrowers.

VINEYARDS - The vineyards are all within a couple of kilometers of the farm-cum-cellar, in the communes of Montalto, Rivoli and Affi. The red grapes for the Bardolino and Chiaretto are Guyot-trained, while the garganega and cabernet use the spurred cordon system. The soils, alluvial with plenty of pebble and gravel, are relatively fertile and produce notably fresh-tasting wines. The winery was certified organic a couple of years ago.

WINES - The choice to go organic was accompanied by the switch to screw caps in 2008, a solution that ensures clean aromas and halves the amount of sulfur previously needed with corks. The wines are direct and ideal for everyday drinking. A typical "Matilde-style" wine is **Bardolino 2013 (●** 65,000 bt), which has just the right degree of fruit and spices on the tannins. A must-buy is **Bardolino Cl. Brol Grande 2013 (●** 6,500 bt), barrel-aged for eight months, a fiesta of aromas and flavor with a super-leisurely, laid-back palate. Bardolino Chiaretto Ròdon 2013 `Everyday Wine` (⊙ 18,000 bt) is tangy and dry and long, great with fish. **Garganega Camporengo 2013 (○** 15,000 bt) is a blossomy, breezy little wine for everyday and all-day supping.

FERTILIZERS none
PLANT PROTECTION chemical, copper and sulphur
WEED CONTROL chemical, mechanical
YEASTS selected
GRAPES 100% estate-grown
CERTIFICATION none

FERTILIZERS manure pellets, green manure
PLANT PROTECTION copper and sulphur, organic
WEED CONTROL mechanical
YEASTS selected
GRAPES 100% estate-grown
CERTIFICATION organic

COLOGNOLA AI COLLI (VR)

Tenuta Sant'Antonio 🍷

Frazione San Zeno
Via Ceriani, 23
tel. 045 7650383
www.tenutasantantonio.it
info@tenutasantantonio.it

GREZZANA (VR)

Cav. G.B. Bertani 🍷

Via Asiago, 1
tel. 045 8658444
www.bertani.net
bertani@bertani.net

---

250 ac - 700,000 bt

PEOPLE - Entrepreneurial flair, a tireless work ethic, passion and experience. Four gifts for the four Castagnedi brothers: Armando (marketing and sales), Massimo (vineyards), Tiziano (logistics) and Paolo (winemaking). The winery's story began in 1989 with 75 acres in the Mezzane zone, which were added to their father's 50 acres in the Cologntola ai Colli area. Now these four musketeers have 247 acres at their command, 75 of which they manage directly. A well-equipped winery building in Monti Garbi was completed in 2002.

VINEYARDS - The 150 acres around the winery are planted on stony, chalky soil (in Veronese dialect, garbo means "hard," "harsh"). The vines range in age from 9 to 45 years. The 100 acres around San Zeno di Cologtola ai Colli are on clayey, silty soil, with vines between 20 and 50 years old. "We want to create an ecosystem in the vineyards, including using bioenergy applied to agriculture," says Massimo.

WINES - In recent years, the Castegnedi brothers' wines are moving towards an increasing refinement, becoming less muscular and powerful. Paolo, supported by the winery's two enologists, is extremely dedicated and takes an almost obsessive care over his work. The winery produces more than 15 different wines; particular standouts include the deep and savory **Soave Monte Ceriani 2012** (○ 20,000 bt) and the **Amarone della Valpolicella Campo dei Gigli 2010** Great Wine (● 15,000 bt), robust and intense, with an assertive character and a perfect balance between acidity and tannins. The fresh and inviting **Valpolicella Sup. La Bandina 2010** (● 30,000 bt) is very good, and is followed by the complex and caressing **Valpolicella Sup. Ripasso Monti Garbi 2012** (● 200,000 bt). It will be worth keeping an eye on the interesting Télos project (from the Ancient Greek for "end," "purpose"), aimed at creating both red and white wines without added sulfites.

495 ac - 1,800,000 bt | 10% discount |

PEOPLE - Tasting an Amarone that has aged for 40 years or more is an experience that only a winery as prestigious as Bertani can offer. An indisputable Valpolicella icon, a pioneer in the repositioning of the area's identity, this distinguished maison – now owned by the Tenimenti Angelini group, but overseen with the same passion as before by the family – remains a reference point for authenticity, quality and meticulous care.

VINEYARDS - Valpolicella, but also Valpantena, Soave and the nearby lakeside areas, like Lugana, Custoza and Bardolino: the Bertanis have always been wholly dedicated to promoting the Veronese wine culture, ever since the founders started their visionary project here in 1857. Villa Novare is worth a mention; as well as being a beautiful estate, it is also a symbol of viticultural research for the whole district.

WINES - Tradition and innovation merge in Bertani's wines, with a range of the highest standard, despite the absence of the winery's flagship Amarone (to be released next year). The **Secco Bertani Original Vintage Edition 2011** (● 80,000 bt) reflects a desire to tell the story of a long winemaking tradition. Made from old clones of corvina, sangiovese, syrah and cabernet, it undergoes a slow fermentation, first in steel and then in wood, and presents subtle, spiced fruit; on the palate it is rugged, with a pervasive tanginess. The **Valpolicella Cl. Sup. Vigneto Ognisanti 2012** Great Wine (● 25,000 bt) once again guarantees absolute quality: elegant, balsamic, with crisp fruit and great gustatory fullness. The powerful and warm **Amarone della Valpolicella Valpantena Villa Arvedi 2011** (● 80,000 bt) offers dark fruit and hints of leather. The **Valpolicella Cl. Villa Novare 2013** (● 130,000 bt) is also good.

FERTILIZERS manure pellets, compost
PLANT PROTECTION organic
WEED CONTROL mechanical
YEASTS selected
GRAPES 100% estate-grown
CERTIFICATION none

FERTILIZERS organic-mineral, manure pellets, natural manure
PLANT PROTECTION copper and sulphur
WEED CONTROL mechanical
YEASTS selected
GRAPES 100% estate-grown
CERTIFICATION none

MEZZANE DI SOTTO (VR)

Corte Sant'Alda

Località Fioi
Via Capovilla, 28
tel. 045 8880006
www.cortesantalda.it
info@cortesantalda.it

47 ac - 80,000 bt | **10% discount**

❝ Corte Sant'Alda is a fortunate concentrate of good planning, farming vision, pragmatism, respect for the land and adherence to local traditions. All values personified by the woman who founded the cellar ❞

PEOPLE - Marinella Camerani, backed by her husband Cesar and daughter Francesca, is the cellar's driving force, the standard-bearer of an original new face for the Valpolicella.

VINEYARDS - Marinella "listens" to her vineyards and tends to the needs of each with rural common sense. Her adoption of biodynamics is her way of embracing an idea of agriculture based increasingly on the equilibrium of the ecosystem. Harmony reigns among the vine rows in the Cavallero vineyard, a very steep strip of land with an exceptional high planting density (9,200 vines).

WINES - Marinella's wines stand out for their character and personality. Drinkability and well-rounded fruit combine to make the subtle, fresh-tasting **Valpolicella Cà Fiui 2013** (● 25,000 bt) very enjoyable indeed. On the other hand, **Valpolicella Ripasso Sup. Campi Magri 2011** (● 20,000 bt) has a rich, potent nose redolent of blackcurrants, bramble, tobacco and spices, followed by a tangy palate and a pleasantly bitter finish. **Soave 2013** (○ 12,000 bt), made with garganega and trebbiano di Soave grapes with a small percentage of chardonnay, is delicate and fresh.

> slow wine **AMARONE DELLA VALPOLICELLA 2010** (● 14,000 bt) At once complex and dynamic, a wine with blood-rich, earthy, inky notes on the nose and a long full finish.

SAN PIETRO IN CARIANO (VR)

Brigaldara

Frazione San Floriano
Via Brigaldara, 20
tel. 045 7701055
www.brigaldara.it
info@brigaldara.it

74 ac - 350,000 bt | **10% discount**

PEOPLE - The perfectly restored 15th-century villa alone is a good enough reason to visit the Cesari family's beautiful winery, where you'll be welcomed by Stefano, the genial and dynamic owner. In just a few years he has successfully managed to strengthen and consolidate the winery established by previous generations, acquiring important vineyards and launching the meticulous production of Amarone, firmly anchored in tradition.

VINEYARDS - Stefano is very proud of the winery's mix of produce: grapes, olives and summer truffles. The extensive woodland also ensures a high level of biodiversity, a sign of the winery's strong ecological awareness. The vineyards, some fairly old, with pergola-trained vines, others recently modernized, are divided between various plots in the municipalities of Grezzana, Marano, San Pietro and San Martino.

WINES - This year, Brigaldara presented three Amarones. Two had already been reviewed two years ago, but they were so excellent that we were happy to come across them again: the Amarone della Valpolicella Case Vecie 2009, in truly excellent form, with crisp fruit and a great sapid finish, and the Amarone della Valpolicella Cl. 2009, rich, balsamic and highly drinkable. They share an impeccable, refined style, combining elegance and dynamism, found also in the **Amarone della Valpolicella Ris. 2007** Great Wine (● 5,000 bt), a subtle, exalted wine, accompanied by hints of leather and spices, supple and caressing on the palate. The **Soave 2013** (○ 15,000 bt) is also well made, very typical, with fruit in the foreground and a dynamic drinkability.

FERTILIZERS compost, biodynamic preparations
PLANT PROTECTION copper and sulphur
WEED CONTROL mechanical
YEASTS native
GRAPES 100% estate-grown
CERTIFICATION biodynamic, organic

FERTILIZERS none
PLANT PROTECTION chemical, copper and sulphur, organic
WEED CONTROL mechanical
YEASTS selected
GRAPES 100% estate-grown
CERTIFICATION none

SAN PIETRO IN CARIANO (VR)

Monte dall'Ora

Via Monte dall'Ora, 5
tel. 045 7704462
www.montedallora.com
info@montedallora.com

16 ac - 35,000 bt

❝ It's impossible to speak about Monte dall'Ora without using the word 'love.' This wine cellar is, in fact, the 'baby' of two young lovebirds, Carlo Venturini and Alessandra Zantedeschi, who decided to leave steady jobs to crown their dream: to farm the land ❞

PEOPLE - They set out from scratch, driven by their love of nature (which they have since passed on to their kids). Since then they have created what is now a fantastic wine cellar in the heart of the Valpolicella.

VINEYARDS - The vineyards, which grow on terraces held up by traditional drystone walls, locally know as marogne, encircle the cellar in the hills of Castelrotto. Here biodiversity reigns, with cherry and olive trees, aromatic herbs and woodland growing side by side with the vines to create a harmonious, balanced whole. Carlo and Alessandra have always farmed organically, tending the vines meticulously and rigorously by hand.

WINES - In the cellar, the grapes are vinified spontaneously in 10-hectoliter truncated cone-shape vats and adequately aged. Monte dall'Ora's are "narrative" wines in which you can read vintage, unmistakable style and typology, always interpreted in textbook fashion. One such is **Amarone della Valpolicella Cl. 2009** (● 6,000 bt), in which partial drying of the grapes hasn't hidden vivid suggestions of cherry and red berry fruits, enhanced by balsamic tinges. **Valpolicella Cl. Sup. Camporenzo 2011** (● 8,000 bt) has a rich nose redolent of leather and tobacco with vaguely smoky tones, and sappy mouthfeel.

> **slow wine** RECIOTO DELLA VALPOLICELLA CL. SANT'ULDERICO **2010** (● 2,000 bt) Refined and enormously enjoyable as ever, a masterwork of a wine in an often hackneyed typology.

FERTILIZERS compost, biodynamic preparations
PLANT PROTECTION copper and sulphur, organic
WEED CONTROL mechanical
YEASTS native
GRAPES 100% estate-grown
CERTIFICATION organic

SAN PIETRO IN CARIANO (VR)

Speri

Frazione Pedemonte
Via Fontana, 14
tel. 045 7701154
www.speri.com
info@speri.com

135 ac - 350,000 bt `10% discount`

PEOPLE - No resting on their laurels for the fifth generation of the Speri family. Instead they have announced a series of innovations: the first, a real source of pride, is the organic certification that will be applied to their wines as of the 2014 vintage. Additionally, work will soon begin to extend and renovate the winery, to facilitate the winemaking process and create the optimal conditions for aging the wines.

VINEYARDS - At the end of 2013, the winery acquired six hectares of land in the same area where it already has 20 hectares on volcanic-origin soil, in Sant'Urbano a Fumane. The plot is still being studied, with the plan being to plant the first two hectares of vines by spring 2015. The first harvests are expected in 10 years. Organic cultivation, only recently introduced, is improving the vineyard ecosystem and the quality of the grapes.

WINES - As in previous years, the wines from this historic winery are of a good quality, with a very precise style deriving from the method of aging in large barrels and tonneaus. The violet-scented **Valpolicella Cl. 2013** (● 100,000 bt) has a fresh, direct flavor. The **Valpolicella Cl. Sup. Ripasso 2012** (● 80,000 bt) is delightful, with lingering notes of morello cherries and violets. The **Valpolicella Cl. Sup. Sant'Urbano 2011** (● 60,000 bt) is obtained from a selection of grapes that are dried for around 20 days; the result is a red of marked elegance, aromatic complexity and structure. The **Amarone della Valpolicella Cl. Vigneto Monte Sant'Urbano 2010** (● 100,000 bt) is still young, but in the glass it shows equilibrium and finesse. Last comes the wine we liked best, the **Recioto della Valpolicella Cl. La Roggia 2011** `Great Wine` (● 10,000 bt): highly enjoyable, intoxicating, dense and weighty without being cloying.

FERTILIZERS natural manure, biodynamic preparations
PLANT PROTECTION copper and sulphur, organic
WEED CONTROL mechanical
YEASTS selected
GRAPES 100% estate-grown
CERTIFICATION organic

SAN PIETRO IN CARIANO (VR)

Villa Bellini

Località Castelrotto di Negarine
Via dei Fraccaroli, 6
tel. 0457 725630
www.villabellini.com
villabellini@villabellini.com

SOMMACAMPAGNA (VR)

Monte Del Frà

Strada Custoza, 35
tel. 045 510490
www.montedelfra.it
info@montedelfra.it

10 ac - 12,000 bt

430 ac - 1,000,000 bt

❝ One face of the Valpolicella, as authentic as it's original, a place where everything is in the right place, from the old vineyards to the lake hidden in the woods, from the 18th-century villa to profound respect for the land and the ecosystem. This is the magical world of Cecilia Trucchi ❞

PEOPLE - Cecilia and her husband Marco Zamarchi bought the cellar in 1987. An enchanting place of sincere people and sincere wines, it's well worth a visit.

VINEYARDS - Century-old pergolas, low-bush training, exclusively local grape varieties, the exaltation of the farming landscape, including the traditional *brolo*, a small orchard surrounded by a stone wall – all important elements of the vineyards, supplemented by organic farming methods. Besides the old vineyards, there's also a small recently replanted one.

WINES - Cecilia's textbook wines are close-focused and original and all bear her hallmark characteristics of refinement and harmony. Don't make the mistake of underrating **Valpolicella Cl. Sup. Taso 2011** (● 4,500 bt); initially timid on the nose, it opens slowly in the glass with a multitudinous array of olfactory nuances – from ripe fruit to Mediterranean scrub to cocoa and many more besides – followed by a long, slightly bitter finish. **Valpolicella Cl. Sotto le Fresche Frasche 2013** (● 6,000 bt) is obviously much weightier altogether: at once bright and elegant, it fuses chewy cherries and spices with pleasant acidity, which then give way to well-balanced softness. This year we were also lucky enough to taste the rare **Recioto della Valpolicella Cl. Uva Passa** (● 1,200 bt).

PEOPLE - Brothers Eligio and Claudio Bonomo have been making wine for over 50 years, working in the vineyard and the winery respectively. Eligio's daughter, Marìca, has dedicated her passion and skill to public relations and hospitality (the winery is always open, even Sunday mornings). The spacious tasting room hosts exhibitions and cultural evenings. Young Silvia and Massimo (a future enologist) are the latest generation to join the winery.

VINEYARDS - The vineyard holdings are truly remarkable, divided between the moraine hills south of Lake Garda and the Valpolicella Classico area, where the Tenuta Lena di Mezzo in Fumane was acquired in 2006. The Custoza vineyards are managed using mechanical means, but the grapes are vinified separately to highlight the diversities of the poor, loose soil. Meanwhile, the 10 or so hectares producing the grapes for Valpolicella and Amarone are managed entirely manually.

WINES - The hand of enologist Claudio Introini joins that of Claudio Bonomo to make elegant, balanced wines with great attention to detail, even when produced in large quantities. As usual, the **Custoza Sup. Cà del Magro 2012** (○ 60,000 bt) has an unmissable finesse and aromatic complexity. The simpler but no less juicy and flavorful Custoza 2013 Everyday Wine (○ 500,000 bt) is also excellent, as is the juicy, stylish and spiced Bardolino 2013 Everyday Wine (● 200,000 bt). The playful **Bardolino Chiaretto La Picia** (◑ 10,000 bt), a creamy and enjoyable extra dry sparkling wine, is very interesting. The **Amarone della Valpolicella Cl. Scarnocchio 2009** (● 10,000 bt) is still young, but already has a beautiful gustatory depth, spiced and with an appealing equilibrium. **Amarone della Valpolicella Cl. Tenuta Lena di Mezzo 2010** (● 30,000 bt) is closer to being ready to drink.

FERTILIZERS compost, biodynamic preparations	**FERTILIZERS** organic-mineral
PLANT PROTECTION copper and sulphur	**PLANT PROTECTION** chemical, copper and sulphur
WEED CONTROL mechanical	**WEED CONTROL** chemical, mechanical
YEASTS native	**YEASTS** selected
GRAPES 100% estate-grown	**GRAPES** 100% estate-grown
CERTIFICATION organic	**CERTIFICATION** none

Garganega Country

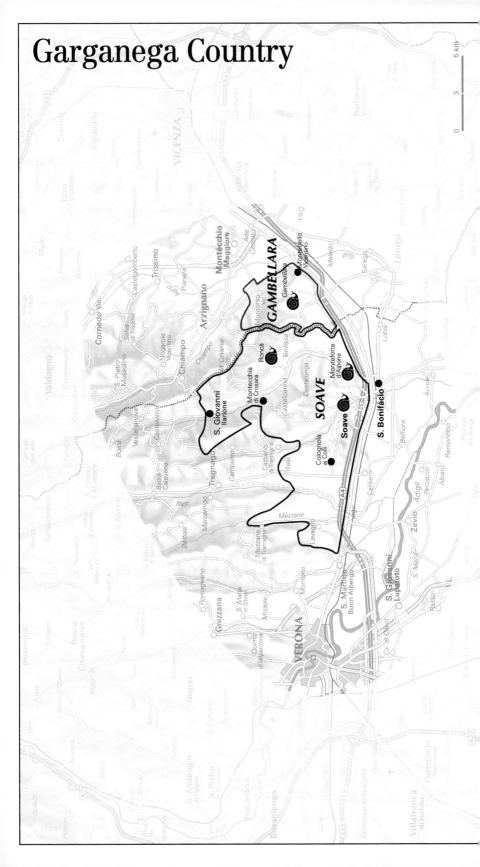

La Biancara

Frazione Sorio
Contrada Biancara, 14
tel. 0444 444244
www.biancaravini.it
biancaravini@virgilio.it

32 ac - 65,000 bt

66 «A good viticulturist has to be concerned with the health and equilibrium of the vines and the soil – says Angiolino Maule – following old values with a scientific vision.» **99**

PEOPLE - Angiolino, a winemaker's winemaker and a precursor of the natural wine movement, founded the cellar in 1988 with his wife Rosamaria. Now the president of the VinNatur association, he lives his life choice coherently and to the full.

VINEYARDS - Helping Angiolino and Rosamaria to run the cellar, which received organic certification two years ago, are their sons Francesco (sales), Alessandro (vineyard and accounts) and Tommaso (vineyard). The vineyards at Gambellara, in the Biancara, Faldeo, Montedimezzo, Taibane and Le Coste districts, rest on volcanic terrains, rich in basalt and silicon. The ones at Sossano, in the Colli Berici, grow on clayey soils. They are farmed without forcing and with maximum respect for the ecosystem. Experimentation work is incessant.

WINES - For the last two years Angiolino has received the collaboration of a friend of his, enologist Franco Giacosa. In the new wine cellar, not far from the old one, the use of chemicals, inoculated yeasts, filtering and clarifying continue to be banned, and fermentations are spontaneous without temperature control. The use of sulfur is limited to a minimum and will gradually be eliminated. "Great land and great grape varieties don't need outside help," says Maule, who's as coherent in the cellar as he is in the vineyard. **Sassaia 2013** (O garganega, trebbiano; 15,000 bt) is tangy and succulent and long. **I Masieri 2013** (O garganega, trebbiano; 20,000 bt) is supple and concentrated.

slow wine **So San 2012** (● 5,000 bt) A very personal interpretation of the tai rosso grape that's all freshness, dynamism, fruity concentration and suppleness.

FERTILIZERS compost, green manure
PLANT PROTECTION copper and sulphur, organic
WEED CONTROL mechanical
YEASTS native
GRAPES 100% estate-grown
CERTIFICATION biodynamic

Dama del Rovere €

Frazione Brognoligo
Via Mezzavilla, 59
tel. 045 6175556
www.damadelrovere.com
info@damadelrovere.com

18.5 ac - 33,000 bt

PEOPLE - The winery was founded in 2003 by brothers Massimo and Davide Prà, at the time in their twenties, but with the experience of three generations of winegrowers behind them. The name comes from a small statute of the Madonna placed inside a hollow in a large oak tree in the Tremenalto vineyard in Brognoligo. The building where the wines are made and aged was constructed recently above the Brenton di Roncà village, surrounded by woods, small vineyards and panoramic views.

VINEYARDS - The vines are trained using either the pergola corta or the Guyot system. The Tremenalto hill is planted with garganega for Soave, while the Brenton vineyards are primarily planted with durella, with a very recent Guyot vineyard, a new experiment. The soil is of volcanic origin, sometimes chalkier, sometimes more basaltic, sometimes even changing composition within the same vineyard.

WINES - Wisdom and skill inherited from their parents and grandparents have helped Massimo and Davide to make an old-school **Soave Cl. Tremenalto 2013** (O 10,000 bt) with an excellent nose and palate, precise and clean. With the Durello, it seems as though the god Bacchus had a hand, or maybe Pan, what with all the youthful creativity and the healthy hunt for pleasure, starting with the Charmat **Lessini Durello Brut Brenton** (O 10,000 bt): very fine bubbles, flavorful and lemony, to drink with a meal. The excellent **Lessini Durello M. Cl. 36 Mesi Extra Brut 2010** (O 5,000 bt) inevitably ends up finished as soon as it is uncorked, and so perhaps there will be a few years of purgatory to pay off, but otherwise ours is a pagan hymn of praise to Dionysus.

slow wine **Lessini Durello M. Cl. 24 mesi** (O 5,000 bt) A perfect and personal interpretation of the variety, exalting the best characteristics: finesse, elegance, assertiveness, depth and character.

FERTILIZERS none
PLANT PROTECTION chemical, copper and sulphur, organic
WEED CONTROL mechanical
YEASTS selected
GRAPES 100% estate-grown
CERTIFICATION none

MONTEFORTE D'ALPONE (VR)

Gini

Via Matteotti, 42
tel. 0457 611908
www.ginivini.com
info@ginivini.com

136 ac - 200,000 bt

PEOPLE - The estate is run by the two Gini brothers – enologist Sandro and Claudio – with Claudio's son, Matteo, in the winery. Their faces, radiant and serene, seem to reflect their healthy vineyards, in equilibrium with the environment. Interestingly, despite their many decades of winemaking, the two brothers have never had to replant a vineyard, thanks to the precious legacy of their father, Olinto, who began working towards organic cultivation as far back as the 1960s.

VINEYARDS - The historic vineyards are planted on volcanic soil in the best Soave zones, with pergola-trained vines, some ungrafted (over 100 years old!). The decision to limit yields has turned into a elixir of longevity for the plants, and given rise to the best crus. Other Guyot-trained rows can be found in Campiano, in a breezy spot with stony soil, also the site of the first planting of pinot nero in 1988.

WINES - The two crus deserve a special mention. The **Soave Cl. La Froscà 2013** Great Wine (O 20,000 bt) opens with mineral notes, white flowers, honey and anise; on the palate the freshness of the earth emerges, as do impressive sapidity and a rare finesse, offering great strength of feeling in a glass. The **Soave Cl. Contrada Salvarenza Vecchie Vigne 2012** (O 10,000 bt) brings intoxicating scents of hay, acacia and ripe fruit, and is savory and almondy in the mouth. The **Soave Cl. 2013** (O 110,000 bt) is clean and dry, less fragrant than the previous vintage. The **Monte Lessini Bianco Sorai 2011** (O chardonnay, garganega, pinot bianco, durella; 5,000 bt) is fragrant and assertive, with flowers from the garganega and buttery tones from the chardonnay. The **Recioto di Soave Re Nobilis 2008** (O 2,000 bt) is a refined and complex passito.

FERTILIZERS natural manure, green manure
PLANT PROTECTION copper and sulphur, organic
WEED CONTROL mechanical
YEASTS native
GRAPES 100% estate-grown
CERTIFICATION organic

MONTEFORTE D'ALPONE (VR)

Le Battistelle €

Frazione Brognoligo
Via Sambuco, 110
tel. 045 6175621
www.lebattistelle.it
info@lebattistelle.it

22 ac - 20,000 bt   10% discount

PEOPLE - Documents show that the Dal Bosco family has owned vineyards since at least the 18th century. Angelo, the father of Gelmino, the current owner, was one of the founders of the Monteforte cooperative winery. In 2002, Gelmino, with the unconditional support of his wife Cristina in the vineyard and with the administration, founded his own winery, producing the first bottles in 2004. Their son Andrea takes care of marketing, and enologist Armando Vesco has long overseen the winemaking.

VINEYARDS - Roccolo del Durlo, 720 feet above sea level, surrounded by woods, is quite a sight: volcanic soils and century-old pergola-trained vines growing on steep slopes that bring to mind heroic viticulture. Here you'll find the experimental vineyard, planted with cuttings from ancient vines. Battistelle and Montesei are two slopes of the same hill, the first at an altitude of 590 feet, the second at 330 feet. The youngest vines are 30 years old.

WINES - While the wines of the welcoming Dal Bosco family are indisputably good, they are also interesting for other reasons, like the incredible work they do in the vineyards under very difficult conditions. A visit is well worth the trip, as is stopping for refreshment at the Roccolo del Durlo viewpoint. While all of volcanic origin, the soils have different characteristics, which can be detected in the wines. The **Soave Cl. Battistelle 2012** (O 4,000 bt) is fresh and mouthfilling. The **Soave Cl. Montesei 2013** (O 12,600 bt) expresses a delicate immediacy. The **Passito Sacripante 2007** (O 200 bt), the traditional Brognoligo Vin Santo, made from garganega grapes, is worthy of note: a rarity for a few – a very few! – connoisseurs.

slow wine **SOAVE CL. ROCCOLO DEL DURLO 2012** (O 2,000 bt) An authentic garganega, expressive and vibrant, revealing depth and length on the palate.

FERTILIZERS organic-mineral
PLANT PROTECTION copper and sulphur
WEED CONTROL chemical, mechanical
YEASTS selected
GRAPES 100% estate-grown
CERTIFICATION none

Daniele Nardello €

Via IV Novembre, 56
tel. 045 7612116
www.nardellovini.it
info@nardellovini.it

Prà

Via della Fontana, 31
tel. 045 7612125
www.vinipra.it
info@vinipra.it

37 ac - 55,000 bt `10% discount`

PEOPLE - Daniele Nardello and his sister Federica represent the new generation at this historic Soave winery. The winemaking business was started recently, following a project to improve the family's estate, which in the past 30 years had been focused only on selling grapes. Since 2009 Daniele and Federica have been able to take advantage of a new, functional and welcoming winery building.

VINEYARDS - Daniele and Federica's great-grandfather was a far-sighted man. He, along with grandfather Domenico and father Gaetano, deserves credit for acquiring the important vineyards that today give the winery a consolidated legacy of old vines in excellent condition. Monte Zoppega in Monteforte and Monte Tondo in Soave are two crus in the classic zone. Some of the plantings are over 50 years old.

WINES - Depth and immediacy combined with character and complexity: That's one way to sum up the style of the Nardellos' wines. The **Soave Cl. Merides 2013** (○ 30,000 bt) is subtle, fresh and delicate in its floral notes, while the **Soave Cl. Monte Zoppega 2012** (○ 5,000 bt), fermented and aged in barrique, is richer and more complex, with an excellent balance between fruity succulence and acidic-sapid verve. We very much liked the Soave Cl. Vigna Turbian 2013 `Everyday Wine` (○ 6,500 bt); the 30% trebbiano di Soave, added to the garganega, brings a more assertive and deep tone, greatly increasing the enjoyability. The unusual but good **Blanc de Fè 2013** (○ 3,000 bt), made from an equal blend of garganega, trebbiano and chardonnay, is very fruity and soft.

82 ac - 285,000 bt `10% discount`

❝ The pursuit of quality and the improvement of the local area are the two missions of Graziano Prà, a virtuous winemaker but also an attentive observer of the market and a strenuous defender of Soave's identity ❞

PEOPLE - In 1983 Graziano, the descendant of a family of winegrowers, decided to build a cellar and bottle his wine. A few years ago he decided to diversify production by buying a good piece of growing land in the Valpolicella.

VINEYARDS - Montegrande, Foscarino, Froscà and Monte Croce are garganega vineyards that Graziano has patiently brought to the limelight, working on them as if they were grands crus. The vines are espalier- and pergola Veronese-trained in equal measure. In both cases they are tended with great care for their natural equilibrium. The Valpolicella vineyards are at an altitude of about 1,600 feet and rest on flaky white morainal soil.

WINES - A range of white wines that combine elegance and flavor. The approachable and delightful **Soave Cl. Otto 2013** (○ 150,000 bt) is wonderfully fruity and tangy. **Soave Cl. Montegrande 2013** (○ 15,000 bt), which has an impeccable, very delicate mineral finish, is more complex, softer and burlier. Moving on to the two red wines from the Valpolicella vineyards, **Valpolicella La Morandina 2013** (● 10,000 bt) is pleasantly fruity and supple, while the distinctly austere and rugged **Amarone della Valpolicella 2009** (● 10,000 bt) displays ripe fruit and robust tannins.

slow wine **SOAVE CL. STAFORTE 2012** (○ 6,600 bt) Elegance and body to the nth degree attended by deep flavor, huge aromatic complexity and a long finish.

FERTILIZERS organic-mineral, mineral
PLANT PROTECTION copper and sulphur
WEED CONTROL mechanical
YEASTS selected
GRAPES 100% estate-grown
CERTIFICATION none

FERTILIZERS organic-mineral, natural manure
PLANT PROTECTION chemical, copper and sulphur
WEED CONTROL mechanical
YEASTS selected
GRAPES 100% estate-grown
CERTIFICATION none

RONCÀ (VR)

Fongaro ⊚⃫

Via Motto Piane, 12
tel. 045 7460240
www.fongarospumanti.it
info@fongarospumanti.it

29 ac - 90,000 bt

66 Set up in 1975 by Guerrino Fongaro, this commendable Roncà cellar deserves credit for believing in the potential of durella, a local grape variety previously underrated for its husky, edgy character 99

PEOPLE - Guerrino celebrated his hundredth birthday this year (congratulations!) but has no plans to retire. He's still active and involved, and supports the work of his grandsons Matteo and Alessandro to whom he's handed over the reins of the business.

VINEYARDS - Fongaro decided to farm his vineyards organically way back in 1985 because he didn't want chemicals to harm his grapes – especially the delicate native durella – in any way. The vineyards run along the slopes of the hill on which the cellar is situated. They are pergola Veronese-trained and rest on lean volcanic soil with good drainage.

WINES - The complex and elegant **Lessini Durello Pas Dosé Ris. 2007** (○ 10,000 bt) has character, pleasing acid grip and delicate, seductive perlage. The durella monovarietal 100x100 Fongaro, which rests for 100 months on the yeasts, was created especially to celebrate granda Guerrino's hundredth birthday. Unfortunately it was only produced in a limited edition of 100 magnums. Not to worry, there's always the evergreen **Lessini Durello Brut 2010** (○ 20,000 bt) to go on with: fragrant and tangy, it's a joy to drink.

---
slow wine LESSINI DURELLO BRUT RIS. **2008** (○ 10,000 bt) A superlative wine, biting and deep, enfolding and flavorsome, headily redolent of citrus and dried fruit. It rests on the yeasts for 40 months and more before being dégorged.

SOAVE (VR)

Monte Tondo €

Via San Lorenzo, 89
tel. 045 7680347
www.montetondo.it
info@montetondo.it

79 ac - 220,000 bt | **10% discount**

PEOPLE - Tenacious and tireless vigneron Gino Magnabosco has passed all of his passion for vines and wine on to his children, Luca, Marta and Stefania. The business was started in 1985 and in 2000 the winery building, clearly visible from the Soave highway toll booths, was completely renovated. This family business has been able to skillfully unite tradition and innovation, while always keeping its feet on the ground.

VINEYARDS - The garganega vineyards are on the same hill (called Monte Tondo) as the winery building, and in two other excellent Soave zones, Monte Tenda and Monte Foscarino. A few years ago, it was decided to make red wines as well as whites, so the winery acquired twelve acres of vineyard in Campiano, in a hilly area characterized by chalky soils rich in the white limestone layers known as scaglia bianca.

WINES - Each of the winery's three Soaves is a synthesis of a distinctive trait linked primarily to its zone of origin and the interpretation given in the winery. We can find a marked minerality and rounded, ripe fruit in the **Soave Cl. Sup. Foscarin Slavinus 2012** (○ 10,000 bt), the result of a late harvest and fermentation in wooden barrels. The grapes for the **Soave Cl. Casette Foscarin 2012** Great Wine (○ 13,000 bt) come from the same area; it offers sensations of flint and citrus, accompanied on the palate by a cutting, pervasive acidity. More obvious fruit, with hints of peach and white flowers, comes from the graceful and zesty **Soave Cl. Monte Tondo 2013** (○ 40,000 bt). The **Amarone della Valpolicella 2010** (● 6,000 bt) is endowed with grace and suppleness.

FERTILIZERS natural manure, green manure	**FERTILIZERS** natural manure
PLANT PROTECTION copper and sulphur	**PLANT PROTECTION** chemical, copper and sulphur
WEED CONTROL mechanical	**WEED CONTROL** mechanical
YEASTS selected	**YEASTS** selected
GRAPES 100% estate-grown	**GRAPES** 100% estate-grown
CERTIFICATION organic	**CERTIFICATION** none

SOAVE (VR)

Leonildo Pieropan

Via Camuzzoni, 3
tel. 045 6190171
www.pieropan.it
info@pieropan.it

99 ac - 400,000 bt

66 If Soave is famous the world over as a great white, then much of the credit must go to Leonildo Pieropan who, with doggedness, intelligence and visions, has raised the profile of his home turf and its bounties 99

PEOPLE - The Pieropan family has been making Soave for a century and more, but it's thanks to Leonildo, grandson of the founder, that the cellar has soared to success. Having learned his lessons, it's now Leonildo's sons Andrea and Dario who are carrying on the tradition.

VINEYARDS - The garganega vineyards are scattered over the best growing areas in the denomination. The 18 acres at Calvarino, one of the cellar's celebrated crus, have basalt and tufa soil, while its other prestigious vineyard grows on limestone and clay soil near the Scala family castle and produces the grapes for La Rocca. The 30-acre vineyard at Cellore d'Illasi, in the Valpolicella, was planted in 1999 to enable Leonildo to try his hand with reds.

WINES - Albeit the fruit of a vintage that fell slightly short in terms of bite and depth, **Soave Cl. Calvarino 2012** (○ 43,000 bt) retains all its customary elegance, austerity and linearity. The wood-aged **Soave Cl. La Rocca 2012** (○ 33,000 bt) is more rounded and expressive. The classically delicate and blossomy **Soave Cl. 2013** (○ 260,000 bt) is fresh-tasting and dynamic on the palate. The excellent **Amarone della Valpolicella Cl. 2010** (● 8,600 bt) has an opulent, soft style supplemented by style and balance. **Valpolicella Sup. Ruberpan 2011** (● 24,000 bt) is packed with flesh and flavor.

SOAVE (VR)

Suavia

Frazione Fittà
Via Centro,14
tel. 045 7675089
www.suavia.it
info@suavia.it

37 ac - 130,000 bt

PEOPLE - The management of this well-established family winery, named after the old term for Soave, is dominated by women. Located in the Fittà frazione, it has 37 acres of vines in the Soave Classico hills. Founded almost 30 years ago by Giovanni Tessari, for the last decade it has been focusing on increasing quality, with the growing involvement of his daughters Valentina, Alessandra, Meri and Arianna.

VINEYARDS - Only white grapes, from the best crus: Castellaro, Le Rive, Carbonare, Tremenalto. In the Carbonare cru, 80-year-old vines use the pergola veronese system, and the other vineyards are all aged over 40 years. The only exception is the new plot of Guyot-trained trebbiano di Soave. The microclimate created by the southwestern exposure and the chalky-basaltic composition of the volcanic-origin soil give the wines freshness, minerality and longevity.

WINES - "It's like having a piece of the land in your glass." Valentina's words introduce the **Soave Cl. Monte Carbonare 2012** Great Wine (○ 30,000 bt), whose 15 months on the lees give it the complexity, elegance, length and equilibrium of a truly great wine. The **Soave Cl. 2013** (○ 80,000 bt) is clean, fragrant and juicy. The **Soave Cl. Le Rive 2010** (○ 7,000 bt), made from late-harvest grapes and aged in wood, is full-bodied and velvety with hints of petrol, spiced and lingering. Notes of citrus are followed by minerals in the **Massifitti 2011** (○ trebbiano di Soave; 13,000 bt), while the **M. Cl. Dosaggio Zero Opera Semplice** (○ trebbiano di Soave; 2,000 bt) is creamy with a fruity, minerally texture. The **Recioto di Soave Acinatium 2008** (○ 4,000 bt) has great aromatic density.

FERTILIZERS none	**FERTILIZERS** natural manure
PLANT PROTECTION copper and sulphur	**PLANT PROTECTION** copper and sulphur
WEED CONTROL mechanical	**WEED CONTROL** mechanical
YEASTS selected	**YEASTS** selected, native
GRAPES 100% estate-grown	**GRAPES** 100% estate-grown
CERTIFICATION none	**CERTIFICATION** converting to organics

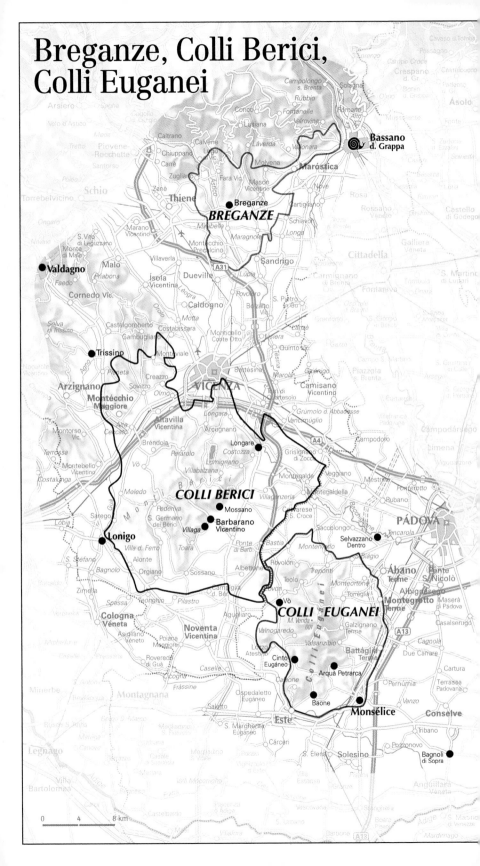

Vigneto Due Santi

Viale Asiago, 174
tel. 0424 502074
www.vignetoduesanti.it
info@vignetoduesanti.it

44 ac - 100,000 bt `10% discount`

❝ Cousins Adriano and Stefano Zonta are skilled winegrowers in love with their job. For them, wine isn't a commodity but the essence of the local area in which they live ❞

PEOPLE - The cellar was set up at the start of the 1960s. Stefano began to work there in 1988, and was joined ten years later by Adriano. Under their guidance Due Santi has made great headway on the road to quality (with elegant, enjoyable, reasonably priced wines) and environmental sustainability, and is now a benchmark for all winemakers in the Bassano area.

VINEYARDS - The property is subdivided into different parcels, all in the same strip of land on the edge of the woods at the foot of the mountains, where a limestone crust is covered by a very fine stratum of relatively unfertile soil. Every vineyard has been planted taking the lie of the land and the slopes into account. It has never been overworked and is now farmed with methods that are virtually organic, though not certified as such.

WINES - The common denominators of all the wines are traditional style and value for money. **Malvasia Campo di Fiori 2013** (○ 3,500 bt) is a lovely white, elegantly aromatic, fresh-tasting and mineral on the palate. Once more outstanding among the reds is Breganze Merlot 2011 Everyday Wine (● 20,000 bt), a weighty, charismatic version of the grape, full of fruit with a nice tangy finish. **Breganze Cabernet 2011** (● 25,000 bt) is subtler, austere and typical, characteristics replicated in its "elder brother" **Breganze Cabernet Vigneto Due Santi 2011** (● 16,000 bt) which, however, has greater flesh and substance. Last but not least, **Breganze Rosso Cavallare 2011** (● 6,000 bt) is dark, full-bodied and enfolding.

FERTILIZERS natural manure
PLANT PROTECTION chemical, copper and sulphur
WEED CONTROL mechanical
YEASTS selected
GRAPES 100% estate-grown
CERTIFICATION none

La Montecchia
Conte Emo Capodilista

Via Montecchia, 16
tel. 049 637294
www.lamontecchia.it
lamontecchia@lamontecchia.it

74 ac - 130,000 bt `10% discount`

PEOPLE - La Montecchia is a charming spot in the Colli Euganei, the Euganean Hills, not far from Padua. This is where Giordano Emo Capodilista guides with a sure hand his historic and impressive winery, maintaining strong links to local tradition. Affable Giordano gives everyone a warm welcome, and a visit to the winery, which includes a golf club and the splendid Villa Capodilista, is highly recommended.

VINEYARDS - The winery's extensive vineyards are divided between two main plots. Each one is planted with the varieties that have become traditional here: cabernet sauvignon, carmenère and merlot. They are joined by moscato Fior d'Arancio, typical of the Euganean Hills, a variety in which Giordano has long invested. The agricultural management, under the control of Patrizio Gasparinetti, is oriented towards sustainability.

WINES - Impeccably crafted wines with confident expressiveness issue from the winery, overseen by enologist Andrea Boaretti. They include two reds of great character: the **Colli Euganei Rosso Villa Capodilista 2011** (● 6,500 bt) is very elegant, but also beautifully concentrated and with a refined tannic weave, while the **Colli Euganei Cabernet Sauvignon Ireneo 2011** (● 6,000 bt) perfectly unites the power of the fruit with a very fine and deep mineral vein. The Piuchebello 2013 Everyday Wine (○ 6,000 bt) is a dry wine made from moscato giallo and moscato bianco grapes, highly enjoyable and with an elegant balance between rounded fruit, aromatic qualities and freshness. Only moscato giallo is used in the **Colli Euganei Fior d'Arancio Passito Donna Daria 2012** (○ 4,000 bt) which is voluptuous and full, with intense apricot and peach notes, and the **Colli Euganei Fior d'Arancio Spumante 2013** (○ 30,000 bt), properly sweet and fragrant.

FERTILIZERS none
PLANT PROTECTION chemical, copper and sulphur
WEED CONTROL mechanical
YEASTS selected, native
GRAPES 100% estate-grown
CERTIFICATION none

Prosecco Hills, Piave and Western Veneto

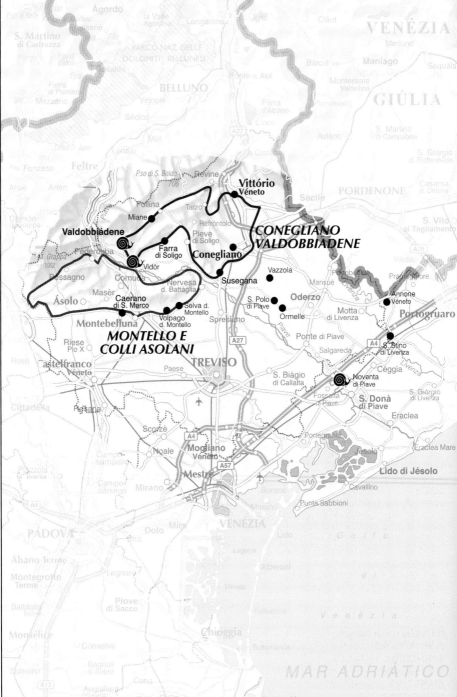

NOVENTA DI PIAVE (VE)

Tessère

Località Santa Teresina
Via Bassette, 51
tel. 0421 320438
www.tessereonline.it
info@tessereonline.it

---

37 ac - 55,000 bt · 10% discount

❝ Known locally as the 'Lady of Raboso,' Emanuela Bincoletto is a beacon for viticulture in the Basso Piave district **❞**

PEOPLE - Tessère opened in 1979 and now also performs educational activities, organizing very interesting, original projects. This year as part of the Cantine Aperte (Open Cellars) event, for example, a systemic orchard was created in the garden of the cellar. Accommodation is also available at the holiday farm.

VINEYARDS - Tessère is an organic and biodynamic cellar. Its vineyards are at Noventa di Piave, in the Piave DOC zone, in an area of eastern Veneto when the reclaimed clayey soils are of alluvial origin. The vines are Guyot- and spurred cordon-trained. The main grape cultivated by the cellar is raboso, which is used to make red, bottle-refermented rosé and passito wines. Merlot, cabernet sauvignon and pinot bianco grapes are also grown.

WINES - Experimentation with the wines is ongoing and recently the range of Piave wines has been supplemented by a Verduzzo and a Refosco di Faedis, made with grapes on an estate the cellar owns in Friuli. This year we tasted and enjoyed the bottle-refermented **Rosato di Raboso Brut Sui Lieviti Redentor 2010** (☉ 1,500 bt), vaguely the color of a red onion: lively and fresh-tasting, with the acidulous note typical of the grape on the palate, it will certainly attract lovers of the typology. We reviewed the exciting and compelling meditation wine Raboso Passito Rebecca 2007, still on sale at the cellar, an excellent interpretation of raisined raboso grapes.

FERTILIZERS green manure
PLANT PROTECTION copper and sulphur, organic
WEED CONTROL mechanical
YEASTS selected
GRAPES 100% estate-grown
CERTIFICATION biodynamic

SUSEGANA (TV)

Malibran

Via Barca II, 63
tel. 0438 781410
www.malibranvini.it
info@malibranvini.it

---

17 ac - 80,000 bt · 10% discount

PEOPLE - An encounter with Maurizio Favrel, the young and passionate enologist who now runs the winery he inherited from his father Girolamo and grandfather Gregorio, is an experience that will teach you much about Prosecco and its various expressive possibilities. Malibran is a family nickname that became their distinctive hallmark, and has nothing to do with the famous Venetian theatre of the same name.

VINEYARDS - The estate is located in Susegana and has 17 acres of vineyards, entirely planted with glera, on the hills that rise towards the castle. Sustainability principles are followed from vine to bottle. The clayey soils produce well-structured wines. The grapes are picked entirely by hand, in order to maximize the quality of the bunches. The work in the winery is meticulous and, says Maurizio, "we make as few interventions as possible."

WINES - These modern wines nonetheless follow in the path of tradition, starting with the **Conegliano Valdobbiadene Extra Brut Cinquegrammi 2013** (○ 3,300 bt), a wine with a perfect foundation, which will last over time. The **Conegliano Valdobbiadene Extra Dry Gorio 2013** (○ 35,000 bt) is excellent, while the **Conegliano Valdobbiadene Brut Ruio 2013** (○ 15,000 bt), with its drinkability and fragrance, will make everyone happy. Those who love sweeter Proseccos shouldn't miss the **Conegliano Valdobbiadene Dry Millesimato 2013** (○ 6,600 bt). Lastly, one of the two versions refermented in the bottle is the sulfite-free **Conegliano Valdobbiadene ColFondo Senza Solfiti Sottoriva 2013** (○ 2,200 bt), which has an evolving acidity.

slow wine · **CONEGLIANO VALDOBBIADENE COLFONDO PER TRADIZIONE SOTTORIVA 2013** (○ 10,000 bt) This traditional wine, fragrant, intense and very flavorful, just gets better every year. "In fact, we've never stopped making it," says Maurizio.

FERTILIZERS natural manure
PLANT PROTECTION chemical, copper and sulphur
WEED CONTROL mechanical
YEASTS selected
GRAPES 20% bought in
CERTIFICATION none

Valdellövo

Frazione Collalto
Via Gramsci, 4/c
tel. 0438 981232
www.valdellovo.it
info@valdellovo.it

Casa Coste Piane

Frazione Santo Stefano
Via Coste Piane, 2
tel. 0423 900219
casacostepiane@libero.it

25 ac - 70,000 bt   10% discount

15 ac - 60,000 bt

PEOPLE - Benedetto and Clotilde Ricci manage this winery, founded in 2000, in tandem, benefitting from Federico Giotto's winemaking consultancy. Benedetto's passion for wine is clearly the result of family imprinting, as he is following in the footsteps of his grandfather Bepi and father Romano. He dedicates himself primarily to production and winemaking, while Clotilde oversees the business side of things. "But we make the important decisions together," they tell us in unison.

VINEYARDS - Though the winery's operations are based in easily reachable Susegana, the vineyards are located in two beautiful and more remote spots. One parcel, inside a wood in the Collalto hills, has five well-tended acres of glera, bianchetta and verdiso, with some very old vines. Another ten acres are found further up in Le Crode, also in a very picturesque setting with a unique microclimate.

WINES - In just a short time, Benedetto and Clotilde's passion for their work has brought them to excellent levels of quality, with fresh, elegant, fragrant wines. The various types of Prosecco rule the roost here. This year we particularly liked the **Conegliano Valdobbiadene Prosecco Sup. Extra Dry Anno Zero 2013** (O 40,000 bt). The winery made its debut with this wine in 2000 and it offers excellent value for money, beautifully full-flavored taste sensations and scents of fruit and flowers. The **Conegliano Valdobbiadene Brut Zero Nove 2013** (O 5,000 bt) is also interesting, dry, with good acidity, and ideal for drinking throughout the meal. The Conegliano Valdobbiadene Col Fondo Bade 2012 Everyday Wine (O 5,000 bt), made partly from dried grapes, has scents of aromatic herbs and a pleasantly bitter finish, making it a very interesting and enjoyable wine.

“ Loris Follador is universally acknowledged as a master. If bottle-refermented Prosecco is enjoying success today, credit is due to him, a producer who has never betrayed the wine, never given up the cause ”

PEOPLE - Loris insists on calling himself "a farmer" and for over 20 years he has been "farming" in his Fol vineyards to produce wine with the CCP label. If you go to meet him, he'll talk to you not only about agronomy but also about local history and poetry with the eloquence of a great orator. He's helped by his wife Sandra and his children Adelchi and Raffaele.

VINEYARDS - The vineyards are in the Fol district, near the small cellar, in a green natural amphitheater of breathtaking beauty. The vine rows are farmed as naturally as possible and, with vines over 100 years old, are a veritable historical treasure. They grow on conglomerates of sandstone and fossils at an altitude of 980-1,300 feet. These vineyards are fully-fledged Valdobbiadene and have to be seen to be believed!

WINES - The two bottle-refermented Proseccos are again a benchmark for their personality and land-rooted recognizability. **Brichet Frizzante Naturalmente 2013** (O 4,000 bt) has a spacious palate but is still annoyingly chalky on the nose, a flaw which a few more months in the bottle will put right.

slow wine **VALDOBBIADENE PROSECCO SUP. FRIZZANTE NATURALMENTE 2013** (O 38,000 bt) A massive testimonial for the typology as always. It has elegant, clean, floral olfactory notes, a piquant palate and a pervasive, zesty finish.

FERTILIZERS compost, green manure	FERTILIZERS organic-mineral, natural manure
PLANT PROTECTION chemical, copper and sulphur	PLANT PROTECTION copper and sulphur
WEED CONTROL chemical, mechanical	WEED CONTROL mechanical
YEASTS selected	YEASTS native
GRAPES 100% estate-grown	GRAPES 100% estate-grown
CERTIFICATION none	CERTIFICATION none

VALDOBBIADENE (TV)

Silvano Follador

Frazione Santo Stefano
Via Callonga, 11
tel. 0423 900295
www.silvanofollador.it
info@silvanofollador.it

9 ac - 20,000 bt

66 Silvano Follador has never shied away from taking tough decisions in his virtuous winemaking career. Which is why his winery has become one of the most impressive in the Prosecco zone 99

PEOPLE - The young Santo Stefano di Valdobbiadene winemaker Silvano Follador embarked on his career in 1999. After years of apprenticeship in which he picked up the ropes of this demanding profession, the first turnaround came 2003, when he developed a precise productive style of his own. A second followed in 2007, when he acquired professional autonomy. His choices have put the cellar where it is today.

VINEYARDS - The four-acre property in the Cartizze district is a "hymn to joy," and on a par with it are the vineyards of Santo Stefano, Saccol and San Giovanni Bigolino, which grow on marly, clayey soil in the heart of the Prosecco production zone. A number of old vines add extra luster to the prestigious whole. The soils are fertilized with natal manure and the vines are treated with eco-friendly organic and biodynamic products.

WINES - The exclusively dry wines place the onus on quality and the essence of the grapes. **Conegliano Valdobbiadene Brut Nature 2013** (O 12,000 bt) is very forthright and full of thrust. It releases aromas of wild flowers and wisteria, delicately rounded off by a whiff of lavender, and a palate of refreshing citrusy tones with an encore of aromatic herbs. Delicious!

slow wine **VALDOBBIADENE SUP. DI CARTIZZE BRUT NATURE 2013** (O 6,600 bt) A paragon of elegance and depth. To the nose it offers exquisite nuances of mint and lemon balm, to the palate white peach with a lingering licoricey finish.

FERTILIZERS natural manure, biodynamic preparations
PLANT PROTECTION copper and sulphur, organic
WEED CONTROL mechanical
YEASTS selected
GRAPES 100% estate-grown
CERTIFICATION none

VIDOR (TV)

Sorelle Bronca

Frazione Colbertaldo
Via Martiri, 20
tel. 0423 987201 987009
www.sorellebronca.com
info@sorellebronca.com

44 ac - 280,000 bt   **10% discount**

66 A winery that's become a symbol of the local area on account of its research and experimentation work (hence its organic certification in 2012) 99

PEOPLE - Grandfather Martino's heritage has been gathered by sister Ersiliana and Antonella, ably assisted by the latter's husband Piero Balcon and the former's daughter Elisa, a budding young enologist. This year they opened a b&b under their famous Particella 68 parcel. All in all, a small but very efficient enterprise.

VINEYARDS - The vineyards are situated in four areas. The one at Colbertaldo rests on a steep hillside and grows glera vines over half a century old. It includes the legendary Particella 68 parcel, which has now been producing very low yield per acre for ten years. At Farrò and Rolle more glera vineyards are flanked by a few olive trees. The central plot at Rua di Feletto, finally, grows still more glera grapes, as well as red grape varieties, Manzoni bianco and olives.

WINES - The winery produces Prosecco with distinctive techniques of its own, such as vat-refermentation with the separate addition of must by different typologies, tangential settling without racking, and the use of native yeasts. Hence very particular wines, such as the bottle-refermented **Conegliano Valdobbiadene Difetto Perfetto 2013** (O 3,000 bt), made with a selection of grapes without added sugars: its bouquet is fruity with lemony notes, its palate crisp and full of verve. **Conegliano Valdobbiadene Extra Dry** (O 120,000 bt) is elegant and stylish. **Conegliano Valdobbiadene Brut 2013** (O 120,000 bt) has good presence.

slow wine **VALDOBBIADENE PROSECCO SUP. BRUT PARTICELLA 68** (O 10,000 bt) A symbol of a terroir and of determination to raise its profile. Its distinctive characteristics are crispness, tanginess and flavor.

FERTILIZERS natural manure, green manure
PLANT PROTECTION copper and sulphur
WEED CONTROL na
YEASTS selected
GRAPES 100% estate-grown
CERTIFICATION organic

FRIULI VENEZIA GIULIA

Normal! That, in a word, is our verdict on the 2013 vintage in Friuli. Yes, everything was alright, everything was OK. Which actually comes as good news after sequence of seriously problematic years. Our opinion was confirmed by the generally high quality of the wines. The only gray area was the estimated 5% drop in white grape production (only glera enjoyed a 10% increase).

Leaving aside our tastings, our judgments on the wines and the impressions we gathered on our visits to cellars, we'd like to reflect for a moment on two interesting questions concerning the Friuli wine world.

Recently a debate opened up among wine producers in the Collio zone–the most important, best known denomination in Friuli, and for many in Italy a synonym of wines of excellent quality–about an alleged loss of appeal on the Italian and international market. The feeling, probably well-founded, stems from a sort of complacency that has taken over the Friulian winegrowing community in recent years in conjunction with the undoubted growth, in terms of real and perceived quality, of other prime-quality Italian white wine production zones. The fact that it's Friulian producers themselves who are wondering what should be done is, we believe, a good sign.

Then there's the much debated "Prosecco affair." At present, about 85% of the Prosecco produced with grapes grown in Friuli is commercialized by cellars whose headquarters are outside the region, mostly in Veneto. Some see this as a problem. We don't, and the fact that the name Prosecco isn't associated with Friuli doesn't bother us one bit. Mainly because, in Italy but even more so abroad, Prosecco is seen not as a *vin de terroir* but as a "universal" brand. We just don't see the point in going on and on about its origin.

snails 🐌

105	MEROI
105	MIANI
107	I CLIVI
109	LE DUE TERRE
109	RONCO SEVERO
110	RONCO DEL GNEMIZ
111	VIGNAI DA DULINE
113	BORGO SAN DANIELE
114	EDI KEBER
115	KANTE
115	SKERK
116	ZIDARICH
116	GRAVNER
117	LA CASTELLADA
117	DAMIJAN PODVERSIC
118	RADIKON
119	SKERLJ

bottles 🍾

108	LE VIGNE DI ZAMÒ
108	AQUILA DEL TORRE
111	VOLPE PASINI
114	RONCO DEL GELSO
118	VIE DI ROMANS
119	ZUANI

coins €

106	PAOLO RODARO
107	GIGANTE
110	VISTORTA

The Plains and Eastern Hills

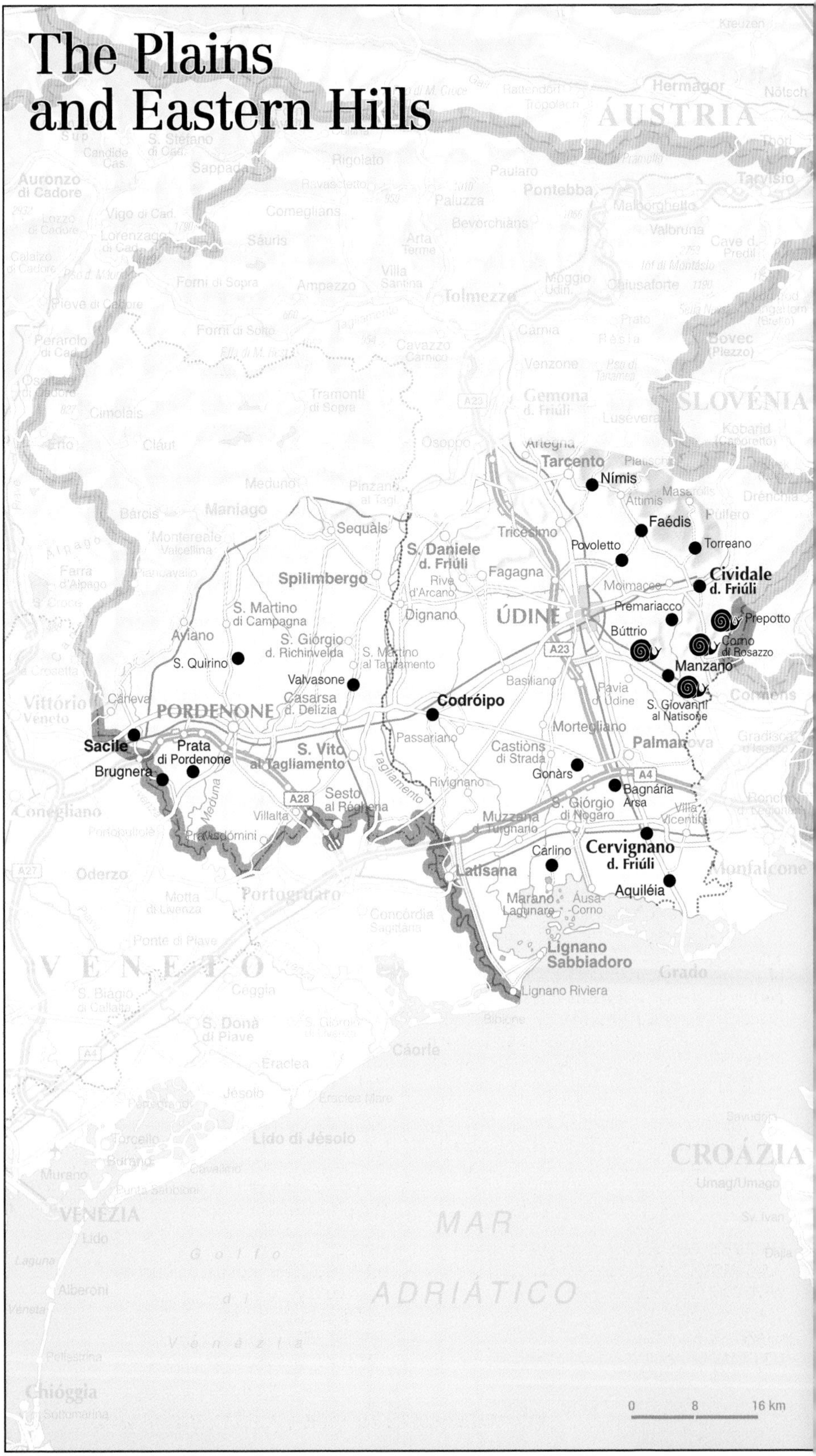

Meroi

Via Stretta, 6 B
tel. 0432 674025
www.meroidavino.com
info@meroidavino.com

Miani

Via Peruzzi, 10
tel. 0432 674327

---

72 ac - 40,000 bt

66 Paolo Meroi produces wines without compare, at the same time raising the profile of the local area 99

PEOPLE - The cellar, hidden behind Al Parco, the family restaurant in the center of Buttrio, may not be pretty but it's certainly functional. Paolo's son Damiano helps him run the business, while talented young Mirko Degan oversees the vineyards and the cellar firsthand.

VINEYARDS - Meroi owns 71 acres of vineyards, of which 49 are currently productive. Dominin, a warm vineyard with old vines, produces the most important reds. The new Zitelle vineyard is on a cooler slope with plenty of potential for whites, and here a project is underway that will be much talked about in years to come. The Merois attach great attention to grape ripening and the health of the soil.

WINES - All the Meroi wines age in small oak casks but, thanks to the skill with which these are used and the quality of the grapes, the wood is never invasive. The reds are spectacular, starting from **FCO Merlot Vigna Dominin 2011** (● 1,800 bt), which shows all the quality, depth and sweetness of fruit typical of the great wines of Buttrio. The rich, flavorsome **FCO Refosco P.R. Vigna Dominin 2011** (2,900 bt) has aromas of spices and berries with a soft, juicy, lingering palate. **FCO Picolit 2011** (○ 600 bt) is all elegance and complexity; on the nose it offers lime blossom, apricot and a touch of freshly mown grass and lemon zest, on the palate it's precise with a delicious sweet-acid contrast. On first tasting the 2013 dry whites seem highly promising. Worthy of mention are the Friulano, the Chardonnay and, a new entry, the first vintage of a great Malvasia.

32 ac - 11.500 bt

66 Enzo Pontoni is a model winemaker, totally devoted to his job. With his daily efforts he has taught many people how vines should be treated 99

PEOPLE - Enzo began working his mother Edda Miani's vines in the early 1990s with two set ideas: extreme viticulture and radical selection. The upshot is that the few bottles he produces are fought over by importers all round the world.

VINEYARDS - Enzo spends much of his time out in the vineyards overseeing the many small plots of land he owns, scattered between Rosazzo and Corno di Rosazzo and the great Vigna delle Zitelle at Buttrio. After scoping the vines and dedicating the time it takes to "listen to" the wines, he often goes back to the cellar to meditate. "The climate's changing," he says, "so I'll have to change too. And so will my wines."

WINES - Methods of vinification, carried out exclusively in barriques, differ vineyard by vineyard. When the growing year permits, as this one did, the wines remain separate, otherwise they are assembled. Enzo shuns our guide's symbols, though **FCO Friulano Filip 2013** (○ 1,000 bt) certainly deserves one and all of them with its huge grip and superb texture, almost unctuous breadth and unique depth and bite. Lighter and suppler is **FCO Friulano Buri 2013** (○ 1,600 bt), albeit no less tangy and thrusting on the palate. Il **FCO Sauvignon Banel 2013** (○ 900 bt) is made with grapes ripened on ponca, hence is buttery, juicy and complexly aromatic. It is the limestone soil instead that makes the aromas of **FCO Sauvignon Saurint 2013** (○ 1,100 bt) subtler and more moderate. The subtly complex **FCO Chardonnay Baracca 2013** (○ 650 bt) is lip-smacking, taut and zesty. In the absence of Calvari, we were delighted by **FCO Rosso Miani 2011** (● 4,000 bt), 60% merlot and 40% refosco, ultra-elegant and bristling with character.

FERTILIZERS manure pellets, natural manure
PLANT PROTECTION chemical, copper and sulphur
WEED CONTROL mechanical
YEASTS selected
GRAPES 100% estate-grown
CERTIFICATION none

FERTILIZERS natural manure
PLANT PROTECTION copper and sulphur
WEED CONTROL mechanical
YEASTS selected, native
GRAPES 100% estate-grown
CERTIFICATION none

Paolo Rodaro €

Località Spessa
Via Cormons, 60
tel. 0432 716066
www.rodaropaolo.it
info@rodaropaolo.it

Eugenio Collavini

Via della Ribolla Gialla, 2
tel. 0432 753222
www.collavini.it
collavini@collavini.it

---

124 ac - 200,000 bt   **10% discount**

37 ac - 1,300,000 bt

PEOPLE - To visit Paolo Rodaro's winery is to travel through the history of the many generations who have helped give this corner of Friuli its great vine- and winegrowing tradition. Paolo is also the spokesperson of a large-scale concern that has innovated and expanded gradually with dedication. Evidence of Rodaro's commitment to the local area is the 17th-century Villa Romano, surrounded by 60 acres of vineyard, which houses the wine cellar.

VINEYARDS - The vineyards at Villa Romano are the result of recent renovation and optimization work that included the introduction of native varieties. The other vineyards stretch over hill and plain and grow the classic Colli Orientali grapes, as well as some international varieties. Worth mentioning are the winery's efforts to raise the profile of picolit, of which Paolo is one of the most authoritative interpreters.

WINES - Let's begin with two "heavyweight" reds made with super-ripe grapes: **FCO Schioppettino Romain 2007** (○ 6,000 bt) is substantial, fleshy and alcoholic, while **FCO Merlot Romain 2009** (○ 9,000 bt) has concentrated ripe fruit on the nose and a dense, rich palate with good supporting acidity. **FCO Friulano 2012** (○ 40,000 bt) is a highly reliable label of delicious brightness and dynamism on the palate. The attractive **FCO Pinot Grigio 2013** (○ 15,000 bt) has a soft, embracing bouquet but grows edgier and more biting in the mouth. Finally, we recommend you invest in **FCO Verduzzo Friulano 2013** (○ 6.000 bt), which has copious ripe fruit and measured sweetness, well set off by pleasing freshness.

PEOPLE - The Collavini brand is a piece of Friulian winemaking history. It appeared on the market more than a century ago and affirmed itself in the 1970s under the tenacious guidance of Manlio Collavini, now flanked by his sons Giovanni, the production controller, and Luigi, the sales manager.

VINEYARDS - The company initially bought in its grapes from a group of trusted growers, subsequently supervise by its own technicians. This still tends to be its approach, although recently it planted a few acres of vineyard with ribolla gialla on its beautiful estate at Poggiobello.

WINES - Collio Bianco Broy 2013 Great Wine (○ 20,000 bt) is back on top form: a clever, measured, highly effective blend of friulano, chardonnay and sauvignon, it's bright and captivating on the nose and full of flavor and chewy fruit on the palate. We were also impressed by the subtle, linear **FCO Ribolla Gialla Turian 2013** (○ 50,000 bt) with its delectable blossomy notes. **Collio Merlot dal Pic 2007** (● 10,000 bt) is soft and enfolding, its big, beefy structure set off by just the right freshness. The cellar's hallmark wine **Ribolla Gialla Brut 2010** (○ 50,000 bt), made with the long Charmat method (resting for more than two years on the yeasts), is as delicious as ever. A very welcome novelty is the revival of a label shelved for many years, **M. Cl. Brut Applause 2009** (○ 8,000 bt), made with chardonnay and pinot nero grapes; it has soft, lingering sparkle, clearcut aromas and deep, punchy, extremely enjoyable acidity and flavor.

FERTILIZERS organic-mineral, mineral, manure pellets, natural manure, green manure
PLANT PROTECTION chemical, copper and sulphur
WEED CONTROL chemical, mechanical
YEASTS selected
GRAPES 100% estate-grown
CERTIFICATION none

FERTILIZERS organic-mineral
PLANT PROTECTION chemical, copper and sulphur
WEED CONTROL chemical, mechanical
YEASTS selected
GRAPES 90% bought in
CERTIFICATION none

Gigante

Via Rocca Bernarda, 3
tel. 0432 755835
www.adrianogigante.it
info@adrianogigante.it

I Clivi

Località Gramogliano, 20
tel. 328 7269979
www.clivi.it
iclivi@gmail.com

62 ac - 110,000 bt

25 ac - 50,000 bt | **10% discount**

PEOPLE - It was 1957 when grandfather Ferruccio bought the house and the friulano vineyard in the Colli Orientali del Friuli, where the cellar now stands, and when Adriano was born. In the 1980s Adriano took over the reins of the estate and with tenacity and passion, helped by his wife Giuliana and his cousin Ariedo, has managed it to this day. He's a pragmatic guy, Adriano Gigante.

VINEYARDS - The vineyards encircle the cellar in the Rocca Bernarda area and include a parcel of friulano planted in the 1930s. It's here that Adriano gives of his best, striving to practice a viticulture that is as sustainable as possible after gradually eliminating weed control, adopting non-invasive farming methods and harvesting entirely by hand.

WINES - Processing is kept essential to get all the typicality of the terroir out of the wines. "I want my wines to be stylish, elegant and very drinkable." This concept is expressed and translated into practice with great efficacy. Confirmation of the fact came with the excellent **FCO Friulano 2013** Great Wine (O 12,000 bt), a real joy to drink by virtue of intense, subtle richness of flavor, nice fruity flesh and a delicious aftertaste of bitter almonds. **FCO Sauvignon 2013** (O 10,000 bt) has an impressive, well-balanced attack, full of body and grip on both nose and palate. Finally, we also liked **FCO Pinot Grigio 2013** (O 6.000 bt), which has fruit on the nose, nice acidity and very enjoyable drinkability.

66 «What we have is what nature has given us – say Ferdinando and Mario Zanusso – all we can do is try to preserve it as best we can» 99

PEOPLE - Ferdinando Zanusso's house-cum-cellar is in the heart of Gramogliano, a hamlet outside Corno di Rosazzo, on the top of a hill surrounded by woodland and old vineyards. Ferdinando has acquired his vast knowledge of winemaking traveling round the world. Today he and his son Mario bring their passion and skill to their vineyard and cellar work and, in practice, oversee the whole distribution chain directly.

VINEYARDS - The vineyards are divided over two estates, one in the Collio DOC zone, the other in the Friuli Colli Orientali DOC zone. Both are 40-60 years' old. All procedures, in the field and in the cellar, are designed to protect the grapes naturally and the wines from unnecessary extra processing.

WINES - Work in the vineyard and in the cellar takes time, but the Zanussos are in no hurry. Hence soft pressing and fermentations as non-invasive as possible with the declared aim of producing elegant, clear-tasting wines. The charismatic **FCO Verduzzo 2013** (O 3,000 bt) has subtle floral notes and plenty of bite on the palate. **Collio Malvasia Vigna 80 anni 2012** (O 3,000 bt) has spicy nuances on the nose and a well-rounded, rich mouthfeel. Expressive and citrusy with plenty of acidity, **Ribolla Gialla 2013** (O 15,000 bt) is an excellent interpretation of the grape variety.

slow wine **FCO FRIULANO CLIVI GALEA 2012** (O 3,000 bt) Fine and refined, flavorful and plump on the palate with a finish of bitter almonds.

FERTILIZERS organic-mineral, natural manure
PLANT PROTECTION chemical, copper and sulphur
WEED CONTROL mechanical
YEASTS selected
GRAPES 100% estate-grown
CERTIFICATION none

FERTILIZERS organic-mineral
PLANT PROTECTION copper and sulphur
WEED CONTROL mechanical
YEASTS native
GRAPES 100% estate-grown
CERTIFICATION organic

MANZANO (UD)

Le Vigne di Zamò 🍶

Località Rosazzo
Via Abate Corrado, 4
tel. 0432 759693
www.levignedizamo.com
info@levignedizamo.com

165 ac - 280,000 bt	10% discount

PEOPLE - The Zamò family began writing the story of Friulian wine in 1978, when Tullio Zamò bought his first vineyard at Ipplis. Since then his sons Pierluigi and Silvano have developed the company and made the Zamò brand the world over. They recently decided to sell a 50% interest to the Eataly group without altering the management team: namely agronomist Adriano Qualizza (with the consultancy of Giovanni Bigot) in the field and enologist Alberto Toso in the cellar under the supervision of Franco Bernabei.

VINEYARDS - The vineyards are spread across three large estates: the historic Vigna del Leon (between Ipplis and Rocca Bernarda, with vines planted over 30 years ago), where the old sauvignon, malvasia and pinot bianco vineyards enjoy sharp night-day temperature swings; Buttrio, where there are 10 acres; and Rosazzo, where the plot round the cellar is the youngest and largest of all.

WINES - The pick of the bunch was **FCO Merlot Vigne Cinquant'anni 2011** Great Wine (● 4,000 bt), which has body and character to spare thanks to full, solid fruit and stylish, velvety tannic texture. The forthright, austere **FCO Friulano Vigne Cinquant'anni 2012** (○ 4,100 bt) moves on quickly from fruit to deep flavor. The bright and breezy **FCO Malvasia 2012** (○ 3,300 bt) has a full, balsamic palate, while the linear **FCO Ribolla Gialla 2013** (○ 27,000 bt) has notes of honey and acacia flowers. Elegant, stately and assertive as always, **FCO Rosazzo Ronco delle Acacie 2011** (○ chardonnay, friulano; 12,000 bt) is a master class in the wood-fermented Burgundy oxidized style. Last but not least, the superlative **FCO Picolit 2006** (○ 2,000 0.5-lt bt) is wonderfully pervasive and symmetrical.

FERTILIZERS natural manure, humus
PLANT PROTECTION copper and sulphur, organic
WEED CONTROL mechanical
YEASTS selected
GRAPES 100% estate-grown
CERTIFICATION none

POVOLETTO (UD)

Aquila del Torre 🍶

Frazione Savorgnano del Torre
Via Attimis, 25
tel. 0432 666428
www.aquiladeltorre.it
info@aquiladeltorre.it

49.5 ac - 60,000 bt	10% discount

PEOPLE - Claudio Ciani bought this property in 1996, spruced up the vineyards and converted the old barn into a winery with cellar. The name Aquila del Torre refers to the shape the vineyards form, reminiscent of the wingspan of an eagle (*aquila* in Italian). Today the company is run by his son Michele, agronomist and production manager, and Francesca, who oversees the point of sale and hospitality.

VINEYARDS - The vineyards cover an area of almost 50 acres in a single plot surrounded by 160 acres of woodland. It is hoped to have the whole area officially recognized as a nature park. The terraced vineyards cover the hillsides to an altitude of 1,150 feet and create a breathtaking spectacle. Different grape varieties alternate to exploit the stratifications of the hill and excellent night-day temperature swings to the full.

WINES - The wines from the 2013 harvest are certified organic and come in three lines: "AT", fresh, steel-aged wines, crus and selections. **Oasi 2012** (○ 2,000 bt) is a captivating dry interpretation of the picolit grape which combines intact fruit with a spacious, enfolding, well-developed palate. Also excellent is **FCO Friulano AT 2013** (○ 6,000 bt), blossomy with a smidgeon of citrus fruit on the nose and fleshy in the mouth with a bright and breezy finish. **FCO Sauvignon AT 2013** (○ 8,000 bt) impresses for its stylish, elegant attack with a mixture of fruit and *fines herbes*. **FCO Sauvignon Vit dai Maz 2012** (○ 1,500 bt) is enjoyable too.

> slow wine **FCO Picolit 2012** (○ 2,000 bt) "A non-sweet sweet wine." That's how the great Italian wine critic Luigi Veronelli memorably described Picolit and the definition suits this stupendous wine to a tee. It's unctuous and creamy but never cloyingly so, braced as it is by vibrant acidity and flavor.

FERTILIZERS natural manure, compost, green manure
PLANT PROTECTION copper and sulphur
WEED CONTROL mechanical
YEASTS native
GRAPES 100% estate-grown
CERTIFICATION organic

Le Due Terre

PREPOTTO (UD)

Via Roma, 68 B
tel. 0432 713189
fortesilvana@libero.it

12 ac - 19,000 bt

66 Knowledge of the local area and respect for eco-equilibrium in the vineyard are the visiting card of this splendid winery. A simple card but a significant one 99

PEOPLE - The name is a tribute to the two vineyards that encircle the house, which doubles as a wine cellar. Since the 1980s, Flavio Basilicata and Silvana Forte have been producing wine here that expresses the true potential of Friulian viticulture. Their daughter Cora is playing an increasingly active role in the business.

VINEYARDS - Flavio Basilicata, *deus ex machina* of the company's production, farms 12 acres of vineyard with care and concern for biodiversity. His is an essential approach to viticulture in which manual and mechanical mowing are reduced to a bare minimum to allow wild herbs and flowers to grow. No fertilizers are used and treatment with copper and sulphur is also limited, the aim being to develop equilibrium in the fruit, hence in the wine.

WINES - Here we have personal healthy wines that encapsulate sense of place, naturalness and potential, seen as the capacity to bring out the best from native grape assemblages. **FCO Bianco Sacrisassi 2012** (O 5,000 bt) is a complex, magical, graceful drink with an abundance of blossom on the nose and exceptional tanginess on the palate, with the friulano adding power and the ribolla gialla mellowing its huskiness. **FCO Merlot 2012** (● 2,700 bt) and **FCO Pinot Nero 2012** (● 4,000 bt) are both elegant and mature.

> slow wine **FCO Rosso Sacrisassi 2012** (● 7,500 bt) One of the all-time great Friulian reds. A blend of schioppettino and refosco in equal measures, a juicy, intriguing, crisp, pervasive wine of incredibly land-rooted pungent spiciness.

FERTILIZERS none
PLANT PROTECTION copper and sulphur
WEED CONTROL mechanical
YEASTS native
GRAPES 100% estate-grown
CERTIFICATION none

Ronco Severo

PREPOTTO (UD)

Via Ronchi, 93
tel. 0432 713340
info@roncosevero.it

20 ac - 25,000 bt   `10% discount`

66 Affable and theatrical, Stefano Novello is the sole creator of his wines, in the vineyard and in the cellar. Without half measures and with the clear ideas he has developed over time with adamancy and a sense of responsibility 99

PEOPLE - An untiring worker, Stefano studied enology before going abroad to work. He came back to the Prepotto hills to run his father's winery, applying a rigorously organic approach to viticulture right from day one. Stefano's spirit is evident in the new labels, which show a small boy doing an acrobatic balancing act on the back of a chair.

VINEYARDS - The vineyards are situated on the wide terraces built in the past to shore up the marly, sandy soil against landslides. Most of the vines are at least 40 years' old. Natural manure, limited treatments with copper and sulphur, grassing among the vine rows and lots and lots of manual labor – these are the simple but rigorous practices adopted.

WINES - All the grapes ferment and macerate in large cone-shaped oak vats. In the rich, austere **Severo Bianco 2011** (O friulano, chardonnay, picolit; 5,000 bt), rugged minerality overwhelms fruity plumpness. **Pinot Grigio 2011** (O 5,000 bt) is nicely concentrated with a somewhat dry, hard finish. The excellent **FCO Schioppettino di Prepotto 2010** (● 3,000 bt) is elegant, wrapped in pepper and spices with tugdid, juicy fruit. Soft and intense, **FCO Merlot Artiul Ris. 2010** (● 4,000 bt) has well-judged close-knit tannins.

> slow wine **FCO Friulano Ris. 2011** (O 5,000 bt) An extraordinary wine in which harmony, finesse and potency complement each other. It has aromas of ripe fruit, spices and officinal herbs followed up by saltiness. The palate is taut and punchy with just the right degree of tannic dryness.

FERTILIZERS natural manure
PLANT PROTECTION copper and sulphur, organic
WEED CONTROL mechanical
YEASTS native
GRAPES 100% estate-grown
CERTIFICATION organic

SACILE (PN)

Vistorta €

Via Vistorta, 82
tel. 0434 71135
www.vistorta.it
info@vistorta.it

198 ac - 250,000 bt　**10% discount**

PEOPLE - Brandino Brandolini D'Adda, who studied Agraian Sciences in France and the United States and worked for a long time at Château Greysac, in the Médoc, runs his family's business with considerable acumen. He is a man with strong, innovative ideas, as he showed when he decided to switch to organic viticulture. Over the next few years, the entire property will become a "laboratory" for agricultural sustainability.

VINEYARDS - The company's property is split into two main plots: the vast and impressive Guyot- and spurred cordon-trained merlot vineyard at Vistorta, and the one at Cordignano, where a variety of grapes, mostly white, are grown. Agronomic management is meticulous (the vie rows are monitored and analyzed one by one) and in constant evolution and like that of the wine cellar, is in the hands of Alec Ongaro.

WINES - This year the company's most important wine, Friuli Grave Merlot Vistorta 2011, was wisely left to age for another year in the bottle. It was worthily replaced by its "kid brother," Friuli Grave Merlot 2012 Everyday Wine (● 33,000 bt), which has the selfsame elegant, sedate style with less flesh and body but an equal level of flavor. **Friuli Grave Friulano 2013** (○ 6,600 bt), elegantly mineral and expressive with lovely notes of almonds on the finish, and **Friuli Grave Pinot Grigio 2013** (○ 65,000 bt), austere and linear but, nonetheless, delicious, are both commendable. The entrancing **Friuli Grave Sauvignon 2013** (○ 20,000 bt), is stylishly varietal and subtle, as is **Friuli Grave Traminer Aromatico 2013** (○ 11,000 bt), aromatic and soft as can be with a palate that develops beautifully. **Friuli Grave Chardonnay 2013** (○ 17,350 bt) is zesty and juicy, bright and deep.

SAN GIOVANNI AL NATISONE (UD)

Ronco del Gnemiz

Via Ronchi, 5
tel. 0432 756238
www.roncodelgnemiz.com
serena@roncodelgnemiz.com

17 ac - 18,000 bt

66 Ronco del Gnemiz's are among the few Italian wines that you'd have no qualms about recommending to a foreign connoisseur unfamiliar with them 99

PEOPLE - The winery is run to the highest standards of quality thanks to the experience that Serena Palazzolo and her companion, enologist Christian Patat, have accumulated over the years.

VINEYARDS - Serena and Christian farm seven acres of vineyards, some rented and some their own. They adopt an uncompromisingly organic approach, no easy task in Friuli, where the unpredictable climate which greatly influences the vegetative cycle. Serena says that, faced with natural adversity, she bends but doesn't break. Which is how she achieves the results she does.

WINES - Output may vary from year to year but hardly ever exceeds 20,000 bottles. The whites have always been the result of field selections but recently the number of crus has increased. The possibilities of comparison that the philosophy offers for sauvignon are intriguing: **FCO Sauvignon Serena Palazzolo & Figli 2013** (○ 2,300 bt) is full-bodied and rich, while **FCO Sauvignon Salici 2013** (○ 2,000 bt) is saltier and more linear. The exceptional **FCO Sauvignon Perì 2012** (○ 660 bt), a paragon for the grape in the region, is a trifle edgy in its attack but has great depth, grip and potential for aging in the bottle. Moving on to the whites, **FCO Friulano San Zuan 2013** (○ 2,060) is elegant on the nose and bright on the palate.

slow wine **FCO Rosso del Gnemiz 2011** (● 1,700 bt) A classic Bordeaux blend (60% merlot, 40% cabernet) of great elegance and personality with juicy, fleshy fruit and soft, well-gauged tannins. The model of a great Friulian red.

FERTILIZERS manure pellets, natural manure, compost	**FERTILIZERS** natural manure, compost, biodynamic preparations, green manure
PLANT PROTECTION copper and sulphur	**PLANT PROTECTION** copper and sulphur
WEED CONTROL mechanical	**WEED CONTROL** mechanical
YEASTS selected	**YEASTS** selected
GRAPES 100% estate-grown	**GRAPES** 100% estate-grown
CERTIFICATION organic	**CERTIFICATION** organic

SAN GIOVANNI AL NATISONE (UD)

Vignai da Duline

Località Villanova
Via IV Novembre, 136
tel. 0432 758115
www.vignaidaduline.com
info@vignaidaduline.com

20 ac - 22,000 bt

❝ For its singularity, for its young history, for its particular approach in the vineyard, Vignai da Duline is one of the most interesting wineries on the whole regional wine scene ❞

PEOPLE - In 1997, Federica Magrini and Lorenzo Mocchiutti, young, dynamic and enthusiastic, decided to steward a few of their relatives' vineyards. Since then they have taken major decisions aimed at protecting the natural balance of the land and the vineyard, which they farm with a critical, never wandering eye.

VINEYARDS - The vineyards are farmed with care and dedication using organic methods. They are an ode to biodiversity, especially the 14 acres on Ronco Pitotti, near Manzano, where the vineyards of a small natural amphitheater encircled by woodland look like an oasis from a distance. Alfalfa is sown between the vine rows to preserve the fertility of the soil and mass planting with very old clones add substance and elegance to the wines.

WINES - Juicy and intriguing, even though it's still young, **Morus Nigra 2012** (● 1,300 bt) is a Refosco with almost chewy flesh and an intriguing dynamic character, which, far from weighing it down, make it linear and velvety. **FCO Chardonnay Ronco Pitotti 2012** (○ 1,000 bt) is complex and juicy. Pinot Nero 2009, yet to be released, is an experiment carried out with just a few vine rows. We can anticipate that it manages to synthesize the delicacy of the grape variety and the force of the terroir.

> **slow wine** **Morus Alba 2012** (○ malvasia istriana, sauvignon; 2,500 bt) All the attentive work in the vineyard manifests itself in this wine. As vital as it's pervasive, it's full of soft nuanced aromas and texture on the palate. A wine sure to age well.

FERTILIZERS green manure, none
PLANT PROTECTION copper and sulphur, organic
WEED CONTROL mechanical
YEASTS native
GRAPES 100% estate-grown
CERTIFICATION organic

TORREANO (UD)

Volpe Pasini

Frazione Togliano
Via Cividale, 16
tel. 0432 715151
www.volpepasini.net
info@volpepasini.it

128 ac - 400,000 bt | **10% discount** |

PEOPLE - Emilio Rotolo bought Volpe Pasini in the mid 1990s. The estate has been farmed since the 17th century, as historical documents attest, and began to specialize in growing vines and making wine at the start of the 20th century, thereby launching a process that has continued to this day. Indeed, Emilio, now helped by his son Francesco and consultant enologist Lorenzo Landi, has pushed the company to the top of the international wine world.

VINEYARDS - The property covers an area of about 130 acres, where over two centuries of farming have individuated the best growing surfaces. In the Prepotto and Togliano zones in particular, Volpe Pasini has selected the two parcels that yield the company's best wines. The agronomic approach is commonsensical and the use of chemical is limited to a bare minimum.

WINES - The Zuc di Volpe logo is reserved for the selections, top of which is **FCO Sauvignon Zuc di Volpe 2013** Great Wine (○ 16.500 bt), which has a complex nose, followed up by a burly, flavor-rich palate enriched by elegant piquancy. **FCO Pinot Bianco Zuc di Volpe 2013** (○ 6,700 bt), elegant with easy floral notes, taut and assertive on the palate, and **FCO Ribolla Gialla Zuc di Volpe 2013** (○ 7,000 bt), with its expansive spring flowers and refreshing, mineral palate, are both very good. For us, the best of the more economical Volpe Pasini line is the wonderful **FCO Friulano 2013** Everyday Wine (○ 9,900 bt), rigorous, austere and very, very tangy. **FCO Ribolla Gialla 2013** (○ 41,200 bt) is full of fruit and a joy to drink, while the well-built **FCO Pinot Grigio Grivò 2013** (○ 130,000 bt) has leisurely fruity, floral notes.

FERTILIZERS natural manure
PLANT PROTECTION chemical, copper and sulphur, organic
WEED CONTROL chemical, mechanical
YEASTS selected
GRAPES 100% estate-grown
CERTIFICATION none

Collio, Isonzo and Carso

CAPRIVA DEL FRIULI (GO)

Russiz Superiore

Via Russiz, 7
tel. 0481 80328
www.marcofelluga.it
info@marcofelluga.it

CORMONS (GO)

Borgo San Daniele ◎꙰

Via San Daniele, 16
tel. 0481 60552
www.borgosandaniele.it
info@borgosandaniele.it

---

124 ac - 200,000 bt

PEOPLE - The historical Istrian Felluga family began to invest in Friuli in the 1940s when they bought a number of acres of vineyard. The decision proved a fortunate one and spawned a number of prestigious properties, among which Russiz Superiore, now run by Roberto Felluga. The estate is situated in the heart of Collio with a breathtaking view of the hills as they tumble down into Slovenia.

VINEYARDS - Limestone and marl form the bases of the soils that characterize the terraces where the company's 120 acres of vineyard (plus another 120 of sowed fields and woods) are situated. Vine density is high, the plants, some of which planted 30 years ago, are Guyot-trained and topping has been abolished on some plots. More in general, the viticultural approach is conventional but also prepared to try out new antidotes to downy and powdery mildew.

WINES - The wines of Russiz Superiore are endowed with stylistic consistency and elegance, their fine noses enhanced by the use of oak. They impress themselves in the imagination as classically Friulian clean, long-lasting whites. **Collio Bianco Col Disore 2011** `Great Wine` (O friulano, pinot bianco, sauvignon, ribolla gialla; 7,000 bt) is impeccable, a super-successful blend in which recherché elegance meets clear-cut, well-defined, intriguing but measured aromas. Also impressive is **Collio Friulano 2013** (O 20,000 bt), which has delicate fruit, faint floral notes and a composed, well-balanced, very varietal palate. Fragrant and succulent with just the right acidity, **Collio Pinot Bianco 2013** (O 11,000 bt) reconciles one with a category that sometimes receives a bad press. **Collio Sauvignon 2013** (O 45,000 bt) is less deep.

44 ac - 56,000 bt   `10% discount`

❝❝ Here at Borgo San Daniele,' say the Mauris, 'wine isn't just wine, it's the precious lifeblood that joins heart, culture, history, passion and ideas ❞❞

PEOPLE - The architects of Borgo San Daniele are Mauro and Alessandra Mauri, who gave life to a wonderful winery when they completed their first bottling in the 1990s. The place is an oasis of peace in the heart of Cormons, a place which stands apart for its hospitality and friendliness.

VINEYARDS - The Mauri brothers' philosophy is to preserve what their grandfather left them as best they can. Hence healthy, very old vines rich in biodiversity. The vineyards are totally grassed with high vine density, the various grape varieties being planted according to their own characteristics and those of the soil.

WINES - The Mauri brothers' philosophy consists of pursuing naturalness in wine and allowing them to express the vintage. As Mauro says, "Our wines are the fruit of ripe grapes, because every wine has a story to tell." **Arbis Blanc 2012** (O 10,000 bt) is a blend in which grape percentages change every year, so it always conjures up different sensations. This year it includes sauvignon, friulano, chardonnay and pinot bianco grapes, and the perception is one of a drinkable, well-structured white with a pleasant "multivarietal" note. It will take time for it to express its exceptional potential.

`slow wine` **FRIULI ISONZO PINOT GRIGIO 2012** (O 13,000 bt) A wine with a very strong personality, miles away from the clichés that often haunt the variety. It offers light, very fine fruity notes on the nose and a flavorsome, plump, elegant, refined palate.

FERTILIZERS organic-mineral, manure pellets, natural manure, green manure
PLANT PROTECTION chemical, copper and sulphur
WEED CONTROL chemical, mechanical
YEASTS native
GRAPES 100% estate-grown
CERTIFICATION none

FERTILIZERS compost, biodynamic preparations
PLANT PROTECTION copper and sulphur, organic
WEED CONTROL mechanical
YEASTS native
GRAPES 100% estate-grown
CERTIFICATION converting to organics

CORMONS (GO)
Edi Keber

Località Zegla, 17
tel. 0481 61184
edi.keber@virgilio.it

Via Isonzo, 117
tel. 0481 61310
www.roncodelgelso.com
info@roncodelgelso.com

---

30 ac - 50,000 bt | **10% discount**

62 ac - 150,000 bt

---

66 Edi Keber is an institution not only in the Collio zone, but also for the whole of the Friuli wine world. In this borderland, he was the first to carry through an idea of wine as a symbol and mirror of the local area 99

PEOPLE - Edi comes from an old farming family, his ancestors settling in the splendid Zegla hills as many as three centuries ago. Today he's helped by his son Kristian, a worthy heir, his wife Silvana and his daughter Veronika.

VINEYARDS - Most of the company's vineyards are below the company headquarters. The ribolla, tocai and malvasia varieties (literally in descending order) are grown with respect for the delicate equilibrium of the land. Research into vineyard management is ongoing, as is constant experimentation with practices aimed at being as non-invasive as possible, such as pruning during the harvest in order to allow the vines to develop naturally.

WINES - Most of the company's vineyards are below the company headquarters. The ribolla, tocai and malvasia varieties (literally in descending order) are grown with respect for the delicate equilibrium of the land. Research into vineyard management is ongoing, as is constant experimentation with practices aimed at being as non-invasive as possible, such as pruning during the harvest in order to allow the vines to develop naturally.

slow wine **COLLIO BIANCO 2013** Collio Bianco 2013 (○ 48,000 bt) The wine impressed us yet again this year with its brightness and compactness. It has intense notes of fruit and blossom on the nose with a soft palate exalted by conspicuous minerality. It's elegant, suave and inviting. In other words, fantastic!

PEOPLE - Self-styled "plains producer" Giorgio Badin learned the ropes of winegrowing by working first in plant nurseries. Slaving at the Rauscedo nursery cooperative and not just rooting all day, he picked up all the basic notions about clones and rootstocks and hence developed the enthusiasm to make his first plantings and start making wine at Cormons.

VINEYARDS - The plantings, which resemble one another, are unilateral Guyot-trained and grow on alluvial soils. The abundant pebbles on a stratum of shallow, dry soil has made Badin opt for 1103 Paulsen and 110 Richter rootstocks. The grape bunches – no more than four and a half pounds per plant – are well exposed to the sun thanks to leaf removal immediately after flowering.

WINES - Apart from malvasia, pinot bianco and riesling, the grapes are barrel-fermented with frequent stirring of the lees to give wines the capacity to age and evolve. At the top of the range is the excellent, intriguing **Friuli Isonzo Malvasia Vigna della Permuta 2013** Great Wine (○ 8,000 bt), whose lovely aromatic tones are enhanced by sweet notes of ripe fruit with hints of aniseed and barley sugar, while the stylishly balanced palate is sumptuous and delicious. We were also very impressed by **Friuli Isonzo Rive Alte Chardonnay Siet Vignis 2012** (○ 16,000 bt) has a tempting mouthfeel with enjoyable evolution, flavor and dryness. With its taut, tangy palate, the subtle **Friuli Isonzo Pinot Bianco 2013** (○ 5,000 bt) works perfectly, as does **Friuli Isonzo Bianco Latimis 2013** (○ 8,000 bt) a soft, flavorsome, aromatic blend of friulano, pinot bianco, riesling and traminer grapes.

FERTILIZERS natural manure, biodynamic preparations, green manure
PLANT PROTECTION copper and sulphur
WEED CONTROL mechanical
YEASTS selected
GRAPES 100% estate-grown
CERTIFICATION converting to organics

FERTILIZERS manure pellets
PLANT PROTECTION chemical, copper and sulphur
WEED CONTROL chemical, mechanical
YEASTS selected
GRAPES 100% estate-grown
CERTIFICATION none

Kante

Frazione San Pelagio
Località Prepotto, 1 A
tel. 040 200255
www.kante.it
kante@kante.it

Skerk

Frazione San Pelagio
Località Prepotto, 20
tel. 040 200156
www.skerk.com
info@skerk.com

---

32 ac - 45,000 bt

❝ How can you be clear-headed if you're in love with what you do?" That's Edi Kante talking. Just a few words, meaningful brushstrokes that express his sense of freedom more than anyone else could ❞

PEOPLE - A winemaker, or rather a farmer, and an artist, Edi spearheaded a movement that spread the word about Carso and its extraordinary terroir all over the world. He was already a believer, the first, over 30 years ago.

VINEYARDS - For Kante, believing in a seemingly inhospitable terrain of rocks and red earth means working it without seeking to tame it. It has to maintain its integrity and stay harsh and real. To cultivate it with very high vine densities and, at the same time, very low yields to get the best out of it is to sublimate it. This *intimiste* vision also embraces the splendid wine cellar, created by hewing into the rock to a depth of 50 feet.

WINES - Kante's wines can be subdivided into classic line and selections, which are released only when Edi deems that the right moment has come. Retasting his wines many years on, there can be no doubt that he wins all hands down, proving that the longevity of Carso wines is a tangible fact. The name of the compelling, complex **Rosso Opera Viva 10 Annate** (● pinot nero, terrano, merlot, cabernet sauvignon; 4,000 bt) refers to all vintages from 2000 to 2010. The excellent **Vitovska 2011** (○ 10,000 bt) offers crisp fruit with notes of aniseed and mint.

---

17 ac - 20,000 bt

❝ Sandi Skerk espoused the philosophy of natural viticulture some time ago. He now proceeds with great abnegation, seeking dialogue with other producers to create a virtuous and constructive team spirit ❞

PEOPLE - Sandi has taken over the reins from his father Boris. His family, all of them dedicated to farming, also run a pretty *osmizza*, a traditional osteria.

VINEYARDS - All the vineyards grow on the red earth of Carso, on small plots on terraces south of the Gulf of Trieste. The vineyards are farmed with organic methods and all the painstaking work involved is designed to produce healthy grapes, reducing interventions with external agents as much as possible.

WINES - All the grapes harvested are fermented with the lees in contact with the must and interventions in the cellar are limited to a bare minimum. After overcoming its initial shyness, **Vitovska 2012** (○ 6,000 bt) expresses thyme and Mediterranean scrub with elegant notes of iodine. The palate is very expressive and complex with a delicate finish of bitter field greens. **Ograde 2012** (○ vitovska, malvasia, sauvignon, pinot grigio; 6,000 bt) has a broad-based, inebriating suite of aromas of bitter orangeade, aromatic herbs, oregano, capers and meadow flowers. Aromatic on the palate, it has a dry finish with an encore of apricots. The rugged **Terrano 2012** (● 4,000 bt) impresses with aromas of red berries and well-integrated spices.

> **slow wine** **MALVASIA 2012** (○ 6,000 bt) Nice and juicy with plenty of creamy, fruity flesh and strong hints of ripe apricot, well balanced by a very delicate vein of acidity and invigorating salty minerality.

FERTILIZERS natural manure
PLANT PROTECTION chemical, copper and sulphur
WEED CONTROL chemical, mechanical
YEASTS selected
GRAPES 100% estate-grown
CERTIFICATION none

FERTILIZERS manure pellets, natural manure, green manure, humus
PLANT PROTECTION copper and sulphur, organic
WEED CONTROL mechanical
YEASTS native
GRAPES 100% estate-grown
CERTIFICATION organic

DUINO AURISINA (TS)

Zidarich ◉⋎

Frazione San Pelagio
Località Prepotto, 23
tel. 040 201223
www.zidarich.it
info@zidarich.it

---

20 ac - 28,000 bt

❝ Measured and solar, Benjamin Zidarich is a painstaking, passionate winemaker, but he's often depressed by the many problems that he's forced to address (red tape, first and foremost). But when you walk into the vineyards with him, you see his eyes light up ... ❞

PEOPLE - The whole family helps Benjamin with the field work and the running of the osmizza, well worth a visit not only for the food and wine but also for the breathtaking view it affords over the Gulf of Trieste.

VINEYARDS - The vines on the small parcels are trained with a modified bush system. Densely planted with canopies, they resemble candelabra and have great longevity. Prulke, Ruje and Lehte produce single-vineyard wines. In dry years, the thin stratum of Carso red earth requires careful complementary irrigation.

WINES - In superlative years, Zidarich creates veritable reserves with wines made with the best grapes. One of the finest is **Carso Vitovska Collection 2009** (○ 1,500 bt), in which well-judged maceration has created a nice balance between soft and iodine notes, elegance and charm. **Prulke 2012** (○ sauvignon, vitovska, malvasia; 5,000 bt) takes time to open on the nose but then offers a very delicate, intriguing palate **Ruje 2009** (● merlot, terrano; 2,500 bt) has a subtle palate and plenty of stuffing. **Terrano 2012** (● 5,000 bt) conjures up all the conviviality of the *osmizza*.

slow wine **Vitovska 2012** (○ 10,500 bt) This, the youngest version of Vitovska, has great character and body with a fragrant, pleasant palate. Yet more proof of the qualities and personality of this grape variety.

GORIZIA (GO)

Gravner ◉⋎

Frazione Oslavia
Località Lenzuolo Bianco, 9
tel. 0481 30882
www.gravner.it
info@gravner.it

---

39 ac - 38,000 bt

❝ For experienced farmer Josko Gravner, every action has a meaning and every choice has a reason. Each new precept he comes up with is an idea anticipating the future ❞

PEOPLE - Josko Gravner is one of the protagonists of the last 30 years of Italian winemaking. It was in the 1970s that he began bottling his steel-aged wines, then he moved over to barriques, unknown in Friuli at the time. Fifteen years ago, he decided to step back in time to ferment his grapes in amphorae. He has been helped along the way by his wife Maria and now his daughter Mateja oversees sales and communication.

VINEYARDS - Gravner's evolution is also visible in the vineyards. Barring ribolla, all the white grape varieties have been explanted and replaced by new bush-trained vines. The stunning Hum vineyard is gradually a definitive structure, while viticultural methods continue to be all-organic.

WINES - Josko's recipes in the cellar are very simple: fermentation in amphorae without the addition of yeasts and temperature control; aging in oak barrels for a few years; bottling with the waning moon without fining or filtering. **Breg 2006** (○ 10,575 bt) is born of this idea: a blend of sauvignon, chardonnay, pinot grigio and riesling, it conflates power and harmony into a palate that sates and satisfies.

slow wine **Ribolla Gialla 2006** (○ 13,965 bt) Taut, salty, lip-smacking, elegant, deep – these are the first epithets that come to mind to describe this label. Sometimes one finds fakes on the market that are indistinguishable from the original. Ribolla di Josko is the original, and you can tell!

FERTILIZERS natural manure	**FERTILIZERS** none
PLANT PROTECTION copper and sulphur	**PLANT PROTECTION** copper and sulphur
WEED CONTROL mechanical	**WEED CONTROL** mechanical
YEASTS native	**YEASTS** native
GRAPES 100% estate-grown	**GRAPES** 100% estate-grown
CERTIFICATION none	**CERTIFICATION** none

La Castellada

Località Oslavia, 1
tel. 0481 33670
www.lacastellada.it
info@lacastellada.it

25 ac - 30,000 bt

66 This winery is named for one of its vineyards. One of the main aims of the Bensa family is to translate a district as magical as Oslavia into wine 99

PEOPLE - It was 1985 when the Bensa brothers, Giorgio and Nicolò, decided to release their first bottles, thereby opening the floodgates to a market of fans all over the world. Today Nicolò's son Stefano oversees the cellar with great dedication.

VINEYARDS - Some of the vineyards are to be found along the road that runs across the ridges of the hills of Oslavia, on the side looking towards Slovenia. The rest are situated on the south-facing hillside opposite the cellar itself. The vines, most of which are half a century old, are single Guyot- and double arch cane-trained.

WINES - Ideal soil and climate conditions, with optimal air circulation and sharp night-day temperature swings, and low yields make for fully ripe fruit, good concentration and brightness. All the grapes ferment on the lees, for different lengths of time according to variety, to produce excellent extracts. The wines age in barriques or large barrels and are bottled without filtering. **Collio Friulano 2009** (O 2,500 bt) has an extremely sensory profile with notes of honey, hay and sandalwood, wonderful grip and a juicy finish. **Collio Bianco della Castellada 2009** (O pinot grigio, chardonnay, sauvignon; 6,300 bt) has tremendous structure and **Collio Ribolla Gialla 2009** (O 5,200 bt) is a joy to drink.

FERTILIZERS natural manure, green manure, humus
PLANT PROTECTION copper and sulphur
WEED CONTROL mechanical
YEASTS native
GRAPES 100% estate-grown
CERTIFICATION none

Damijan Podversic

Via Brigata Pavia, 61
tel. 0481 78217
www.damijanpodversic.com
damijan.go@virgilio.it

25 ac - 30,000 bt

66 There are only three important things to take into account: the minerality of the soil, the crispness of the fruit and the rhythm of the growing year. If you manage to put these three things in the glass, then you've achieved your goal.' This is how Damijan Podversic sums up his productive philosophy and everyday work. Once he has achieved his goal, wine acquires its truest essence as food for the soul 99

PEOPLE - Damijan was but a slip of a lad when he began to spend time in the vineyards. He learned to make wine from the man he regards as his master, Josko Gravner. His wife Elena joins him in the "complicated" business of running the company, which has its farmhouse-cum-office at Doberdò del Lago, vineyards on Monte Calvario and cellar at Scriò, on the border with Slovenia.

VINEYARDS - Most of the vineyards are on the southern slopes of the Calvario in a terraced natural amphitheater surrounded by woodland. With his 100% natural viticulture, which respects and regenerates the soil and the flora, Damijan has helped preserve this beautiful, unspoiled environment.

WINES - A range of excellent wines, all fermented on the lees. Top of the list is Primeggia la **Malvasia 2010** (O 4,000 bt), spacious, lip-smacking and full of fruit and intense, delicate notes of Mediterranean scrub with a tangy, lingering finish. **Nekaj 2010** (O friulano; 3,000 bt) is dry, austere and alcoholic, while **Kaplja 2010** (O chardonnay, friulano, malvasia; 7,000 bt) is pervasive and complex. **Prelit 2010** (● merlot, cabernet; 3.000 bt) is soft and spicy with perfectly crafted tannins.

slow wine **RIBOLLA GIALLA 2010** (O 7,000 bt) As always, a great masterpiece, a rich, enjoyable, fruity Ribolla with a never-ending vein of acidity and minerality.

FERTILIZERS green manure, none
PLANT PROTECTION copper and sulphur
WEED CONTROL mechanical
YEASTS native
GRAPES 100% estate-grown
CERTIFICATION organic

GORIZIA (GO)

Radikon

Località Tre Buchi, 4
tel. 0481 32804
www.radikon.it
info@radikon.it

MARIANO DEL FRIULI (GO)

Vie di Romans

Località Vie di Romans, 1
tel. 0481 69600
www.viediromans.it
viediromans@viediromans.it

---

30 ac - 30,000 bt

❝ Stanko Radikon was one of the first winemakers to rediscover the ancient technique of macerating white grapes, a controversial practice that challenges the credos of conventional enology. He's been devoting himself to it with great belief for the last 20 years and more ❞

PEOPLE - Stanko is now flanked by his son Saša, a young man with a rugby player's physique and impeccable manners, a graduate in enology who has created a line of his own within the company range.

VINEYARDS - The winery is situated in the Tre Buchi district. The name means "three holes" and maybe refers to the damage felt by bombs during World War I. The historic vineyard is to be found below the cellar on one side of small valley that climbs up towards San Floriano. The uppermost part, sunny with good air circulation, is given over to ribolla. The vines, which carry five bunches each, are planted on very narrow terraces and bush-trained.

WINES - Americans call them "orange wines," a term which, albeit neither here nor there, has now entered common parlance and which Stanko accepts with a shrug of his shoulders. He ferments his wines in 650-gallon vats, then leaves them on the lees for different lengths of time according to grape variety. He draws off the lees from the Pinot Grigio and Slatnik ("Saša's wines") after 10-12 days, while the classic Ribolla, Jakot and Oslavja may macerate for months on end. **Pinot Grigio 2012** (○ 8,000 bt) is ultra-tangy with notes of citrus fruits and damp soil. **Oslavje 2007** (○ pinot grigio, chardonnay, sauvignon; 2,500 bt) has strength and **Jakot 2007** (○ friulano; 2,500 bt) has complexity, but it's **Ribolla Gialla 2007** (○ 3,000 bt) which, after four years in barrels and another two in the bottles, best crystallizes the concept and the commitment behind this very special way of making wine. It's intense, it's soft, it's linear and it's thrilling.

124 ac - 250,000 bt

PEOPLE - Vie di Romans isn't just any winery. Thanks to the effort the Gallo family have always put into research and to the distinctiveness of their wines, its name and its labels are among the best known and admired internationally. Since 1978 the winery has been managed by Gianfranco, the brains behind the visionary, enterprising strategies that have taken it where it is today, one of the very first to exalt the cru concept.

VINEYARDS - Visiting the Vie di Romans vineyards is a unique experience. Their high vine density, deliberately chosen by Gianfranco and his staff, makes them stand out in the classic local landscape. The purpose of the approach is to favor not only concentration but also the depth and minerality of the grapes, both essential ingredients for the longevity of the wines.

WINES - The quality of Gianfranco's wines is as impressive as ever, so it's hard to say which we prefer. Let's say **Flors di Uis 2012** Great Wine (○ 21,000 bt), a marvelous blend of malvasia, friulano and Riesling, full-bodied, delicious, fragrant and succulent, that makes the palate (and the heart) sing. Topnotch too are **Friuli Isonzo Chardonnay Ciampagnis Vieris 2012** (○ 35,450 bt), with its impeccable ripe fruit, and **Friuli Isonzo Sauvignon Piere 2012** (○ 45,300 bt), a textbook label for the variety that releases a constant interweave of vegetal and fruity notes followed up by a tangy, satisfying palate. **Dut'Un 2011** (○ 4,150 bt), an assemblage of equal amounts of chardonnay and sauvignon with a gutsy, persuasive personality, and **Friuli Isonzo Malvasia Istriana Dis Cumieris 2012** (○ 6,830), with its seductive aromas and dynamic palate, are both very good indeed.

FERTILIZERS natural manure, compost, green manure	**FERTILIZERS** organic-mineral, manure pellets, humus
PLANT PROTECTION copper and sulphur, organic	**PLANT PROTECTION** chemical, copper and sulphur
WEED CONTROL mechanical	**WEED CONTROL** chemical, mechanical
YEASTS native	**YEASTS** selected
GRAPES 100% estate-grown	**GRAPES** 100% estate-grown
CERTIFICATION none	**CERTIFICATION** none

SAN FLORIANO DEL COLLIO (GO)

Zuani

Località Giasbana, 12
tel. 0481 391432
www.zuanivini.it
info@zuanivini.it

SGONICO (TS)

Skerlj

Frazione Sales, 44
tel. 040 229253
www.agriturismoskerlj.com
info@agriturismoskerlj.com

---

37 ac - 75,000 bt

PEOPLE - Patrizia Felluga is a woman with a strong character, forthright and very practical. Now that her presidency of the Consorzio Collio Carso has elapsed, she devotes all her time to her winery, where she's helped by her children Caterina and Antonio Zanon. We were accompanied on our visit by Antonio, who showed us the winery's new and attractive guest accommodation consisting of five rooms at the top of the hill on which the spectacular vineyards grow.

VINEYARDS - The vines grow round the slopes of the hill and the cellar is situated at the top. The new plantings are Guyot-trained while the older ones are *casarsa*- and double-arched cane trained. To valorize the aromatic grapes, they are spared treatment with copper which, after flowering, isn't used on any of the other varieties either. Only two wines are produced, each with the same grape blend.

WINES - The grapes are fermented at controlled temperatures and the sauvignon and friulano varieties are subjected to brief macerations. Collio Bianco is made with friulano, chardonnay, sauvignon e pinot grigio, with a few variables according to vintage and the addition of grapes from the younger vineyards. Made with slightly riper grapes, **Collio Bianco Zuani Ris. 2011** (○ 10,000 bt) ages in barriques, a third of which new. In the glass it is full of flavor and fruit, after which a leisurely finish is accompanied by notes of dried fruit and spices, the latter even more evident after time in the bottle.

 COLLIO BIANCO VIGNE 2013 (○ 65,000 bt) The usual very effective blend of friulano, chardonnay, sauvignon and pinot grigio, a wine full of identity and an emblem of the Collio Bianco typology. On the nose emerges a vast suite of ripe fruit and wild herbs, while the well-defined palate is enfolding, complex and extremely elegant.

---

4 ac - 4,000 bt

66 Matej Skerlj is a young winemaker, but also a farmer, a horticulturalist, a livestock breeder, a *charcutier* and a restaurateur who processes and serves the fruit and vegetables and the meat from the animals he raises. In short he's a countryman through and through with strong passions for the land of his birth, the Carso 99

PEOPLE - Matej divides his time between vineyard and cellar, which he oversees firsthand, and his family's *osmizza*, an old-fashioned country inn where he and his sister Kristina and his servants serve their own wine, cured meats and other foodstuffs.

VINEYARDS - The family's vineyards are divided into six parcels of land where the soil is composed of a top stratum of a couple of feet of red earth over Carsic stone. Some plantings are very old, others were made recently by Matej, whose approach is very simple, almost minimalist in style: hence no fertilizers, herbicides or other chemicals and treatments only with copper and sulphur.

WINES - Matej intervenes as little as possible on the must and the wine, macerating all the grapes to ensure that the end product has *goût de terroir*. **Vitoska 2011** (○ 1,500 bt), with its subtle hints of flowers, citrus fruits and aromatic herbs, has quality to spare. After a measured attack it follows up with a distinctively zesty, salty palate. The excellent and expressive **Terrano 2011** (● 1,000 bt) conflates the roughness of the grape (hard tannins and high acidity) and fruity, soft delicacy.

MALVASIA 2011 (○ 1,500 bt) Intense sensations of ripe apricot and delicate aromaticity lead into a very rich, sumptuous but approachable palate and a long, refreshing finish.

FERTILIZERS natural manure, green manure
PLANT PROTECTION chemical, copper and sulphur
WEED CONTROL mechanical
YEASTS selected
GRAPES 100% estate-grown
CERTIFICATION none

FERTILIZERS natural manure
PLANT PROTECTION copper and sulphur
WEED CONTROL mechanical
YEASTS native
GRAPES 100% estate-grown
CERTIFICATION none

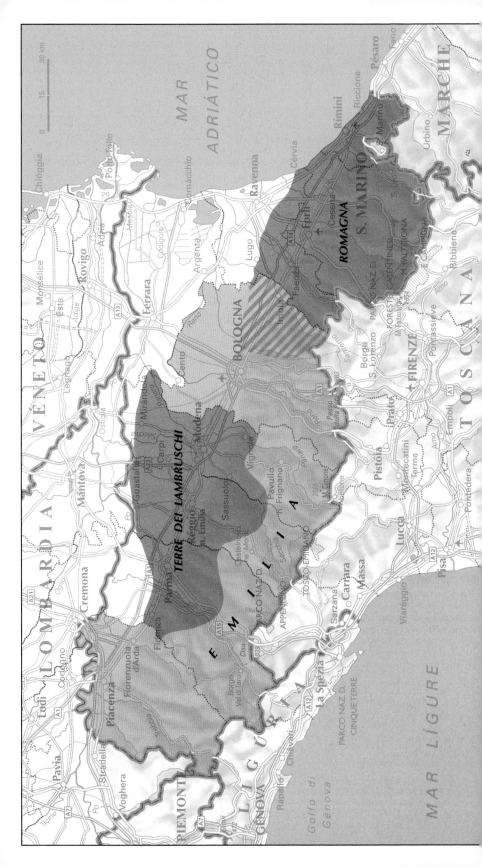

EMILIA-ROMAGNA

Paradoxically, it may appear undynamic and directionless, but over the last few years the Emilia-Romagna region has actually shown itself to be a lively, complex winegrowing area. The reality is that there's a lot going on, albeit not in the most homogeneous and consistent of fashions. Shining out among the large cooperative and private colossi are a host of small cellars run by virtuous producers in pursuit of wines that express different forms of identity – living proof that new ways of vineyard and cellar management really are possible. Our impression is that Colli Piacentini is the zone that least exploit the beauty of their terroir and wealth of biodiversity. And yet something is moving and we're delighted to report great steps forward in two different directions. The first is the new trend to bottle-refermented white wines, mainly those made with the ortrugo and malvasia grapes, a method that promises to help Ortrugo the wine in particular to find an identity and market niche of its own – at last. The second is actually more a confirmation than a truly new development: we believe in fact that the presence of the aromatic malvasia di Candia grape can turn the Colli Piacentini into one of the most important zones for the production of passito (not forgetting other singular wines such as Vin Santo di Vigoleno) in Italy.

Terre dei Lambruschi continues to be the most significant, exciting growth area. The 2013 vintage produced full-bodied, fragrant wines combining subtlety and essentiality, especially those in the naturally bottle-refermented typology wine lovers now prefer.

The native pignoletto grape is easily the most representative of the Colli Bolognesi zone. The 2013 vintage gave us wines of excellent quality with the beneficial spring rains and good day-to-night temperature swings throughout the summer until the harvest allowing the grapes' typical aroma to develop nicely. Albeit sadly not widespread, the old method of bottle-refermentation yields convincing expressions of Pignoletto with a real sense of place. Today, almost 50 years on from the creation of the Sangiovese di Romagna DOC, we can safely say that production has increasingly concentrated on quality thanks to the constant effort and passion of numerous small producers, among whom the number who support natural viticulture is growing all the time. The 2013 vintage recorded high levels of performance with a host of fragrant highly enjoyable Sangioveses, and the 2011 Reserves, the products of a troublesome growing year, nonetheless held a few surprises in store.

Last but not least, Albana, made from the important native Romagna grape of the same name; we are very pleased to report that many producers are concentrating their efforts on interpretation and quality.

In short, Emilia-Romagna is in a state of ferment – or should that be refermentation!

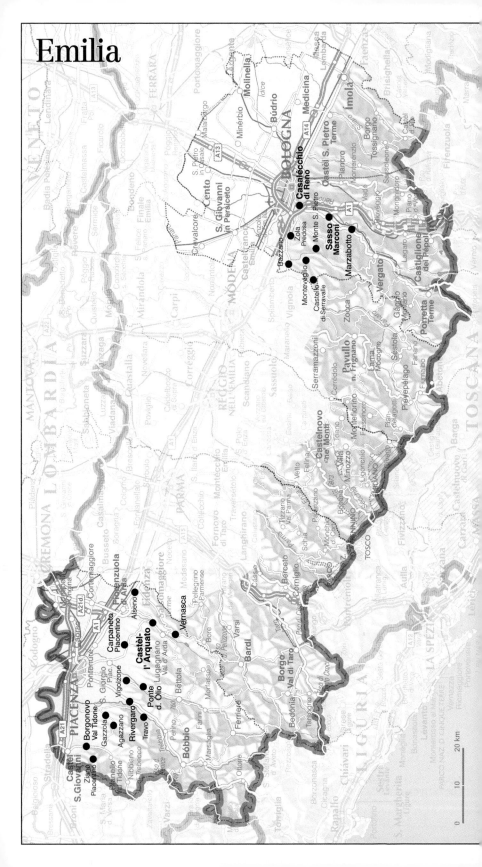

Emilia

VIGOLZONE (PC)

Barattieri

Località Albarola
Via Dei Tigli, 100
tel. 0523 875111
www.aziendabarattieri.com
ottobarattieri@libero.it

ZIANO PIACENTINO (PC)

Lusenti

Località Casa Piccioni di Vicobarone, 57
tel. 0523 868479
www.lusentivini.it
info@lusentivini.it

---

86 ac - 125,000 bt   `10% discount`

42 ac - 120,000 bt

PEOPLE - The historic Barattieri family cellar is housed in a 19th-century palazzo and warrants a visit. Today it's run by Massimiliana and her brother Alberico with the help of the latter's wife Francesca. Cellar operations are guided by the indestructible Romano Dondi and his young assistant Davide Bolzoni, helped by enologist Stefano Testa.

VINEYARDS - The company vineyards, managed by agronomist Camillo Rossi, are split into two distinct plots at altitudes that vary between 650 and 980 feet. Both have the same type of soil, composed of clay with sizable quantities of iron. The company practices integrated pest management among the vine rows and grows traditional Piacenza grapes and international varieties that were brought here in the Napoleonic period.

WINES - Barattieri's wines are undergoing a small revolution which is making them more precise and well-defined with more emphasis on the characteristics of their grape varieties. Gutturnio Frizzante 2013 `Everyday Wine` (● 25,000 bt), fruity with floral and vegetal hints, has a soft attack in the mouth followed up by a dry finish. The well-crafted, linear **C.P. Sauvignon Frizzante 2013** (○ 13,000 bt) has a beautifully calibrated body with notes of chewy fruit, a tangy palate and fine, silky perlage, Il **Gutturnio Cl. Ris. 2011** (● 1,500 bt) offers weight with an almond twist. **C.P. Malvasia Secca Frizzante 2013** (○ 5,000 bt) is a simple, textbook wine.

`slow wine` **C.P. VIN SANTO ALBAROLA 2004** (○ 800 bt) Superlative as ever, this icon of a wine was first made in 1823 and is barrel-aged for nine years. Sumptuous, velvety and balsamic, it's endowed with great elegance and symmetry, which fuse into never-ending brightness and length.

PEOPLE - The affable, ever smiling Lodovica Lusenti infects everyone who visits her winery, a veritable institution for the wines of the Colli Piacentini, in especial Valtidone, with her warmth and friendliness. In the cellar she can count on the contribution of Stefano Testa, a key figure in the movement to re-establish the identity of the local area.

VINEYARDS - The wine world can't afford to rest on its laurels. Lodovica is well aware of the fact and over the last few years she has invested hefty resources in experimentation and research. The most significant challenge she has to face is the conversion to organics, a decision she has taken talking to fellow winemakers, with whom she shares many of her strategies.

WINES - We like the wines for their combination of recognizability, consistency with the traditions of the Valtidone, and personality. The latter is one of the qualities of the original and masterfully crafted **C.P. Malvasia Frizzante Emiliana 2013** `Everyday Wine` (○ 6,000 bt), a bottle-fermented wine that should be "shaken before pouring" to bring out its sparkle and complex, snappy, aromatic identity. **Gutturnio Frizzante 2013** (● 35,000 bt) is characterized by huskiness and fruitiness. The bottle-aged **Gutturnio Frizzante Tournesol 2011** (● 4,200 bt) is an interesting wine with a complex, dynamic palate. **C.P. Bonarda La Picciona 2008** (● 2,000 bt) has moderate tannins and lingers on the palate. **Martin 2012** (● barbera, croatina, merlot; 3,500 bt) is enjoyably simple.

FERTILIZERS organic-mineral, manure pellets
PLANT PROTECTION chemical, copper and sulphur
WEED CONTROL chemical, mechanical
YEASTS selected
GRAPES 100% estate-grown
CERTIFICATION none

FERTILIZERS natural manure
PLANT PROTECTION copper and sulphur
WEED CONTROL mechanical
YEASTS selected
GRAPES 20% bought in
CERTIFICATION converting to organics

Lambrusco Country

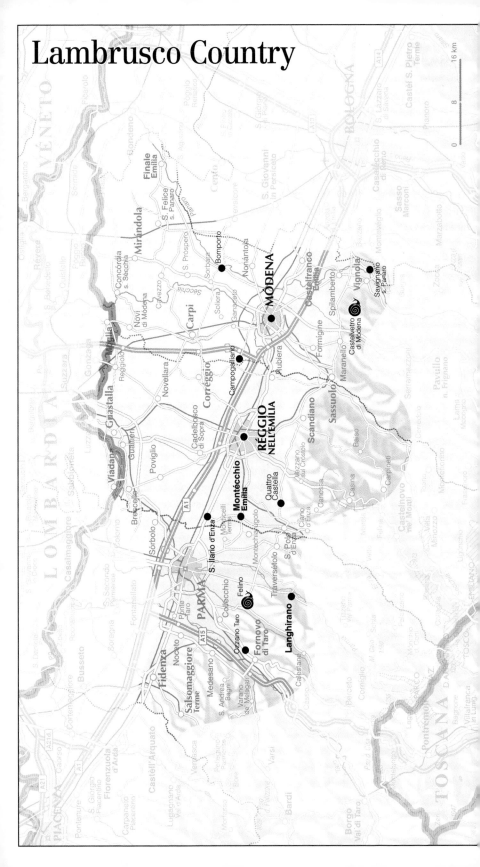

CASTELVETRO (MO)

Cleto Chiarli

Via Belvedere, 8
tel. 059 3163311
www.chiarli.it
italia@chiarli.it

FELINO (PR)

Camillo Donati

Frazione Barbiano
Via Costa, 3 A
tel. 0521 637204
www.camillodonati.it
camillo@camillodonati.it

247 ac - 900,000 bt   **10% discount**

37 ac - 90,000 bt

PEOPLE - The story of Lambrusco in Modena has interwoven with that of the Chiarli ever since Cleto set up this now prestigious winery a year before the unification of Italy. Today the business is run by Anselmo and Mauro Chiarli, and owns seven estates, among which Cleto, founded in 2001 with the clear aim of making high quality wines by vinifying the grapes from its vineyards with consummate skill.

VINEYARDS - The grasparossa vineyards are in the hill-foot district of Castelvetro, where the soil is mostly clayey with copious gravel. The sorbara grapes, instead, grow on the flat land between Soliera and Sozzigalli, where the River Secchia has enriched the soil with sand and silt, which give the wines acidity and finesse.

WINES - The technical team of Franco De Biasi, Michele Faccin and Stefano Tedeschini use cutting-edge technology to present wines of enviably consistent quality every year. One such is the impeccable bottle-refermented Lambrusco di Sorbara del Fondatore 2013 Everyday Wine (● 12,000 bt), once more a convincing interpretation of the typology by virtue of its constant precision, enjoyable freshness and soft tangy finish. On a par is Lambrusco Grasparossa di Castelvetro Vigneto Cialdini 2013 Everyday Wine (● 50,000 bt) is genuine and stylish on the nose, spacious on juicy on the palate, and dry on the finish. **Lambrusco di Sorbara Vecchia Modena Premium M.H. 2013** (● 60,000 bt) offers great drinkability with well-balanced supporting acidity, **Lambrusco Grasparossa di Castelvetro Villa Cialdini 2013** (● 80,000 bt) is dynamic and refined.

❝ «I live wine, I don't make it» is Camillo Donati's favorite adage. And, for him, living wine means having a philosophy of life and a *modus operandi* in the vineyard and in the cellar whose aim is to change whatever natural cycles impose as little as possible. ❞

PEOPLE - The company was formed in 1930; and is now managed by Camillo with the help of his wife Francesa and his niece Monia. Certified organic since 2001, it adopts a rational approach to biodynamic agriculture to make its wines express the local area as naturally and authentically as possible.

VINEYARDS - The vineyards are split up between the Bottazza and Sant'Andrea estates, both in the hills round the cellar. Though they have similar silty pale clay soils, the microclimates are different.

WINES - All the wines are bottle-refermented according to tradition, without the use of selected yeasts or temperature control. **Il Mio Trebbiano 2013** (○ 5,000 bt) is fragrant, flavorsome and subtle with an enjoyable approachable palate. **Il Mio Sauvignon 2013** (○ 5,000 bt) is lip-smackingly juicy and zesty. **Il Mio Lambrusco 2012** (● 6,000 bt) has a forthright character with distinctive earthy notes, good fruit and plenty of tannic huskiness. **Il Mio Barbera 2012** (● 7,000 bt) contends with the Malvasia for the title of flagship wine; this year it's juicy and full-bodied with very lively acidity and a wonderfully tangy finish.

slow wine **IL MIO MALVASIA 2012** (○ 6,000 bt) A textbook Malvasia that conflates character and drinkability. The aromas on the nose are contained with subtle notes of citrus fruit and fresh flowers, while the palate is full-bodied and tangy, flavorsome and fragrance.

FERTILIZERS organic-mineral, green manure	**FERTILIZERS** none
PLANT PROTECTION copper and sulphur, organic	**PLANT PROTECTION** copper and sulphur
WEED CONTROL mechanical	**WEED CONTROL** mechanical
YEASTS selected	**YEASTS** native
GRAPES 100% estate-grown	**GRAPES** 100% estate-grown
CERTIFICATION none	**CERTIFICATION** organic

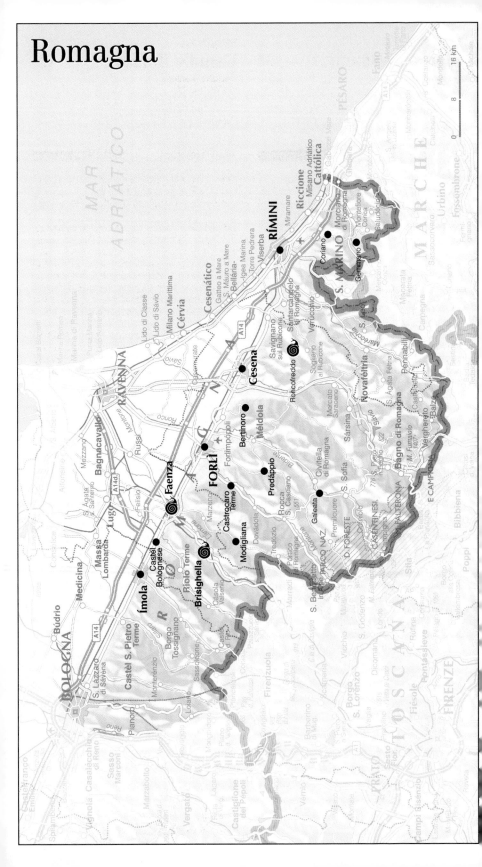

Vigne dei Boschi

Via Tura, 7/A
tel. 0546 51648
www.vignedeiboschi.it
vignedeiboschi@alice.it

Fattoria Zerbina

Frazione Marzeno
Via Vicchio,11
tel. 0546 40022
www.zerbina.com
info@zerbina.com

---

160 ac - 13,000 bt | **10% discount**

66 Katia Alpi and her companion Paolo Babini are the heart and soul of this, a small craft winery that has raised the profile of the Brisighella area with agronomic practices designed to preserve the soil and the surrounding environment 99

PEOPLE - The work of this devoted couple of winemakers is based on the belief that "Good wine is made in the vineyard, not in the cellar," so care for the vines is their first priority.

VINEYARDS - Thanks to biodynamic practices and a very limited use of copper and sulphur, the vines have established a steady balance with the soil and developed their natural defense mechanisms optimally. The vineyards stand at an altitude of about 1,150 feet in excellent locations with good air circulation and significant night-day temperature swings. The sandy, marly soil adds finesse and expressiveness to the structure of the wines.

WINES - The fruit of meticulous hard work and respect for the rhythms of nature, Katia and Paolo's wines are a convincing expression of the terroir. **16 Anime 2012** (O riesling; 2,500 bt) has a backbone of acidity that gives the palate verve and length. **Malbo Borgo Stignani 2010** (● 4,000 bt) is dark and deep with close-knit tannins and hints of licorice, while **Malbo Settepievi 2008** (● 3,000 bt) stands out for its intense notes of incense and austere structure. **Poggio Tura 2009** (● 1,500 bt) and **Poggio Tura 2010** (● 3,500 bt) are monovarietal Sangioveses that are exemplary reflections of their respective vintages. The first is defined by well-developed fruit, the second has an intense nose of crisp berries and is fresh, juicy and delicately tangy.

72 ac - 200,000 bt | **10% discount**

66 Fattoria Zerbina is telling the whole world that a new way of wine making and, above all, of vine growing is possible in Romagna 99

PEOPLE - Whoever would have imagined that the Romagna wine Risorgimento would be set off by a woman from the Brianza district of Lombardy. In the 19980s, in fact, Maria Cristina Geminiani gave her heart and soul to this generous region. Viewing the past with a critical eye, she has never taken short cuts to achieve top quality wines.

VINEYARDS - Cristina has revived the traditional bush-training technique, abandoned during the years of industrialization because it was deemed uneconomical and hard to manage. Cristina's return to this approach allows her to grow very high quality, beautifully balanced grapes in old vineyards. The terroir is Marzeno, a small subzone in the foothills between Faenza and Brisighella.

WINES - Fattoria Zerbina's Sangioveses have always conveyed power, burly tannins and warmth. It came as a surprise therefore to note the change in style and extreme elegance of **Romagna Sangiovese Sup. Pietramora Ris. 2011** Great Wine (● 15,000 bt), with its distinctive floral notes – especially violet, typical of the grape – and bittersweet tones redolent of cocoa; on the palate it's dynamic, despite its corpulence and juiciness. It's one of the best versions ever of this reserve. Excellent too is the second release of **Romagna Albana Bianco di Ceparano 2013** Everyday Wine (O 8,500 bt), a lean wine with a reductive style, highly original for its typology. It exploits the contrast between the fruity sweetness of the grape and sharp acidity. A good table wine, Cristina sees it as the beginning of an interesting new approach for albana.

FERTILIZERS biodynamic preparations, green manure
PLANT PROTECTION copper and sulphur, organic
WEED CONTROL mechanical
YEASTS native
GRAPES 100% estate-grown
CERTIFICATION biodynamic, organic

FERTILIZERS organic-mineral, manure pellets, green manure
PLANT PROTECTION chemical, copper and sulphur
WEED CONTROL chemical, mechanical
YEASTS selected
GRAPES 100% estate-grown
CERTIFICATION none

FAENZA (RA)

Paolo Francesconi

Località Sarna
Via Tuliero, 154
tel. 0546 43213
www.francesconipaolo.it
info@francesconipaolo.it

18.5 ac - 20,000 bt `10% discount`

66 *"Nature is amazing,"* says Paolo Francesconi, *"and you never stop learning from her. You think you know everything but nature's always there to take you aback. This is the beauty and the burden of my job* 99

PEOPLE - Paolo is, without doubt, a brilliant winemaker. The organic and biodynamic work he does in the vineyard is exceptional, as you can tell from the wild herbs and ladybirds that invade his vine rows. The "good and the clean and the fair" sought after by Slow Food is here for all to see.

VINEYARDS - The vineyards are situated in an area with no great reputation for winegrowing at an altitude of 260 feet in the hills inland from Faenza. The soil, typical of the old Lamone river bed, is composed of red clay and silt. The estate explodes with luxuriant nature in which the equilibrium between flora and fauna is extraordinary. This allows the Guyot-trained albana grapes and the spurred cordon-trained sangiovese grapes to give of their best.

WINES - Paolo's wines tell the terroir exactly how it is, encapsulating the flavor of the grapes, the soil and all the many hours of hard work. They are unfussy wines made without temperature control and with the use of solely native yeasts. Made with albana grapes macerated in terracotta jars, the extremely complex **Antiqva 2013** (O 500 bt) has refined aromas of black tea and chamomile with a taut, acidic palate and a superb salty finish. **Romagna Sangiovese Sup. Limbecca 2012** (● 9,000 bt) has notes of red berries and **Luna Nuova 2013** (O trebbiano; 1,500 bt) is fresh and vegetal.

> slow wine **ARCAICA 2013** (O 2,000 bt) A beautifully crafted Albana made with long maceration on the lees. Hence very elegant notes of dried flowers and ripe fruit with a rich, tannic, complex tangy palate.

FERTILIZERS biodynamic preparations, green manure
PLANT PROTECTION copper and sulphur
WEED CONTROL mechanical
YEASTS native
GRAPES 100% estate-grown
CERTIFICATION organic

IMOLA (BO)

Tre Monti

Località Bergullo
Via Lola, 3
tel. 0542 657116
www.tremonti.it
tremonti@tremonti.it

106 ac - 180,000 bt `10% discount`

PEOPLE - The Navacchia family have played an important role in the history of Romagna winemaking. It was in the 1970s that Sergio Navacchia bought his first acres of land in the hills west of Imola and planted them with new vineyards. Now his sons David and Vittorio run the company, the former working as sales manager, the latter supervising work in the vineyards and cellar.

VINEYARDS - The white grapes are grown round the cellar in the Serra subzone on the pale gray soils that run down towards the River Sanguinario. The oldest sangiovese vineyards whose grapes go into the (southeast facing) Petrignone and (south-facing) Thea selections are at Petrignone in the Oriolo subzone, where the clay is darker and, in some places, very pebbly. Both estates have been converted to organics.

WINES - Tre Monti has always produced precise, charismatic wines at affordable prices. Both the Sangiovese selections are good, especially the **Romagna Sangiovese Oriolo Thea Ris. 2011** `Great Wine` (● 7,000 bt), which is extraordinarily compact and stylish with a racy entry onto the palate and a vibrant finish. More robust but less spacious, **Romagna Sangiovese Oriolo Petrignone Ris. 2011** (● 24,000 bt) is full of fruity flesh. **Romagna Sangiovese Sup. Campo di Mezzo 2013** (● 40,000 bt) is enjoyable and lean, while **Romagna Sangiovese SoNo 2013** (● 20,000 bt), with no added sulphites, is even more delicious and supple. Last but by no means least, two excellent whites: **Romagna Albana Secco Vigna Rocca 2013** (O 24,000 bt) is very typical and full-bodied on the palate, **Romagna Trebbiano Vigna Rio 2013** (O 10,000 bt) is more lightweight but no less interesting.

FERTILIZERS natural manure
PLANT PROTECTION copper and sulphur
WEED CONTROL mechanical
YEASTS selected
GRAPES 100% estate-grown
CERTIFICATION organic

MODIGLIANA (FC)

Torre San Martino

Località Casone
Via San Martino in Monte
tel. 06 89786312
torresanmartino@gmail.com

RONCOFREDDO (FC)

Villa Venti

Frazione Villa Venti
Via Doccia, 1442
tel. 0541 949532
www.villaventi.it
info@villaventi.it

25 ac - 18000 bt

17 ac - 27,000 bt   **10% discount**

PEOPLE - In 2001 architect Maurizio Costa decided to put in order and improve a few hectares of vineyard in the sangiovese growing area of Modigliana. And that's how Torre San Martino was born. We were told how it all happened by enologist and agronomist Francesco Bordini during our visit. Franco himself is a key figure behind the success of the small winery, which he oversees in both field and cellar.

VINEYARDS - The wooded hills of the province of Faenza are among the best growing areas for sangiovese. The vineyards are situated at an altitude of about 1,150 feet and enjoy good air circulation with sharp night-day temperature swings. The marly soil ensures plenty of acidity for the grapes. The decision to conserve an old bush-trained vineyard made up entirely of original sangiovese clones shows just how much the winery respects tradition.

WINES - Refined, clean wines, accomplished interpretations of the terroir that conflate tannic texture and dynamism. The exemplary **Romagna Sangiovese Vigna 1922 Ris. 2011** Great Wine (● 3,000 bt), made with grapes from a very old vineyard (hence the name), is deep and caresses the palate with mellow tannins and good supporting acidity: it's a masterpiece of elegance and equilibrium. Juicy and ebullient, **Romagna Sangiovese Gemme 2013** (● 8,000 bt) develops well in the mouth. **Colli di Faenza Chardonnay 2013** (○ 2,000 bt) has lean, vibrant body with heady aromas of peaches and apricots and blossom, while **Colli di Faenza Vigne della Signora 2013** (○ 4,000 bt) is all fresh and fruity. The austere **Colli di Faenza Rosso 2011** (● 4,000 bt) is a blend of cabernet sauvignon and franc and merlot.

66 The journey undertaken in 2002 by Mauro Giardini and Davide Castellucci has been tough, but with talent and application they have managed to give life to this small, virtuous wine cellar 99

PEOPLE - On the steep hills of Roncofreddo, these two partners in business and friends in life practice sustainable, eco-friendly agriculture. Everything lives in harmony in this pretty natural landscape.

VINEYARDS - Situated at an altitude of 650 feet, the vines are candelabra-trained (a type of vertical cordon system) round the farmhouse, which also provides accommodation. The soil, composed of red and sandy clay, adds oomph and structure to the wines and the frequent winds mitigate the summer heat. Agronomist Remigio Bordini always has a say in decisions regarding vineyard management.

WINES - The consultant enologist is Francesco Bordini, an expert on the terroir and the potential of the sangiovese grape. The wines of the Longiano enclave are characterized by intense fruit and close-knit tannins to which the Villa Venti microclimate adds finesse and brightness. The harmonious **Romagna Sangiovese Longiano Ris. 2011** (2 4,000 bt), has floral and delicately balsamic notes with well extracted tannins. The aromaticity of the grape characterizes **Serenaro 2013** (○ 1,500 bt), a pervasive wine with plenty of grip.

slow wine **ROMAGNA SANGIOVESE LONGIANO SUP. PRIMO SEGNO 2012** (● 15,000 bt) A superlative Sangiovese that matures solely in steel vats. Hints of fresh berries accompany a succulent palate with good acid backbone and the follow-through is deep and persistent.

FERTILIZERS manure pellets
PLANT PROTECTION copper and sulphur
WEED CONTROL chemical, mechanical
YEASTS selected
GRAPES 100% estate-grown
CERTIFICATION none

FERTILIZERS none
PLANT PROTECTION copper and sulphur
WEED CONTROL mechanical
YEASTS native
GRAPES 100% estate-grown
CERTIFICATION organic

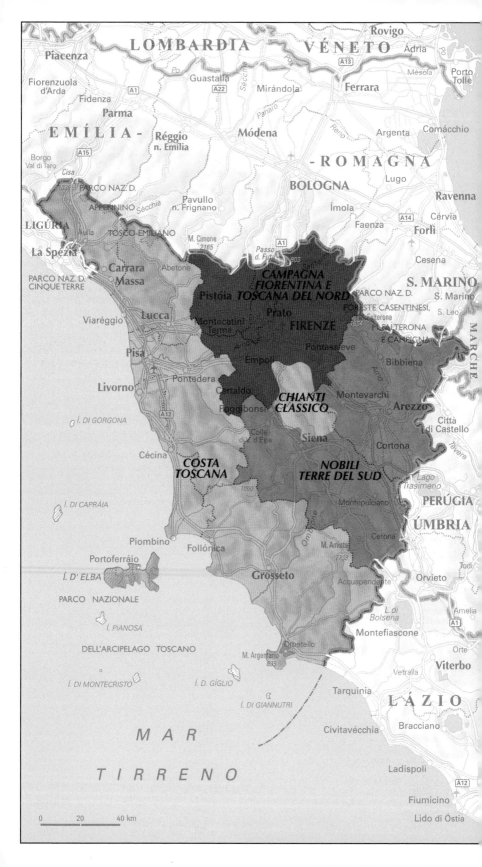

TUSCANY

The present situation in Tuscany needs to be carefully analyzed. Which is normal for a region with about 160 acres of vineyards, in which diverse enological eras are stratified, scattered here and there over its many, many glorious denominations. Our report is based on direct knowledge and experience of each single terroir acquired through visits to each single wine cellar. At Montalcino the 2009 harvest was adversely affected by an unusually warm growing year. In general, however, producers showed skill and coherence in their wines, focused more on approachability than on aging potential, albeit increasingly in line with the sangiovese monovarietal textbook. Good news came from Montepulciano, where the denomination replicated the vivacity we remarked upon last year. Chianti Classico has added another arrow to its bow – the Gran Selezione – though, in our view, it continues to be a "dark object." The Consortium intended it to be the peak of the quality pyramid but the truth of the matter is that, at our tastings, the "new" Chianti Classico showed no more quality than what it had already. The Tuscan coast is a veritable mosaic of terroirs, hard to sum up in a few words. What we can say is that, from Massa-Carrara to Grosseto, we noted improving viticulture at last – at least in some areas – free from enological tampering and geared more to the specific aptitudes of the single denominations. In the pages that follow, pay special attention to the winegrowing areas that border with the Apennines – Lunigiana, Rufina, Garfagnana, Mugello, and Casentino – which all treated us to interesting and original pearls. Moving on to whites, finally, alongside the ever chirpy Vernaccia di San Gimignano, a number of trebbiano-based wines are coming to the fore with intriguing sensory profiles and relaxed, laid-back flavor.

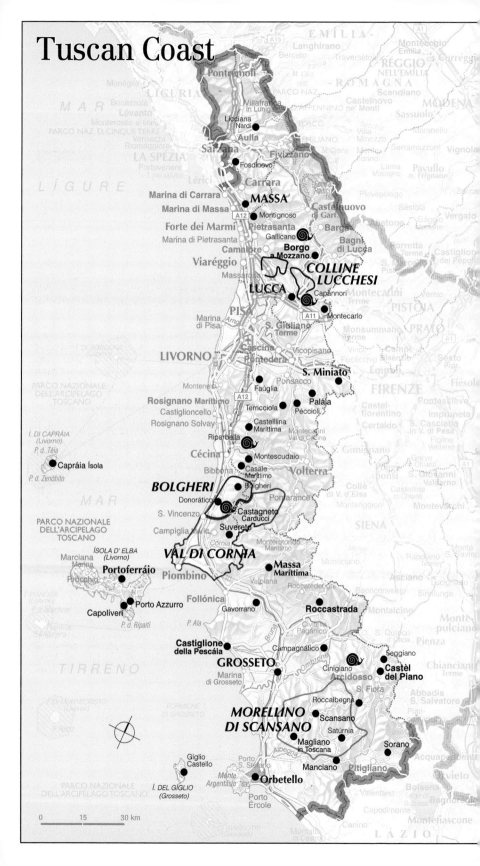

Tuscan Coast

BOLGHERI (LI)

Tenuta San Guido 🍾

Località Capanne, 27
tel. 0565 762003
www.sassicaia.com
info@sassicaia.com

CAMPAGNATICO (GR)

Poggio Trevvalle €

Località Arcille
Podere Ex E.M., 348
tel. 0564 998142
www.poggiotrevvalle.it
valle@poggiotrevvalle.it

---

215 ac - 740,000 bt

33 ac - 60,000 bt   `10% discount`

PEOPLE - One approaches the cellar that gives life to one of Italy's legendary wines with a certain deference. "Will there be any secrets or novelties to report?" one wonders. "In San Guido the novelty is that there are no novelties," says Marchese Niccolò Incisa della Rocchetta, thus summing up both his company's philosophy and his own measured, elegant, discreet approach.

VINEYARDS - If any alchemies exist behind the amazingly consistent quality of Sassicaia, they are to be sought mainly in the vineyard: in the best hillside positions in the Bolgheri area, including the historic Castiglioncello plot, and the finest too on the plain down towards the sea, which are carefully managed with minimal impact on the environment, and where any interventions carried out are purely for consolidation purposes.

WINES - Recent work on the sober, functional wine cellar hasn't altered the minimalist, concrete approach to vinification operations, which the Marchese performs himself. **Bolgheri Sassicaia 2011** `Great Wine` (● cabernet sauvignon and franc; 200,000 bt) is mature and generous on the nose with notes of redcurrants, soil and graphite, lovely background florality, fine tannins, full body and substance; it engulfs and pushes with elegance and suppleness and persistent. **Guidalberto 2012** (● cabernet sauvignon, merlot; 240,000 bt) is still a little stiff but, with its excellent stuffing, is sure to improve. **Le Difese 2012** (● cabernet sauvignon, sangiovese; 240,000 bt) has well-judged fruit with a fresh, snappy palate.

PEOPLE - Poggio Trevvalle is situated at Campagnatico, which marks a sort of ideal boundary between two denominations, Morellino di Scansano and Montecucco. Brothers Umberto and Bernardo Valle began making wine in the late 1990s harnessing all the enormous agronomic knowhow accrued managing a large farm in Puglia. They adopted organic viticulture right from the beginning and now produce land-rooted wines full of character and expressive naturalness.

VINEYARDS - The vineyards are spread out round the cellar on clayey soil containing a good deal of gravel, especially in the top part of the vineyards. The owners' farming skills can be seen in their respect for the oldest vineyards where they "listen" to the land to understand its productive potential. Virtuous soil management ensures the vines plenty of water, a *sine qua non* at these latitudes.

WINES - The winery advocates clean viticulture and produces wines consistent with this approach. Interventions in the cellar are thus reduced to a bare minimum, just enough to ensure the right amount of sulfur, and racking according to necessity. We were impressed by the fragrance of **Morellino di Scansano Pàssera 2013** `Everyday Wine` (● 25,000 bt), which is floral, juicy and forthright. The cask-aged **Morellino di Scansano Larcille Ris. 2011** (● 2,000 bt) is a more heavyweight wine with noble ripe fruit and balsamic hints and dynamic but well-structured development on the palate. The well-crafted **Montecucco Rosso 2011** (● sangiovese, merlot, cabernet; 5,000 bt) is full of bulk and warmth. **Morellino di Scansano 2012** (● 5,000 bt) has delicate floweriness and a light palate with fine tannins.

FERTILIZERS organic-mineral, natural manure, green manure
PLANT PROTECTION chemical, copper and sulphur
WEED CONTROL mechanical
YEASTS native
GRAPES 15% bought in
CERTIFICATION none

FERTILIZERS manure pellets, green manure
PLANT PROTECTION copper and sulphur
WEED CONTROL mechanical
YEASTS native
GRAPES 100% estate-grown
CERTIFICATION organic

CAPANNORI (LU)

Tenuta di Valgiano

Frazione Valgiano
Via di Valgiano, 7
tel. 0583 402221
www.valgiano.it
info@valgiano.it

52 ac - 80,000 bt	10% discount

66 The wines of Valgiano reflect unconventional research and original flavor. They are characterized by finesse and enjoyability and exalt the flavor of the grapes 99

PEOPLE - Saverio Petrilli, an enologist converted to the country life, Moreno Petrini and Laura Collobiano run a democratic "pirate ship" and are always willing to listen to their experienced collaborators' opinions. Here no one has a fixed role; as on farms in the old days, everyone does a bit of everything. They also breed pigs and grow fruit and vegetables and old cereal varieties for good measure.

VINEYARDS - In 1993, the trio began with the idea of making and selling wine. In 1997 they repudiated chemicals and in 2001 converted to biodynamics, a fortunate choice that has served to improve the vines and the wines. The former grow mostly under the farmhouse in the shadow of the towering Pizzorne massif and overlook the plains round Lucca below. The soils are composed of *alberese* rock and *macigno toscano*, a local sandstone, which give the wines structure and finesse.

WINES - Vinification is traditional, grapes being piled into open containers and trodden. The bright and enjoyable **Colline Lucchesi Palistorti Bianco 2013** (○ vermentino, malvasia, trebbiano; 5,000 bt) offers flowery notes. **Colline Lucchesi Tenuta di Valgiano 2011** (● syrah, sangiovese, merlot; 11,000 bt) is a top-notch complex red with fruity, balsamic aromas that grow salty and mineral on the palate against a fresh, crisp, wonderfully stylish background. The company chose to defer the tasting of Colline Lucchesi Palistorti Rosso 2012 to next year.

CASTAGNETO CARDUCCI (LI)

Fornacelle

Località Fornacelle, 232 A
tel. 0565 775575
www.fornacelle.it
info@fornacelle.it

20 ac - 40,000 bt	10% discount

PEOPLE - Fornacelle is a small Castagneto winery with a long history behind it. It has been owned by the Billi family for four generations. Everything began with a parcel the Conti della Gherardesca granted to the great-grandfather of Stefano, who now manages it with his wife Silvia. The estate now has new plantings but preserves part of the original mixed farming system, growing also secular olives, fruit trees and cereals.

VINEYARDS - The vineyards are almost all on the plain south of Bolgheri on mixed soils with patches rich in gravel. Most of the red grape vineyards were planted in 1998 with vermentino, sauvignon, sémillon and fiano only being planted from 2000 onwards. The vineyards are grassed and fertilized only with manure, while weeding is mechanical.

WINES - The wines are very fine and elegant and clearly reveal the winery's style. **Bolgheri Sup. Guardaboschi 2011** (● cabernet sauvignon and franc, merlot; 7,000 bt) has nice fruity, spicy notes, a bulky body and a lingering finish. **Fornacelle 2013** (○ sémillon; 2,500 bt) offers a very blossomy bouquet, strong flavor and an agreeable finish. It's a huge pleasure to sip is the anything but banal **Bolgheri Bianco Zizzolo 2013** (○ vermentino; 10,000 bt), fresh-tasting and lip-smacking. The pleasant **Bolgheri Rosso Zizzolo 2012** (● merlot, cabernet sauvignon; 30,000 bt) has a balsamic nose and a harmonious palate.

slow wine FOGLIO 38 2011 (● cabernet franc; 3,200) An enfolding nose with fresh aromas and a grassy entry into the mouth evolving into mature notes. The finish is vegetal and full of verve. A dazzling red, the product of attentive farming with an artisan approach.

FERTILIZERS biodynamic preparations
PLANT PROTECTION organic
WEED CONTROL mechanical
YEASTS native
GRAPES 100% estate-grown
CERTIFICATION biodynamic

FERTILIZERS manure pellets, natural manure
PLANT PROTECTION copper and sulphur
WEED CONTROL mechanical
YEASTS native
GRAPES 100% estate-grown
CERTIFICATION none

CASTAGNETO CARDUCCI (LI)

I Luoghi

Località Campo al Capriolo, 201
tel. 0565 777379
www.iluoghi.it
info@iluoghi.it

CINIGIANO (GR)

Salustri

Località La Cava
Frazione Poggi del Sasso
tel. 0564 990529
www.salustri.it
info@salustri.it

8.5 ac - 14,000 bt

❝ The company's philosophy is disarmingly simple. 'We aren't interested in quantity or excessive extracts. We only want quality because we love elegant wines!' Period! ❞

PEOPLE - When Stefano Granata began telling me the story of I Luoghi, I had to pinch myself to make sure I was living in the present era, not in the world of make-believe. The fact is that this small winery has become one of the leading players in the Bolgheri style revolution in next to no time.

VINEYARDS - Stefano and his wife Paola De Fusco speak openly about how they decided upon their style of vineyard management. They were in the Chianti Classico zone when, all of a sudden, they found themselves standing by a vineyard that belonged to agronomist Gioia Cresti, so well kept that they decided there and then that she would be the consultant enologist for them. The vineyards are a couple of miles from the cellar and are unilateral and bilateral spurred cordon-trained according to grape variety and soil.

WINES - When I visited, they were finishing work on the simple and functional new cellar. The interesting **Bolgheri Sup. Campo al Fico 2011** (● cabernet sauvignon e franc; 3,000 bt) has complex, balsamic aromas with a bright, coherent palate, not exactly expansive but, nonetheless, nicely natural.

> **slow wine** **BOLGHERI SUP. PODERE RITORTI 2011** (● cabernet sauvignon and franc, merlot, syrah; 10,000 bt) We'll never cease to lavish praise on this red, whose complex aromas are characterized by notes of berry fruits and iron filings. On the palate it's reactive, bright and invigorating with modulated raciness and silky tannins and a long, punchy finish.

64 ac - 120,000 bt

❝ Leonardo Salustri is unique in his genre, an artist of viticulture and enology without compare. With his great energy he was one of the people who brought the Montecucco DOC to life in the first place ❞

PEOPLE - Leonardo has confirmed his theory about the recovery of old vineyards by regrafting old vines, some of which originally planted over 50 years ago, on their own roots. In this way he reinvigorates them to produce better wines. He is helped in the cellar by his son Marco.

VINEYARDS - Salustri loves anything old, which is why 40% of his vines have an age of 50-70 years. The rest were planted 15 years or so ago with a density of 10,000 per acre. An experimental vineyard monitored by Pisa University contains as many as 400 clones. The grapes from the vineyard with the oldest vines, selected by Leonardo after years of hard work and a great deal of passion, are fermented and matured exclusively in wood barrels.

WINES - The wines capture the very essence of the terroir and fresh, mineral aromas can be detected in all of them. **Narà 2013** (○ vermentino; 20,000 bt) exudes character with varietal brightness and notes of Mediterranean scrub, and brings to the palate minerality and pleasant acidity. **Montecucco Sangiovese Santa Marta 2011** (● 35,000 bt), made only with grapes from the new vineyards, expresses brightness with hints of red berries and elegant varietal tannins. **Montecucco Rosso Marleo 2012** (● 35,000 bt) has blossomy hints with a racy, well-calibrated palate and a sappy finish.

> **slow wine** **MONTECUCCO SANGIOVESE GROTTE ROSSE 2011** (● 12,000 bt) Produced with grapes from the oldest vines, a fresh, mineral, elegant wine with a massive attack on the palate, the one which has helped the denomination to grow and spread its fame.

FERTILIZERS green manure
PLANT PROTECTION copper and sulphur, organic
WEED CONTROL mechanical
YEASTS native
GRAPES 100% estate-grown
CERTIFICATION organic

FERTILIZERS natural manure, green manure
PLANT PROTECTION copper and sulphur
WEED CONTROL mechanical
YEASTS native
GRAPES 100% estate-grown
CERTIFICATION organic

GALLICANO (LU)

Podere Concori

Frazione Fiattone
Località Concori, 1
tel. 0583 766374
www.podereconcori.com
info@podereconcori.com

10 ac 12,000 bt

❝ Gabriele Da Prato's wines are disarmingly natural. And moreish: one sip, then another to the end of the bottle. A magical balance of sweetness, acidity and fruit ❞

PEOPLE - This unspoiled place, set between the hills and the mountains, is 40 miles up the Serchio Valley from Lucca. Here the volcanic Gabriele Da Prato, in love with his job and the land of his birth, tests out new ways of producing wine. Until a few years ago, in fact, in the Garfagnana district, on the border between Tuscany and Emilia, nobody would have dreamed of planting vines."

VINEYARDS - The quality and the originality of the wines come from the spectacular vineyards. Vigna Piezza is a natural terrace at an altitude of 1,300 feet overlooking the Serchio, and some of its vines were planted over 60 years ago. The loose soils are rich in sand and minerals, and the terrain is blessed by sun during the day and cooled by night by the breezes that descend from the Apennines.

WINES - **Vigna Piezza 2012** (● syrah; 1,800 bt) has a nose enriched by hints of white pepper and ripe cherries, a complex palate and an expansive, tangy finish. **Pinot Nero 2012** (● 1,400 bt), made with grapes from a northwest-facing vineyard encircled by chestnut groves, is elegant and thirst-quenching with a blossomy aroma. **Podere Concori Bianco 2013** (○ pinot bianco, chenin blanc; 2,500 bt) is an explosion of summer flowers and peach with notes of graphite on the finish.

> **slow wine** **MELOGRANO 2012** (● syrah, ciliegiolo, carrarese, merlot; 7,000 bt) Intriguing, expansive and deep, a veritable thoroughbred of a wine. Elegance, length and character – a minor masterpiece.

FERTILIZERS biodynamic preparations
PLANT PROTECTION copper and sulphur
WEED CONTROL mechanical
YEASTS native
GRAPES 100% estate-grown
CERTIFICATION biodynamic

RIPARBELLA (PI)

Caiarossa

Località Serra all'Olio, 59
tel. 0586 699016
www.caiarossa.com
info@caiarossa.com

79 ac - 90,000 bt

❝ Caiarossa is the protagonist of an exemplary winemaking career in which biodynamics has interwoven with perfect enology to produce marvelous wines ❞

PEOPLE - Dominique Genot welcomed me to his luminous tasting room and told me where his wine is born, of the harmony that exists between man and land, and of the importance of work in the vineyard and painstaking aging in the cellar.

VINEYARDS - Most of the vineyards are situated in a single semicircular property in front of the wine cellar. Another 39 acres are to be found in the Niccolino district at Riparbella. The soils are heterogeneous, ranging from zones with pebbly clays to saline red earth. Just small quantities of copper and sulfur are used in the vineyards and only compost to fertilize the soil.

WINES - The wines have distinctive personality. Harvests and vinification and aging processes are kept separate until the final assemblage. The remarkable **Caiarossa Bianco 2012** (○ chardonnay, viognier; 1,700 bt) is aromatic, well-structured, vegetal and fresh. **Aria di Caiarossa 2011** (● cabernet sauvignon and franc, syrah, merlot; 14,000 bt) offers fresh, vegetal aromas, a well-developed linear palate and balanced acidity. **Pergolaia 2011** (● sangiovese, cabernet sauvignon and franc, merlot; 32,000 bt) is juicy and drinkable. **Oro di Caiarossa 2011** (○ petit manseng; 850 bt) is a very enjoyable passito.

> **slow wine** **CAIAROSSA 2011** (● sangiovese, cabernet sauvignon & franc, merlot, alicante, syrah, petit verdot; 42,000 bt) has great fruit and a fresh, edgy finish. A red wine that bowled us over with its class, elegance and depth.

FERTILIZERS natural manure, biodynamic preparations
PLANT PROTECTION copper and sulphur, organic
WEED CONTROL mechanical
YEASTS native
GRAPES 100% estate-grown
CERTIFICATION biodynamic, organic

ROCCASTRADA (GR)

Ampeleia

Frazione Roccatederighi
Località Meleta
tel. 0564 567155
www.ampeleia.it
info@ampeleia.it

---

86 ac - 110,000 bt | **10% discount**

PEOPLE - We like to think that it was the magic of the place and the breathtaking landscape that prompted Elisabetta Foradori and Giovanni Podini to buy this property at the start of the century. It's at the foot of the spur of rock on top of which the tiny village of Roccatederighi nestles in the heart of the Maremma. The cellar is run by Marco Tait, a young man who came here when he was only 20. Sales manager is Simona Spinelli.

VINEYARDS - The vineyards and wine cellar are in the Meleta district at an altitude of about 1,900 feet, where the oldest vines were planted in the early 1990s. Another two plots, planted in 2002 are situated between Roccastrada and Paganico and at Roccatederighi. Here the soils and planting density are slightly different, hence the vines produce grapes with different nuances. The cellar is currently converting to biodynamics.

WINES - The cellar has always set itself an ambitious mission: to produce wines that have warm Mediterranean tones, but are never heavy or "boring." Top of the range **Ampeleia 2011** (● cabernet franc, sangiovese, grenache, mourvèdre, carignano, alicante bouschet; 20,000 bt), made with grapes from the oldest vineyards, is full-bodied with soft, velvety mouthfeel. **Alicante 2013** (● 4,000 bt), produced with the very best grapes from a single parcel, is dull red in color with elegant blossomy aromas and tangy, almost seawater-salty flavor. **Un Litro 2013** (● mix cellar's grapes; 50,000 bt) comes in an unusual format and is supple in the mouth.

slow wine **KEPOS 2012** (● grenache, mourvèdre, carignano, alicante bouschet; 30,000) Fermented and aged in cement vats, a wine that releases scents of fresh fruit and maquis onto a dry, aromatic palate. The Mediterranean in a glass.

FERTILIZERS biodynamic preparations, green manure
PLANT PROTECTION copper and sulphur, organic
WEED CONTROL mechanical
YEASTS native
GRAPES 100% estate-grown
CERTIFICATION converting to biodynamics

TERRICCIOLA (PI)

Casanova della Spinetta

Località Casanova
Via Provinciale Terricciolese
tel. 0587 690508
www.la-spinetta.com
toscana@la-spinetta.com

---

160 ac - 225,000 bt

PEOPLE - The Piedmontese Rivetti family embarked on their Tuscan adventure almost for fun in 2001. It was Giorgio Rivetti who wanted to try his hand with the sangiovese grape, which at the time was being grubbed up and replaced with international varieties. Now, years on, what began as a game has materialized into a splendid 160-acre estate in the commune of Terricciola. It grows mainly native grape varieties which, as the Rivettis has predicted, no one would dream of grubbing up any more.

VINEYARDS - There are two different terroirs. Most of the vineyards surround the cellar, where the soil is sandy and jam-packed with fossils, a reminder of the fact that the area was once covered by the sea. Another 35 acres are at Casciana Terme where the clay and limestone soil contains traces of travertine. As we said, the grapes grown are mostly native, hence sangiovese, prugnolo gentile and colorino.

WINES - **Nero di Casanova 2010** (● sangiovese; 140,000 bt) has a balsamic, earthy bouquet with a well-developed, linear palate. **Gentile di Casanova 2009** (● prugnolo gentile; 15,000 bt) has deep fruit with oriental spice and tinges of sweetness and a close-knit, pervasive palate. **Colorino di Casanova 2009** (● 15,000 bt), which ages in large casks for two years, has delicate, blossomy aromas expanded by a streak of vanilla and a spherical, enfolding palate with luscious acid verve. **Chianti Ris. 2009** (● 23,000 bt) offers sweet aromas with hints of blossom in the background and delicious fragrance. Fresh-tasting, lip-smacking **Vermentino 2013** (○ 32,000 bt) is almost tropical in style.

FERTILIZERS natural manure, compost, green manure
PLANT PROTECTION copper and sulphur
WEED CONTROL mechanical
YEASTS native
GRAPES 100% estate-grown
CERTIFICATION none

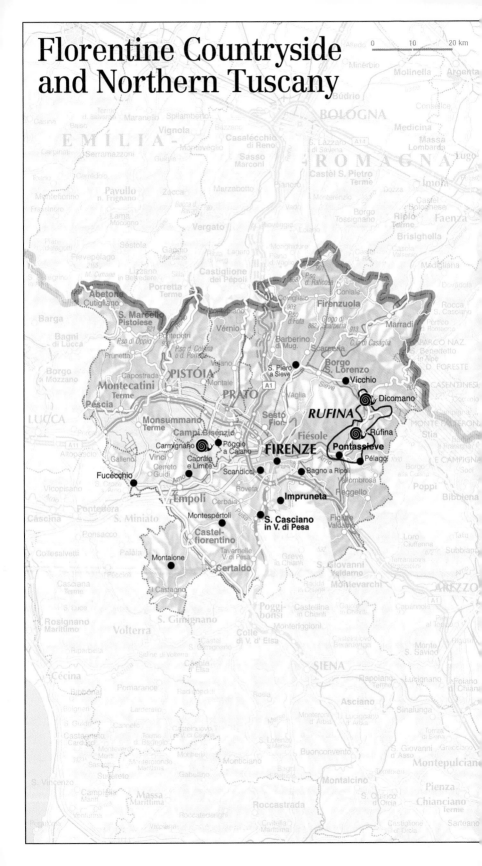

Florentine Countryside
and Northern Tuscany

Fattoria di Bacchereto ⓢ⤳ Terre a Mano

Via Fontemorana, 179
tel. 055 8717191
terreamano@gmail.com

Tenuta di Capezzana

Via Capezzana, 100
tel. 055 8706005
www.capezzana.it
capezzana@capezzana.it

---

20 ac - 23,000 bt

❝ Fattoria di Bacchereto is a fascinating place both for the type of viticulture is practiced there and for the way in which agricultural labor is experienced in toto, with all its fascination and inevitable fatigue ❞

PEOPLE - Rossella Bencini Tesi has preserved the beauty of the place she has inherited, protecting it from the menace of urbanization and adopting a biodynamic approach to exalt its fruits.

VINEYARDS - The company applies biodynamics attentively and precisely. "With the increasingly bizarre climate trends we are seeing, biodynamics is a great help for the equilibrium of the vines and the health of the soil," explains enologist Marco Vannucci. Green manure is used specifically to meet the needs of each plot, 500 and 501 field spray preparations are employed, and chemical treatments are reduced to a bare minimum.

WINES - We tasted wines from the latest harvests, separated by vineyard, from mid-sized casks. Rossella was at Raw Vienna, the artisan wine fair. "One day we'd like to isolate a cru wine. Sometimes it's a pity to lose the incredible nuances the different parcels are capable of offering." Not a bad idea, I thought as I tasted a magnificent Sangiovese from the Vignone parcel. **Carmignano Terre a Mano 2011** (● sangiovese, cabernet sauvignon, canaiolo; 10,000 bt) is the fruit of an assemblage of grapes from the best vineyards. Its edgy attack is tinged by dark, almost corpulent tones. The body is still stiff, enervated by splendid acidity. A wine for the future.

slow wine **SASSOCARLO 2012** (○ trebbiano, malvasia; 3,000 bt) Hints of ripe apricot and minty tones on the nose and a well-developed, laid-back palate with a tanginess that defines the body and makes for memorable drinkability. A splendid interpretation of Tuscan white grape varieties.

215 ac - 500,000 bt   `10% discount`

PEOPLE - The Contini Bonaccorsis, counts of Mantuan origin, have owned the Tenuta di Capezzana estate, a jewel of art and culture set in the Carmignano hills, for generations. We were welcomed by Vittorio Contini Bonaccorsi, "born and bred" in the vineyards and a dispenser of pearls of wisdom about his vineyards and the change of thinking that has led him in recent years to switch from conventional viticulture to organics.

VINEYARDS - The cellar's 250 acres or so of vineyard are scattered over the whole Carmignano area and afford the traveler spectacular views. New plantings alternate with old ones and native grape varieties live side by side with high-ranking international ones. The meticulously kept vine rows are checked more than once a week, to avoid unexpected, harmful "intrusions." The grassed vineyards are a sight for sore eyes and produce fresh grapes, well sheltered from the sun's rays.

WINES - **Carmignano Trefiano Ris. 2009** (● 18,500 bt) has a sexy bouquet and explodes in the mouth with aromatic "special effects." The delicate **Ghiaie della Furba 2009** (● cabernet, merlot, syrah; 15,000 bt), is pleasing on nose and palate, never over-the-top. **Carmignano Villa di Capezzana 2010** (● 60,000 bt) is the wine that made the cellar famous, its nose and palate both brimming over with terroir. **Barco Reale di Carmignano 2012** (● 200,000 bt) is refreshing, lively and quaffable ... just as it should be! The **Monna Nera 2013** (● sangiovese, merlot, cabernet, syrah; 50,000 bt) is a joy to drink, too.

slow wine **VIN SANTO DI CARMIGNANO RIS.** 2007 (○ 1,000 bt) Dedicated to anyone keen to taste a traditional, complex, elegant, textbook Vin Santo. *Bellissimo!*

FERTILIZERS green manure
PLANT PROTECTION copper and sulphur, organic
WEED CONTROL mechanical
YEASTS native
GRAPES 100% estate-grown
CERTIFICATION organic

FERTILIZERS organic-mineral, green manure
PLANT PROTECTION copper and sulphur, organic
WEED CONTROL mechanical
YEASTS native
GRAPES 100% estate-grown
CERTIFICATION converting to organics

Frascole

Località Frascole, 27 A
tel. 055 8386340
www.frascole.it
frascole@frascole.it

39 ac - 50,000 bt

66 All the wines offer elegance and finesse thanks to patient parcelization in the vineyard and fermentation of small batches of grapes in the cellar. Plus organic certification and great respect for naturalness 99

PEOPLE - Enrico Lippi says that when he used to go back to Frascole in the evening in the early days, his heart used to pound with emotion. It's a declaration of the rapport Enrico and his wife Elisa Santoni have with the land where they've decided to live and produce wine. The story began with the family vineyards in the Cavaliere district, not far from Dicomano, and proceeded with the purchase of Frascole in 1992.

VINEYARDS - The 40 acres of vineyard are situated at different altitudes on very different soils, with marls and sandstones downstream and rocks at 1,600 feet. The variations have necessitated the selection of parcels that are harvested separately to allow each plot to give of its best.

WINES - In **Albis 2012** (O trebbiano; 2,000 bt) is a wine made with grapes from five-stage multiple-pass harvesting, the result of which is concentrated aromas and great harmony. **Bitornino 2012** (● sangiovese, canaiolo, colorino; 15,000 bt) is delicious and approachable, excellent for everyday drinking. **Chianti Rufina 2012** (● 30,000 bt) is symmetrical and juicy. **Limine 2009** (● merlot; 2,000 bt) is balsamic, succulent and complex. **Vin Santo del Chianti Rufina 2005** (O trebbiano, malvasia; 1,000 bt) is superlative.

> **slow wine** CHIANTI RUFINA RIS. 2011 (● 6,000 bt)
> A concentrated, potent red that combines beef with beauty admirably, a sure sign of longevity.

FERTILIZERS natural manure, green manure
PLANT PROTECTION copper and sulphur, organic
WEED CONTROL mechanical
YEASTS native
GRAPES 100% estate-grown
CERTIFICATION organic

Colognole

Via del Palagio, 15
tel. 055 8319870
www.colognole.it
info@colognole.it

67 ac - 100,000 bt `10% discount`

PEOPLE - The Spalletti family have farmed in Colognole since the 19th century. In the sharecropping period they lived in Rome and used to come here on holiday. Then came the new system and, with it, the family's passion for the local area, for the rural world and agriculture. While mother Gabriella represents continuity with the past, Cesare oversees promotion and sales, his brother Mario administration. The enologist is Andrea Giovannini and agronomist Massimo Achilli sees to all the rest.

VINEYARDS - The vineyards are situated at an altitude of 900-1,700 feet and are surrounded by woods and olive groves (of which there are almost 20 acres). The vine are planted at a density of about 2,000-2,500 per acre on clayey soil rich in *galestro* marl. The replantings, made from 1995 to 1997 produce the grapes for Sinopie. The ones planted in 1999 produce sangiovese, colorino and also a few merlot grapes. The Rogaie vineyard, planted in 2003, gives the grapes for Riserva di Sangiovese. In 2007-2009, more sangiovese and chardonnay were planted. Talk about dynamism!

WINES - Colognole's wines are characterized by elegance and longevity, not to mention normally close-knit tannins. In **Chianti Sinopie 2012** (● 22.000 bt), which reveals all the fragrance of the fruit, the entry into the mouth, the development linear and crisp. **Chianti Rufina 2011** `Everyday Wine` (● 30,000 bt) evolves with a pleasing streak of acidity and concludes with delicious tannins. **Chianti Rufina Collezione 2007** (● 4,000 bt), produced solely in vintages deemed worthy, is a wine of class with notable aging potential it has elegant aromas and velvety, fully flavor. **Chianti Rufina Ris. 2009** (● 13,000 bt) offers complex aromas, juice, structure and minerality on the palate and a lingering finish.

FERTILIZERS organic-mineral, compost, green manure
PLANT PROTECTION chemical, copper and sulphur, organic
WEED CONTROL mechanical
YEASTS selected
GRAPES 100% estate-grown
CERTIFICATION none

RUFINA (FI)

Fattoria Selvapiana

Località Selvapiana, 43
tel. 055 8369848
www.selvapiana.it
selvapiana@tin.it

RUFINA (FI)

Podere Il Balzo

Via del Poggiolo, 12
tel. 055 8397556
podereilbalzo@alice.it

---

148 ac - 240,000 bt   `10% discount`

66 The concepts of custodianship,
conservation and protection are very much
in evidence among the Chianti hills of
Selvapiana. Anyone lucky enough to pass
through this magic landscape will understand
why 99

PEOPLE - The winery is a symbol and an
institution in the area and Federico Giuntini
runs it conscientiously with vision, respect
and gratitude.

VINEYARDS - The soils at Selvapiana are
generally arid and pebbly with some clay
and a certain amount of *galestro* and *alberese* marl. The vine rows are cover-
cropped and enriched by the sowing of different plant varieties. At Rufina the climate is
quite cool and the altitude of the vines, from
650 to 980 feet, ensures good air circulation
and precious night-day temperature swings.

WINES - The wines' extraordinary aging potential is the result of painstaking, respectful work in a generous, highly promising terroir. The Sangioveses of Selvapiana, especially those from very old vintages,
are not only great wines but also represent
a precious historic memory. The earthy
**Chianti Rufina Vigneto Bucerchiale Ris.
2011** (● 40,000 bt) is a nuanced, beautifully symmetrical wine with a balsamic bouquet and juicy palate. Very enjoyable too is
Chianti Rufina 2012 `Everyday Wine` (● 120,000
bt), which has notes of violet and cherry, a
harmonious palate with plenty of grip and
stylishly integrated tannins, and a silky, lingering finish. **Vin Santo del Chianti Rufina
2006** (○ trebbiano, malvasia; 6,000 bt)
opens with notes of dates and dried fruit,
which lead into a sweet palate with bracing,
body-building acidity.

16 ac - 7,000 bt

PEOPLE - *Balzo* is a word that refers to
the boundary of a property. Paolo Ponticelli,
farmer, cellarman, and sales assistant, runs
the cellar with the help of his mother and
sister. He inherited it from his father, also
a farmer, as was his grandfather, an estate
manager at Poggiolo. The first Chianti Rufina saw the light in 2006 with the encour-
agement of Federico Giuntini and the consultancy of Franco Bernabei. In 1990 Paolo
began to modernize first the vineyards, then
the cellar, completing the project in 2009.

VINEYARDS - The oldest vineyards were
planted in the 1970s and are situated near
the wine cellar. Here experimental canaiolo,
malvasia nera, malvasia bianca, and trebbiano clones grow on clayey-marly soils. The
younger parcels are higher up, at an altitude
of more than 1,300 feet, where the soils are
composed of clay and limestone and the air
circulation is good. Here the sangiovese can
express itself to the full and acquire acidity
and brightness. This year the cellar bought
new terrains where it intends to grow sangiovese and malvasia nera.

WINES - The company bottled its first
wines in 2006. It has two cellars: one in the
cool basement under the farmhouse with
cement vats and barriques for aging the
wines, the other on the ground floor with
steel fermentation vats and a small store-
room. Chianti Rufina Podere Il Balzo 2011
`Everyday Wine` (● 3,500 bt), bright ruby red
in color, has a bouquet of violets and black
berries, and a tangy palate with a streak
of acidity that doesn't quite manage to ab-
sorb all the tannins. Making its debut this
year, the elegant, well-balanced **Chianti
Rufina Podere Il Balzo Ris. 2011** (● 3,500
bt) has a faintly fruity nose with a nicely
chewy palate characterized by full flavor and
understated tannins.

FERTILIZERS organic-mineral, natural manure,
green manure
PLANT PROTECTION copper and sulphur
WEED CONTROL mechanical
YEASTS selected
GRAPES 100% estate-grown
CERTIFICATION converting to organics

FERTILIZERS organic-mineral, green manure
PLANT PROTECTION copper and sulphur
WEED CONTROL mechanical
YEASTS native
GRAPES 100% estate-grown
CERTIFICATION none

Chianti Classico

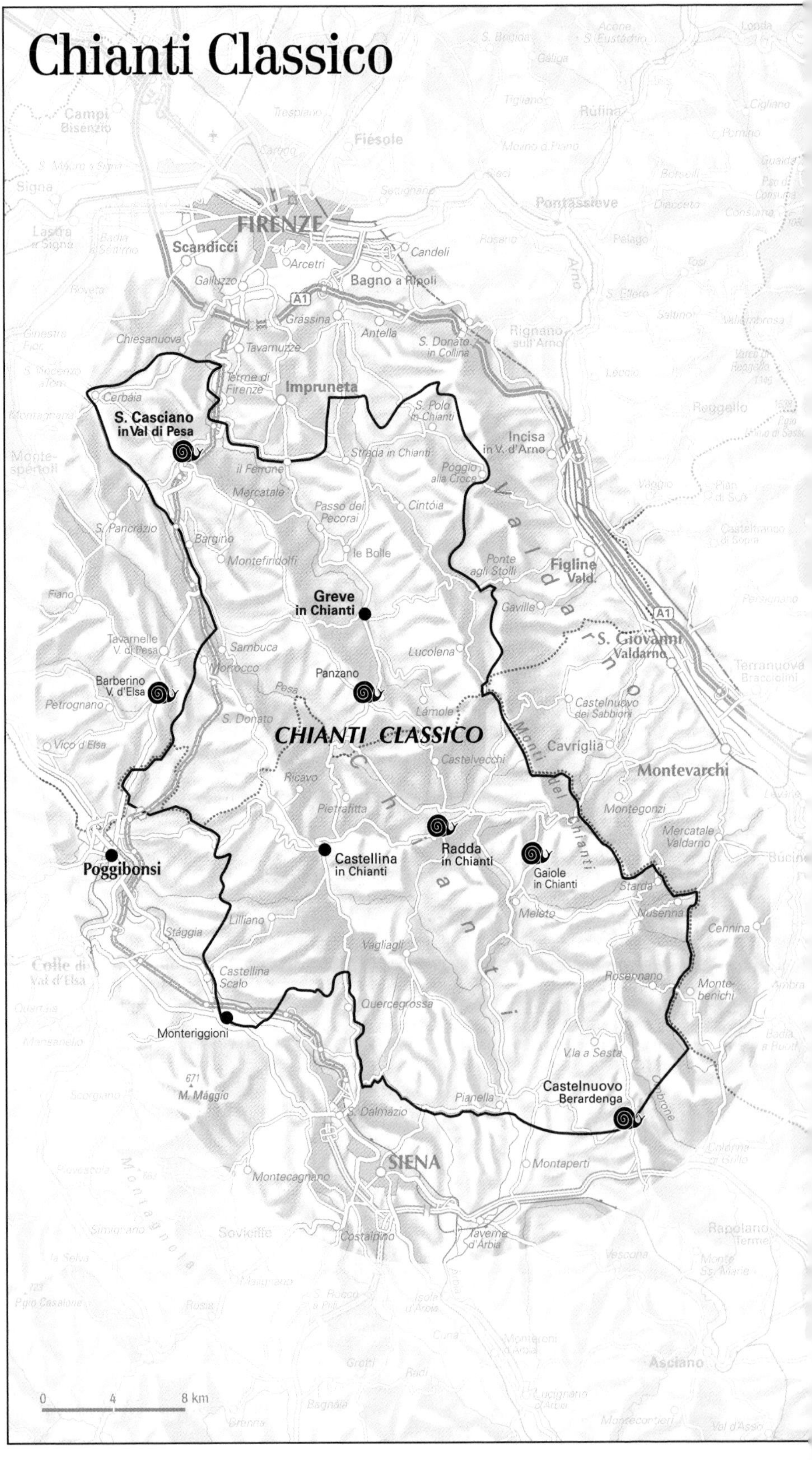

BARBERINO VAL D'ELSA (FI)

Isole e Olena

Località Isole, 1
tel. 055 8072763
office@isoleolena.it

CASTELNUOVO BERARDENGA (SI)

Fattoria di Fèlsina

Via del Chianti, 101
tel. 0577 355117
www.felsina.it
info@felsina.it

---

111 ac - 200,000 bt

66 The production standards of Isole e Olena are very high both in the sense of the place expressed by wines made with traditional grapes and in the stylistic coherence of those made with 'historic' international varieties 99

PEOPLE - The splendid country villages of Isole and Olena are part of the property bought by the De Marchi in 1956, when the sharecropping system still existed. Paolo De Marchi, Piedmontese by birth, still tells the story of the difficult transition which ultimately led to the rebirth of winegrowing in the Chianti area.

VINEYARDS - Geologically speaking, the zone is at the confluence of soils with different characteristics, which Paolo handles with great sensitivity. The company's many vineyards are divided by woodland at an altitude of about 1,300 feet and create a landscape of rare and breathtaking beauty with a proven vocation for winegrowing.

WINES - The superlative **Cabernet Sauvignon 2010** (● 6,000 bt) is rich and potent but also stylish and elegant with very Chianti-style raciness and brightness. The warm growing years is detectable in **Cepparello 2011** (● sangiovese; 30,000 bt), which is enfolding, concentrated and leisurely, but also full of depth. **Syrah 2008** (● 5,000 bt) is somber and moody. **Vin Santo del Chianti Cl. 2005** (○ trebbiano, malvasia; 7,000 bt) is rich and complex and beautifully balanced.

slow wine CHIANTI CL. **2012** (● 125,000 bt) A delicious red, stupendously land-rooted, sharp, nervy and linear with luscious crisp fruit

185 ac - 500,000 bt | **10% discount**

66 History, love of nature, local culture, respect for the grape – Fèlsina is all this and more 99

PEOPLE - The story of Fèlsina began in the mid 1960s, when, showing vision and insight, Domenico Poggiali decided to invest in the land. The winery was run for years by Domenico's son-in-law Giuseppe Mazzocolin, who raised the profile of he place and made it an institution for the whole area. Today the reins have been taken over by Domenico's grandchildren Caterina Mazzocolin and Giovanni Poggiali.

VINEYARDS - Since 2000 not a single chemical molecule has been used at Fèlsina and all the farming is now organic. The property is split into five estates. It is situated in the southern part of the denomination (Castelnuovo Berardenga), a real borderland where Chianti stone runs into the lush Siena countryside.

WINES - The immediately impressive **Fontalloro 2011** (● sangiovese; 43,000 bt) is well balanced and elegant with hints of ripe red berries and stylishly integrated tannins backed up by enjoyably leisurely drinkability. **Chianti Cl. Gran Selezione 2009** (● 3,000 bt) has notes of toast and toffee and is harmonious and full of character. The well-crafted **Chianti Cl. Rancia Ris. 2011** (● 47,000 bt) has balsamic notes, sweet nuances of wood and good flesh. **Chianti Cl. 2012** (● 240,000 bt) has caressing fruit and a laid-back, warm, wonderfully juicy palate. Soft and deep, **Maestro Raro 2011** (● cabernet sauvignon; 6,000 bt) is varietal but not to be taken for granted. **Vin Santo del Chianti Cl. 2005** (○ trebbiano, malvasia; 8,000 bt) has well-calibrated sweetness and a long, progressive finish.

FERTILIZERS organic-mineral, natural manure, compost
PLANT PROTECTION copper and sulphur
WEED CONTROL mechanical
YEASTS selected
GRAPES 100% estate-grown
CERTIFICATION none

FERTILIZERS biodynamic preparations, green manure
PLANT PROTECTION copper and sulphur
WEED CONTROL mechanical
YEASTS selected
GRAPES 100% estate-grown
CERTIFICATION converting to organics

Badia a Coltibuono

Località Badia a Coltibuono
tel. 0577 746110
www.coltibuono.com
info@coltibuono.com

Riecine

Località Riecine
tel. 0577 749098
www.riecine.it
info@riecine.com

---

130 ac - 250,000 bt

37 ac - 60,000 bt

---

66 The wines are disarmingly authentic, a true expression of the finest Chianti sangiovese with a style as natural as can be 99

66 In the cellar, now being renovated to make it more functional, the relatively non-invasive natural productive approach is written to an enological grammar of great precision and cleanness 99

PEOPLE - At Coltibuono you breathe in the history of agriculture in this corner of Chianti Classico. The result today of farming and change is a huge property of almost 2,000 acres with manifold complementary and synergic activities. Here, besides wine, they produce excellent extra virgin olive oil and there are also a restaurant and accommodation. The brains behind the whole enterprise are sister and brother Emanuela and Roberto Stucchi.

PEOPLE - Sean O' Callaghan was recently joined by a group of foreign investors in the management of the company, but this has in no way affected the virtuous process that has taken Riecine to the top of the Chianti Classico tree. A lucid and talented *condottiero*, Sean is helped in the cellar by Ilda Rocci and receives precious advice from consultant agronomist Ruggero Mazzilli.

VINEYARDS - This, one of the first of the larger Tuscan wineries to believe in organic farming, is now testing the use of natural plant protection products. As Roberto said when we were visiting the vineyards together, "In the long run even copper is a form of soil pollution." The vineyards are in the Monti district at an altitude of about 1,400 feet and encircle the modern wine cellar.

VINEYARDS - The vineyards, with their different soil compositions are carefully and sustainably farmed: Casina, where there is heavy sand; Vertine, where it is calacerous and pebbly; and Riecine, where it contains clay and *galestro* marl. The latter encircles the wine cellar and is home to the oldest vines, planted in 1968. Sean valorizes the different soil characteristics with separate fermentations and maturing processes for each single vineyard.

WINES - Chianti Cl. Cultus Boni 2010 (● 8,000 bt) adds to the classic grape variety small percentages of minor ones (foglia tonda, malvasia and ciliegiolo) to conjure up a truly unique *goût de terroir*. Unfussy, authentic and real, **Chianti Cl. 2012** (● 160,000 bt) has mineral, flinty notes on the nose with grip and almost salty sappiness on the palate. Finally, another classic, **Vin Santo del Chianti Cl. 2007** (○ trebbiano, malvasia; 8,000 bt) has almonds and burnt cream on the nose and explodes into candied peel and dried fruit in the mouth.

WINES - We were enchanted by the new wine that has taken the place of the Chianti Classico Riserva, no longer produced: **Riecine 2010** Great Wine (● 5,000 bt) is one of the best expressions of Riecine in Chianti. The aromatic profile is dazzlingly spacious and citrusy, the palate is elegant, juicy and piquant, deep and flawless. **Chianti Cl. 2011** (● 40,000 bt) has well-judged warmth, exuberant fruit and gorgeous floweriness with a deliciously long finish. Dark, potent and spicy, **La Gioia 2009** (● sangiovese; 9,000 bt) has a fuller body but is still waiting to develop. The rosé **For Jasper 2013** (◉ sangiovese; 6,000 bt) is saline, earthy and sharpish.

> slow wine **CHIANTI CL. RIS. 2010** (● 28,000 bt) A wine incontrovertibly worthy of its fame. Austere with earthy notes, it has a very, linear palate with bracing rich, juicy tannins.

FERTILIZERS compost, green manure
PLANT PROTECTION copper and sulphur
WEED CONTROL mechanical
YEASTS native
GRAPES 100% estate-grown
CERTIFICATION organic

FERTILIZERS compost, biodynamic preparations, green manure
PLANT PROTECTION copper and sulphur, organic
WEED CONTROL mechanical
YEASTS native
GRAPES 10% bought in
CERTIFICATION organic

Rocca di Castagnoli 🍷

Località Castagnoli
tel. 0577 731004
www.roccadicastagnoli.com
info@roccadicastagnoli.com

San Giusto a Rentennano 🍷

Località San Giusto a Rentennano
tel. 0577 747121
www.fattoriasangiusto.it
info@fattoriasangiusto.it

---

544 ac - 780,000 bt `10% discount`

PEOPLE - It's been a year of change for this winery, owned by Calogero Calì, a lawyer, who has just sold one of his Chianti Classico properties, Castello di San Sano, to the Antinori family. Not that he's stepping down in any way. On the contrary, as group manager Rolando Bertacchini told us, the reorganization is the starting point for a new phase in the winery's history. This year in fact it will officially convert to organics.

VINEYARDS - It was Rolando who took us to see the principal vineyards in an unspoiled natural environment near the pretty village of Castagnoli. Not only the vineyards are well kept but also the surrounding woodland, with attention to very single detail. The places that stick in the memory are Stielle, a magnificent bush-trained vineyard resting on *galestro* marl, and the parcels at Poggio a' Frati, which produce the grapes for the Riserva.

WINES - The quality of the wines is so dependable and consistent that it's hard to establish to make a list of preferences. He one that excited us most was **Chianti Cl. Capraia Ris. 2011** `Great Wine` (● 30,000 bt), made with grapes from the Castellina in Chianti property, wine with a blossomy bouquet and deftly complex mouthfeel. Splendid too is **Chianti Cl. Stielle Gran Selezione 2010** (● 12,000 bt), fermented with some of the grape stalks, which releases metallic notes followed by beautifully close-knit texture on the palate. **Chianti Cl. Poggio a' Frati Ris. 2011** (● 30,000 bt) has acid backbone, volume and enfolding tannic texture. Blossomy, fresh-tasting **Chianti Cl. 2012** (● 300,000 bt) has simple, but well-defined flavor.

77 ac - 80,000 bt

PEOPLE - A historic Tuscan cellar managed by the Martini di Cigala family with all the focus, conscientiousness and consistency typical of anyone, like them, who feels real passion for their work and for their local area. Luca oversees the farm work and his brother Francesco the winemaking proper, while their sister Elisabetta is in charge of administration. Agronomist Ruggero Mazzilli and enologist Attilio Pagli are the external consultants.

VINEYARDS - The vineyards, about 70 acres in all, are in the southernmost strip of the Chianti Classico zone. They are situated on three different hillsides with very different soils: rich in *galestro* marl and *alberese* rock towards the Arbia; tufa with sand and pebbles in the central part; clay and sand northwards. The vineyards are tended to constantly and interventions are minimal and timely to preserve the peculiarities of the grapes and the soil.

WINES - The wines produced are a faithful reflection of the terroir. They have character and personality without falling short in terms of finesse and naturalness. As always, **Percarlo 2010** (● sangiovese; 16,000 bt) impresses for the concentration and richness of its aromas, ripe fruit and floral notes: cocoa and sweet spiciness attest to 22 months' aging in barriques (20% of which new), while the palate is deep, long and bulky with a lovely floral finish – a wine with great aging potential. **Chianti Cl. 2012** (● 40,000 bt) is scent-drenched with ebullient fruit, fresh flavor and imposing tannins. **Chianti Cl. Le Baroncole Ris. 2011** (● 11,000 bt) offers the nose ripe fruit, spice and minerality, the palate length, tautness and warmth with robust tannins. **La Ricolma 2011** (● merlot; 4,000 bt) is a deep, potent wine.

FERTILIZERS organic-mineral, manure pellets	**FERTILIZERS** natural manure, compost
PLANT PROTECTION copper and sulphur	**PLANT PROTECTION** copper and sulphur, organic
WEED CONTROL mechanical	**WEED CONTROL** mechanical
YEASTS native	**YEASTS** native
GRAPES 100% estate-grown	**GRAPES** 100% estate-grown
CERTIFICATION converting to organics	**CERTIFICATION** organic

I Fabbri €

Località Lamole
Via Casole, 52
tel. 055 2345719
www.agricolaifabbri.it
info@agricolaifabbri.it

Querciabella

Via di Barbiano, 17
tel. 055 85927777
www.querciabella.com
info@querciabella.com

25 ac - 35,000 bt **10% discount**

PEOPLE - Susanna Grassi's whole life is at Lamole. This is where everything started and she's here now to carry on the good work. In love with the land of her birth, about 15 years ago she came back here and settled down with her family at nearby Casole. She has since made the area her own. Her team is made up of ... herself (you guessed!) plus three able farmers who know the area like the back of their hands.

VINEYARDS - The view from the highest vineyards is majestic and stretches as far as the sea. Most of the plantings are spurred cordon-trained and it's nice to see that the vine rows are grassed. The sangiovese grape prevails but the merlot vineyard is also beautiful in its own right. Production is never intensive and yields are kept low to ensure top-quality grapes. The cellar is inside the main farmhouse among the vineyards and, albeit small, is perfect and fully equipped.

WINES - Chianti Cl. Lamole 2012 (● 12,000 bt) has a generous nose of fruit and an agreeably earthy flavor. The land-rooted **Chianti Cl. Terre di Lamole 2011** (● 6,000 bt) is thirst-quenching with faint notes of coffee. In the unmistakable **Chianti Cl. I Fabbri Ris. 2011** (● 5,000 bt) the fruit blends nicely with spicy notes before blood-rich meat begins to linger on the finish. The commendable **Chianti Cl. I Fabbri Gran Selezione 2011** (● sangiovese; 2,300 bt), produced only in the best vintages, has complexity and impact. **Duedonne 2011** (● sangiovese, schioppettino; 600 bt) is the outcome of an interesting new project, half Tuscany and half Friuli: it's worth a try. Refreshing and powerful, **Doccio 2011** (● merlot; 2,000 bt) adds an international touch.

222 ac - 220,000 bt **10% discount**

PEOPLE - Giuseppe Castiglioni started cultivating five acres of vineyard as a hobby in 1974. But then his passion grew so much that two years later the area had increased to about 200. Giuseppe went organic ten years ago and today his son and successor Sebastiano is even planning vegetarian biodynamics. In fact, his desire to improve is so great that there's never a dull moment for enologists Guido De Santi and Manfred Ing, assisted by agronomist Dales D'Alessandro.

VINEYARDS - The vineyards are scattered round the most beautiful, most important places in Chianti – Greve, Gaiole and Radda in Chianti – and now in Maremma too. All require different approaches according to their altitudes, which range from 1,000 to 2,000 feet. Thanks to all-biodynamic farming, the vegetation is lush and nature is allowed to bear its most delectable fruits.

WINES - At Querciabella they make structurally faultless wines. **Camartina 2011** (● cabernet sauvignon, sangiovese; 10,000 bt) has fruity notes of cherry and a direct, powerful attack on the palate with evocative intensity. **Batar 2012** (○ chardonnay, pinot bianco; 13,000 bt) has hugely piquant and mineral impact with ethereal and blossomy hints. **Chianti Cl. 2012** (● 90,000 bt) offers notes of rose and cherry and a palate that has all the character and density of the sangiovese grape. A novelty this year is **Chianti Cl. Ris. 2011** (● 20,000 bt), balsamic with distinct notes of red berries on the nose, and an elegant palate. **Turpino 2011** (● syrah, cabernet franc, merlot; 30,000 bt) is fresh and spicy with suggestions of rose and pepper. **Mongrana 2012** (● sangiovese, merlot, cabernet sauvignon; 75,000 bt) is eminently quaffable.

FERTILIZERS green manure
PLANT PROTECTION copper and sulphur
WEED CONTROL mechanical
YEASTS native
GRAPES 100% estate-grown
CERTIFICATION organic

FERTILIZERS biodynamic preparations, green manure
PLANT PROTECTION copper and sulphur
WEED CONTROL mechanical
YEASTS native
GRAPES 100% estate-grown
CERTIFICATION biodynamic

Castello dei Rampolla

Via Case Sparse, 22
tel. 055 852001
castellodeirampolla.cast@tin.it

Fontodi

Via San Leolino, 89
tel. 055 852005
www.fontodi.com
fontodi@fontodi.com

---

79 ac - 80,000 bt

66 For the Di Napoli family making wine has always been a matter of 'light,' non-invasive farming, in which the impact of human activities on the land is minimal, with respect for the needs of the plants, fundamental for maintaining and preserving the life of the soil 99

PEOPLE - On breathes in a different air as soon as one arrives at the winery. Tranquility, silence, a penetrating sense of peace. Maurizia Di Napoli Rampolla, owner with her brother Luca of this almost legendary estate, infects one with the same sensation.

VINEYARDS - The land on which the vineyards grow faces south and enjoys a perfect microclimate. The soils are composed of limestone with dark clay and pebbles, and altitudes vary from 900 to 1,300 feet. Albeit not as yet certified, the farm has been adopting biodynamic methods since 1994. The chief grape variety is sangiovese and there are also some French grapes planted by father Alceo Di Napoli with the intention of making great international wines – which he promptly proceeded to do.

WINES - The wines have a very strong sense of place and express a philosophy of life. **Chianti Cl. 2012** (● 22,000 bt) is a red wine of great aromatic intensity with a complex palate, stylish tannins, great structure and a fresh, sappy finish. The interesting **Cabernet 2012** (● 1,900 bt) is fermented without added sulfides in Impruneta terracotta pitchers; fresh and enjoyable, it develops well on the palate. **Sammarco 2010** Great Wine (● cabernet sauvignon, merlot, sangiovese; 6,000 bt) is balsamic and fruity on the nose, long and weighty on the palate. Very good too is **D'Alceo 2010** (● cabernet sauvignon, petit verdot; 7,000 bt), fine, elegant and very clean on the nose, full-bodied, soft and leisurely on the palate with a tangy finish.

---

205 ac - 270,000 bt

66 Far removed from the logic of the market, Fontodi has created a precise identity for itself with a new take on the self-sufficient Tuscan farm model and a multifunctionality that elevates the vineyards, the Chianti landscape and the history of the place 99

PEOPLE - Born in the 1960s, the winery has grown progressively, always seeking to respect the environment and to valorize the land. It has succeeded in the task. Admirably so.

VINEYARDS - The vineyards are situated in the natural amphitheater of Panzano's Conca d'Oro, a unique ecosystem anywhere in the world. This stunning valley has soil of calcareous origin, composed of *galestro* marl, clay and pebbles, and enjoys a microclimate conducive to the development of vines and the ripening of the grapes. Visiting the vineyards with Giovanni Manetti is an experience to relish, a true lesson in agronomy and viticulture in the field.

WINES - **Il Meriggio 2012** (○ sauvignon; 7,000 bt) is a white wine that might have been produced in Alto Adige judging by its intense aromatic attack and the bright, tangy note that permeates the palate. **Chianti Cl. Fontodi 2011** (● 170,000 bt) has a rich suite of aromas with earthy, blood-rich notes and a juicy, mineral palate. **Chianti Cl. Vigna del Sorbo Gran Selezione 2011** (● 28.000 bt), the company cru, offers a fruity nose with vegetal and spicy nuances that lead into a complex, spacious, lingering palate. The stupendous **Flaccianello della Pieve 2011** Great Wine (● 60,000 bt), is a selection of perfectly ripe grapes: it has deftly mature fruit with aromatic, spicy nuances and a palate in which raw tannins domineer the fresh, long, leisurely vegetal texture.

FERTILIZERS biodynamic preparations	
PLANT PROTECTION copper and sulphur, organic	
WEED CONTROL mechanical	
YEASTS native	
GRAPES 100% estate-grown	
CERTIFICATION none	

FERTILIZERS natural manure, compost, green manure	
PLANT PROTECTION copper and sulphur	
WEED CONTROL mechanical	
YEASTS native	
GRAPES 100% estate-grown	
CERTIFICATION organic	

Le Cinciole

Via Case Sparse, 83
tel. 055 852636
www.lecinciole.it
info@lecinciole.it

29 ac - 45,000 bt

" The project is to tell the story of the local area through hard work and a model of sustainable agriculture. In the course of time it has achieved its goals partly thanks to the professionalism and passion of the protagonists of this magnificent story "

PEOPLE - In the heart of Chianti Classico, in a beautifully lush landscape on the northwest side of Panzano, Luca Orsini and Valeria Viganò decided in 1991 to embark on their adventure.

VINEYARDS - During our visit Luca told us that the aim in the vineyard is to maintain the equilibrium of the vegetation by working in-depth, treating the soil with mulch, and fertilizing with the compost they produce with the cuttings from pruning. The soil in the vineyards near the cellar is composed of clay and shale and the sangiovese vines (bunched and loose) are Guyot- and Tuscan tear-trained.

WINES - The wines clearly reflect the cellar's philosophy and fully express the intentions of Luca, who supervises ever stage of production firsthand. Rich in floral, fruity aromas, **Rosato 2013** (☉ sangiovese; 2,500 bt) has a tangy, bright, soft palate. The simple but by no means uninteresting **Cincio Rosso 2012** (● sangiovese, cabernet, merlot; 9,000 bt) releases clear-cut, fresh fruity and floral aromas and is a joy to drink.

> **slow wine** CHIANTI CL. 2011 (● 25,000 bt) We were all highly impressed by the way this wine offers all the nuances of the terroir with perfectly ripe fruit and earthy, blood-rich aromas. On the palate it's enjoyable, spacious and bright with nicely developed vegetal tannins.

FERTILIZERS natural manure, compost, green manure
PLANT PROTECTION copper and sulphur
WEED CONTROL mechanical
YEASTS native
GRAPES 100% estate-grown
CERTIFICATION organic

Vecchie Terre di Montefili

Via San Cresci, 45
tel. 055 853739
www.vecchieterredimontefili.it
info@vecchieterredimontefili.it

29 ac - 50,000 bt

PEOPLE - Roccaldo Acuti, a great wine enthusiast, decided to buy a Chianti winery after attending a course for sommeliers. After looking at a number of farms, he came upon Montefili and fell in love with the position and, above all, the old vineyard that occupied the whole of a natural amphitheater in front of the place. Today the enterprise is run by Roccaldo's daughter Maria, who has inherited all his verve and enthusiasm, and his son-in-law Tommaso Paglione.

VINEYARDS - The vineyards rest on pebbly soils composed of *galestro* marl and *alberese* rock with traces of gray clays. The main grape grown is sangiovese, which is part spurred cordon-trained and part Guyot-trained. Over the last three years, the cellar has converted to organic farming. Another point worth mentioning is that vine rows are sowed alternately with oats and barley to keep downy mildew at bay, to create mulch, and to keep the soil fresh.

WINES - The structure of the terrains and the positions of the vineyards give the wines acidity. The well-crafted **Chianti Cl. 2011** (● 20,000 bt) has a bouquet of blossom and fruit, a juicy, spicy palate, and good drinkability. **Anfiteatro 2009** Great Wine (● 5,000 bt) is a pedigree Sangiovese with a fruity, spicy nose and a dry palate with fine tannins braced by supporting acidity. The more international **Bruno di Rocca 2009** (● cabernet sauvignon, sangiovese; 7,000 bt), has an intriguing suite of aromas with soft tannins and a warm, fruity finish. **Montefili Rosso 2011** (● cabernet, canaiolo, sangiovese; 6,000 bt) is sound and drinkable.

> **slow wine** CHIANTI CLASSICO RIS. 2010 (● 4,000 bt). A very complex wine with blossom on the nose, vegetal tannins on the concentrated palate, and a linear, lingering finish.

FERTILIZERS manure pellets, green manure
PLANT PROTECTION copper and sulphur
WEED CONTROL mechanical
YEASTS selected
GRAPES 100% estate-grown
CERTIFICATION converting to organics

Caparsa

Case sparse Caparsa, 47
tel. 0577 738174
www.caparsa.it
caparsa@caparsa.it

29 ac - 20,000 bt `10% discount`

❝ Paolo Cianferoni says that the nice thing about wine is its unpredictability, that the important thing is to have "living" wines capable of changing. For him the idea that they should always be the same is an absurdity ❞

PEOPLE - Thanks to Paolo, founder and jack of all trades (who has been devoting himself exclusively to winemaking ever since 1965) and to his organic philosophy, Caparsa has become one of the most virtuous wineries in all Chianti.

VINEYARDS - The vineyards, which are given over mainly to sangiovese, are all round the estate where Paolo lives with his numerous family. It's a pleasure to see the enthusiasm in his eyes when he speaks about how he got the winery started. Walking through the steep vineyards he shows us the various types of soil composed of *galestro* marl, clay and *alberese* rock. The drainage is optimal and almost all the vines have been replanted with the new clones of the Chianti 2000 project.

WINES - The range of wines released varies from year to year according to quality. If Paolo isn't satisfied with a wine, he simply doesn't bottle it. **Chianti Cl. Doccio a Matteo Ris 2011** (● 6,666 bt) has enfolding aromas and is dark in color; it has a strong impact on the palate and reveals not only sense of place but also great naturalness. Completing the range, which doesn't include Rosso di Caparsa, **Bianco di Caparsino 2012** (○ trebbiano, malvasia; 2,000 bt) is reminiscent of the wines of yesteryear, forthright, somewhat husky and distinctly unfussy.

slow wine CHIANTI CL. CAPARSINO RIS. 2010 (● 4,800 bt) An intensely land-rooted sangiovese with blossom on the nose and close-knit tannins and tangy grip on the palate.

FERTILIZERS manure pellets, natural manure
PLANT PROTECTION copper and sulphur
WEED CONTROL mechanical
YEASTS native
GRAPES 100% estate-grown
CERTIFICATION organic

Castello di Radda
Agricole Gussalli Beretta

Località Il Becco
tel. 0577 738992
www.castellodiradda.it
info@castellodiradda.com

79 ac - 100,000 bt

PEOPLE - Situated at the foot of the hill that climbs to Volpaia, Castello di Radda is part of a sizable number of companies owned by the Gussalli Beretta group. It has 80 acres in different places in the commune of Radda. It's directed by Stefano Peruzzi, and in vineyard and cellar it's possible to detect the Piedmontese hand of Marco Mascarello, one of the editors of Slow Food's *A Wine Atlas of the Langhe.*

VINEYARDS - The viticultural approach is serious and sustainable, and experiments with organics are being performed on about 10 acres of land. Treatments are kept down to a bare minimum and chemical weedkillers are used only on certain plots. "In my view, the grass under the vines damages the grapes," says Marco. "If I didn't weed our cordon-trained rows, there'd be too much vigor at a crucial stage in the vine's growth."

WINES - The company's property consists of the vineyards of Poggio Selvale, above the cellar, Vertine, and the parcel in the Il Corno district, not far from Volpaia. In the cellar they take the expressiveness of the grapes from each single vineyard into account. The excellent **Chianti Cl. Gran Selezione 2010** (● 3,000 bt), which ages in large oak barrels, has a blossomy, citrusy nose that preludes a palate of massive, succulent dynamism. We also loved **Chianti Cl. 2011** `Great Wine` (● 20,000 bt), made largely with grapes from the Poggio Selvale vineyard; its style is sweet and delicate with fruit to the fore plus flavorful verve. The cask-aged **Chianti Cl. Ris. 2011** (● 9,000 bt) has well-developed bulk braced by supporting acidity; its bouquet of citrus zest and flower petals glides into a highly concentrated palate.

FERTILIZERS manure pellets, natural manure, green manure
PLANT PROTECTION chemical, copper and sulphur
WEED CONTROL chemical, mechanical
YEASTS selected
GRAPES 100% estate-grown
CERTIFICATION none

Monteraponi

Località Monteraponi
tel. 0577 738208
www.monteraponi.it
mail@monteraponi.it

Montevertine

Località Montevertine
tel. 0577 738009
www.montevertine.it
info@montevertine.it

---

24 ac - 45,000 bt   `10% discount`

66 Michele Braganti runs his farm with respect for nature. Untiring and coherent, he works every day to produce wines with a sense of place. His aim is to preserve the equilibrium between land, vines and human labor 99

PEOPLE - It was his father Antonio who bought the property in 1974, but it was Michele who took a step forward in 2003 when he received organic certification. The upshot was an important place on the Chianti Classico wine scene.

VINEYARDS - The south-facing vineyards grow at various altitudes on wooded slopes round the small medieval village of Monteraponi, where the air circulation is good. The Campitello vineyard, at 1,500 feet, grows on *galestro* marl while, further up, the Baron Ugo, at 1,800 feet, grows on *alberese* rock and its vines, some of which 40 years' old, are Guyot-trained. The position affords a magnificent view over the whole property.

WINES - The cellar is simple and well organized. Interventions are minimal and manual out of respect for the work done in the vineyard. Wines are cement-fermented and mostly barrel-aged. Sangiovese grapes are used to make the two crus, different expressions of the same terroir. The beefy **Chianti Cl. Campitello Ris. 2011** (● 4.500 bt) has notes of blossom and undergrowth on the nose and a warm fragrant palate. **Chianti Cl. Baron' Ugo Ris. 2010** `Great Wine` (● 3,500 bt) has terrific lingering aromatic complexity and a broad, potent, linear palate. We enjoyed the fruity, spicy **Chianti Cl. 2012** (● 35,000 bt) for its elegance and drinkability. **Vin Santo del Chianti Cl. 2005** (○ 1,000 bt) has aromas of officinal herbs and dried fruit.

---

44 ac - 80,000 bt

66 Over the years Martino Manetti acquired a penchant and a passion for viticulture, partly thanks to the precious lessons of his father Sergio, the founder, enologist Giulio Gambelli and land agent Bruno Bini, unforgettable protagonists of one of the most important and renowned Chianti wineries 99

PEOPLE - The generational turnover at Montevertine has been a natural process and respect for tradition, from vineyard to cellar, has remained unaltered.

VINEYARDS - Most of the vineyards are in the stunning hills of Montevertine, where the farmhouse, wine cellar and historic Pergole Torte are situated. The latter, planted in 1968 is Guyot-trained, covers an area of five acres and, unusually, faces north-northeast. This "super cru" is exceptional not only for its age but also for the abundance of minerals contained in its soil. The consultant agronomist is Ruggero Mazzilli.

WINES - Martino explains that the methods used in the cellar are traditional and that interventions are limited to a bare minimum. In this way, he says, the wines are an authentic expression of the characteristics of the terrain. The highly complex **Le Pergole Torte 2011** `Great Wine` (● sangiovese; 23,000 bt) has gorgeous blossomy, fruity notes on the nose and a deep, warm, enfolding palate with close-knit but well-integrated tannins. The wonderful **Pian del Ciampolo 2012** (● sangiovese, canaiolo, colorino; 25,000 bt) is exceptionally drinkable. The consultant enologist is Paolo Salvi, a pupil of Giulio Gambelli, who Martino pays homage to in the 2011 labels.

> `slow wine` **MONTEVERTINE 2011** (● sangiovese, canaiolo, colorino; 24,000 bt) Notes of ripe fruit prelude to a palate in which the symmetry between softness and acidity is close to perfection. An enjoyably elegant wine with velvety tannins, it's a memorable version of the label.

FERTILIZERS manure pellets, green manure	**FERTILIZERS** natural manure, compost
PLANT PROTECTION copper and sulphur, organic	**PLANT PROTECTION** copper and sulphur
WEED CONTROL mechanical	**WEED CONTROL** mechanical
YEASTS native	**YEASTS** native
GRAPES 100% estate-grown	**GRAPES** 100% estate-grown
CERTIFICATION organic	**CERTIFICATION** none

RADDA IN CHIANTI (SI)

Val delle Corti

Località La Croce
Case Sparse Val delle Corti, 144
tel. 0577 738215
www.valdellecorti.it
info@valdellecorti.it

17 ac - 28,000 bt | 10% discount

❝ The wines of Val delle Corti are beautifully crafted and land-rooted; they express at once cleanness, precision and technical coherence. Delightful and alluring, delicious and light, they go wonderfully well with food ❞

PEOPLE - Roberto Bianchi is a lucid, tenacious winemaker. The old Val delle Corti estate was purchased by his father in the 1970s. Since his death in 1999, Roberto has managed it firsthand and, by virtue of his enthusiasm and passion, it is now one of the purest, most representative expressions of Radda, a great winegrowing terroir dear to lovers of true, essential Chianti Classico.

VINEYARDS - The vineyards are mostly east-facing and mixed with woodland. They stand at an altitude of 1,600 feet in a stunning natural setting on loose soils rich in *galestro* marl. They are farmed naturally with total respect for the environment and the biodiversity of the place. The oldest was planted 40 years ago and produces the *riserva*. It is still trained with the old Tuscan systems, whereas the more recent plantings are Guyot- and spurred cordon-trained.

WINES - The warmth and maturity of the vintage are commendably handled in the two DOCG wines submitted for tasting. The long, laid-back **Chianti Cl. 2011** (● 15,000 bt) has typically Chianti floweriness, fleshy fruit and soil (lots of it!). **Rosato 2013** (⊙ sangiovese; 4,000 bt) has character and bright tanginess. **Straniero 2012** (● merlot, sangiovese; 4,000 bt) is simple with well-gauged fruit.

slow wine CHIANTI CL. RIS. **2011** (● 7,000 bt) An earthy, deep wine, beautifully poised between enfolding ripe fruit and punchy acid grip.

FERTILIZERS natural manure, compost, biodynamic preparations
PLANT PROTECTION copper and sulphur, organic
WEED CONTROL mechanical
YEASTS native
GRAPES 25% bought in
CERTIFICATION organic

SAN CASCIANO IN VAL DI PESA (FI)

Corzano e Paterno

Frazione San Pancrazio
Via San Vito di Sopra, 9
tel. 055 8248179
www.corzanoepaterno.it
info@corzanoepaterno.it

44 ac - 75,000 bt

❝ The inscription on the wall in the new cellar, 'Drinking wine isn't bad for you, it's drinking bad wine that isn't good for you,' attests that wine quality is the winery's prime objective, one it achieves with impeccable sustainable agriculture ❞

PEOPLE - Corzano e Paterno is a gem of a winery, in which the choral work of the family is shouldered passionately but also shared out logically. Since 2004 it's been Arianna Gelpke, the house enologist, who's had the last word before bottling. Her brother Tillo is in charge of the livestock and dairy farming, while her cousin and head of the family Aljoscha Goldshmidt oversees work in the vineyards and sales.

VINEYARDS - Despite rain in the days leading up to our visit, Aljoscha was nevertheless able to take us round the vineyards anyway, because cropping, in part natural and in part deliberate, had dried up the surface water. "Important for our wines," says Aljoscha, "is not only the soil, composed of polished stones known as *pilloli*, but also the favorable southwest position of the vineyards. And we also use different forms of training: from Guyot for the whites, to bush and high trellis for the reds."

WINES - Chianti Terre di Corzano 2012 **Everyday Wine** (● 22,000 bt) is fruity on the nose, and juicy with mellow tannins on the palate and a punchy finish – a textbook interpretation of the denomination. **Il Corzano 2011** (● sangiovese, cabernet, merlot; 5,500 bt) lives up to its reputation: albeit slightly reticent on the nose, it follows through with a slow tempo into a concentrated palate of great brightness and flavor. **Chianti I Tre Borri 2011** (● 5,000 bt) performs well again too with its blossomy, fruity bouquet, nicely acid palate and long finish. **Corzanello Rosato 2013** (⊙ sangiovese; 5,000 bt) and **Corzanello Bianco 2013** (○ chardonnay, sémillon, petit manseng; 25,000 bt) are both wonderful summer drinks.

FERTILIZERS natural manure
PLANT PROTECTION copper and sulphur
WEED CONTROL mechanical
YEASTS selected
GRAPES 100% estate-grown
CERTIFICATION converting to organics

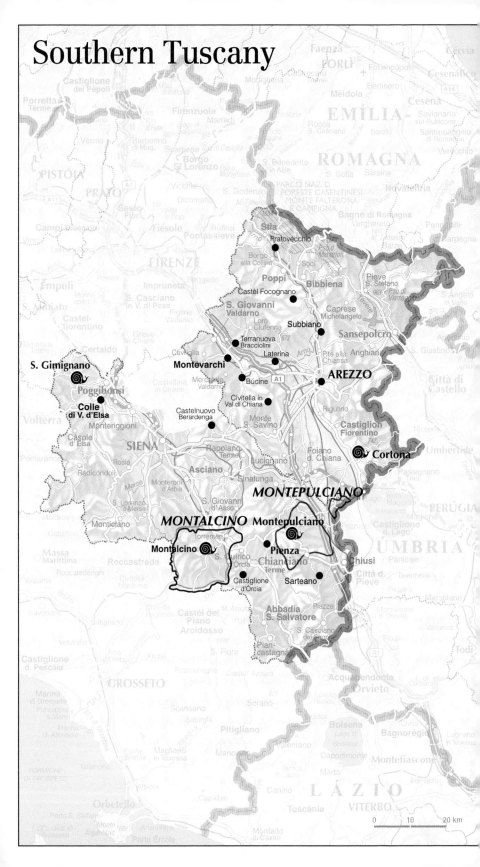

Southern Tuscany

Petrolo 🍷

Frazione Mercatale Valdarno
Località Petrolo, 30
tel. 055 9911322
www.petrolo.it
petrolo@petrolo.it

66 ac - 70,000 bt

PEOPLE - People have been farming and growing vines on this land since Etruscan and Roman times. The estate was bought by the grandfather of the present owner, Luca Sanjust, in 1947. It's divided in two by the old Via Cassia Vetus and was likely an inn and coach house. The number of acres of vineyard and olive groves have remained the same as that recorded in 18th-century documents.

VINEYARDS - It was in the winery's vineyards, which tumble down from the high Chianti hills towards the Valdarno on soils of *galestro* marl, pure or mixed with clay, that Giulio Gambelli had the notion of planting the merlot grapes that now go into Galatrona. In 2001 a small cabernet sauvignon vineyard was planted under walls of the tower of Galatrona. This grape, like all Petrolo's, is grown organically and the consequent absence of non-invasive techniques help balance the soil.

WINES - Extreme care in the vineyard and the very natural vinification techniques applied by Carlo Nesterini and Stefano Guidi give Petrolo's wines an elegant personal feel. **Valdarno di Sopra Boggina 2012** Great Wine (● sangiovese; 6,000 bt) has weight and elegance; tangy and flavorful, it's a red of rare finesse, unique even. **Valdarno di Sopra Bogginanfora 2012** (● sangiovese; 800 bt) is well-balanced and enjoyable to drink. **Galatrona 2011** (● merlot; 15,000 bt) captures the grape variety to perfection: deep and spacious on both nose and palate, its luscious fruit is all-pervading. Debut wine **Campolusso 2011** (● cabernet sauvignon; 800 bt) is packed with personality, while **Torrione 2012** (● sangiovese, merlot, cabernet sauvignon; 45,000 bt) is very stylish. The sangiovese monovarietal **Valdarno di Sopra Inarno 2013** (● 60,000 bt) is very approachable indeed.

FERTILIZERS none
PLANT PROTECTION copper and sulphur
WEED CONTROL mechanical
YEASTS native
GRAPES 100% estate-grown
CERTIFICATION converting to organics

Podere Il Carnasciale 🍷

Località Mercatale Valdarno
tel. 0559 911142
bettinarogosky@caberlot.eu

12 ac - 9,000 bt

PEOPLE - The cellar came into being after the big freeze of 1985 on land that had previously been given over to olive growing. The idea of planting the first vineyard of caberlot, a spontaneous cross between merlot and cabernet franc, came about in a meeting between Wolf Rogosky and the agronomist Remigio Bordini, who still have a few plants of this unique grape. Today this brilliant notion is being carried forward with unfailing passion by Wolf's widow Bettina and his son Moritz.

VINEYARDS - We were accompanied on our tour of the historic densely planted, bush-trained vineyard by enologists Peter Shilling and Marco Maffei. It's part of a total of 12 acres of vineyard, if which about eight are productive. The area is stunningly beautiful and the vineyard offers a stunning panoramic view as far as the medieval tower of Galatrona. The *galestro* marl soil contains a large amount of iron and drains very well. The vineyard stands at an altitude of 1,400 feet meters and is farmed manually and non-invasively with great respect for the environment.

WINES - Caberlot production begins in the vineyard with the selective manual harvesting of only perfectly ripe grapes. These are refrigerated immediately to a temperature of 50-53 °F, then transferred to 10-15 quintal vats to ferment. The winery's philosophy may be evinced from the fact that it is gradually converting to biodynamics but without applying for certifications. As Peter says, "Viticulture is a generational contract implemented by leaving soils active, productive and healthy." **Caberlot 2011** Great Wine (● 3,600 magnum) is produced only in magnums and is packed with personality. Deep and potent on the nose with forest fruits and sweet spices against a balsamic, slightly vegetal background, it conflates complexity and drinkability on the juicy, well-rounded palate, perfectly poised between fruit and toasty, spicy notes with a very leisurely, elegant finish.

FERTILIZERS organic-mineral, biodynamic preparations, green manure
PLANT PROTECTION copper and sulphur
WEED CONTROL mechanical
YEASTS native
GRAPES 100% estate-grown
CERTIFICATION none

Stefano Amerighi

Poggiobello di Farneta
tel. 0575 648340
www.stefanoamerighi.it
info@stefanoamerighi.it

21 ac - 23,500 bt · **10% discount**

66 Biodynamics is a philosophy of life for Stefano Amerighi, who adopts it in everything he does and makes with admirable passion 99

PEOPLE - In his constant quest for quality with natural, sustainable practices, Stefano counts on the help of Federico Staderini. Thanks to the recent addition of a livestock unit, his can now be defined as a closed-loop farm, self-sufficient for its every need.

VINEYARDS - The vines are a situated in splendid positions in the rolling hills of Poggiobello di Farneta, west of Cortona, and rest on prevalently clayey soil. Vine density, about 1,500 per acre, is high, and interventions are made using biodynamic methods, following the stars and natural cycles. The principal grape variety is syrah, now typical of the zone and the vines are Guyot-, canopy- and cordon-trained.

WINES - The cellar has a low impact on the environment and was built according to criteria of sustainability. Interventions on the grapes are kept to a bare minimum without correctives or artifices. **Cortona Syrah 2011** (● 22,000 bt) confirms our impressions of previous vintages. It has a lingering spicy, mineral bouquet, a long, taut palate, and polished tannins set off by acid sparkle that makes for enjoyability in the glass.

> **slow wine** **CORTONA SYRAH APICE 2010** (● 1,500 bt) As the name makes clear, this wine is made with grapes from the top of the vineyards. We were impressed by its complexity on the nose, with typical notes of spice and balsam, followed up by minerals and raw meat. The palate is austere and linear, and develops in breadth and in length with velvety tannic structure.

FERTILIZERS biodynamic preparations, green manure
PLANT PROTECTION copper and sulphur, organic
WEED CONTROL mechanical
YEASTS native
GRAPES 100% estate-grown
CERTIFICATION biodynamic, organic

Baricci

Località Colombaio di Montosoli, 13
tel. 0577 848109
baricci1955@libero.it

12 ac - 30,000 bt

66 The cellar is the domain of Federico Buffi, who explains how he only meddles with ripe grapes when necessary, always bearing in mind the lessons he learned from his grandfather Nello. His wines have very traditional stylization and freshness on the palate 99

PEOPLE - Our annual visit to Baricci revealed to us the unusual role, humble but granitic, of Nello's daughter Graziella, who the family see as the real "motor" of the winery today. Graziella's husband Pietro and their sons Federico and Francesco define themselves as the "body." Together they form a tried and tested team, but they still listen to Nello's words of advice on his rare visits to the vineyard and the cellar.

VINEYARDS - Francesco points out that there are six vineyards: "The one at the house, the one over the wall, the one at the crossroads, the new one, the little one and the one down the road," is what he calls them. They are all inside the Brunello zone at an altitude of 900 feet, facing south-south-east and resting on a mixture of *galestro* marl, sands, shale, quartz and fossil detritus in an ideal microclimate for Brunello grapes.

WINES - **Brunello di Montalcino 2009** (● 13,600 bt) has all its customary pragmatic goodness. The aromas are complex with well-developed, spicy and earthy notes, while the palate is soft and pleasurable. It caresses the mouth and develops through delicious, smooth tannins into a leisurely finish with encores of spice.

> **slow wine** **ROSSO DI MONTALCINO 2012** (● 18,000 bt) A masterpiece of enjoyableness in which the sangiovese unleashes all its varietal elegance. The attack on the palate is caressingly bright, then its natural energy takes the upper hand and rolls into a long tangy finish. A wine worth a round of applause.

FERTILIZERS manure pellets
PLANT PROTECTION copper and sulphur
WEED CONTROL mechanical
YEASTS native
GRAPES 100% estate-grown
CERTIFICATION none

Jacopo Biondi Santi Tenuta Greppo

Località Villa Greppo, 183
tel. 0577 848087
www.biondisanti.it
biondisanti@biondisanti.it

62 ac - 100,000 bt

PEOPLE - Speak of Brunello di Montalcino and this cellar immediately springs to mind. The two go together like peas in a pod, a fact that's a worthy tribute to the Biondi Santi family who, since the 19th century, have demonstrated how the wine produced here in Montalcino is one of the finest, most age-worthy on the world. At the helm of the winery is Jacopo Biondi Santi, son of Franco, who made such a huge contribution to the area.

VINEYARDS - We were taken on a short stroll through the vineyards by Alessandro Alì, who was at pains to point out that yields are managed not by the acre but by the vine, without any forcing. He also showed us how the grape bunches are geometrically arranged on the same row with as the spurred cordon to allow them to ripen perfectly. The vineyards are situated at an altitude of 1,150-1,870 feet and face in every direction possible.

WINES - At the cellar we tasted the wines both of Biondi Santi and those of Castello di Montepò, at Scansano. It was an incredible range and, unfortunately, we are unable to review all of them. The fabulous **Rosso di Montalcino 2010** (● 30,000 bt) is a huge pleasure to drink. The classic **Brunello di Montalcino 2009** Great Wine (● 70,000 bt) releases complex aromas redolent of blossom and earth, the sangiovese grape coming to the fore in the mouth with all its juice, after which the beautifully balanced palate then eases into long and leisurely flavorsome finish. The massive, austere **Brunello di Montalcino Ris. 2008** (● 13.000 bt) has a complex nose that develops rigorously and vigorously with pervasive salinity. **Morellino di Scansano Braccale 2011** (● 20,000 bt) and **Sassoalloro 2011** (● sangiovese; 100,000 bt) are both enjoyable.

FERTILIZERS	organic-mineral
PLANT PROTECTION	chemical, copper and sulphur
WEED CONTROL	mechanical
YEASTS	native
GRAPES	100% estate-grown
CERTIFICATION	none

Camigliano

Località Camigliano
Via d'Ingresso, 2
tel. 0577 816061
www.camigliano.it
info@camigliano.it

222 ac - 350,000 bt   **10% discount**

PEOPLE - In 1957 Walter Ghezzi came down from Milan and decided to invest in Camigliano, a quiet, sunny rural spot, then needy of improvement work. Half a century has gone by since then and Walter's project has been taken over by his son Gualtiero and his daughter-in-law Laura, who have revived the tiny village, a stupendous terrace over the hills of Montalcino, with cash, time and bundles of enthusiasm. The new piazza is a gift from the Ghezzi to all the inhabitants.

VINEYARDS - The vineyards of Camigliano stretch out over the hills that surround the village and it's possible to see the cell from virtually all of them. The positions are very good, and climate and altitude ate conducive to the switch to organics, now underway across the farm. Camigliano has a strong urge to evolve and, given the vastness of its properties, the move to natural farm management will require a huge deployment of men and machines. But it will be worth the effort.

WINES - In the cellar, the new deal imposed by Beppe Caviola is certainly making itself felt. **Rosso di Montalcino 2012** (● 100,000 bt) has fragrant tones of black cherry and leather and is evolving towards agreeable minerality. **Gamal 2013** (○ vermentino; 6,000 bt) is an explosion of wild flowers, broom and acacia. **Sant'Antimo Campo ai Mori 2008** (● 6,000 bt) has a herby, spicy nose and well-developed full flavor. The moreish **Moscadello di Montalcino L'Aura 2010** (○ 1,500 bt) has notes of almond and dried fruit. **Poderuccio 2012** (● merlot, cabernet sauvignon; 30,000 bt) is grapey and enjoyable.

> **slow wine** **BRUNELLO DI MONTALCINO 2009** (● 160,000 bt) A spicy wine with fruity tones and a palate with intriguing entry. One of the year's best at an affordable price, it surprised and amazed us.

FERTILIZERS	manure pellets, natural manure, green manure
PLANT PROTECTION	copper and sulphur
WEED CONTROL	mechanical
YEASTS	selected, native
GRAPES	100% estate-grown
CERTIFICATION	converting to organics

Collemattoni

Frazione Sant'Angelo in Colle
Podere Collemattoni, 100
tel. 0577 844127
www.collemattoni.it
collemattoni@collemattoni.it

17 ac - 50,000 bt `10% discount`

PEOPLE - The Buccis are a family of wine-growers who lay their roots in the Montalcino area. At Sant'Angelo in Colle Adon Bucci and his son Marcello have found an exceptional ecosystem that allows them to express their skills to the full. In 2012 they converted to organics. Another eco-friendly move has been the installation of photovoltaic panels on the cellar roof which ensure 80% energy self-sufficiency.

VINEYARDS - Driven by his love of nature, Marcello addresses all the delicate factors that affect organic farming to produce impeccably healthy wines. In the vineyard, a place of perpetual motion, he banks on the industry of a set of untiring workers–bees! Among other things, he makes a mean mille-fiori honey. Among the vine rows, the red soil is a witness to the nuances of the Bucci family's Brunello's.

WINES - During our tasting what stood out most was Marcello's personal pursuit of well-balanced, subtle wines. Between cover cropping and racking, he carries on his quest for the perfect alchemy with consummate skill in both vineyard and cellar. Hence, the product of a great vintage, **Brunello di Montalcino Vigna Fontelontana Ris. 2007** (● 2,400 bt), bright ruby red in color and a nose of great complexity and quick reflexes; a wine that amazes for discretion and velvety tannins at every sip. **Rosso di Montalcino 2012** (● 14,000 bt) has ethery tertiary aromas redolent of myrrh, followed by tannins that are free and full of verve.

slow wine **BRUNELLO DI MONTALCINO 2009** (● 20,000 bt). The fruit is rich and juicy and its great nose-palate symmetry has one eye on equilibrium and the other on the terroir. The wine comes at the right price and is certified organic.

FERTILIZERS	green manure
PLANT PROTECTION	copper and sulphur
WEED CONTROL	mechanical
YEASTS	native
GRAPES	100% estate-grown
CERTIFICATION	organic

Fattoi

Località Santa Restituta
Podere Capanna, 101
tel. 0577 848613
www.fattoi.it
info@fattoi.it

22 ac - 50,000 bt `10% discount`

66 A true rural Montalcino DOC cellar producing terroir-based wines, that respect the grape and the land. Something of a rarity these days 99

PEOPLE - It was Lucia Fattoi, a member of the younger generation, who told us his family's history. His grandfather Ofelio Fattoi bought the estate in the 1970s. His experience allowed him to see the huge wine-growing potential of this excellent farmland.

VINEYARDS - The vineyards are at Santa Restituta, a good growing area on the west side of the denomination. The Fattoi family exploit the favorable microclimate – plenty of sunshine and constant ventilation – which regulates the temperature and acts as a natural barrier against harmful pathologies. Here the soils are rich in clay and pebbles. In the best vintages, the Brunello Riserva is made with grapes from a splendid plot that was planted about 40 years ago.

WINES - Lucia oversees marketing and tastings in the cellar, skills that have become necessary over the last few years as the company's wines have gradually acquired international fame. Even while we were there, a number of people turned up looking for Brunello Fattoi. **Brunello di Montalcino 2009** (● 22,000 bt) has delicate notes of blossom and citrus fruit on the nose and runs over the palate accompanied by lots of juice and acid brightness which set off rich extracts.

slow wine **BRUNELLO DI MONTALCINO RIS. 2008** (● 3,300 bt) The nose offers tertiary aromas of soil, rust and blood-rich meat, while the reactive palate is exalted by edgy saline tannins.

FERTILIZERS	organic-mineral
PLANT PROTECTION	chemical, copper and sulphur
WEED CONTROL	mechanical
YEASTS	selected
GRAPES	100% estate-grown
CERTIFICATION	none

Il Paradiso di Manfredi ◉

Via Canalicchio, 305
tel. 0577 848478
www.ilparadisodimanfredi.com
info@ilparadisodimanfredi.com

5 ac - 9,500 bt

❝ A visit to Il Paradiso di Manfredi reconciles one with the world of wine. Here it's nature, quiet and harmony with the land that prevail ❞

PEOPLE - We were welcomed by owner Florio Guerrini, who patiently took us round the terraces where five acres of vines grow. He explained how he has carried on the work begun by his father-in-law Manfredi. Then his wife Rosella joined us and we moved on to the wine cellar.

VINEYARDS - Walking among the vine rows, one notes the heterogeneousness of the top soil, the color of which varies from red and white to yellow-ochre. Florio points out that the vines rest on strata of mineral sediment over a strip of rock that dates to the Pliocene. Among the wines grew olive trees, fruit trees, wild flowers and herbs to create a miniature ecosystem in which nature is allowed to express itself.

WINES - The great Paradiso reds are the fruit of minimal interventions in the vineyard, a virtually virgin environment and soils that nourish the vines with precious minerals. The functional cellar receives healthy grapes faithful to the vintage that ferment in large Slavonian oak barrels. **Rosso di Montalcino 2012 (●** 2,500 bt) is more approachable than in the past but still display sheer class. The bouquet is dominated by notes of blossom and red berries, the palate is warm and sweet and the finish is saline and flavorful.

slow wine BRUNELLO DI MONTALCINO 2009 (● 7,000 bt) A wine which, as Florio says, holds you back with its austerity but then opens out and releases the quintessence of sangiovese. Red berries leather and a shot of iodine prelude a palate that conflates uncompromising potency and elegant brightness.

FERTILIZERS none
PLANT PROTECTION copper and sulphur
WEED CONTROL mechanical
YEASTS native
GRAPES 100% estate-grown
CERTIFICATION none

Le Chiuse ◉

Località Pullera, 228
tel. 055 597052
www.lechiuse.com
info@lechiuse.com

20 ac - 30,000 bt | **10% discount**

❝ The soils are conducive to stylish, elegant wines. Only native yeasts, moderate macerations and large barrels are used in the cellar, according to tradition. The result is a perfect synthesis between the regal elegance of the sangiovese and a sense of place ❞

PEOPLE - We were welcomed by Lorenzo Magnelli, a member of the young generation of this family of Montalcino producers whose DNA has always contained the Brunello. Passionate and knowledgeable despite his youth, he displays all the desire and energy of someone keen to carry on and improve the work of his predecessors. He works under the watchful eye of his mother Simonetta Valiani and his father Niccolò.

VINEYARDS - The property consists of three distinct vineyards, all north-facing and all round the cellar, just down from Montalcino. The soils are rich in clay with a significant presence of *galestro* marl and fossil matter. The youngest parcel is eight years' old, the others 22 and 27 respectively, and are planted with a density that varies from 1,700 plants per acre in the oldest parcel to 2,500 in the youngest. Organic certification was received in 2005.

WINES - **Brunello di Montalcino 2009 (●** 11,000 bt) is an emblematic wine with notes of flint and dried orange peel on the nose and a stylish, chewy, refreshing palate. Another great, albeit simpler wine is **Rosso di Montalcino 2012 (●** 9.000 bt), which has a blossomy bouquet and a velvety palate with delicately tangy fruit. The 2008 vintage was deemed unworthy for the production of the reserve.

FERTILIZERS manure pellets, green manure
PLANT PROTECTION copper and sulphur
WEED CONTROL mechanical
YEASTS native
GRAPES 100% estate-grown
CERTIFICATION organic

Pian delle Querci €

Località Pian delle Querci
tel. 0577 834174 - 333 9940016
www.piandellequerci.it
info@piandellequerci.it

Pietroso

Podere Pietroso, 257
tel. 0577 848573
www.pietroso.it
info@pietroso.it

---

21 ac - 53,000 bt

PEOPLE - The Pinti family have been farming for four generations. With long experience and considerable knowhow under his belt, Vittorio Pinti converted the farm from livestock breeding to winegrowing with the greatest of ease. The wines he produces are naturally expressive with a strong sense of place. Today his son Angelo and daughter-in-law Angelina Ndreca help him run the estate.

VINEYARDS - The work in the vineyard is done by Angelina's younger brothers Martin and David Ndreca, both experienced farmers, under Vittorio's watchful eye. Methods have low impact on the environment and only copper and sulfur are used as treatments. The vines are spurred cordon trained with an "old-fashioned" density of 1,600 plants per acre. The single plot stands on a slight slope on clayey soil rich in gravel.

WINES - The wines are steel-fermented and matured in 14 50-hectoliter Slavonian oak barrels. The Pinti family's recipe is pretty simple: healthy grapes, long fermentations and adequate bottle-aging. **Rosso di Montalcino 2012** (● 15,000 bt) is blossomy, fragrant and extremely enjoyable. **Brunello di Montalcino Ris. 2008** (● 6,000 bt) has a blood-rich impact on the nose with notes of rust that veer into balsamic suggestions. The wine develops well with great breadth braced by supporting acidity and vigorous tannins.

> **slow wine** **BRUNELLO DI MONTALCINO 2009** (● 30,000 bt) The wine offers earthiness and dried flowers on the nose, then develops harmoniously and smoothly to gradually enwrap the palate and line it with juice. An excellent interpretation of the vintage at a tempting price.

12 ac - 35,000 bt   **10% discount**

PEOPLE - The winery was set up in the 1970s by enthusiast Domenico Berni, and since the 1990s has been run with passion and dedication by his nephew Gianni Pignattai. In the meantime, Gianni has been joined by his son Andrea, who manages the cellar, and his wife Cecilia Brandini, who is in charge of the administrative side of the business. The consultant enologist is Alessandro Dondi, and since 2013 the agronomist has been Federico Becarelli.

VINEYARDS - The company owns vineyards in three different Montalcino zones. The west-facing Pietroso is on a terrace at an altitude of 1,640 feet alongside the cellar. In the hilly Canalicchio area, the Fornello vineyard faces east, while Colombaiolo, finally, overlooks the abbey of Sant'Antimo. The company also rents a south-facing vineyard with vines 40 years old on the lovely hill of Montesoli at an altitude of 650 feet.

WINES - We tasted the wines in the new glass-walled tasting room with a breathtaking view over the vineyards of Montalcino. Gianni ascribes the complexity and elegance of his wines to two main factors: the richness of the grapes from the different vineyards and attentive traditional management of vineyard and cellar. He's at pains to point out that, "We aren't organic but this doesn't mean that we don't work conscientiously. If and when we intervene, we do so specifically and only in cases of real necessity." The expressive, intriguing **Brunello di Montalcino 2009** Great Wine (● 12,500 bt) is intense with earthy, balsamic notes, followed by a palate that, far from being austere, is elegant and pleasurable. **Rosso di Montalcino 2012** (● 20,000 bt) is a sound wine, fruity and balsamic, fragrant and well-balanced.

FERTILIZERS organic-mineral, natural manure	FERTILIZERS manure pellets, none
PLANT PROTECTION copper and sulphur	PLANT PROTECTION chemical, copper and sulphur
WEED CONTROL mechanical	WEED CONTROL mechanical
YEASTS native	YEASTS selected
GRAPES 100% estate-grown	GRAPES 25% bought in
CERTIFICATION none	CERTIFICATION none

Podere Salicutti 🍾

Località Podere Salicutti, 174
tel. 0577 847003
www.poderesalicutti.it
leanza@poderesalicutti.it

10 ac - 18,000 bt | **10% discount**

PEOPLE - Podere Salicutti is where Francesco Leanza has grown up as a winegrower. Since coming to Montalcino in 1990, Francesco has become a sensitive interpreter of the terroir, using the best terrains to grow wines with total respect for the landscape. As he walked with us through the vineyards, he still continued to observe everything with curiosity and interest, qualities that have made him one of Brunello's to producers.

VINEYARDS - The Sorgente vineyard grows on clay and limestone soil, whereas Piaggione, the top part of which was planted in 2012, and Teatro rest on a deep stratum of rock. Leanza is amazed by his own plots. "In 2009 the Sorgente vineyard provided grapes for the Brunello for the first time, he says with a smile. This, actually, is proof of the effectiveness of the farming, capable of exalting the single vineyards despite the variability of vintages.

WINES - "Wine has to narrate time and the seasons; bottles are witnesses of the history of a place. Every year it's a different story." That's how Leanza sums up his work in the cellar, which consists of accompanying the fermentation without enological tampering. **Brunello di Montalcino Ris.** 2008 (● 1,333 bt) is a wine of extraordinary olfactory concentration with blood-rich earthy notes; the mouthfeel is austere, braced by tannins that give it massive length. The excellent **Rosso di Montalcino Sorgente 2011** (● 6,600 bt) has fragrant fruity expressiveness.

> **slow wine** BRUNELLO DI MONTALCINO TRE VIGNE **2009** (● 10,000 bt) A wine that reflects a vintage geared to early drinking. It opens on a vegetal note, which leads into a dynamic, juicy palate closed by very deep tannins.

Sesti 🍾
Castello di Argiano

Frazione Sant'Angelo in Colle
Località Castello di Argiano
tel. 0577 843921
www.sestiwine.com
elisa@sesti.net

23 ac - 65,000 bt

PEOPLE - In the early days, back in the 1970s, this was Giuseppe Sesti's country retreat, the place where he used to hide away to write his astronomy treatises. Then, in view of the natural context and the enviable position of the terrains, he decided to produce classic wines with a sense of place. Since then Castello di Argiano has become one of the stars in the Montalcino firmament, and much of the credit for this must go to Giuliano Bernazzi.

VINEYARDS - The winery's 25 acres of vineyard are spread over various plots round the old tower for which it's named. The soils are very mineral and rich in sand and marine fossils, and the vineyards stand at an average altitude of about 980 feet. "The wines are left to grow on their own without any coaxing in both vineyard and cellar. The various processing phases are carried out following the moon's waning cycle," says Giuseppe with pride.

WINES - The cellar's wines stand out for their natural amalgam and distinctive mineral note. **Brunello di Montalcino Phenomena Ris.** 2008 **Great Wine** (● 2,000 bt) is certainly one of the finest in its category: austere, nuanced, rich and complex on the nose, it's elegant with a finish of restorative saltiness. On a par is **Brunello di Montalcino 2009** (● 13,000 bt), with its intriguing bouquet of Mediteranean scrub and earth and taut, edgy but relaxed and well-balanced palate. **Rosso di Montalcino 2012** (● 10,000 bt) is floral in tone and deliciously thirst-quenching. **Grangiovese 2012** (● 22,000 bt) is another authentic example of a young local Sangiovese. **Sauvignon 2013** (○ 5,000 bt) is an outsider to bank on for lovers of assertive, blunt, dry mineral whites.

FERTILIZERS natural manure	FERTILIZERS natural manure, compost
PLANT PROTECTION copper and sulphur	PLANT PROTECTION copper and sulphur
WEED CONTROL mechanical	WEED CONTROL mechanical
YEASTS native	YEASTS native
GRAPES 100% estate-grown	GRAPES 100% estate-grown
CERTIFICATION organic	CERTIFICATION none

MONTEPULCIANO (SI)

Boscarelli

Frazione Cervognano
Via di Montenero, 28
tel. 0578 767277
www.poderiboscarelli.com
info@poderiboscarelli.com

35 ac - 100,000 bt **10% discount**

66 A benchmark winery for the denomination whose whole range is characterized by incredible quality. Results like this aren't the fruit of chance 99

PEOPLE - It's always a pleasure to pop in to see the De Ferrari brothers at Montepulciano. Luca and Niccolò combine agronomic training and commercial nous to give their wonderful Cervognano vineyards the visibility they deserve."

VINEYARDS - The aim as always is to grow grapes that are as healthy as possible. To do so they apply rigorous farming practices to the already conducive terrain. So far they have adopted a conventional approach but are now more attentive to the health of the soil and have carried out trials in the vineyard using quasi-organic methods.

WINES - The company's wines have exceptionally light flavor and delicate extracts. You only have to taste one of the old vintages to appreciate their aging potential. **Nobile di Montepulciano Il Nocio dei Boscarelli 2010** Great Wine (● 5,000 bt) is one of the best wines tasted in Tuscany this year. Its bouquet has floral and balsamic notes, while the body is delicious and spacious with supporting acidity that makes for a leisurely finish. **Nobile di Montepulciano Ris. 2009** (● 10,000 bt) has ripe but well-judged fruit with grip and deftness on the palate. Though it comes from a warm harvest, **Nobile di Montepulciano 2011** (● 58,000 bt) is notably dynamic. **Rosso di Montepulciano Prugnolo 2013** (● 15,000 bt) is, as always, an example of fragrance and drinkability.

MONTEPULCIANO (SI)

Lunadoro

Frazione Valiano
Località Terrarossa-Pagliareto
tel. 0578 748154
www.lunadoro.com
info@lunadoro.com

29 ac - 65,000 bt

PEOPLE - We visited the beautiful new cellar, work on which was completed last year. Husband and wife team Gigliola Cardinali and Dario Cappelli had it built to place Lunadoro inside the denomination physically. It's situated near Valiano, where they own 30 acres of vineyard. Designed to be functional, it will enable the owners to adopt a more flexible approach to winemaking, which will obviously have positive repercussions on the quality of the wines.

VINEYARDS - If on the one hand the cellar is brand-new, on the other the company is fortunate enough to own vineyards at least 40 years old that ensure balanced vine growth and grapes that guarantee sensory complexity in the wines. The vineyards in the hills at Valiano are planted on clayey, pebbly soil. They benefit from the in-depth knowhow of Dario, who also farms acre upon acre of cereals in the Val d'Orcia.

WINES - We were welcomed by the new enologist Fabio Romegialli, who has good professional experience at the Ar.Pe.Pe cellar under his belt and believes that the best wine is born from the terroir and should be accompanied by attentive but non-invasive enological techniques. **Nobile di Montepulciano 2011** (● 30,000 bt) is fruity with streaks of alcohol on the nose, intact and velvet on the palate, which is spliced by edgy acidity and robust tannins. **Nobile di Montepulciano Quercione Ris. 2010** (● 7,000 bt) reveals arguably too much spiciness from the wood, but comes back with a beautifully textured palate. Rosso di Montepulciano Primo Senso 2012 Everyday Wine (● 10,000 bt) has fruity fragrance and is ready to drink: the palate is supple and juicy and nicely dynamic.

FERTILIZERS natural manure, green manure	FERTILIZERS natural manure, green manure
PLANT PROTECTION chemical, copper and sulphur	PLANT PROTECTION copper and sulphur
WEED CONTROL chemical, mechanical	WEED CONTROL mechanical
YEASTS native	YEASTS native
GRAPES 100% estate-grown	GRAPES 100% estate-grown
CERTIFICATION none	CERTIFICATION none

MONTEPULCIANO (SI)

Poderi Sanguineto I e II

Frazione Acquaviva
Via Sanguineto, 2/4
tel. 0578 767782
www.sanguineto.com
sanguineto@tin.it

9 ac - 30,000 bt | **10% discount**

    ❝ Sanguineto is a unique, unrepeatable place of inestimable agricultural and enological worth **❞**

PEOPLE - Dora Forsoni and Patrizia Brogi are the stars of this winery, which has been bottling Nobile di Montepulciano since 1997. Dora inherited it from her father and, rather than delegating duties, she has preferred to assert her own talent with wines of extraordinary character. Her secret is an old-fashioned approach to viticulture, unlike any other in Montepulciano, consisting of empathy with the land and obedience to nature.

VINEYARDS - The treasure of Sanguineto is a vineyard of about eight acres, "Lived in" day by day and never disregarded. "Look, we remove the shoots from the bottom," says Dora. "They're young at the top but at the bottom, the part that interests me, the roots are 60 years old." Treatments are kept to a bare minimum and carried out with a skill that comes from rebellion against set models and acute observation, a gift now rare among contemporary vine dressers."

WINES - Patrizia Brogi draws the white wine from a cement vat. It's a wine that's hard to find, very interesting. To our minds, Patrizia has brought equilibrium and a certain rationality to Dora's sometimes unpredictable inventiveness. The white is a blend of trebbiano and malvasia leaves the mouth with a sense of salinity and a taste of gooseberry. "Most of this ends up in Japan," laughs Patrizia. **Rosso di Montepulciano 2012 (●** 17,000 bt) is a wine of incredible natural expressiveness, floral, blood-rich and compelling.

> **slow wine** **NOBILE DI MONTEPULCIANO 2011 (●** 9,000 bt) A thrilling sequence of notes on the nose runs from floral to spicy. On the plate it bowls you over with juice, tannic power and genuine flavor. A liquid synthesis of the winery and a paradigm of Nobile.

FERTILIZERS none
PLANT PROTECTION chemical, copper and sulphur
WEED CONTROL mechanical
YEASTS native
GRAPES 100% estate-grown
CERTIFICATION none

SAN GIMIGNANO (SI)

Montenidoli

Località Montenidoli
tel. 0577 941565
www.montenidoli.com
montenidoli@valdelsa.net

59 ac - 90,000 bt | **10% discount**

    ❝ The wines of Montenidoli have soul, character and flavor. Natural and expressive, they reflect the peculiarities of the land and the vintage vividly and faithfully **❞**

PEOPLE - Elisabetta Fagiuoli is a charismatic woman of great sensibility and culture, not to mention great humanity. Her latest noble brainchild is the Fondazione Sergio il Patriarca, set up in memory of her late partner Sergio Muratori. The aim of the foundation is to promote charity, assistance and welfare initiatives. One such is to provide for hospitality for deprived young and old people in cottages made available by the winery.

VINEYARDS - "Sono Montenidoli" (I am Montenidoli) appears on all the winery's labels. Let Elisabetta explain what it means: "I don't make the wines and neither does anyone else," she says. "It's the place, Montenidoli, that makes them and speaks through them." Hence her vineyard management geared to maximum respect for the land and its fruits using all-natural, non-invasive methods.

WINES - The charismatic **Vernaccia di San Gimignano Tradizionale 2012** (○ 13,000 bt) is salty and citrusy. **Vernaccia di San Gimignano Carato 2010** (○ 6,000 bt) has class, elegance and density and promises to age well. The delicious **Vinbrusco 2012** (○ trebbiano, malvasia; 4,000 bt) is oddly "grapeskin-flavored," very tangy. **Canaiuolo 2013** (⊙ 10,000 bt) has backbone, zesty juice and intriguing aromas. The forthright, slightly rugged **Chianti Colli Senesi Montenidoli 2011** (● 6,000 bt) is good at the table.

> **slow wine** **TEMPLARE 2010** (○ vernaccia, trebbiano, malvasia; 6,000 bt) An austere, pebbly, deep, sappy wine whose refreshing supporting acidity makes for a long, lingering finish.

FERTILIZERS green manure
PLANT PROTECTION copper and sulphur
WEED CONTROL mechanical
YEASTS native
GRAPES 100% estate-grown
CERTIFICATION organic

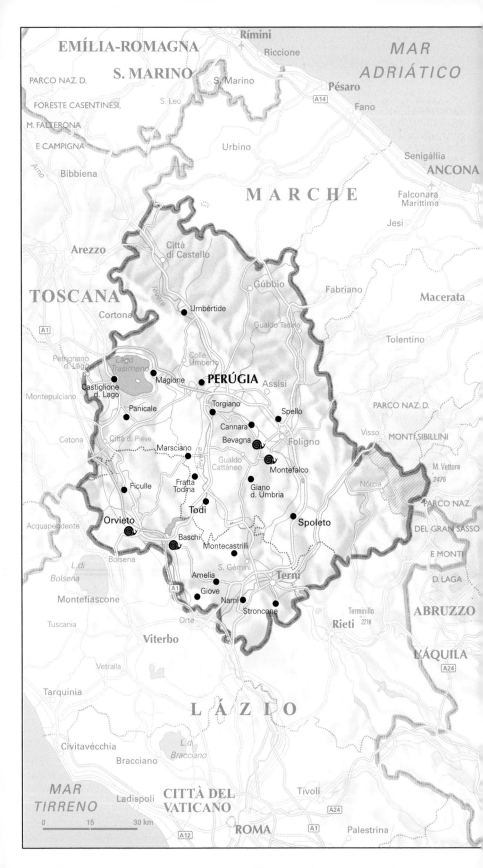

UMBRIA

We weren't far off the mark in previous editions when we described Umbria as an "enological laboratory." We realized that amid apparent immobilism a new generation of winemakers was emerging, capable of adding color to a regional picture cocooned by two overpowering denominations: Montefalco and Orvieto. This is precisely what has happened and this year we can, at long last, speak of a new-look, productive wine region. You might say Umbria was in a state of ferment! Beware, however: we advise you to read the pages that follow carefully, as the new development are to be found not only in our usually recommendations, but also in the wineries we are including for the first time. There are four of them, quite a number considering the size of the region: Fattoria Calcabrina at Montefalco, Cantina Cenci at Marsciano (run by the young, determined Giovanni Cenci), Fattoria Mani di Luna at Torgiano and Trentaquerce at Lugnano in Teverina. We were impressed by all of them for their direct approach to viticulture and the enthusiasm they put into their own personal ideas of wine. We can also confirm that Ciliegiolo is being given increasingly interesting interpretations in various parts of the region, though its main production area is still round Amelia-Narni. Orvieto again came up with wines of national importance, but not many novelties. Montefalco, instead, has stepped up an acquisition of enological personality that we believed was only beginning. Our tastings of a few challenging versions of Sagrantino di Montefalco showed that the denomination is now capable of interpreting the grape as it deserves, replacing the enological caricatures of the past with wines of aromatic complexity followed by great structure and dynamism. Summing up, this time round Umbria put us in good spirits and we hope it will have the same effect on you.

BASCHI (TR)

Barberani - Vallesanta ☺♪

Località Cerreto
tel. 0763 341820
www.barberani.it
barberani@barberani.it

135 ac - 350,000 bt   `10% discount`

66 In its promotion of tradition, Barberani is doing a precious job. By virtue of the quality and the ethics of its viticulture, the winery now has benchmark status in the local area 99

PEOPLE - Luigi Barberani set up the business in 1961. Since then, three generations of the family have developed the initial spirit of the enterprise, which is to be in sync with the Baschi area in order to produce good quality, healthy wines. Today the winery is run by Niccolò, an enologist who monitors every phase in production, and Bernardo, the sales manager.

VINEYARDS - The cellar affords a wonderful view over Lake Corbara, which gives the hills a special microclimate, with a high rate of humidity and sharp night-day temperature swings. The winery received organic certification in 2014, though the Barberani family had actually been controlling its impact on the environment for years. There are 135 hectares of vineyard, all resting on prevalently limestone-clay soil.

WINES - Calcaia Muffa Nobile, the company's star wine, was missing this year, but the overall quality of the wines submitted for tasting made up for its absence. **Orvieto Cl. Sup. Castagnolo 2013** (O grechetto, procanico, chardonnay, riesling; 100,000 bt) is a wine of character with refreshing aromas of fruit and makes a grand entrance on a palate braced by elegance and equilibrium. **Lago di Corbara Rosso Villa Monticelli Polvento 2009** (● sangiovese, cabernet, merlot; 10,000 bt) is fleshy and pleasurable thanks to barrique-aging. **Moscato Passito Villa Monticelli 2009** (O 5,000 bt) is deep and concentrated on nose and plate both.

slow wine ORVIETO CL. SUP. VILLA MONTICELLI LUIGI E GIOVANNA 2011 (O grechetto, procanico; 10,000 bt.) A wine of personality, structure and equilibrium that fuses the essence of the grechetto grape with noble rot (5%).

FERTILIZERS green manure
PLANT PROTECTION copper and sulphur
WEED CONTROL mechanical
YEASTS native
GRAPES 100% estate-grown
CERTIFICATION organic

BEVAGNA (PG)

Adanti ☺♪

Località Arquata
Via Belvedere, 2
tel. 0742 360295
www.cantineadanti.com
info@cantineadanti.com

74 ac - 160,000 bt   `10% discount`

66 This winery has always shone like a beacon for Montefalco thanks to its unique, elegant wines made with a sensitive, terroir-oriented approach to farming 99

PEOPLE - Excellence is the fruit of tradition married with innovation and respect for the environment. This is the view of Daniele Palini, the life and soul of Adanti along with his father Alvaro. The two are never without the support and assistance of the owners, Donatella, Daniela and Pietro Adanti. The technicians are enologist Maurizio Castelli and agronomist Massimo Bianconi.

VINEYARDS - The Arquata vineyard is a cru in a perfect location with good air circulation and compact, clayey soil, ideal for the sagrantino grape. The other vineyard, Colcimino, is higher up at an altitude of about 1,150 feet with pebblier soil and usually yields fresher, more elegant grapes. Harvesting and pruning are carried out separately and manually, and the winery prides itself on the work it does on the buds.

WINES - For Daniele Palini, high quality is a matter of time and method. Six hours after the harvest, the grapes are already in the vats, after which they skin are worked delicately. Aeration is gradual and the wines are released after six to seven years. **Montefalco Sagrantino Il Domenico 2008** (● 5,000 bt), aged for 42 months in large oak barrels, is fruity, elegant and harmonious. **Montefalco Rosso 2010** (● 60,000 bt) has red berries and mature tannins. **Montefalco Bianco 2013** (O 20,000 bt) displays fragrance and slightly piquant flavor. **Montefalco Sagrantino Passito 2007** (● 8,000 bt) has a dry finish and **Grechetto Colli Martani 2013** (O 10,000 bt) is a real joy to drink.

slow wine MONTEFALCO ROSSO RIS. 2009 (● 8,000 bt) A wine of extreme aromatic finesse with rarefied notes of fresh blossom and balsamic undertones. The tannins are concentrated, the finish long and graceful.

FERTILIZERS natural manure
PLANT PROTECTION copper and sulphur
WEED CONTROL mechanical
YEASTS selected
GRAPES 100% estate-grown
CERTIFICATION none

BEVAGNA (PG)

Fattoria Colleallodole 🐌

Vocabolo Colle Allodole, 228
tel. 0742 361897
www.fattoriacolleallodole.it
info@fattoriacolleallodole.com

49 ac - 70,000 bt | **10% discount**

❝ Wine as contact with nature but, above all, as rural culture, which Francesco still hands down with the flavors that characterize every bottle he produces ❞

PEOPLE - "My wines are like pictures." This is how Francesco Antano describes his art of winemaking. Since 1967, the year in which his father and a handful of other pioneers embarked on their Sagrantino adventure, the wines of Colleallodole have carved out a niche for themselves on the wine scene at home and overseas.

VINEYARDS - The 30 acres of vineyard are in the rolling hills that join Bevagna to Montefalco. The vines are spurred cordon trained and some of them were planted 30-35 years ago. The soil that gives Francesco's wines their proverbial character is prevalently clayey, and the favorable position of the vineyards and painstaking farming do the rest.

WINES - **Montefalco Rosso 2011** (● 25,000 bt) is packed with red berries and has lengthy mouthfeel. The sensational **Montefalco Sagrantino 2010** (● 7,000 bt), a terrific match with food, amazes for the depth of its aromas and length on the palate. For some years now the winery has been exploring the world of whites. We recommend **Grechetto Antano 2012** (○ 5,000 bt), elegant and bright with nuances that range from rose to apricot and peach. Be sure to try it to see for yourself how the winery is developing an increasingly deft touch in this particular typology.

> **slow wine** Rosso di Montefalco Ris. 2010 (● 3,000 bt) A wine that starts moody and earthy, then opens out into notes of dried roses. The development on the palate is sumptuous and engulfing.

MONTEFALCO (PG)

Antonelli San Marco 🐌

Località San Marco
tel. 0742 379158
www.antonellisanmarco.it
info@antonellisanmarco.it

124 ac - 300,000 bt | **10% discount**

❝ Antonelli's wines have helped to consolidate the wine heritage of the area through consistent quality and clean farming ❞

PEOPLE - The Antonelli winery, run by Filippo Antonelli, is situated in a breathtaking natural setting and makes a significant contribution to the valorization of Umbrian winemaking, of Montefalco in particular. Credit for its constant improvements in quality, innovations and increasingly rigorous selections is due to the team coordinated by enologist Massimiliano Caburazzi and agronomist Alessio Moretti, who have been working together for years.

VINEYARDS - Work in the vineyards, which cover an area of about 125 acres, is regulated with supplement nutrients and mechanical and natural systems on variegated, mostly clayey soils. The vines are Guyot-trained and mainly native grapes are grown on the soils most conducive for the production of charismatic wines combining innovation and tradition.

WINES - **Grechetto dei Colli Martani 2013** (○ 30,000 bt) is high on acidity and drinkability. The exceptionally typical **Trebbiano Spoletino 2013** (○ 11,000 bt), as versatile and vigorous as the vines it comes from, is splendidly tangy and mineral. The pick of the red range, **Montefalco Rosso 2011** (● 130,000 bt), opens on a vivacious tannic note and youthful hints of fruit.

> **slow wine** Montefalco Sagrantino 2009 (● 27,000 bt) Thickset and vigorous on the palate, a wine of well-defined structure, equilibrium and elegance with a beautifully leisurely aromatic finish. An ideal primer for anyone keen to explore the denomination.

FERTILIZERS green manure
PLANT PROTECTION copper and sulphur
WEED CONTROL mechanical
YEASTS selected
GRAPES 100% estate-grown
CERTIFICATION none

FERTILIZERS natural manure, compost
PLANT PROTECTION copper and sulphur
WEED CONTROL mechanical
YEASTS selected
GRAPES 100% estate-grown
CERTIFICATION organic

MONTEFALCO (PG)

Paolo Bea

Località Cerrete, 8
tel. 0742 378128
www.paolobea.com
paolobea@viniveri.net

MONTEFALCO (PG)

Raìna

Frazione Turri Case Sparse, 42
tel. 0742 621356
www.raina.it
info@vini-raina.it

27 ac - 55,000 bt

25 ac - 50,000 bt   `10% discount`

66 Passing fads aside, Bea has defended and raised the profile of the wine of Montefalco as an expression of a century-old culture and respect for the land 99

PEOPLE - Giampiero Bea's natural approach to viticulture and his bond with nature can be detected in everything about him, from his care for the vineyards and the soil to cellar practices that allow the wine to live and evolve, to his wonderment at natural cycles, to idea for the new cellar.

VINEYARDS - The vineyards are characterized by low plant spacing based on old farming practices. It's a rarity worth seeing to get an idea of how the Umbrian rural landscape must have looked in the past, with the old trebbiano spoletino vines growing round the field maples that have survived the explanation brought about by the mechanization of the countryside on the plain that surrounds the old village.

WINES - All the wines produced by the cellar convey personality, reflect the seasons, and conjure up memory and emotion. **Arboreus 2011** (○ trebbiano spoletino; 9,300 bt), macerated on the lees for four months, is full in color with definite, concentrated aromas, notable acidity and a bitter finish that promises a long life ahead. **Montefalco Sagrantino Cerrete 2007** (● 3,933 bt) is opulent and complex with a soft palate and smooth tannins. **San Valentino 2009** (● sangiovese, sagrantino, montepulciano; 10,300 bt) is a dry, slightly tannic red, a pleasure to drink, approachable with lots of fruit. **Rosso de Vèo 2008** (● 3,380 bt) is made with young sagrantino grapes and is full of attractive brightness.

PEOPLE - Enthusiast Francesco Mariani set up this winery in 2002, converted it to organics in 2006 and to biodynamics in 2012. His aim was to achieve grapes rich in substance, an expression of the terroir and his own personality. Agronomist Andrea Mattioli oversees the vineyards and the cellar, helped by Fabio Primavera, an expert on natural practices.

VINEYARDS - The vines grow in the hills that run eastwards towards Montefalco. They were planted from 2002 to 2010, round the beautifully restructured old farmhouse. The sagrantino vines rest on calcareous alluvial soil with plenty of gravel at an altitude of 985 feet and are delimited by hedges and trees. The other varieties are a little further down where the soil is more fertile. The trebbiano spoletino is Guyot-trained, while the other varieties are spurred cordon-trained.

WINES - Raìna was the nickname of the world farmer who used to work the estate. Francesco named the winery from him, as well as the vineyard that produces its flagship wine: **Montefalco Sagrantino Campo di Raìna 2010** (● 6,600 bt), which ages for 15 months in small wood casks, has rich aromas and develops confidently on the palate, where the tannic texture is well-knit and the flavor mellow. The stylish, well-balanced **Montefalco Sagrantino Passito 2011** (● 1,000 bt) is long and palate-cleansing. **Montefalco Rosso 2012** (● 15,000 bt) has notes of aromatic herbs. **Trebbiano Spoletino 2013** (○ 1,500 bt), which is macerated for 24 hours on the skins, has notes of almond paste on the nose and refreshing flavor. Rosso della Gobba 2012 `Everyday Wine` (● sangiovese, sagrantino, montepulciano; 15,000 bt) is quaffable without being banal.

FERTILIZERS compost, green manure
PLANT PROTECTION copper and sulphur
WEED CONTROL mechanical
YEASTS native
GRAPES 100% estate-grown
CERTIFICATION organic

FERTILIZERS biodynamic preparations, green manure
PLANT PROTECTION copper and sulphur, organic
WEED CONTROL mechanical
YEASTS native
GRAPES 100% estate-grown
CERTIFICATION converting to biodynamics

Tabarrini

Frazione Turrita
tel. 0742 379351
www.tabarrini.com
info@tabarrini.com

40 ac - 70,000 bt `10% discount`

66 Knowhow and lots and lots of passion are the main ingredients of this winery, run by the one and only Giampaolo Tabarrini 99

PEOPLE - Giampaolo never stops! Even when he's standing still, his eyes are always peeled and taking in every single detail. When he talks about wine it's like listening to a series of exciting adventure stories and his explanations of the various aspects of the winery are in-depth, technical analyses. Other members of the team include consultant enologist Emiliano Falsini and manager Daniele Sassi.

VINEYARDS - Giampaolo's day-to-day contact with his vineyards and his profound knowledge of the soil have allowed him to identify the characteristics that best suit the sagrantino grape and establish his three crus. After being valorized in climatically different vintages, these now ensure top-quality Sagrantinos every year. Another gem is the trebbiano spoletino grape, some of whose vines are 150 years' old.

WINES - **Montefalco Rosso Colle Grimaldesco 2011** (● 18,000 bt) is spicy and toasty on the nose with a warm, grassy almost bitter palate. **Montefalco Sagrantino Colle Grimaldesco 2010** (● 15,000 bt) is packed with fruit and has more concentrated alcohol. **Montefalco Sagrantino Colle alle Macchie 2010** (● 3,300 bt), minty with a fruity, almost sweet finish, is harmonious and likely the most ready of the bunch. **Montefalco Sagrantino Campo alla Cerqua 2010** (● 3,300 bt) veers between tanginess, spiciness and toastiness.

> **slow wine** **ADARMANDO 2012** (○ trebbiano spoletino; 8,000 bt) A master class in the use of trebbiano spoletino, which the winery was one of the first to revaluate. The rich bouquet is redolent of minerals and spices and the palate steers through citrus fruit and almonds into a long lingering finish.

FERTILIZERS manure pellets, green manure
PLANT PROTECTION copper and sulphur
WEED CONTROL mechanical
YEASTS native
GRAPES 100% estate-grown
CERTIFICATION none

Palazzone

Località Rocca Ripesena, 68
tel. 0763 344921
www.palazzone.com
info@palazzone.com

59 ac - 140,000 bt `10% discount`

66 A beacon for the Umbrian wine world, Palazzone captures all the laid-back magnificence of the Orvieto area 99

PEOPLE - The Dubini family has produced consistently high-quality wine and promoted the local area since 1969, holding their heads high despite the problems that dog the denomination.

VINEYARDS - The winery's 60 acres of vineyard grow on hillsides, some of them steep, where the soil is sedimentary and clayey. The vines are trained with the single-arched Guyot system, an excellent compromise between quality and manageability. Jack of all trades Giovanni oversees vineyards, cellar and production with a careful eye. The wines are built to last and, since the 2009 vintage, a certain quantity of Campo del Guardiano is aged in a cave.

WINES - Orvieto Cl. Sup. Terre Vineate 2013 `Everyday Wine` (○ 60,000 bt) is a textbook Orvieto, well-balanced, moreish and chewy, a wonderful wine for day-to-day drinking. **Grechetto Grek 2013** (○ 7,000 bt) has a scent-drenched varietal nose, a full-bodied palate and vivacious mouthfeel. The quaffable **Pinot Grigio Tixe 2013** (○ 8,000 bt) is long and fragrant. **Piviere 2012** (● 4,000 bt) is a varietal Sangiovese, husky and enjoyable. **Armaleo 2011** (● cabernet sauvignon and franc; 3,000 bt) has an elegant suite of aromas, a lean, reactive body and a finish of jam with whiffs of mint.

> **slow wine** **ORVIETO CL. SUP. CAMPO DEL GUARDIANO 2012** (○ 10,000 bt) A wine made with grapes from the oldest part of the vineyard. It opens with tranquil notes of fern, rust and chamomile, then shifts to peach, honey and beeswax. The deftness of its architecture comes through with great expressive power and rich, tangy succulence.

FERTILIZERS organic-mineral, natural manure, green manure
PLANT PROTECTION chemical, copper and sulphur
WEED CONTROL mechanical
YEASTS selected
GRAPES 100% estate-grown
CERTIFICATION none

0
15
30 km
MAR
ADRIÁTICO
Ravenna
EMÍLIA-
-ROMAGNA
Cérvia
Cesena
A14
Rímini
S. MARINO
Riccione
S. Marino
Pésaro
S. Leo
Fano
Urbino
Senigállia
Falconara
Maríttima
MARCHE DEL NORD
ANCONA
M. Conero
Jesi
Città
di Castello
Loreto
Recanati
Civitanova
Marche
Fabriano
Gúbbio
Macerata
Tévere
S. Severino Marche
Fermo
Tolentino
Lago
Trasimeno
PERÚGIA
Camerino
COLLINE MACERATESI
E PICENO
Assisi
PARCO NAZ. D.
A14
MONTI SIBILLINI
S. Benedetto
d. Tronto
Foligno
Visso
Áscoli
Piceno
Tévere
ÚMBRIA
M. Vettore
Nórcia
Giulianova
PARCO
Todi
Spoleto
Orvieto
NAZ.
Téramo
Roseto
d. Abruzzi
DEL
A1
Amélia
GRAN SASSO
A24
Montefiascone
Terni
Gran Sasso E
d'Itália
2912
Terminillo
2216
Orte
MONTI
Rieti
Viterbo
D. LAGA
L'ÁQUILA
Vetralla
A25
ABRUZZO
LÁZIO
A24
L. di
Bracciano

MARCHE

The Marche region confirmed its penchant for white wine. The 2013 vintage allowed both the verdicchio and the pecorino grapes to express their characteristic acid-saline profile. This is part of their DNA but was overwhelmed slightly in the previous two vintages by high temperatures. Wines proved very elegant, fresh but not sharp, with balanced flavor and aroma. Artemisia by Spinelli and Donna Orgilla by Fiorano are at the cutting edge but they are flanked by a host of very good, reliable labels. Verdicchio – the two Jesi varieties and Matelica – is top of the league with wines that show impeccable varietal clarity and sense of place in every price range. The 2013 versions are intriguing, having benefited from a very cool year that brought out the acid-saline profile of the grapes. The 2012 wines are very good, ready to drink and refined, while the 2011s suffered the above-average climate, though there are a few beautifully balanced exceptions. The one that stands out is the incredibly vivacious, reactive Il Cantico della Figura by Andrea Felici up in Apiro.

Moving on to reds, Piceno leads not only for output but also for its diffuse capacity to tame the character of montepulciano with adequate structure and aromatic freshness. Rosso Piceno Superiore and the Offida DOCG, now with a high percentage of montepulciano, demonstrated plenty of balance, fruity flesh and drinkability. The Conero peninsula is showing signs of improvement; though the Conero DOCG suffers from overextraction, a flaw that affects its drinkability, here and there, it is now shifting to expressions that exalt its fruit and balanced structure. With Cumaro and, even more so, Campo San Giorgio, Umani Ronchi showed that balance and finesse can live side by side with the character of montepulciano. Lacrima shows stylistic and varietal coherence, qualities most to the fore in vintage versions. Ribona is on the road to growth and shows greater coherence than in the past, while Bianchello del Metauro seemed to lack the flesh needed to countervail the freshness of the vintage.

snails 🐌

171 ANDREA FELICI
173 COLLESTEFANO
174 PIEVALTA
175 FATTORIA LA MONACESCA
175 FATTORIA SAN LORENZO
177 BUCCI
177 LA STAFFA
180 AURORA
181 FATTORIA DEZI

bottles 🍾

171 SANTA BARBARA
172 GIOACCHINO GAROFOLI
174 CANTINE BELISARIO
176 UMANI RONCHI
179 VELENOSI

coins €

172 TENUTA DELL'UGOLINO
173 COLONNARA
176 MAROTTI CAMPI
179 DE ANGELIS
180 LE VIGNE DI FRANCA
181 SAN FILIPPO

Northern Marche

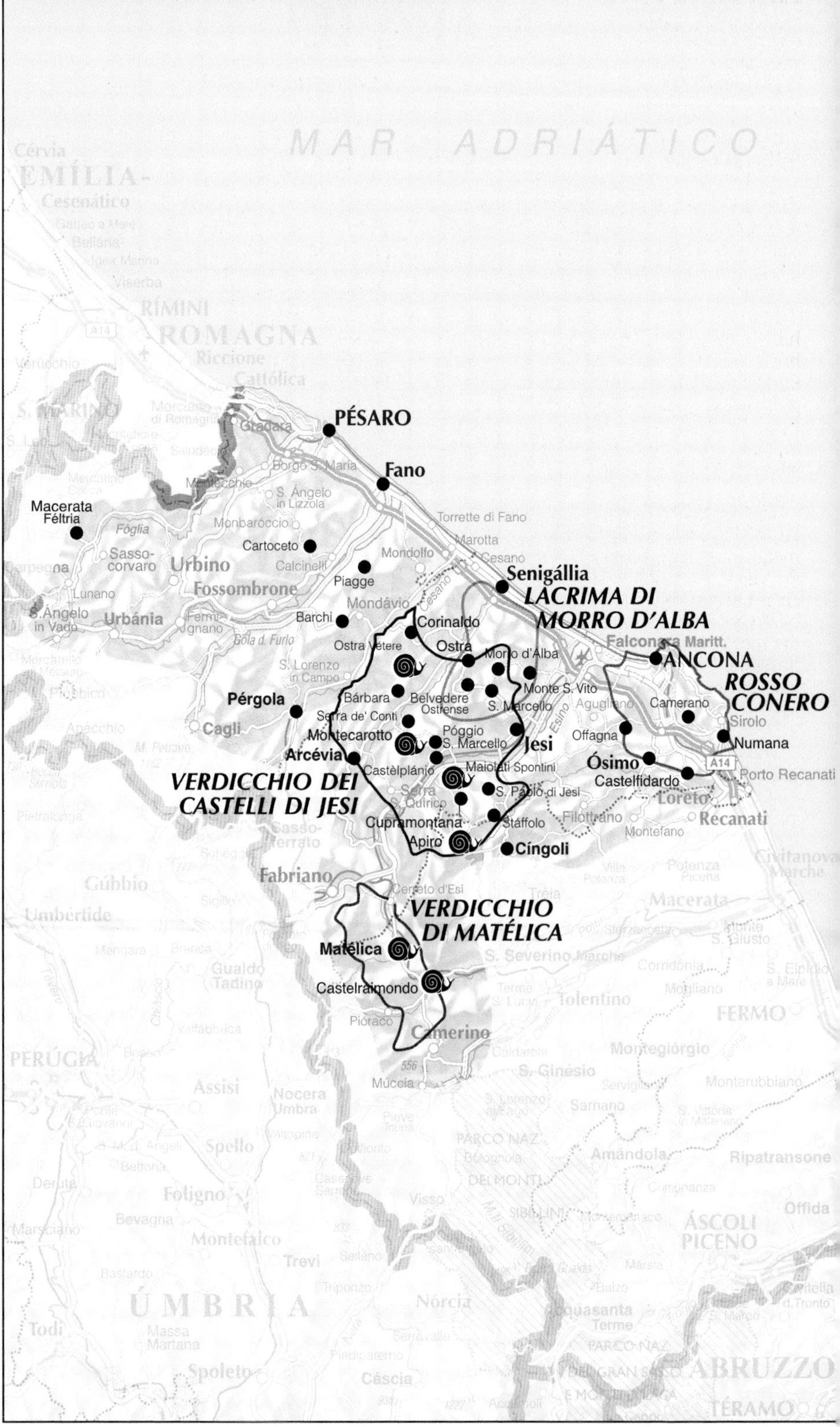

APIRO (MC)

Andrea Felici 🐌

Contrada Sant'Isidoro
tel. 0733 611431
www.andreafelici.it
leo@andreafelici.it

32 ac - 40,000 bt | **10% discount**

66 Andrea and Leo Felici, a winning team from Apiro who combine sustainability in the field with stylistic modernity in the cellar to produce refined wines with a sense of place 99

PEOPLE - Just a year ago we described him as the golden boy of the local *movida*, but now he's a family man! Leopardo, better known as Leo, is leapfrogging through life as he has done through winemaking. His rational, well-organized approach allows him to monitor every detail, which is why the results are always so good.

VINEYARDS - While Leo oversees the cellar, his dad Andrea farms the vineyards. A meticulous hard worker, Andrea pampers the vineyards as if they were a garden lawn. He prunes the vines and trims the leaves and works the land with painstaking care in an attempt to achieve the greatest equilibrium possible. These are the secrets behind his healthy grapes, enhanced by the freshness and saltiness of the Apiro terroir.

WINES - The skill of a winemaker is best judged in difficult years, and the warm 2011 and cool, damp 2013 certainly put the Felicis to the test. But the end results were excellent. Verdicchio dei Castelli di Jesi Cl. Sup. Andrea Felici 2013 Everyday Wine (○ 33,000 bt) expresses the freshness of the vintage with all the clarity of the grape, a lively palate and long saline complexity, all served up with meadow flowers, peach and apricot, aniseed and mint.

slow wine CASTELLI DI JESI VERDICCHIO RIS. CL. IL CANTICO DELLA FIGURA 2011 (○ 7,000 bt) A high-altitude Verdicchio that's elegant and refined, despite the warm growing year. Serious and severe in appearance but with gentle manners, it releases mineral aromas, herbs, aniseed and citrus fruit, which intersect constantly. The palate is juicy and taut, bright and saline.

FERTILIZERS natural manure, green manure
PLANT PROTECTION copper and sulphur
WEED CONTROL mechanical
YEASTS selected, native
GRAPES 100% estate-grown
CERTIFICATION organic

BARBARA (AN)

Santa Barbara 🍾

Borgo Mazzini, 35
tel. 071 9674249
www.vinisantabarbara.it
info@vinisantabarbara.it

173 ac - 650,000 bt | **10% discount**

PEOPLE - Santa Barbara saw the light in 1984 and a few years later Stefano Antonucci, fed up with his bank job, decided to opt out and devote himself to wine full-time. Thirty years on, he's still at the forefront, more determined and inspired than ever, as his impeccable range of wines demonstrates. The thread that sews his original and more terroir-based interpretations together is the constantly positive response of the market.

VINEYARDS - The cellar owns 60 acres of vineyard, the rest being leased or managed by third parties across the Barbara area and in the best Castelli zones. The area is vast but soil management is nonetheless rigorous, tailored to position and composition, as is the care devoted to the vines. The variety of locations makes for grapes suited to every need.

WINES - Every year a novelty appears to brighten an already broad, dynamic panorama. Elegance is in the DNA of Castelli di Jesi Verdicchio Ris. Cl. Stefano Antonucci 2012 Great Wine (○ 35,000 bt), whose fruity, spicy aromas fuse into a sinuous, tonic, highly complex palate to create a wine that's refined in every sense. Verdicchio dei Castelli di Jesi Cl. Tardivo ma non Tardo 2011 (○ 5,000 bt), a blend of sweet aromas and aniseed that pervades a supple, snappy palate, and the fresh-tasting, thirst-quenching Verdicchio dei Castelli di Jesi Cl. Le Vaglie 2013 (○ 170,000 bt) are as dependable as ever. Stefano Antonucci 2011 (● merlot, cabernet, montepulciano; 10,000 bt) combines structure, raciness and aromatic dynamism. Mossone 2011 (● merlot; 1,300 bt) is a huge, soft easy-drinker.

FERTILIZERS organic-mineral
PLANT PROTECTION chemical, copper and sulphur
WEED CONTROL mechanical
YEASTS selected, native
GRAPES 10% bought in, wine bought in
CERTIFICATION none

CASTELFIDARDO (AN)

Gioacchino Garofoli

Località Villa Musone
Via Marx, 123
tel. 071 7820162
www.garofolivini.it
mail@garofolivini.it

124 ac - 2,000,000 bt | **10% discount**

PEOPLE - No Garofoli, no Verdicchio. With 50 grape harvests under his belt, Carlo, a model of Marche sobriety, is one of the "founding fathers," one of the winemakers who contributed to the wine's resurgence under the banner of quality in the 1980s. He still holds the baton firmly in his hands, but his daughter Beatrice is in the running to take it in the future. He and his cousins Gianluca and Caterina represent tradition and continuity.

VINEYARDS - The verdicchio's heart beats in the Cupo delle Lame at Montecarotto, a single plot on clayey-sandy soil at an altitude of 1,100 feet. The vineyard was replanted between 1999 and 2005 and is pampered by its guardian of many years Natale Bellucci. The main montepulciano vineyard was planted 15 years ago near the sea among woods and olive groves on the slopes of Mount Conero, in the Piancarda district, where the soil is calcareous. The rest of the vineyards grow on the clay soil of Paterno.

WINES - The wines are impeccable and full of class with clear-cut varietal aromas. It sounds like an advertising slogan, but this really is the style of this historic cellar. **Verdicchio dei Castelli di Jesi Cl. Sup. Podium 2012** Great Wine (○ 60,000 bt) is a paragon of finesse as always: it has all the forwardness typical of warm vintages but is also lively and vigorous with a rich bouquet, succulent texture and a snappy finish. The **Verdicchio dei Castelli di Jesi Cl. Sup. Macrina 2013** (○ 150,000 bt) has stylish, delicate aromas and a fresh-tasting palate. **Rosso Conero Grosso Agontano Ris. 2009** (● 33,800 bt) offers fruit and notes of coffee to the nose and good, albeit somewhat alcoholic mouthfeel. **Verdicchio dei Castelli di Jesi M. Cl. Brut Ris. 2008** (○ 24,000 bt) has varietal brightness and soft fizziness.

CASTELPLANIO (AN)

Tenuta dell'Ugolino   €

Località Macine
Via Copparoni, 32
tel. 071 812569 - 360 487114
www.tenutaugolino.it
cantina@tenutaugolino.it

15 ac - 37,000 bt | **10% discount**

PEOPLE - Despite his young age, Andrea Petrini is already a verdicchio veteran. Mannerly but astute, he has stepped up the progress of the winery founded by his father. Working hard and with passion, a little at a time and with not a few concerns, taking important decisions, he has now found the right dimension for the company. For some years he has been helped by Matteo Foroni and his friend and technical manager Aroldo Bellelli.

VINEYARDS - The winery owns about ten acres of vineyard (the rest it rents) in a small valley surrounded by woodland. The largest property on a hillside on very dry calcareous-sandy soil consists of a vineyard planted 15 years ago and another 40 years ago. On richer, cooler soil near the cellar, a two-acre plot grows the grapes for Balluccio. Andrea doesn't farm organically but he hasn't practiced weed control for years, he fertilizes with manure pellets and only sprays with systemic pesticides at the start of the season.

WINES - Andrea deserves praise for preserving the varietal profile of verdicchio and expressing it with clear-cut, fragrant aromas. In warm years, the wines show a streak of enviable verve, while in cooler years, such as 2013, they guarantee juicy, never biting acidity. **Verdicchio dei Castelli di Jesi Cl. Le Piaole 2013** (○ 31,000 bt) is compelling for its elegance, and also for its price, its forthright bouquet and well-integrated acidity boost drinkability without making it banal.

slow wine **VERDICCHIO DEI CASTELLI DI JESI CL. SUP. VIGNETO DEL BALLUCCIO 2013** (○ 5,600 bt) A wine that expresses the grape variety in crystalline fashion. Its supple body and acid-saline profile give it balance and style, and its aromatic dynamism emerges with aniseed, spring flowers and aromatic herbs.

FERTILIZERS organic-mineral, mineral, manure pellets, natural manure, green manure
PLANT PROTECTION chemical, copper and sulphur
WEED CONTROL chemical, mechanical
YEASTS selected
GRAPES 50% bought in, wine bought in
CERTIFICATION none

FERTILIZERS manure pellets, green manure
PLANT PROTECTION chemical, copper and sulphur
WEED CONTROL mechanical
YEASTS selected
GRAPES 100% estate-grown
CERTIFICATION none

CASTELRAIMONDO (MC)

Collestefano ⊚↵

Frazione Rustano
Località Colle Stefano, 3
tel. 0737 640439
www.collestefano.com
info@collestefano.com

69 ac - 120,000 bt

❝❝ Collestefano is an emblem of 'good, clean and fair' wine. It's exciting, it's the product of healthy farming and it's sold at affordable prices – despite all the accolades it has received ❞❞

PEOPLE - Fabio Marchionni is the archetype of the modern *vigneron*. After studying enology and working abroad, he came home and revolutionized the local farming world, especially winemaking, to which he applied a mixture of rural wisdom and academic expertise, hence respect for the land and technical knowhow.

VINEYARDS - The cellar now owns and rents a total of 70 acres of vines in the southern part of the Matelica plateau. The verdicchio grapes grow on soil rich in limestone, kept alive by cover cropping and fertilization with manure, in a continental climate with sharp night-day temperature swings and good air circulation. Organic farming methods are the natural consequence of Fabio's ideas and *modus operandi*.

WINES - Collestefano may be increasing the number of acres and of the bottles it produces, but the reliability and land-rootedness of its wines never alter. According to Fabio, "The only variable is the weather, which adds character to wine." Thanks must go therefore to the 2013 growing year if he's managed to produce one of his best labels for years. Not to mention **Rosa di Elena 2013** (⊙ sangiovese, cabernet; 5,000 bt), a graceful blossomy rosé.

slow wine **VERDICCHIO DI MATELICA COLLESTEFANO 2013** (○ 110,000 bt) A refined cohesion of floral, fruity, vegetal notes with hints of minerals. The palate has plenty of grip thanks to its juicy acidity and salinity and develops into an elegant finish.

CUPRAMONTANA (AN)

Colonnara ©

Via Mandriole, 6
tel. 0731 780273
www.colonnara.it
info@colonnara.it

296 ac - 1,000,000 bt   **10% discount**

PEOPLE - Colonnara is a sustainably scaled cooperative which allows its many small member producers to manage their estates (which have an average area of 4 acres of vineyard) on their own, thereby keeping Cupra wine production alive and avoiding the digging up of vineyards. The cellar thus plays a vital social role in the area.

VINEYARDS - The cooperative's property is made up of a host of "micro-estates" scattered all over the communal territory and the district. The small member producers manage their plots and the cooperative provides them with technical assistance. The estates are positioned to exploit locations, soils and clonal diversity to the full and about 60 acres are farmed organically.

WINES - There's a lot of verdicchio in Colonnara's bottles, with different interpretations and nuances that produce very expressive, varietal wines. The standout wine is **Verdicchio dei Castelli di Jesi Cl. Sup. Cuprese 2013** Everyday Wine (○ 65,000 bt) in which fresh, salty, racy mouthfeel is countervailed by and intense aromatic profile that ranges from meadow flowers to sweet fruit to almond. After long aging, Castelli di Jesi **Verdicchio Ris. Cl. Tufico 2010** (○ 10,000 bt) has soft olfactory notes of saffron, aniseed and chamomile, followed by a well-rounded, caressing palate that a tangy finish attempts to balance. **Verdicchio dei Castelli di Jesi M. Cl. Ubaldo Rosi Ris. 2008** (○ 10,000 bt) is tops in its typology for aromatic finesse, equilibrium and saltiness with the added value of perfect mousse.

FERTILIZERS manure pellets, natural manure, green manure
PLANT PROTECTION copper and sulphur, organic
WEED CONTROL mechanical
YEASTS selected, native
GRAPES 25% bought in
CERTIFICATION organic

FERTILIZERS manure pellets, green manure
PLANT PROTECTION chemical, copper and sulphur
WEED CONTROL mechanical
YEASTS selected
GRAPES 100% estate-grown, wine bought in
CERTIFICATION part of the vineyards certified organic

MAIOLATI SPONTINI (AN)

Pievalta

Frazione Moie
Via Monteschiavo, 18
tel. 0731 705199
www.baronepizzini.it
pievalta@baronepizzini.it

65 ac - 110,500 bt · **10% discount**

66 Pievalta focuses on the grapes' structure, acidity and salinity naturally without being dazzled by passing fads and fashions 99

PEOPLE - In 2002 the Franciacorta wine company Barone Pizzini decided to invest in verdicchio and put its faith in the skilled young enologist Alessandro Fenino. Since then Alessandro has worked with modesty and passion, developing his own personal agronomic and enological interpretation of the grape. Initial difficulties have now been resolved, growth has been continuous and Pievalta has become well respected in the sector.

VINEYARDS - The measured use of organic and biodynamic techniques underpins work in the vineyard. Fifty hectares of vines, of which 32 over 40 years' old, grow on fresh limestone marl round the cellar at Maiolati. Another 12 hectares of vine rows grow a variety of grapes on the tufa soil at San Paolo, in Contrada Follonica, at an altitude of 1,000 feet.

WINES - Native yeasts, fermentation in steel vats and lees contact heighten the flavor of the grapes. Verdicchio dei Castelli di Jesi Cl. Sup. Pievalta 2013 Everyday Wine (O 60,000 bt) is a masterpiece: it has substance, juiciness, not oversharp acidity, uniform texture and lots of salt, and the bouquet alternates meadow flowers, wild fennel, aniseed and mint. **Verdicchio dei Castelli di Jesi Cl. Sup. Dominè 2013** (O 7,000 bt) is fruity with intriguing acid verve. **M. Cl. Extra Brut Perlugo** (O verdicchio; 20,000 bt) has a delicate mousse with hints of aniseed and licorice.

> **slow wine** CASTELLI DI JESI VERDICCHIO RIS. CL. SAN PAOLO 2012 (O 14,000 bt) A wine of great personality that grows sip by sip. The nose offers deft aromas of peach and apricot, aniseed and crusty bread and the tapered, saline tannins faithfully interpret the tufa soil of San Paolo.

FERTILIZERS	manure pellets, natural manure, compost, biodynamic preparations, green manure
PLANT PROTECTION	copper and sulphur, organic
WEED CONTROL	mechanical
YEASTS	selected, native
GRAPES	100% estate-grown
CERTIFICATION	biodynamic, organic

MATELICA (MC)

Cantine Belisario

Via Vittorio Bachelet, 1
tel. 0737 787247
www.belisario.it
belisario@belisario.it

741 ac - 850,000 bt · **10% discount**

PEOPLE - The Camerino district has become one of the Marche region's most important industrial hubs over the last 30 years. As built-up areas grew, so the number of vineyards, a traditional source of income locally, decreased. It was in this context that the Cooperativa Belisario, set up in the early 1970s, played a vital role from a social point of view, by accruing dozens of acres of vineyard that otherwise would have been dug up. Today the cooperative is a thriving concern that provides income for many local farmers.

VINEYARDS - Belisario doesn't buy in grapes but controls whole vineyards either directly or by instructing its members. In this way historic plots, some of which planted over 40 years ago, are kept alive. Every effort is made to keep the soil fertile, to regulate budding with careful pruning, and to reserve the health of the grapes with specific treatments.

WINES - The Belisario range is always impeccable. At the lower end of the price range Verdicchio di Matelica Del Cerro 2013 Everyday Wine (O 100,000 bt) is a condensation of varietal clarity that is developing a personality of its own: very well-balanced and saline, it has lingering suggestions of meadow flowers, aniseed and mint. The fresh, tonic, thirst-quenching **Verdicchio di Matelica Terre di Valbona 2013** (O 450,000 bt) is even cheaper. Moving up a category, Verdicchio di Matelica Cambrugiano Ris. 2011 Great Wine (O 60,000 bt) exhibits balance in a fusion of oaky hints and fruitiness; the palate is sexy and dynamic, the finish very, very complex. **Verdicchio di Matelica Meridia 2011** (O 13,000 bt) conjures up a delicious blend of saffron, fruit and honey on its sinuous palate, which is pepped up by a streak of saltiness.

FERTILIZERS	organic-mineral, manure pellets, natural manure, green manure
PLANT PROTECTION	copper and sulphur
WEED CONTROL	mechanical
YEASTS	selected
GRAPES	100% estate-grown
CERTIFICATION	organic, none

Fattoria La Monacesca 🐌

Contrada Monacesca
tel. 0733 672641
www.monacesca.it
info@monacesca.it

---

66 ac - 180,000 bt

❝ This verdicchio has never been ruffled by the wind of fashion, preferring instead to stick to the job of interpreting terroir, though not without finesse and personality ❞

PEOPLE - A small hilltop village just outside Matelica, surrounded by woodland, fields of cereals and vineyards – this is the where Aldo Cifola runs the winery founded by his father in the early 1970s. Aldo is a modern winemaker who prefers facts to formalities, a philosophy that has allowed him to turn out sincere, land-rooted, elegant wines for years.

VINEYARDS - Verdicchio occupies most of the company's vineyards, with small plots of land also given over to chardonnay, sangiovese and merlot, which do well at the high altitudes. Verdicchio La Monacesca is the result of mass selection and the replantings were made with grafts from a mother vineyard. Aldo's pragmatism leads him to prefer his own clones to those from nurseries.

WINES - Every year it all seems so easy and automatic. The wines never disappoint and interpret vintages in exemplary fashion. Steel vats are the preferred containers to heighten the aromaticity of the grape and the environment does the rest. As the Verdicchio di Matelica and the red Camerte mature, the flagship wine lives up to expectations in a version of refined varietal expressiveness. Its readiness is an invitation to buy it.

slow wine VERDICCHIO DI MATELICA MIRUM RIS. 2012 (○ 20,000 bt) A refined blend of apples and pears, aniseed, field greens and chamomile, approachable with a clear-cut, sculpted bouquet, which runs softly into an acid, saline palate with a lively texture.

FERTILIZERS mineral
PLANT PROTECTION chemical, copper and sulphur
WEED CONTROL chemical, mechanical
YEASTS selected
GRAPES 100% estate-grown
CERTIFICATION none

Fattoria San Lorenzo 🐌

Contrada San Lorenzo, 6
tel. 0731 89656
az-crognaletti@libero.it
info@fattoriasanlorenzo.com

---

74 ac - 80,000 bt

❝ 'The vine's happy with me. With the attention I give it and the chemicals I don't, it's as if I were caressing it.' Natalino's words sum up his *modus operandi* ❞

PEOPLE - Natalino Crognaletti is an untiring, friendly winemaker. What's striking about him is his ability to make work in the vineyard – meticulous and precise in every detail – look like the easiest thing in the world. For him naturalness in every intervention isn't the hardest way possible, it's the only one.

VINEYARDS - Near the cellar, in an area with good air circulation at an altitude of 1,150 feet, the Oche vineyard's splendid vines, planted 50 years ago from 17 verdicchio clones, lay their roots in clayey soil with a high limestone component. Natalino observes the vines and manages them without set protocols, grassing and cover cropping and using biodynamic products according to necessity.

WINES - Natalino's wines are rich, spontaneous and flavorful. Verdicchio dei Castelli di Jesi Di Gino 2013 Everyday Wine (○ 20,000 bt) is simple but impresses with its juicy, lip-smacking structure with complex hints of peach and apricot, acacia honey and aniseed: once you stat drinking it you can't stop. The top-of-the-range **Verdicchio dei Castelli di Jesi Cl. Sup. Campo delle Oche 2011** (○ 10,000 bt) is dynamic and never cloying, despite the sweetness of its aromas, with a palate that is pervaded by ripe and candied fruit and honey. **Verdicchio dei Castelli di Jesi Cl. Le Oche 2012** (○ 15,000 bt) has a varietal profile but its sugary sweetness detracts from its dynamism. **Rosso Piceno Di Gino 2012** (● 13,000 bt) is pleasantly fruity.

FERTILIZERS natural manure, compost, biodynamic preparations, green manure
PLANT PROTECTION copper and sulphur
WEED CONTROL mechanical
YEASTS native
GRAPES 100% estate-grown
CERTIFICATION organic

Marotti Campi €

Via Sant'Amico, 14
tel. 0731 618027
www.marotticampi.it
wine@marotticampi.net

Umani Ronchi

Via Adriatica, 12
tel. 071 7108019
www.umanironchi.it
wine@umanironchi.it

168 ac - 220,000 bt **10% discount**

570 ac - 2,800,000 bt **10% discount**

PEOPLE - If you visit the cellar, you'll likely be welcomed by trusty cellarman and vine dresser Ivano Belardinelli. The present owner Lorenzo Marotti Campi is often abroad to promote and speak about Lacrima and Verdicchio. The Marotti Campi family has been farming and making wine since the mid 19th century, a fact well documented by newspapers and other writings from the period. The old mansion among the vineyards is still used for hospitality purposes.

VINEYARDS - The farm covers an area of 320 acres of land. It grows vines on 140 of them and rents another 30 for the same purpose. The vineyards are split into a number of plots adjacent to the wine cellar. Only 17 acres are given over to international grapes (chardonnay, sauvignon and petit verdot), all the rest being equally divided between lacrima and verdicchio. On prevalently clayey soil grow vines over 30 years old as well as denser modern plantings.

WINES - The common denominators of the range are stylistic precision and value for money. **Lacrima di Morro d'Alba Rubico 2013** (● 50,000 br) has aromatic verve and an enjoyable, ingratiating entry with lots of fresh flavor. Best of the whites is **Castelli di Jesi Verdicchio Ris. Cl. Salmariano 2011** (○ 15,000 bt), whose nuanced olfactory notes range from fruit to white pepper to meadow greens and whose soft, caressing palate would bee really deep if it just had that extra streak of raciness. **Verdicchio dei Castelli di Jesi Cl. Sup. Luzano 2013** (○ 60,000 bt) is fresh and almondy with close-focused mouthfeel.

> **slow wine** **LACRIMA DI MORRO D'ALBA SUP. ORGIOLO 2011** (● 26,000 bt) Aged in second-use barrels for a year, a wine that displays varietal linearity and amalgamates rounded aromas and poised flavor to perfection. It develops snappily with tannins that lend character to the palate.

PEOPLE - Umani Ronchi occupies an important place in the history of wine in the Marche. Founded by Gino Umani Ronchi in the 1950s, the cellar was subsequently taken over, developed and consolidated by Massimo Bernetti. The latter's son Michele has been in charge for the last few years, running the business with passion and a desire to innovate. In the cellar he is flanked by the bright young enologist Giacomo Mattioli and receives the consultancy of Beppe Caviola.

VINEYARDS - The agronomist Luigi Piersanti has been called in to coordinate the staff who manage the vineyards in districts of differing soil and weather conditions (Conero, Castelli di Jesi, Abruzzo). More specifically, the company boasts eight great crus, of which the Busche di Montecarotto, Torre di Cupramontana and San Lorenzo di Osimo estates produce the best grape selections. It also owns 75 acres of vineyard, which it farms organically, in the hills round Teramo. In all cases, the viticulture practiced places the onus on environmental sustainability.

WINES - The distinctive features of the range are varietal profile, dynamism, and refined mouthfeel. **Conero Cumaro Ris. 2010** (● 45,700 bt), a genuine, delightful Montepulciano has impressive character with laid-back, well-poised mouthfeel, tannic verve and aromatic amalgam. **Conero Campo San Giorgio Ris. 2009** Great Wine (● 2,814 bt) is a refined example of Burgundy style: it caresses the palate, unfolds sinuously, closes with tannins of rare elegance, and releases a mixture of red berries and herbs spliced by spices on the nose. **Verdicchio dei Castelli di Jesi Cl. Sup. Vecchie Vigne 2012** (○ 16,000 bt) is robust and dynamic, taut and tangy with a complex suite of aromas pepped up by dried flowers and aniseed.

FERTILIZERS organic-mineral
PLANT PROTECTION chemical, copper and sulphur
WEED CONTROL chemical, mechanical
YEASTS selected
GRAPES 100% estate-grown
CERTIFICATION none

FERTILIZERS manure pellets, green manure, humus
PLANT PROTECTION chemical, copper, sulphur, organic
WEED CONTROL chemical, mechanical
YEASTS selected, native
GRAPES 20% bought in
CERTIFICATION part of the vineyards converting to organics

Bucci

Località Pongelli
Via Cona, 30
tel. 071 964179
www.villabucci.com
bucciwines@villabucci.com

76 ac - 120,000 bt `10% discount`

66 Bucci's production philosophy is encapsulated in its classical, personal interpretation of the verdicchio grape. Every sip is different from the one before and this makes the wine all the more compelling 99

PEOPLE - Bucci is a piece of the history of viticulture in the Castelli di Jesi zone. The brand owes its reputation to its rootedness in the terroir. The wines have grown up with a combination of quality, personality and stylistic refinement. And credit is due to Ampelio for steering them over the sea of the market with a style that has never altered.

VINEYARDS - The cellar owns 76 hectares of vineyards on the clayey active limestone soils of the hills of Serra de' Conti e Montecarotto. Work in the vineyard is easy, according to Gabriele Tanfani, the company's trusty agronomist. "Before doing anything new," he says, "we look at what we did in the past." His words sum up all the tradition and all the modernity of Bucci."

WINES - Every year Bucci, the entry level Verdicchio, is overwhelmed by the supremacy of the flagship wine, Villa Bucci. But this year, though its "big brother" is as impeccable and refined as ever, our preference goes to this year's version of Bucci, which captures the varietal heart of the grape with elegance and refinement. **Castelli di Jesi Verdicchio Ris. Cl. Villa Bucci 2012** (○ 13,000 bt) is readier than usual, in fact it's perfect: it has a well-defined nose, a rich, juicy palate, uniformity and lip-smacking expansion. **Rosso Piceno Villa Bucci Rosso 2010** (● 5,000 bt) is well-structured and delicate, **Rosso Piceno Pongelli 2011** (● 20,000 bt) expresses fruit and intensity.

> **slow wine** VERDICCHIO DEI CASTELLI DI JESI CL. SUP. BUCCI **2013** (○ 75,000 bt) The quintessence of the verdicchio grape, a wine in which the broad-based, tonic palate is enhanced by flavor and clear-cut aromas.

FERTILIZERS manure pellets, biodynamic preparations, green manure, none
PLANT PROTECTION copper and sulphur, organic
WEED CONTROL mechanical
YEASTS selected, native
GRAPES 100% estate-grown
CERTIFICATION organic

La Staffa

Via Castellaretta, 19
tel. 0731 779810 - 338 1551329
www.vinilastaffa.it
info@vinilastaffa.it

20 ac - 30,000 bt `10% discount`

66 Riccardo Baldi is an *enfant prodige*. Just five years ago he was studying at university with his peers and no way did he know how to prune a vine or what a press was. Then he saw the light, changed his mind and developed a passion for viticulture 99

PEOPLE - Maybe Riccardo might have become a good economist, but what's certain is that he's a very good winemaker, attentive and humble with a desire to grow. He has the character to lead the way, so let's hope that light keeps shining!

VINEYARDS - Contrada Castellaretta is on the ridge opposite Salmagina. The valley is a historic one for Staffolo, the best for winegrowing, where saltwater springs ensure plenty of structure and saltiness. Forty-year-old vines share soils in which clay and limestone with more recent plantings. The latest gamble is the decision to lease some old properties, which Riccardo is putting back on their feet simply through land management and pruning.

WINES - As the young man grows, so does quality and the levels achieved by the wines over the last few years are nonpareil. Their DNA contains Staffolo and the character of verdicchio and they transude the passion of the work done in the vineyards and the cellar. The excellent **Verdicchio dei Castelli di Jesi Cl. La Staffa 2013 Everday Wine** (○ 18,000 bt) draws on the cool growing year to exalt the more floral, vegetal soul of the grape, which refreshes the fruity, spicy texture, then its heart starts beating on the palate and expands sinuously without losing its saline grip. **Amor mio 2013** (○ malvasia; 3,000 bt) is lean, fruity and fragrant.

> **slow wine** VERDICCHIO DEI CASTELLI DI JESI CL. SUP. RINCROCCA 2012 (○ 4,000 bt) The emblem of the grape variety – wild fennel, aniseed, apples and pears – all expressed with complexity, suppleness and a salty, deep finish. A masterpiece to taste in one gulp.

FERTILIZERS manure pellets, green manure
PLANT PROTECTION copper and sulphur
WEED CONTROL mechanical
YEASTS selected, native
GRAPES 100% estate-grown
CERTIFICATION converting to organics

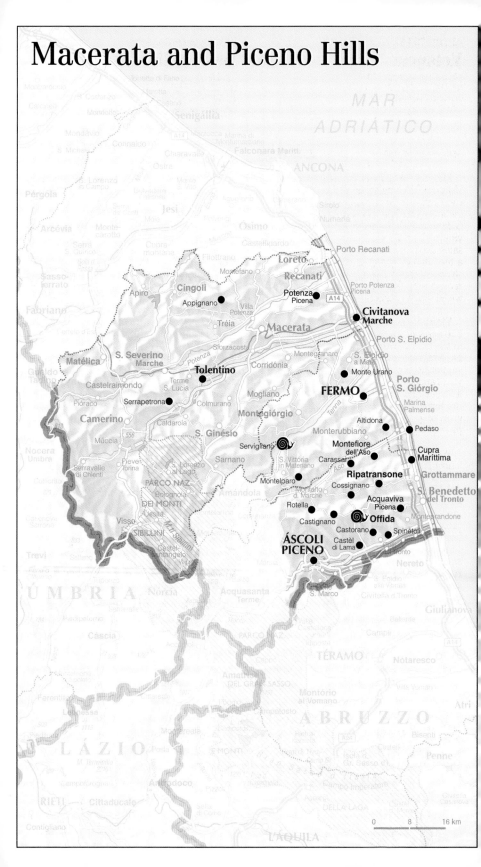

Macerata and Piceno Hills

ASCOLI PICENO

Velenosi

Via dei Biancospini, 11
tel. 0736 341218
www.velenosivini.com
info@velenosivini.com

CASTEL DI LAMA (AP)

De Angelis

Contrada San Francesco, 10
tel. 0736 87429
www.tenutadeangelis.it
info@tenutadeangelis.it

---

368 ac - 2,500,000 bt   `10% discount`

PEOPLE - Angela is the heart and soul of Velenosi, the engine on a train that speeds round the world spreading the word about Piceno. With her travel a first-rate team of collaborators who work with passion in the vineyard, in the wine cellar, and also in the sales department. Angela is professional to a tee, always giving of her best, meticulously, leaving nothing to chance. Which is the reason why the cellar is present on all the world's best markets.

VINEYARDS - The company owns about 250 acres of vineyard and rents another 100 in the Piceno district and round Morro d'Alba. Velenosi has expanded its property to support its constant growth over the last few years and its estates at Castel di Lama, Ascoli Piceno and Castorano are situated right in the heart of the area. The sunny vineyards grow on prevalent clayey-sandy soil, in some places irrigated to give the vines equilibrium.

WINES - It was hard to choose which Velenosi labels were most deserving of inclusion in the guide. **Rosso Piceno Sup. Roggio del Filare 2010** (● 50,000 bt) is more international than usual, conspicuous softness mellowing the flavor without erasing character; the nose is a perfect fusion of black berries, quinine and spice. **Offida Pecorino Villa Angela 2013** (○ 45,000 bt) has a rich, succulent, nicely tonic body and a bouquet redolent of tropical and citrus fruit and blossom. Both fell just short of the Great Wine podium. Rosso Piceno Sup. Brecciarolo 2012 `Everyday Wine` (● 600,000 bt) is sheer value for money, its customary fruity crispness, delicate and never cloying, adding luster to the reactive juicy palate. **Metodo Cl. Brut The Rose 2009** (☉ pinot nero; 15,000 bt) has stylish perlage, a mellow bouquet and a mild, fluent taste profile.

---

124 ac - 500,000 bt   `10% discount`

PEOPLE - From one Alighiero, De Angelis, to another, Alighiero Fausti. The origins of this Castel di Lama cellar are entwined with its future: in-between, 30 years of change and growth thanks to Quinto Fausti, son-in-law of the founder, who moved the business on from the sale of unbottled wine to that of bottled. Now the future is in the hands of Quinto's son Alighiero, who manages foreign sales, and his sister Elisa, who oversees administration.

VINEYARDS - The company owns 125 acres of vineyard in the heart of the Piceno zone. Most of them are near the gullies and the church of Santa Maria della Rocca di Offida in a sunny dale with fertile soil. The rest are round the cellar at Castel di Lama. Mainly local grapes are grown but a few acres are also given over to international varieties, all grown organically.

WINES - De Angelis grows a heck of a lot of grapes and produces a heck of a lot of hectoliters, but it manages nonetheless to keep its focus on local wines. The charismatic **Rosso Piceno Sup. Oro 2010** (● 12,000 bt) has a beautifully turned, enfolding palate with rounded aromas, tannic equilibrium and perfect texture that is sure to mellow in the bottle. The impeccable Rosso Piceno Sup. 2012 `Everyday Wine` (● 150,000 bt) has fruity flesh attenuated by vegetal suggestions, a supple palate and lively tannins. Its affordable price is an added value. Standing out among the whites is **Offida Pecorino 2013** (○ 50,000 bt) which has eschewed its once characteristic mildness to reveal its true personality: it exhibits fruity fullness, hints of blossom and a luscious palate with a freshness that gives it balance and makes it a joy to drink.

FERTILIZERS natural manure, green manure	FERTILIZERS manure pellets
PLANT PROTECTION copper and sulphur	PLANT PROTECTION copper and sulphur
WEED CONTROL mechanical	WEED CONTROL mechanical
YEASTS selected	YEASTS selected
GRAPES 40% bought in	GRAPES 100% estate-grown
CERTIFICATION none	CERTIFICATION organic

Le Vigne di Franca €

Contrada Santa Petronilla, 69
tel. 335 6512938
www.levignedifranca.it
info@levignedifranca.it

Aurora

Località Santa Maria in Carro
Contrada Ciafone, 98
tel. 0736 810007
www.viniaurora.it
enrico@viniaurora.it

---

11 ac - 25,000 bt `10% discount`

PEOPLE - Claudio Paulich, son of an Istrian farming family, studied in Turin and traveled the world before deciding to settle down in Fermo. "I fell in love with the Marche for the beauty of the hills and their colors," he says. A reserved guy of rare pragmatism but at once affable and sentimental, he dedicates his adventure in the Marche wine world to the memory of his late wife Franca, who, alas, was unable to share it with him. Since 2009 he has been translating his own well-developed sense of beauty into wine.

VINEYARDS - The cellar's 11,500 montepulciano, merlot and cabernet vines were planted in 2001 in two adjoining vineyards surrounded by secular olive trees. The land, round the lovely farmhouse at Santa Petronilla is Claudio's domain, a magical dale on the outskirts of Fermo, three miles from the sea, where the breeze is constant and the warm microclimate is perfect for winemaking. "I don't believe in organics," says Claudio, never a one to mince his words.

WINES - Wines are steel-fermented and barrique- and tonneau-aged, and their style is characterized by elegance and fruity fleshiness. Waiting for Crismon 2012 (our tasting of the 2011 confirmed all last year's finesse and elegance), the stage is hogged by its "younger brother," **Rubrum** 2012 `Everyday Wine` (● montepulciano, merlot; 8,000 bt), a Bordeaux-style wine of perfect aromatic cohesion with notes of red berries and vegetal nuances whose well-balanced, juicy palate leaves whiffs of citrus fruit and zest. The house's first white, **Lumen 2013** (○ malvasia, pinot nero; 6,000 bt) makes an impressive debut with wonderfully delicate aromas of peach and apricot braced by mint and herbs, followed up by a well-poised, saline palate.

---

26 ac - 53,000 bt

❝ Passion, dedication, sharing, hospitality – these are the ingredients of Aurora's winning recipe. The difference is made not by individuals but by the combined daily actions of all of them put together ❞

PEOPLE - You'll leave your heart in Aurora. It's far too simplistic to consider the place a "normal" farm. It is, rather, a refuge where you can rediscover life lived to the rhythms of nature, where they work the land simply, implementing a project launched more than 30 years ago by four friends.

VINEYARDS - The "boys" were adamant from the outset that Aurora would practice clean agriculture. After receiving organic certification some years ago, they have subsequently adopted biodynamic criteria. They started off with a vine rows but have since added 24 acres planted with native grape varieties, pecorino in particular on the clayey, sandy soil of the Ciafone hills.

WINES - There's no set pattern to the winemaking, just gallons of spontaneity and a desire to bring out the flavor of the grapes. **Offida Pecorino Fiobbo 2012** (○ 8,000 bt) is a wine with warm caressing tones, spiced up a tad by tanginess and the lightest of tannins; the bouquet is redolent of honey and ripe, roasted fruit. **Morettone 2013** (● 4,000 bt), a ciliegiolo clone without added sulphites stands out for its grapeyness and fruity fragrance. **Rosso Piceno Sup. 2011** (● 8,000 bt) has fleshiness, verve and biting tannins.

`slow wine` **OFFIDA ROSSO BARRICADIERO 2011** (● 4,000 bt) A solid but supple montepulciano redolent of black cherry and blackcurrant and spices. The palate is laid-back and lingering with robust tannins that follow through into the finish.

FERTILIZERS compost, green manure
PLANT PROTECTION chemical, copper and sulphur
WEED CONTROL mechanical
YEASTS selected
GRAPES 20% bought in
CERTIFICATION none

FERTILIZERS biodynamic preparations, green manure
PLANT PROTECTION copper and sulphur
WEED CONTROL mechanical
YEASTS native
GRAPES 100% estate-grown
CERTIFICATION organic

San Filippo €

Contrada Ciafone, 17 A
tel. 0736 889828
www.vinisanfilippo.it
info@vinisanfilippo.it

Fattoria Dezi

Contrada Fontemaggio,14
tel. 0734 710090
fattoriadezi@hotmail.com

---

86 ac - 54,000 bt

PEOPLE - Vine grafter Giuseppe Stracci's experience has aided the professional growth of his sons Fabrizio and Lino, for the last two years helped by the family's young enologist Loris, who is now reviving a brand that had grown somewhat static. Since 1999 the cellar has increased production volumes and sales, and we believe that Loris's fresh, professional approach will become a benchmark for future growth.

VINEYARDS - The cellar farms about 85 acres of vineyard, some of which it owns, others of which it rents. It grows mainly white local grapes on warm, very clayey soils. Most of the white grapes are Guyot-trained in northeast-facing vineyards, while the red ones enjoy sunnier locations and are cordon-trained. The vineyards are meticulously cared for with fertilization with black field bean manure, only lateral topping in June and rigorously organic farming methods.

WINES - The wines are more refined and display more personality and balance than in the past. A tangible example of this is **Offida Pecorino 2013** Everyday Wine (○ 10,000 bt), full of verve and elegance thanks to the cool growing year: its bouquet of peach, dried fruit and blossom is echoed in a well-poised, rich, delicious palate. **Offida Passerina 2013** (○ 10,000 bt) has a sweet, slightly cloying aromatic profile and a simple palate, while **ViMunn 2013** (○ 3,000 bt), a blend of pecorino and passerina without added sulfites, is an interesting work in progress that's getting better all the time.

> slow wine **OFFIDA ROSSO LUPO DEL CIAFONE 2011** (● 5,000 bt) A wine that forcefully expresses the very soul of the montepulciano grape, a concentrate of fruit that goes forth and multiplies on a robust but unobtrusive palate. The finish has character, tannic equilibrium and complexity.

---

37 ac - 42,000 bt `10% discount`

❝ The wines interpret the native grapes without set patterns or styles. It's their personality that makes them so intriguing ❞

PEOPLE - Davide and Stefano Dezi are brothers: the former is shy and retiring, the latter volcanic and restless. The two have taken over the reins of the family business, founded by Romolo and Remo, steering it from mass production towards quality. Their growth has been rapid but, given the energy the brothers have put into the shift, it's only fair that accolades should arrive fast.

VINEYARDS - In Contrada Fontemaggio, an open, ventilated valley looking onto the Ete, the colors of the cereals growing in the fields run into those of the olive groves, symbol of a countryside that still conserves all its lushness and variety. Here, on warm, clayey soil, 37 acres of land are planted with vines, some of which over 40 years' old. Management isn't strictly organic but it is very attentive to the environment.

WINES - The wines from warm growing years are packed with aromatic density. **Regina del Bosco 2008** (● 2,500 bt), a selection of montepulciano matured for 48 months, is a fruity velvet shot with threads of spice; the palate is full of zip, soft but not heavy, with uniform tannins and complexity. **Regina del Bosco 2012** (● 6,000 bt) has comparable aromas but more pronounced fruity sweetness, well-rounded alcohol and tannic verve to add symmetry to the palate. **Solo 2012** (● sangiovese; 6,000 bt) is wrapped in glycerine-rich sweetness and lacks its customary verve. The commendable **Dezio 2012** (● montepulciano, sangiovese; 18,000 bt) is a concentrate of red berries and stylish tannins, which add symmetry.

FERTILIZERS natural manure, green manure
PLANT PROTECTION copper and sulphur, organic
WEED CONTROL mechanical
YEASTS selected
GRAPES 100% estate-grown
CERTIFICATION organic

FERTILIZERS natural manure, green manure
PLANT PROTECTION copper and sulphur, organic
WEED CONTROL mechanical
YEASTS native
GRAPES 100% estate-grown
CERTIFICATION none

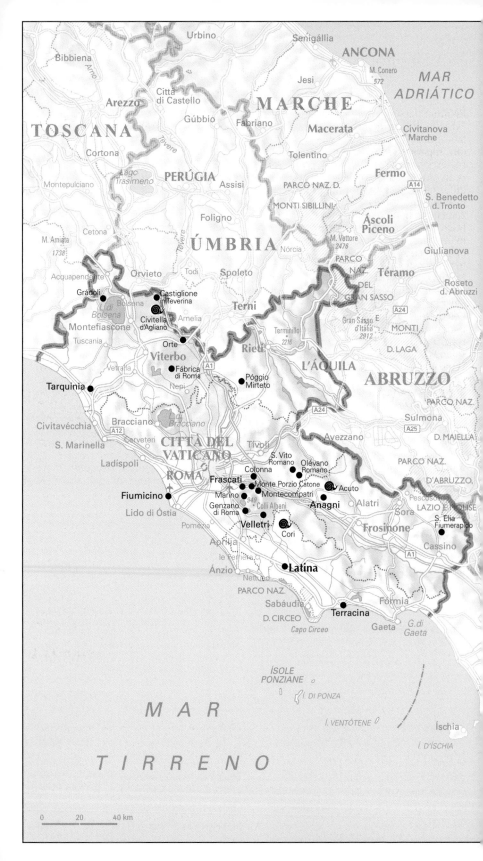

LAZIO

Beautiful Lazio, a land of many colors, is, to quote Dante in *The Divine Comedy*, still "among those who are suspended." The region is also lazy, artful, imprecise, not very far-sighted. The last few vintages have been iffy to say the least and we need to keep our fingers crossed for a truly disconcerting 2014. Even after analyzing the results of regional tastings, we were still unable to come to a reassuring uniform judgment. This is, in part, a matter of logic, since the grape varieties and soil and climate conditions differ notably between the Agro Pontino and Viterbese zones, say, or between Castelli Romani and Ciociaria. And fragmentation is still excessive even inside the different zones: the hope of finding some common denominator, even if only for each different microcosm, keeps having to be put off from one year to the next. As does any attempt to interpret possible lines of evolution in the various contexts consistently in the course of time. This is not entirely the case, however, each ambit revealing, fortunately and to varying degrees, distinctive features that recur year by year. Quality-wise, Northern Lazio continues to produce good Grechetto and rapidly improving Aleaticos – and it also boasts the youngest producers, by the way. Between Piglio and Olevano, the same old masters, along with a handful of bold emulators, continue to produce excellent Cesanese. The same goes for the Castelli Romani, where a Linus security blanket or two managed to infuse warmth and certainty, and this made it possible to avoid surrendering to the temperature swings of last year. Last but not least, the Agro Pontino soldiered on commendably with native and non-native grapes.

What is lacking is the daring exploit, the truly exciting new development, even from admirable loose cannons. Such as the producers in the Viterbo area, for example, who have reconstructed a Rhone-inspired context; or the extreme viticulturists on the island of Ponza; or the women Aleatico producers who are making laudable attempts to subvert the established order; or the winemakers in the Atina who continue to do their own thing with historically significant, albeit not always well-focused, recue work.

Welcome back, finally, to the cellars which spread the word about Castelli Romani, now back in vogue, in the past. To be quite frank, the producers who really do need to find a proper balance are the ones who, serious though they are, are struggling more and more to combine high outputs with quality. It's among them, alarmingly, that routine is starting to creep in …

snails 🐌	bottles 🍾
184 Casale della Ioria	184 Emme
185 Sergio Mottura	Vigneti Massimi Berucci
	185 Trappolini

ACUTO (FR)

Casale della Ioria

Località Agnani
Strada Provinciale 118 Anagni-Paliano km.
4,200
tel. 0775 56031
www.casaledellaioria.com
info@casaledellaioria.com

94 ac - 65,000 bt `10% discount`

❝ The microclimate of the area in which the vineyards are situated and the skills of the company team give life to robust wines that respect tradition and, at the same time, possess nose-palate symmetry and are well-crafted and modern in style ❞

PEOPLE - Paolo Perinelli is the heart and soul of this historic cellar whose mission is to raise the profile of the typical wines of the Frosinone area through a style privileging elegance and drinkability.

VINEYARDS - Cesanese, the principal grape variety of the Ciociaria district, is the most used in Perinelli wines. Another important grape is passerina, while olivella, a red grape on the verge of distinction, is a rarity. The vineyards grow at an altitude of about 1,300 feet and are farmed with great care and attention. Cellar techniques are non-invasive and eco-friendly.

WINES - Passerina Colle Bianco 2013 (○ 9,000 bt) is straw yellow in color and, with its faint notes of flowers and fruit, is an ideal accompaniment to fish and vegetable dishes. The very reasonably priced Cesanese del Piglio Campo Novo 2013 `Everyday Wine` (● 15,000 bt) has red berries and spicy notes with burly tannins and nice acidity. **Cesanese del Piglio Tenuta della Ioria 2012** (● 35,000 bt), which is more complex and will take time to open up, conflates power and elegance with hints of sour cherry, silky tannins and an alcoholic kick: it's a wine to go with roast meats, game and mature cheeses. The enjoyable **Très 2011** (● cesanese, cabernet sauvignon, merlot; 5,000 bt) is an international-style red in which the cesanese grape shines through.

ANAGNI (FR)

Emme
Vigneti Massimi Berucci

Località Isidoro
Via Casilina Km 63
tel. 0775 769960
www.agricolaemme.it
agricolaemme@agricolaemme.it

59 ac - 110.000 bt

PEOPLE - Società Agricola Emme is a major winery in the province of Frosinone with about 59 acres of vineyards. Owners Anatolio and Pietro Piccirilli are currently gearing their production towards increasingly high production standards. In 2011 the group was joined by the San Lorenzo in Valle dairy so that now its terroir-based wines are flanked by prime-quality craft cheeses.

VINEYARDS - The grapes cultivated are cesanese for the red wines and passerina for the whites, and the vineyards, of different ages, are concentrated within the communal boundary of Piglio. Under the management of Lorenzo Costantini, work in the vineyard and cellar is designed to keep yields low with vinifications that respect and exalt the sensory characteristics of each wine with the intelligent use of oak barrels.

WINES - Passerina Hyperius 2013 (○ 20,000 bt) is fresh and fruity with pronounced acidity. **Passerina Casal Cervino 2013** (○ 7,000 bt) is more complex and nuanced with good body and blossomy, mineral notes that close with faint suggestions of bitterness. The excellent **Cesanese del Piglio Hyperius 2013** (● 26,000 bt) is balanced with evident hints of red berry fruits, slightly astringent tannins and refreshing acidity. **Cesanese del Piglio Vigne Nuove 2011** (● 3,000 bt) still needs time to open up and evolve; in the meantime, the alcohol is potent but well amalgamated.

`slow wine` CESANESE DEL PIGLIO CASAL CERVINO 2011 (● 10,000 bt) In our view, not only the cellar's best wine but also the best wine in its category. It has heavyweight body with suggestions of cherry and black cherry, and elegant tannins that make for wonderful drinkability.

FERTILIZERS green manure	FERTILIZERS mineral, manure pellets
PLANT PROTECTION copper and sulphur	PLANT PROTECTION copper and sulphur
WEED CONTROL mechanical	WEED CONTROL mechanical
YEASTS selected	YEASTS selected
GRAPES 100% estate-grown	GRAPES 100% estate-grown
CERTIFICATION none	CERTIFICATION none

Trappolini
Via del Rivellino, 65
tel. 0761 948381
www.trappolini.com
info@trappolini.com

Sergio Mottura

Via Poggio della Costa, 1
tel. 0761 914533
www.motturasergio.it
vini@motturasergio.it

67 ac - 200,000 bt

89 ac - 100,000 bt · **10% discount**

PEOPLE - The Trappolini family have been making wine for more than 50 years. Today Paolo and Roberto Trappoloni run a winery that has progressively refined its style with passion and competence. The turnaround in quality came in the early 1990s, when they began to select grapes to make wines with a strong sense of place.

VINEYARDS - The winery's land extends from the Tiber Valley to the border with Umbria and comprises zones in which the microclimate and soil composition are perfect for winegrowing. The grapes planted are the classic ones for the area and vineyard management has a low impact on the environment. The vines are spurred cordon- and Guyot-pruned. The company recently added a new monovarietal procanico wine to its already comprehensive range.

WINES - The broad range of wines submitted for tasting was top-notch. It was spearheaded by **Paterno 2012** (● sangiovese; 45,000) with its complex nose of cocoa and preserved cherries and full-bodied palate in which the grape's typical acidity fuses with the tannins and leads into a long, entrancing finish with refined spicy notes. **Cenereto 2013** **Everyday Wine** (● sangiovese, montepulciano; 40,000 bt) is a chirpier, vivacious red, but no less well crafted, as quaffable as it is affordable. Noteworthy among the whites is **Grechetto 2013** (○ 10,000 bt), which has an intense, varietal nose redolent of aromatic herbs and a tangy, powerful, long, gutsy palate. We were also enticed by the drinkable **Procanico 2013** (○ 6,000 bt) with its elegant aromas of apple and medlar bright and well-balanced palate.

66 It's not easy to condense different values such as top quality, defense and promotion of the native grapes and the local area and sustainable, certified organic agriculture into a single winery as Sergio Mottura has done over the last few years 99

PEOPLE - It's always a pleasure to meet Sergio, a native of Piemont now very much at home at Tana dell'Istrice, or Porcupine's Den, his farmhouse. This year the winery completed its fiftieth harvest and Sergio's children Giuseppe, Francesca and Alessandra help him to run it.

VINEYARDS - The vineyards, which have always been farmed organically, are spread round the cellar, which is situated under the village, on volcanic soil rich in minerals. They grow native and international grape varieties, which are fermented traditionally, then aged in new and used French barriques. Some of the wines are bottled with screw caps to follow the evolution in the cellar of grechetto, a grape that has always shown a certain aging capacity.

WINES - **Latour a Civitella 2011** **Great Wine** (○ grechetto; 18,000 bt), back after a "gap year," is fermented and aged in wood casks; spacious and elegant, it has delicate notes toasty notes and great minerality with an intense, lingering palate. **Poggio della Costa 2013** (○ grechetto; 45,000 bt) has outstanding body with hints of fruit and minerals. **Orvieto Tragugnano 2013** (○ grechetto, procanico; 12,000 bt), is fermented in steel vats and has a blossomy, fruity nose. **Orvieto 2013** (○ 20,000 bt) is fresh and quaffable. The elegantly structured **Syracide 2011** (● shiraz; 2,800 bt) has hints of spice with red berries very much to the fore, while **Nenfro 2011** (● montepulciano; 5,000 bt) is bright and leisurely. Both wines are barrique-aged.

FERTILIZERS natural manure, green manure	**FERTILIZERS** none
PLANT PROTECTION copper and sulphur	**PLANT PROTECTION** copper and sulphur
WEED CONTROL mechanical	**WEED CONTROL** mechanical
YEASTS selected	**YEASTS** selected
GRAPES 100% estate-grown	**GRAPES** 100% estate-grown
CERTIFICATION none	**CERTIFICATION** organic

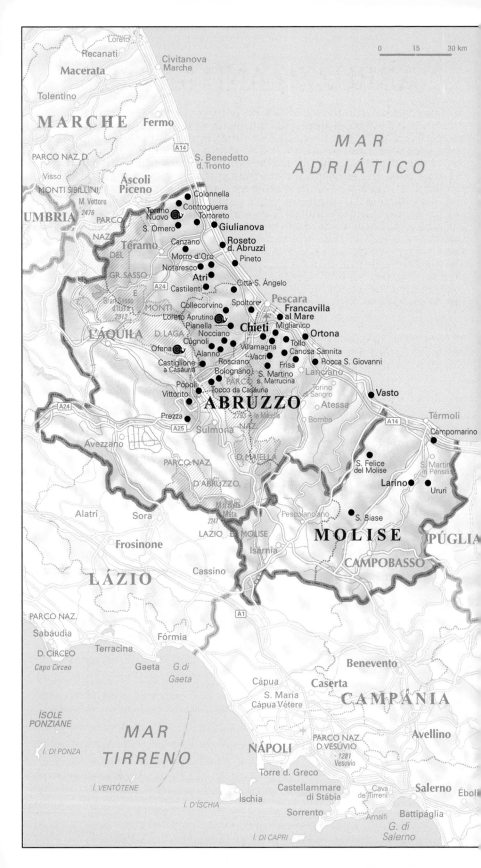

ABRUZZO AND MOLISE

Abruzzo is present and correct. Despite the dismal economic situation in Italy, wine production in the region is responding with unexpected vitality and character. Part of the credit must go to the generational turnover in many wineries and a new wave of young winemakers keen to valorize their local areas with a different approach from that of their parents. During the months we spent visiting cellars, we noted growing concern for sustainability. More and more producers are converting to organics, convinced that this is the best way to manage their vineyards. Results vary from one area to another, but this year it is only right and fair to celebrate the success of a new range of Montepulciano d'Abruzzos. After years of concentrations, long aging on wood and high alcohol content, the montepulciano grape is now returning to more varietal interpretations in which fruit and suppleness dominate. The new wines are bright and lean, vinified no longer on wood but increasingly in stainless steel and cement vats. The trend demands patience if it is to express itself to the full, hence longer bottle-aging prior to market release. This productive turnaround also imposes new methods of vineyard management, with climate change influencing healthy grape ripening more than in the past. Moving on to whites, Trebbiano d'Abruzzo is the star turn, showing yet again that, with due care in the vineyard and grape selection, not to mention fewer interventions in the cellar, it possesses the wherewithal to age supremely well. The 2013 Pecorinos also performed commendably, with a range of fragrant, juicy, personality-packed wines, as did bottles made with other native white grapes such as cococciola, passerina and montonico. The year also shined on Cerasuolo d'Abruzzo, which never ceases to amaze for freshness, structure and complexity. Worthy of mention too is the enthusiasm shown by Abruzzo producers towards sparkling wines produced with local grapes using the Charmat and Classico methods, sometimes with appreciable results.

The quality of wine in Molise is improving progressively thanks to a group of producers highly motivated to emerge beyond the regional boundaries. By banking a lot on the tintilia grape, they are improving the quality of their wines year by year.

snails ◉

189 TORRE DEI BEATI
189 VALENTINI
190 CATALDI MADONNA
190 VALLE REALE
191 PRAESIDIUM
193 EMIDIO PEPE

bottles ▮

188 CONTESA
192 FATTORIA LA VALENTINA

coins €

188 COLLEFRISIO
193 TENUTA TERRAVIVA

COLLECORVINO (PE)

Contesa

Contrada Capparrone, 4
tel. 085 8205078
www.contesa.it
info@contesa.it

FRISA (CH)

Collefrisio

Località Piane di Maggio
tel. 085 9039074
www.collefrisio.it
info@collefrisio.it

---

59 ac - 240,000 bt | **10% discount**

89 ac - 350,000 bt

PEOPLE - Rocco Pasetti and his wife Patrizia's gamble has paid off. Combining their love of the land, pursuit of quality and business acumen, they set up their winery in the Collecorvino hills almost 15 years ago. Now their children are laying an active part in their project in progress, too. Especially their firstborn Franco, a trained enologist who oversees the wine cellar with the assistance of Antonio Circelli.

VINEYARDS - Most of the vineyards, well kept with a good vegetative-productive balance, are spread out over the rolling, sunny hills round the cellar. The majority of the vines are spurred cordon-trained, apart from the Guyot-pruned pecorino. A great deal of care is taken over work in the fields, the grapes being treated only with copper and sulphur, and scrupulously selected.

WINES - The average quality of the wines submitted for tasting was good as always, proof of the company's reliability. Cerasuolo d'Abruzzo Contesa 2013 Everyday Wine (◉ 16,000 bt) offers red berries and brilliant acidity and works well. **Montepulciano d'Abruzzo Contesa 2012** (● 16,000 bt) has notes of blackcurrant and bramble, prominent tannins and a spicy finish. **Montepulciano d'Abruzzo Contesa Ris. 2009** (● 8,000 bt) is a wine with plenty of grip that grows in the glass with vegetal, spicy brushstrokes. Moving on to the whites, **Abruzzo Pecorino Contesa 2013** (○ 18,000 bt) has clear-cut aromas and linear flavor. **Pecorino Sorab 2012** (○ 8,000 bt) has a delicate nose of blossom and dried fruit and a bright and breezy palate. **Trebbiano d'Abruzzo Contesa 2013** (○ 16,000 bt) is enjoyable, too.

PEOPLE - Ten years on from its birth, a dynamic winery in constant evolution and now, to all intents and purposes, a well-established institution on the variegated Abruzzo winemaking scene. Credit for this is due to the owners, Antonio Patricelli and Amedeo De Luca, farsighted in their planning and determined in their decision-making. Duties are equally shared between the two: Antonio is responsible for communication and marketing, Amedeo for work in the wine cellar.

VINEYARDS - The organically farmed vineyards are split between three main hillside properties near Giuliano Teatino (arid, heavy soil and red clay), Frisa (light limestone, pebbly soils) and Valle del Moro (prevalently clayey, pebbly soils). Most are trained with the traditional Abruzzo pergola system, apart from a few acres of rows of montepulciano.

WINES - The wines presented this year were stylistically precise and convincing. The excellent **Trebbiano d'Abruzzo Vignaquadra 2011** Great Wine (○ 5,000 bt) is a sumptuous white with a rich blossomy bouquet, elegant and soft on the palate with well-calibrated supporting acidity and a deep, tangy finish. On a par is **Montepulciano d'Abruzzo 2012** (● 100,000 bt), land-rooted with a bright personality, enviable acid-tannic texture and a nice spicy finish. **Cerasuolo d'Abruzzo 2013** (◉ 20,000 bt) is bright and satisfying, tangy and fruity. **Montepulciano d'Abruzzo Vignaquadra 2010** (● 48,000 bt) has a more modern profile with sweet spices dominating delicate red berries. **Passerina Vignaquadra 2013** (○ 13,000 bt) is fragrant and quaffable.

FERTILIZERS natural manure, green manure
PLANT PROTECTION copper and sulphur, organic
WEED CONTROL chemical, mechanical
YEASTS selected
GRAPES 100% estate-grown
CERTIFICATION none

FERTILIZERS natural manure, green manure
PLANT PROTECTION copper and sulphur, organic
WEED CONTROL mechanical
YEASTS selected
GRAPES 100% estate-grown
CERTIFICATION organic

LORETO APRUTINO (PE)

Torre dei Beati

Contrada Poggioragone, 56
tel. 333 3832344
www.torredeibeati.it
info@torredeibeati.it

LORETO APRUTINO (PE)

Valentini

Via del Baio, 2
tel. 085 8291138

---

45 ac - 100,000 bt

66 With passion, application and humility, Adriana Galasso and Fausto Albanesi have built their lives step by step with their baby, a small winery that just grows and grows 99

PEOPLE - Adriana and Fausto, with their customary attention to detail and dynamism, are currently restructuring a few old farm cottages to provide accommodation for guests. They have also recovered extra space in their underground cellar, where they continue to experiment, partly out of fun, partly to put themselves to the test. Something tells us they have surprises in store for the future.

VINEYARDS - Most of the vineyards surround the cellar at Poggio Ragone, while other parcels are to be found in the hills of Contrada Scannella, protected by the Voltigno plateau, to which another 19 acres were added in 2014. The soil is sandy and clayey and the vines, most of which planted over 30 years ago, are pergola-trained. The younger ones are high-trained, but with a wider planting pattern to provide more shade for the white grapes.

WINES - The wines are once more of a very high standard. The **Abruzzo Pecorino Giocheremo con i Fiori 2013** Everyday Wine (O 25,000 bt) is fragrant and pleasant, while the barrel-fermented **Abruzzo Pecorino Bianchi Grilli 2012** (O 1,800 bt) is more structured and complex. As always, it's hard to choose between the two Montepulciano selections: the reflective, Burgundy-like **Montepulciano d'Abruzzo Cocciapazza 2011** (● 10,000 bt) has crisp fruit, whereas **Montepulciano d'Abruzzo Mazzamurello 2011** (● 5,000 bt) conflates fruit, spices and fine tannins.

slow wine TREBBIANO D'ABRUZZO BIANCHI GRILLI 2012 (O 3,000 bt) A commendable interpretation of the grape. Balsamic in tone, it is full-bodied and packed with peach and apricot with deftly vegetal nuances and lingering minerality.

---

163 ac - 50.000 bt

66 When you meet Francesco Valentini, you inevitably end up talking more about vines than about wines. But besides being a very good farmer, he's also something of a rural intellectual, so his conversation is always stimulating and full of insight 99

PEOPLE - Following in his father's furrow, Francesco dedicates himself as much to vineyard management as to study and research. What with climate change and the recent sequence of problematic growing years, his main concern is to grow healthy grapes to the right degree of ripeness and help the vines to adapt to the new, changeable conditions.

VINEYARDS - An unusually warm autumn, a brusque drop in temperature at the end of November 2013 and, finally, a heavy snowfall devastated 74 acres of old arbor-trained vines much loved by Edoardo yesterday and Francesco today. With a sizable outlay, 56 acres have been rescued, but the other 21, all given over to trebbiano grapes, have been lost for good.

WINES - In view of the "ferment" in the so-called natural wine world these days, thoughts wander "spontaneously" to the Valentini family, who have been practicing "spontaneous fermentations" – no temperature control, no filtration – for well nigh two centuries. This year Valentini presented only its Trebbiano d'Abruzzo, releasing the 2010 after the 2011. So no Cerasuolo and, more importantly, no Montepulciano, though Francesco is cautiously optimistic about recent vintages that are now aging in the cellar.

slow wine TREBBIANO D'ABRUZZO 2010 (O 22,000 bt) Distinctive mineral notes on the nose with deep, taut flavor sustained by lively acidity, in which the fruit gradually prevails over the mineral tones.

FERTILIZERS natural manure, green manure	**FERTILIZERS** none
PLANT PROTECTION copper and sulphur	**PLANT PROTECTION** copper and sulphur
WEED CONTROL mechanical	**WEED CONTROL** mechanical
YEASTS selected	**YEASTS** native
GRAPES 100% estate-grown	**GRAPES** 100% estate-grown
CERTIFICATION organic	**CERTIFICATION** none

OFENA (AQ)

Cataldi Madonna

Località Piano
tel. 0862 954252
www.cataldimadonna.com
cataldimadonna@virgilio.it

77 ac - 250,000 bt · 10% discount

66 Apparently conservative but with an eye to the future, Luigi Cataldi Madonna's winery takes the challenges of modernity in its stride without losing its sound rural tradition and its place in the history of Abruzzo winemaking 99

PEOPLE - The Cataldi Madonna has been working the land and making wine in the countryside round Ofena for more than a century. Now Luigi is flanked by a new generation in the persons of his daughter Giulia and nephew Lorenzo.

VINEYARDS - The aim is to grow vines capable of capturing the characteristics of the terroir. Ofena stands at an altitude of about 1,300 feet on a small plateau at the foot of the Gran Sasso, where the geological conformation and the Calderone glacier have created a unique microclimate, very hot in the summer but with sharp night-to-day temperature swings.

WINES - The absence of the top-of-the-range label, Montepulciano d'Abruzzo Toni, was amply made up for by two very impressive Cerasuolo d'Abruzzos: **Cerasuolo d'Abruzzo Piè delle Vigne 2012** (☉ 3,000 bt), dark in color with a fully, fruity, slightly earthy nose and a complex, tannic spacious palate; and the quaffable, tasty Cerasuolo d'Abruzzo 2013 Everyday Wine (☉ 40,000 bt) with its lovely notes of cherry and fresh, tangy palate. The brand new Rosato **Cataldino 2013** (☉ montepulciano; 2,000 bt) is simple, fresh and enjoyable, while **Pecorino Giulia 2013** (○ 35,000 bt) is fragrant.

> slow wine | **MONTEPULCIANO D'ABRUZZO MALANDRINO 2012** (● 90,000 bt) A masterful old/new generation interpretation of the montepulciano grape, fermented in stainless steel and cement vats. Elegant with notes of bramble and spices on the nose, it unbends on the plate with plenty of juice and body.

FERTILIZERS natural manure
PLANT PROTECTION copper and sulphur
WEED CONTROL mechanical
YEASTS selected
GRAPES 100% estate-grown
CERTIFICATION converting to organics

POPOLI (PE)

Valle Reale

Località San Calisto
tel. 085 9871039
www.vallereale.it
info@vallereale.it

121 ac - 270,000 bt

66 Leonardo Pizzolo, born in Veneto but now perfectly integrated in the rural culture of Abruzzo, seethes with ideas, which he puts into practice with virtuous, unbending pragmatism 99

PEOPLE - First the foundation and development of the winery, then conversion to organics and experiments with biodynamics, spontaneous fermentations in the cellar and, last but not least, an organic garden – these are the various stages in Leonardo's wholehearted, passionate progress in the Abruzzo mountains.

VINEYARDS - The two vineyards are at Popoli, near the cellar, and Capestrano. The soil and climatic conditions in the two areas are very different indeed: at Popoli, the soil is leaner and the climate more rigid and windy; at Capestrano, the soil is rich and the weather sunnier with sharp temperature swings. The vines are pergola- and high-trained.

WINES - **Trebbiano d'Abruzzo 2013** (○ 20,000 bt) is lively and drinkable with bracing acidity. The elegant **Cerasuolo d'Abruzzo 2013** (☉ 95,000 bt) is fresh and fruity. **Montepulciano d'Abruzzo 2013** (● 20,000 bt) has good acidic and tannic texture with plenty of fruit. **Montepulciano d'Abruzzo San Calisto 2013** (● 8,000 bt) impresses with polished tannins and perfectly balanced flavor. **Trebbiano d'Abruzzo Vigneto di Popoli 2012** (○ 5,000 bt) has typically lively acidity and full flavor.

> slow wine | **TREBBIANO D'ABRUZZO VIGNA DI CAPESTRANO 2012** (○ 2,700 bt) One of the most must-have Abruzzo labels. The nose is packed with fruit and ginger and blossom, the palate is full and tangy, and the long finish is dominated by intriguing mineral notes.

FERTILIZERS natural manure, biodynamic preparations, green manure
PLANT PROTECTION copper and sulphur
WEED CONTROL mechanical
YEASTS native
GRAPES 100% estate-grown
CERTIFICATION organic

PREZZA (AQ)

Praesidium 🐌

Via Nazzareno Giovannucci, 24
tel. 0864 45103
www.vinipraesidium.it
vinipraesidium@tiscali.it

12 ac - 26,000 bt `10% discount`

66 The Pasquale family are firm believers in the potential of the Valle Peligna. The results of the work they've been doing in their vineyards for 25 years shows they are right 99

PEOPLE - Enzo Pasquale and his son and daughter Ottaviano and Antonia, who share the vineyard and cellar work equally, form a well-knit team. They are perfectly synchronized in their pursuit of the family's two great ideals: wine and environmental protection.

VINEYARDS - The Pasquale family's approach to viticulture is to observe the vines and respect the environment and the seasons. Their ten-acre vineyard is situated in Contrada Cavate, in the lower part of the Prezza district, where there are good air circulation and significant temperature swings. This year the montepulciano plantings were flanked by a small plot given over to trebbiano.

WINES - Two labels, two types of wines and a single grape, montepulciano, joined by the same production philosophy: the pursuit of a wine that relates the natural context in which it was born in the glass. **Cerasuolo d'Abruzzo 2013** (⊙ 6,000 bt) is a dark rosé with austere fruity notes; potent and staid on the palate, it closes with pleasant spiciness. The cellar also makes an excellent Ratafià by infusing montepulciano grapes and black cherries.

slow wine **MONTEPULCIANO D'ABRUZZO RIS. 2009** (● 14,800 bt) After two years' maturing in steel vats and another two aging in oak barrels, this wine shows massive character and personality. Black berries interweave deftly with spices on the nose, and the tangy palate is full of density and follow-through.

FERTILIZERS natural manure, green manure
PLANT PROTECTION copper and sulphur
WEED CONTROL mechanical
YEASTS native
GRAPES 100% estate-grown
CERTIFICATION organic

SAN FELICE DEL MOLISE (CB)

Claudio Cipressi Vignaiolo

Contrada Montagna
tel. 0874 874535
www.claudiocipressi.it
info@claudiocipressi.it

40 ac - 50,000 bt `10% discount`

PEOPLE - Claudio Cipressi has changed the face of his company, restyling is image and opting for organic farming. An agronomist who picked up experience in the field with his grandfather, Claudio, with the consultancy of enologist Vincenzo Mercurio, has believed right from the outset in the potential of the native tintilia grape and has been working for some time with Campobasso University on yeasts and other native species.

VINEYARDS - Green, green and more green ... that's Molise. The spurred cordon-trained vineyards grow at an altitude of 1,500 feet, face south-southeast and look out to sea and, faraway on the horizon, the Tremiti Islands. "It's great country for farming," says Claudio, and he has a point. The topsoil is clayey with a stratum of limestone just below and the climate is cooled by the sea breeze that wafts up in the evening to refresh the vineyards, as many as 28 acres of which are given over to tintilia.

WINES - The turning point for Claudio was 2013, when he put new labels on wines that perfectly reflected his new strategies: total control of the distribution chain, limited quantities and natural vinification methods to make his wines more compelling. **Molise Macchianera 2010** (● montepulciano, tintilia; 9,000 bt) is austere and spicy. **Falanghina Voira 2013** (⊙ 10,000 bt) is bright, soft and mineral. **Molise Decimo 2011** (● 10,000 bt) is a montepulciano with a lingering suggestion of licorice. **Molise Rosato Colle Quinto 2013** (⊙ montepulciano; 3,000 bt) shows structure, acidity and elegance.

slow wine **TINTILIA MACCHIAROSSA 2010** (● 20,000 bt) The customary, compelling interpretation of the tintilia grape. It entrances with its elegant wild rose nose and enthralls with its follow-up of spices enhanced by a balsamic note.

FERTILIZERS none
PLANT PROTECTION copper and sulphur
WEED CONTROL mechanical
YEASTS selected
GRAPES 100% estate-grown
CERTIFICATION organic

SANT'OMERO (TE)

Valori

Via Torquato al Salinello, 8
tel. 0861 88461
luigivalori@hotmail.it

SPOLTORE (PE)

Fattoria La Valentina

Via Torretta, 52
tel. 085 4478158
www.lavalentina.it
lavalentina@fattorialavalentina.it

---

64 ac - 150,000 bt

PEOPLE - Love of the countryside and love of wine have always been one and the same thing for Luigi Valori. It was this passion of his that led him, in 1997, to set up his own winery. Since then, harvest by harvest, the wines he has produced have been increasingly impressive. Luigi prefers to be out working in the country rather than concerning himself with matters like sales and marketing, which, not surprisingly, he entrusted to Masciarelli Distribuzione some years ago.

VINEYARDS - The vineyards cover an area of about 64 acres, some round the cellar, some in excellent winegrowing country in the Controguerra hills. The altitude varies from 520 to 980 feet, the soils are lean and sandy, and the south-southeast-facing position is perfect for the vines. The oldest vine rows were planted almost 50 years ago and their grapes go into the cellar's reserve.

WINES - The style of Valori's potent, alcoholic but stylish wines is firmly terroir-based. Montepulciano d'Abruzzo 2013 Everyday Wine (● 110,000 bt), still one of the best wines for the typology, is a coherent expression of the grape which offers fruit to the nose and develops well on the nose, dynamically and deeply with a classic aftertaste of licorice. **Montepulciano d'Abruzzo Bio 2013** (● 6,700 bt) is a little less biting. **Montepulciano d'Abruzzo Vigna Sant'Angelo 2009** (● 7,000 bt), marked by ripe fruit and spices, is full-bodied on the palate and a tad dry on the finish. The dense **Merlot Inkiostro 2010** (● 3,000 bt) has a fruity, slightly grassy bouquet. **Trebbiano d'Abruzzo 2013** (○ 13,000 bt) has notes of fruit and blossom and **Abruzzo Pecorino 2013** (○ 6,500 bt) is interesting.

98 ac - 350,000 bt

PEOPLE - An exemplary winery inspired, albeit understatedly, by ethical and eco-friendly principles. Brothers Sabatino, Andrea and Roberto Di Properzio are the brains behind the place, which will celebrate its 25th anniversary in 2015. Other key roles are covered by Luca D'Attoma (enology) and Paride Marino (sales). The winery also co-produces Binomio wines with its friend and partner Stefano Inama.

VINEYARDS - More than a third of the vineyards will be certified organic from the 2014 harvest. They are spread over three good growing areas on a variety of plots: two in Spoltore, round the cellar and on the hillside opposite; two at Scafa and San Valentino, in the Val Pescara and at the fot of the Majella; and, finally, in area between Loreto Aprutino and Pianella. Most are given over to montepulciano, the rest to trebbiano, pecorino and fiano.

WINES - The whites and rosés aren't a surprise any more, while the Montepulciano d'Abruzzos have always been the cellar's strong point. The Bellovedere selection wasn't produced in the 2009 vintage, so spearheading the range is **Montepulciano d'Abruzzo Spelt 2010** Great Wine (● 45,000 bt), which has long, crisp fruit and silky tannins. We liked the new style of **Montepulciano d'Abruzzo Binomio 2010** (● 10,000 bt), which has concentrated fruit enriched by balsamic undertones. **Montepulciano d'Abruzzo La Valentina 2012** (● 150,000 bt) is a valid introduction to the typology. **Cerasuolo d'Abruzzo Sup. Spelt 2013** (◉ 3,500 bt) is one of the best wines in its category. **Trebbiano d'Abruzzo Spelt 2013** (○ 10,000 bt) and **Pecorino 2013** (○ 37,000 bt) are both tangy and develop well over the palate.

FERTILIZERS organic-mineral, natural manure, humus
PLANT PROTECTION copper and sulphur, organic
WEED CONTROL mechanical
YEASTS native, selected
GRAPES 100% estate-grown
CERTIFICATION organic

FERTILIZERS organic-mineral, mineral, biodynamic preparations, green manure, none
PLANT PROTECTION copper and sulphur, organic
WEED CONTROL mechanical
YEASTS selected
GRAPES 40% bought in
CERTIFICATION none

Emidio Pepe 🐌

Via Chiesi, 10
tel. 086 1856493
www.emidiopepe.com
info@emidiopepe.com

37 ac - 70,000 bt

66 A visit to this winery is always an unforgettable experience. Here you see how respect for nature and natural equilibrium is one of the priorities of the Pepe family 99

PEOPLE - It's no coincidence that this historic winery, founded at the end of the 19th century and run with application and passion for generations – from patriarch Emidio to his daughters Sofia and Daniela and granddaughter Chiara – is a recognized point of reference across the region and beyond.

VINEYARDS - The belief that the terroir give of its best with interventions in the cellar reduced to a bare minimum demands impeccable vineyard management, meaning solely natural treatments and hardly any plowing. Biodynamics also helps to draw a sense of place out of the soil. The vineyards are a combination of old pergola-trained vines and younger high-trained plantings.

WINES - Here everything is done by hand. After the grape harvest the white grapes are trodden, while the montepulciano grapes are destemmed by rubbing the bunches on metal grilles over wooden tubs. Native yeasts and bottle-aging do the rest. This isn't a bucolic fairytale but a way of winemaking that has never changed. Its efficacy comes out in the wines. The excellent **Trebbiano d'Abruzzo 2012** (○ 20,000 bt), for example, has a full-flavored, lip-smacking palate of peaches and apricots.

slow wine MONTEPULCIANO D'ABRUZZO 2011 (● 20,000 bt) Thanks to a very warm growing year, this wine is already ready to enjoy. Let it breathe for a moment in the glass and you'll immediately perceive the complexity and depth of this red with its fragrant notes of fruit and spices and fresh fleshy palate.

FERTILIZERS natural manure, biodynamic preparations, green manure
PLANT PROTECTION copper and sulphur
WEED CONTROL mechanical
YEASTS native
GRAPES 100% estate-grown
CERTIFICATION biodynamic, organic

Tenuta Terraviva €

Via del Lago, 19
tel. 0861 786056
www.tenutaterraviva.it
info@tenutaterraviva.it

45 ac - 46,000 bt   **10% discount**

PEOPLE - This small winery just grows and grows. Production is up, albeit by just a few bottles, and a few new labels have appeared, but the *modus operandi* is the same as ever and the quality of the wines improves every year. The credit for this belongs to Pietro Topi and Martino Taraschi who, since they set up in 2006, have skillfully turned the potential of this beautiful Abruzzo terroir into reality.

VINEYARDS - The vineyards are situated near the company headquarters in a single property on a slight slope in a narrow valley between the mountains and the Adriatic. The soils are lean and barren, a fact which contains production, especially in the driest years. Ten acres of vineyards, including the 42-year-old trebbiano plot whose grapes produce Mario's, are trained with the Abruzzo pergola system, and 32 are high-trained with the Guyot and spurred cordon systems.

WINES - All the wines presented impress for quality and sense of place. We were particularly taken by Trebbiano d'Abruzzo Terraviva 2013 Everyday Wine (○ 6,500 bt), fruity and mineral, structured and sappy, and Solo Rosso 2012 Everyday Wine (● sangiovese; 2,000 bt), which has exuberant notes of flowers and undergrowth on the nose set off by a sedate, tannic palate. **Pecorino Ekwo 2013** (○ 4,000 bt) is slightly undeveloped on the nose but has a well-balanced taste profile and unfolds easily on the palate, poised between thrusting minerality and subtle citrusy acidity. **Trebbiano d'Abruzzo Mario's 40 2012** (○ 5,000 bt), full-bodied and tangy, and **Montepulciano d'Abruzzo CO2 2013** (● 3,000 bt), bright and juicy, are both very interesting.

FERTILIZERS natural manure
PLANT PROTECTION copper and sulphur
WEED CONTROL mechanical
YEASTS native
GRAPES 100% estate-grown
CERTIFICATION organic

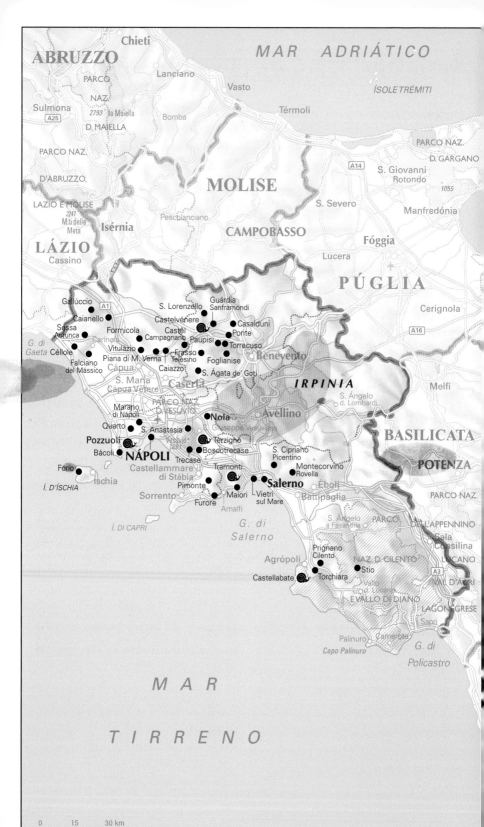

CAMPANIA

Campania produces just over one and a half million hectoliters of wine a year. Little more than a drop in the national ocean, a niche for enthusiasts alone. The fact is that the intensive agriculture of the plains has always relegated vines to the hills of the hinterland. This structural factor also has an upside, with the province of Avellino standing out for quality and, thanks to its three DOCGs (Taurasi, Fiano di Avellino and Greco di Tufo), achieving a national, indeed international dimension.

We'd like to make a mention of Benevento too, a province which, by virtue of reorganization of its DOCs, is now making great steps forward. The 864,000 hectoliters of wine it produces account for half the region's total output, and its two leading wines, Aglianico and Falanghina, are paragons of quality.

In this edition of the guide, we have shifted our attention to the Irpinia and Sannio districts in an attempt to record these two macro-trends. One of the reasons for this stems from our tastings, as precisely in the two provinces in question, Avellino and Benevento, though single cellars interpret their grapes in different ways, we did recognize a common sensory and taste profile.

There are of course outstanding "soloists" in other areas, men and women who make sacrifices to assert the idea of wine we have always advocated: hence eco-compatible viticulture and wines that express the soil they come from and refuse to bend to easy, undemanding flavors. Significant examples are Vesuvio and Campi Flegrei in the province of Naples, and Costiera Amalfitana in the province of Salerno. Just making wine in these areas isn't easy, never mind making it well.

Moving on to grape varieties, the fiano-greco-falanghina "trident" performed superlatively, confirming Campania's vocation for white wines. Other grapes, such as biancolella, asprinio, coda di volpe, pallagrello bianco and coda di pecora, provide further incontrovertible proof of the fact. Taurasi – ie, the aglianico grape – also impressed and now deserves to be considered one of Italy's great reds. Once again, though, the real novelty was the growth of piedirosso, a grape relatively unknown outside the region, an exciting marriage of ancient and modern.

This, then, is our analysis of what, as we have said, is a niche viticulture but which continues to improve. Year by year, an inch at a time.

CASTELLABATE (SA)

Maffini

Località Cenito
tel. 0974.966345
www.luigimaffini.it
info@luigimaffini.it

27 ac - 100,000 bt

66 Luigi Maffini is like an oak tree: he never bends. Either to fashion or, above all, to difficulties. When he's hung-up, he climbs onto his tractor and drives round the vineyards to recover his composure. He then goes on working to produce precise, very distinctive, very personal wines with a sharp sense of place. A certainty in the Cilento district in particular and the Campania region in general 99

PEOPLE - This impressive estate in the Cilento National Park can be summed up in: a) the decision to live on the new property at Giungano; b) solid, uncompromising low-profile consistency of its wines; c) their quality, year in, year out.

VINEYARDS - Methods, already rigorous, are now in the process of being converted to organics. The vineyards are favorably located on a hillside with good air circulation at an altitude of 1,150 feet. Another two hectares are about to be planted with the grafts from the first vineyard selection made by Luigi's father in the 1970s.

WINES - Kratos 2013 (O fiano; 50,000 bt) is a white you can trust thanks to the quality of its fruit. Fermented exclusively in stainless steel vats, it's already nicely fresh and well-balanced. **Cilento Fiano Pietraincatenata 2012** (O 7,000 bt) shows how the winery is progressively reducing its use of wood to bring out acidity, hence more edge, elegance and finesse on the palate. Like the other vintages, it promises to evolve well in the course of time. Waiting for Kleos, whose release has been wisely delayed for a year, we enjoyed the rosé made with aglianico grapes, **Denazzano 2013** (⊙ 5,000 bt).

> **slow wine** **Cilento Aglianico Cenito 2010** (● 4,000 bt) A well-structured red, spot-on given the good vintage and its basic symmetry. A label that tells the story of an entire terroir.

FERTILIZERS natural manure, green manure
PLANT PROTECTION copper and sulphur
WEED CONTROL mechanical
YEASTS native
GRAPES 100% estate-grown
CERTIFICATION converting to organics

CASTELLABATE (SA)

San Giovanni

Località Punto Tresino
Parco Nazionale del Cilento
tel. 0974 965136
www.agricolasangiovanni.it
info@agricolasangiovanni.it

10 ac - 20,000 bt

66 Viticulture as a choice of life and love. Ida and Mario are now reaping the fruits of almost 20 years of sacrifice and privation, during which even electricity and a telephone line were a chimera. Now, thanks to them, the Cilento district has a beacon and a paragon of quality farming 99

PEOPLE - There's never a dull moment for Ida Budetta and Mario Corrado in a typical day on their splendid estate where the vines grow on a sheer drop over the sea. Working with their consultant enologist Michele D'Argenio, they have defined the profile of their wines according to criteria of essentiality and elegance.

VINEYARDS - The single nine-acre vineyard is immersed in an area of unspoiled natural beauty, hemmed in between the sea and the Mediterranean scrub, a place without electricity until only a few years ago. Albeit not certified, it's run using organic methods. The grapes cultivated are fiano and greco, a patch of trebbiano planted by their father in the 1980s, aglianico and piedirosso.

WINES - The two whites are mind-blowing. They show how, if you give the fiano grape the respect it deserves, it'll perform stupendously even in the hottest climes. **Paestum 2013** (O fiano, trebbiano, greco; 7,000 bt), pumped up with greco and trebbiano, is full of exciting acidity, already ready to drink; on the nose it gives notes of blossom and apples and pears. **Tresinus 2013** Everyday Wine (O 3,000 bt) comes from a selection of the oldest vineyard and is aged, as ever, only in stainless steel vats; fresh and tangy, it shows great aging potential. The two reds are fantastic too: **Castellabate 2012** (● aglianico, piedirosso; 7,000 bt), fermented in steel vats, is tangy and fresh; **Maroccia 2011** (● aglianico; 2,500 bt) is deep and promises to improve even more.

FERTILIZERS manure pellets, natural manure
PLANT PROTECTION copper and sulphur
WEED CONTROL mechanical
YEASTS selected
GRAPES 100% estate-grown
CERTIFICATION none

CASTELVENERE (BN)

Antica Masseria Venditti 🎖️⌇

Via Sannitica, 120/122
tel. 0824 940306
www.venditti.it
masseria@venditti.it

27 ac - 65,000 bt   **10% discount**

❝ Maybe stylistic and personal coherence aren't as appreciated as they used to be. But Nicola Venditti couldn't care a fig. "Man of Steel" might be his moniker seeing how steel is the only material he's ever used; for whites and reds indifferently. He went organic earlier than most and he's now in the process of launching an intriguing project for wines without added sulfites ❞

PEOPLE - Nicola Venditti makes wine with terrier-like tenacity, unrelentingly following a philosophy that has remained unchanged since the late 1960s, when he embarked on his adventure. His wife Enza and children Andrea and Serena provide their unconditional support.

VINEYARDS - To suss out the Venditti approach, take the tour of the vineyard alongside the cellar. Its ten vine rows are tantamount to an ID card, the face of the vines that produce the grapes. Then there are parcels spread out over the best growing areas in the countryside round Castelvenere: Bosco Caldaia, Marraioli, Foresta and Fragneto.

WINES - Sannio Falanghina Assenza 2013 (○ 2,660 bt) teases the palate with unobtrusive supporting acidity. **Sannio Barbera Barbetta Assenza 2013** (● 2,660 bt) is a distillation of delicious fragrant fruit. **Sannio Falanghina 2013** (○ 10,000 bt) has minerality to spare; sample it with Sannio white truffle, if you can find it. **Solopaca Bacalat Bianco 2013** (○ falanghina, grieco di Castelvenere, cerreto; 1,333 bt) dazzles for its acidity-body balance. **Sannio Barbera Barbetta 2011** (● 7,000 bt) hits the nose with berries and violets, which recur on the palate. **Sannio Aglianico Marraioli 2009** (● 6,000 bt) is nicely tannic.

FRASSO TELESINO (BN)

Cautiero €

Contrada Arbusti
tel. 338 7640641
www.cautiero.it
info@cautiero.it

10 ac - 16,000 bt   **10% discount**

PEOPLE - Fulvio Cautiero and his wife Immacolata are two young faces on the Campanian wine scene. Many a word has already been spent on their "flight" from the city for a life among the vineyards of Frasso, where they have doggedly created a new future for themselves. A family and a story, one of many in this generous land of Campania. Good, clean and fair!

VINEYARDS - The vineyards that surround the cellar contain a rich variety of historic grape varieties that grow on generally clayey, gravelly soil. The gentle hillsides afford the vines plenty of sunshine, and painstaking day-to-day labor ensures quality grapes that require minimal manipulation in the wine cellar to express all their typicality.

WINES - Sannio Falanghina Fois 2013 **Everyday Wine** (○ 4,500 bt) is one of the finest versions of the typical grape of the Sannio district. Vivacious and bright on the eye, it offers the nose a broad suite of floral aromas, followed by notes of citrus fruit and blossom, while on the palate it's dry and tangy with plenty of acid thrust. **Sannio Greco 2013** (○ 3,000 bt) has markedly salty tones. **Campania Fiano Erba Bianca 2013** (○ 2,000 bt) is very fruity with attractive toasty notes. **Campania Piedirosso 2013** (○ 1,000 bt) is concentrated, fresh-tasting and fruity with delicate streaks of spice. **Sannio Aglianico Fois Rosso 2011** (● 4,500 bt), redolent of red berries and vanilla, has good structure and goes well with good hearty rural cooking.

FERTILIZERS organic-mineral, green manure
PLANT PROTECTION copper and sulphur
WEED CONTROL mechanical
YEASTS selected
GRAPES 100% estate-grown
CERTIFICATION organic

FERTILIZERS green manure
PLANT PROTECTION copper and sulphur
WEED CONTROL mechanical
YEASTS selected
GRAPES 100% estate-grown
CERTIFICATION organic

Marisa Cuomo

Via Lama, 14
tel. 089 830348
www.marisacuomo.com
info@marisacuomo.com

Contrada Salandra

Via Tre Piccioni, 40
tel. 0815265258
www.dolciqualita.com
dolciqualita@libero.it

---

49 ac - 100,000 bt

PEOPLE - A family working in a cellar hewn into the rock, where there's never enough room ... all credit due then to Andrea Ferraioli, Marisa Cuomo and their children Raffaele and Dorotea for the reliability and consistent quality of their wines, the consequence of in-depth knowledge of their land, suspended between sky and sea, and the painstakingly precise consultancy of Luigi Moio.

VINEYARDS - Gliding on the special monorail over the spectacular vineyards round the cellar, planted on terraces in the most impenetrable gullies and caves, is an unforgettable experience in itself, well worth the journey on its own. Andrea performs his experimental work all along the coast, from Vietri to Furore, where the vineyards enjoy constant ventilation, face mostly south and are high-trained.

WINES - **Costa d'Amalfi Furore Bianco 2013** Great Wine (○ falanghina, biancolella, fenile, ripoli, ginestra; 30,000 bt), which amazes for its stylistic perfection, richness and brightness, is mineral and citrusy with a supple, tangy palate. **Costa d'Amalfi Bianco Fiorduva 2012** (○ fenile, ripoli, ginestra; 19,000 bt), made with grapes planted 80 years ago, is shaped to reduce wood in favor of fruitiness. The excellent **Costa d'Amalfi Ravello Bianco 2013** (○ falanghina, biancolella; 12,000 bt) has a compelling iodine bouquet with freshness and flavor on the palate. **Costa d'Amalfi Furore Rosso 2013** (● piedirosso, aglianico; 23,000 bt) is enjoyably quaffable. The two Riservas – **Costa d'Amalfi Furore Rosso Ris. 2010** (● aglianico, piedirosso; 8,000 bt) and **Costa d'Amalfi Ravello Rosso Ris. 2010** (● aglianico, piedirosso; 5,500 bt) – are both concentrated.

11 ac - 16,000 bt · 10% discount

66 Peppino Fortunato runs a clean, healthy, vital vineyard. By virtue of the perfect equilibrium created down the years, it gives life to the two most interesting wines in all Campania. Here time is no object and a bottle leaves the cellar only when it's ready. A sentinel of biodiversity in a difficult but absorbing terroir 99

PEOPLE - "We've got to decide whether we're party of nature or not," says Peppino, a man who's generous with his land. With his wife Sandra Castaldo, he has brought into being a microcosm of bees, very low-impact crops and a virtuous circle of apprentices keen to learn the ropes.

VINEYARDS - A small winery comprising the vineyards round the cellar and Peppino's cherished new planting at Monteruscello – 11 acres in all. The new vineyard should be fully productive in a couple of years' time. Last but not least, the winery is also responsible for the direct management of another vineyard. It grows only ungrafted piedirosso and falanghina and there's a nursery for selecting the best scions.

WINES - "When a queen bee is born or the vines start to blossom, it's a huge thrill." Peppino Fortunato is immersed in this splendid world of bees and grapes, and his labels are emblematic of this. Campi Flegrei Falanghina 2012 Everyday Wine (○ 10,000 bt) macerates for 24 hours then rests on the lees until April with continuous pumpovers. It's a white that is never released earlier than two years after the harvest, and rightly so as this allows it to express all the minerality of the local soil, direct, complex aromas, tanginess and freshness. For the long, elegant **Campi Flegrei Piedirosso 2012** (● 6,000 bt), the grapes are harvested between the middle and end of October, pumped over and oxygenated with racking.

FERTILIZERS none	FERTILIZERS natural manure, green manure
PLANT PROTECTION copper and sulphur	PLANT PROTECTION copper and sulphur, organic
WEED CONTROL mechanical	WEED CONTROL mechanical
YEASTS selected	YEASTS selected
GRAPES 70% bought in	GRAPES 100% estate-grown
CERTIFICATION none	CERTIFICATION none

TERZIGNO (NA)

Villa Dora 🐌

Via Bosco Mauro, 1
tel. 081 5295016
www.cantinevilladora.it
info@cantinevilladora.it

32 ac - 63,000 bt | **10% discount**

❝ Vesuvius looms menacingly over the vineyards and olive groves of the Ambrosio family, who have been making Lacryma Christi for 15 years now after a life in the oil trade. In an area characterized by a "here today, gone tomorrow" sales philosophy, their decision to give their white wine time to develop is an admirable one ❞

PEOPLE - The Ambrosio family made name for themselves for their excellent extra virgin olive oil. For them it was short step to viticulture with a strong sense of identity and success was guaranteed.

VINEYARDS - Motivated by strong ties to his roots, Vincenzo Ambrosio has preserved this gorgeous estate of olive trees and vine rows under the shadow of Vesuvius. Here the typical pergola vesuviana training system is very much in evidence, shading the piedirosso grapes from the hot summer heat.

WINES - The estate enologist is Fabio Mecca. This year the two whites were on top form. The vibrant **Lacryma Christi Bianco 2013** (○ coda di volpe, falanghina; 7,000 bt) is very typical, mineral, racy and salty. **Lacryma Christi Bianco Vigna del Vulcano 2012** (○ coda di volpe, falanghina; 16,000 bt) marries elegance and energy and, as it has already proved in the past, is sure to age well. **Gelso Rosa 2013** (◉ piedirosso, aglianico 3,000 bt) has intriguing, distinctive aromas, a tad smoky with notes of orange zest, and a lively, juicy palate. **Lacryma Christi Rosso 2012** (● piedirosso, aglianico; 10,000 bt) has typical aromas of geranium and cherry, while the deep, gutsy **Lacryma Christi Rosso Gelso Nero 2012** (● piedirosso, aglianico; 20,000 bt), made with pergola vesuviana-trained grapes, has body to spare.

FERTILIZERS green manure	
PLANT PROTECTION copper and sulphur	
WEED CONTROL mechanical	
YEASTS selected	
GRAPES 100% estate-grown	
CERTIFICATION organic	

TRAMONTI (SA)

Tenuta San Francesco 🐌

Via Solficiano, 18
tel. 089 876748 - 856190
www.vinitenutasanfrancesco.it
aziendasanfrancesco@libero.it

25 ac - 60,000 bt

❝ Gaetano Bove loves to rove his vineyards, encircled by oak and chestnut trees. A vet by profession, he has built up this winery pursuing quality and accepting seemingly impossible challenges without seeking easy ways out. Hence little big masterpieces that have achieved cult status among wine lovers ❞

PEOPLE - Gaetano Bove, Vincenzo D'Avino and Luigi Giordano embarked on their adventure ten years ago. Work on the cellar has now been completed and, with the help of enologist Carmine Valentino, turns out reliable base wines and thrilling selections that are increasing in number with the passing of time.

VINEYARDS - The distinctive feature of this small winery is the way it protects its giant pre-phylloxera vines, planted before the last world war. This fascinating genetic heritage is managed with non-invasive methods, facilitated by the altitude and sharp night-day temperature swings and constant breezes from the mountains and the sea.

WINES - The wonderfully fresh **Costa d'Amalfi Tramonti Bianco 2013** (○ falanghina, biancolella, pepella; 18,000 bt) has delicate floral aromas and an enjoyable palate. Very rich and aromatic, **È Iss Prefilloxera 2011** (● tintore; 4,500) has a husky tone. **Costa d'Amalfi 4 Spine Ris. 2010** (● aglianico, piedirosso, tintore; 6,500 bt) is beautifully balanced and elegant with forthright fruit and well-judged wood. **Costa d'Amalfi Tramonti Rosso 2012** (● aglianico, piedirosso, tintore; 13,000 bt), finally, is a simple wine.

slow wine **COSTA D'AMALFI PEREVA 2013** (○ fenile, pepella, ginestra; 6,500 bt) A wine from the highest vineyard. Driven by vibrant acidity and a superabundance of crunchy white-fleshed fruit, it encapsulates Amalfi and its stupendous coastline.

FERTILIZERS green manure	
PLANT PROTECTION copper and sulphur	
WEED CONTROL mechanical	
YEASTS selected	
GRAPES 5% bought in	
CERTIFICATION none	

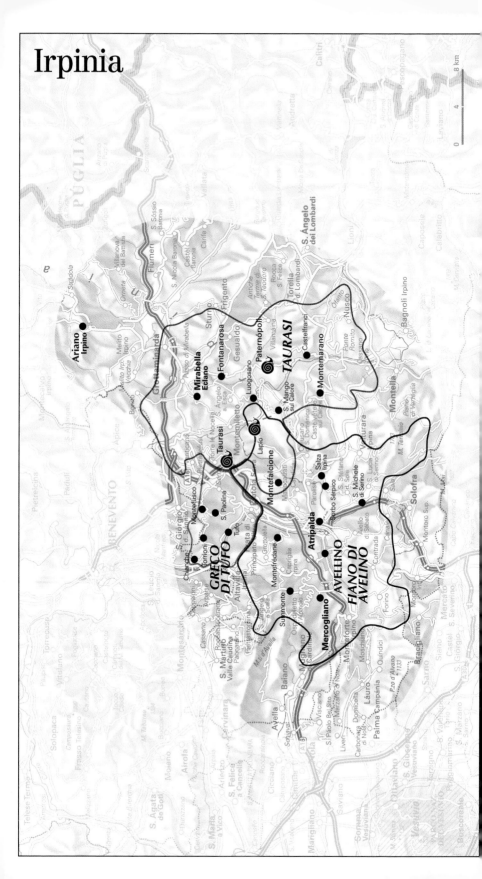

LAPIO (AV)

Colli di Lapio 🍷

Via Arianiello
tel. 0825 982184
www.collidilapio.it
info@collidilapio.it

---

15 ac - 70,000 bt

❝ Twenty years on and she's still there, the "signora del Fiano," dictating the tempo at Lapio. Clelia Romano's tenacity and simplicity and farness from the madding crowd are important seeds she has sown across a terroir which is growing more than any other in Campania ❞

PEOPLE - Clelia Romano, her husband Angelo, her children Carmela and Federico, and low profile enologist Angelo Pizzi – the secret of this winery, now celebrating its 20th harvest, is arguably the industry of its protagonists, the strength of a united family and a professional approach totally devoid of any form of performance anxiety.

VINEYARDS - New projects are in the pipeline: one such is the extension of the vineyards to reach the target of 100% estate-grown grapes. In Contrada Arianello, made famous by the winery, vines grow in a favorable location at an altitude of about 1,600 feet. The soil is calcareous-clay and the climate characterized by sharp night-day temperature swings caused by cold winds from the Terminio massif.

WINES - **Greco di Tufo 2013** (○ 4,000 bt) is proof of a good growing year for the variety. The elegant, subtle **Irpinia Campi Taurasini Donna Chiara 2012** (● 4.000 bt) is a monovarietal aglianico whose fruity aromas are countervailed by pleasant balsamic, herby notes. After skipping 2009, a difficult year for red grapes due to heavy October rain, **Taurasi Andrea 2010** (● 4,000 bt) is concentrated but with bracing freshness and promises to evolve well.

> **slow wine** FIANO DI AVELLINO **2013** (○ 54,000 bt) Much richer, much more sumptuous than the previous vintage. With bundles of fruit, good acidity and already excellent acidity, in some respects it's redolent of the legendary lingering, mineral 1999.

FERTILIZERS green manure
PLANT PROTECTION chemical, copper and sulphur
WEED CONTROL mechanical
YEASTS selected
GRAPES 20% bought in
CERTIFICATION none

MONTEFREDANE (AV)

Pietracupa 🍾

Contrada Vadiaperti, 17
tel. 0825 607418
pietracupa@email.it

---

18 ac - 45,000 bt

PEOPLE - Sabino Loffredo is now a leader in the Montefredane area. He has achieved this status by virtue of the constant reliability, high quality, and impressive elegance and precision of his wines, which embrace all the three DOCG zones of Irpinia. The farmhouse-cum-wine cellar is part of the building purchased by his father Peppino in the 1970s.

VINEYARDS - Sabino farms conventionally. Soil and weather conditions make this possible with non-invasive practices almost everywhere in Irpinia, all the more so in his cool, south-facing hills ventilated by breezes from the nearby Partenio. The fiano vineyard is near the cellar, where the soil is volcanic. The greco grapes come from parcels in nearby Santa Paolina, historically a good area for growing this particular variety.

WINES - The three flagship DOCG wines performed exceptionally at our tasting. **Greco di Tufo 2013** (○ 16,000 bt) is arguably the most backward of the trio but is impressive nonetheless, with its lusciously exuberant citrusy, sulfurous bouquet and bright, tangy forceful palate. The excellent **Fiano di Avellino 2013** Great Wine (○ 16,000) already shows the elegant style that will characterize it throughout its evolution. Both whites are steel-fermented until June and beyond. The big surprise is **Taurasi 2009** (● 5,000 bt): Sabino is noted for his white wines and he only began making reds in the 1990s. This version is arguably the best so far, despite a problematic growing year. Wood and fruit are perfectly fused and the wine is packed with character on both nose and palate, which is dynamic and goes on and on into an elegant finish. A real collector's piece!

FERTILIZERS green manure
PLANT PROTECTION copper and sulphur
WEED CONTROL mechanical
YEASTS selected
GRAPES 100% estate-grown
CERTIFICATION none

PATERNOPOLI (AV)

Luigi Tecce

Via Trinità, 6
tel. 0827 71375
ltecce@libero.it

10 ac - 10,000 bt

❝ Every year the "Aglianico anarchist," as he's nicknamed, treats us to a variety of emotions and wine lovers are duty-bound to follow his work with love and dedication. His wines are part of the denomination, sure, but they are also always one-off creations. His declared objective, in fact, is never to make them equal but to commemorate each single vintage in the best way possible ❞

PEOPLE - Luigi Tecce is a man of culture. Family ups and downs have meant that he devotes himself exclusively to his vines, which he tends with love and from which he achieves exceptional results. Geared as it is to bring out the peculiarities of the vintage, his style of winemaking is anything but invasive.

VINEYARDS - Luigi has the good fortune to own a historic vineyard left to him by his father, which yields the grapes he needs to achieve the results he has accustomed us to. The vines are trained with the old local *starzeto* method and other crops used to be grown beneath them. Their location in the upper part of Paternopoli, at an altitude of about 1,950 feet, is optimal and the air circulation is good too.

WINES - What comes through most in **Campi Taurasini Satyricon 2011** (● 5,200 bt) is the fruit, with sour cherry and mulberry giving way to balsamic, spicy notes. Supple on the palate by virtue of its standout freshness, it's a juicy, satisfying drink. The whites have yet to be released.

slow wine **TAURASI POLIPHEMO 2010** (● 4,500 bt) Made exclusively with grapes from a historic 50-year-old vineyard. Long fermentations and painstaking selection during the grape harvest do the rest. Apart from the fruit, we noted unorthodox but enjoyable tertiary aromas such as topsoil, tar, even a whiff of tobacco. The body is full, the acidity bracing and the finish very long indeed.

FERTILIZERS	green manure
PLANT PROTECTION	copper and sulphur
WEED CONTROL	mechanical
YEASTS	native
GRAPES	100% estate-grown
CERTIFICATION	none

SORBO SERPICO (AV)

Feudi di San Gregorio

Località Cerza Grossa
tel. 0825 986611
www.feudi.it
feudi@feudi.it

620 ac - 4,000,000 bt

PEOPLE - Year by year, Antonio Capaldo and Pierpaolo Sirch are charting new routes for the flagship of winemaking in Campania. Now that they have reorganized their vineyards, they are experimenting with the wines with the two Studi labels, dedicated to Fiano di Sorbo Serpico and Fiano di Arianiello, at Lapio. They are also pushing wine and food matches at their Marennà restaurant and the new wine bar at Naples airport. Last but not least, they are investing in the Vulture zone and have purchased Azienda Agricola Cefalicchio, a farming estate in Puglia.

VINEYARDS - From Irpinia to Vulture, from Murgia to Manduria – Feudi is the wine company with the vastest area of vineyards in the South of Italy. The vines are pruned with methods developed by Sirch according to the criteria of eco-compatible viticulture and respect for native grape varieties. In the province of Avellino, vines grow at altitudes that vary from 1,000 feet at Taurasi to 2,000 at Sorbo Serpico on mostly clayey, volcanic soils. Many old plants have ben preserved in the Taurasi area.

WINES - White wines are improving with every vintage and starred once again this year in our tastings. **Fiano di Avellino Pietracalda 2013** (○ 30,000 bt) has an attractive bouquet of fruit and Mediterranean scrub, a snappy, fresh-tasting, full-bodied palate, and a wonderfully clean, precise finish. **Greco di Tufo Cutizzi 2013** Great Wine (○ 40,000 bt) is also up to the mark thanks to sulfurous, citrusy notes on the nose, vibrant acidity and a very long finish. **Irpinia Campanaro 2012** (○ fiano and greco; 20,000 bt) has now achieved excellent balance. The wine that impressed us most was "new entry" **Fiano di Avellino Arianello 2012** (○ 2,000 bt), made with grapes from the area of the same name, the first of a series to be made according to a production-by-zoning system. **Taurasi 2010** (● 60,000) is still working towards wood-fruit symmetry.

FERTILIZERS	none
PLANT PROTECTION	copper and sulphur
WEED CONTROL	mechanical
YEASTS	selected
GRAPES	10% bought in
CERTIFICATION	none

TAURASI (AV)

Antonio Caggiano

Contrada Sala
tel. 0827 74723
www.cantinecaggiano.it
info@cantinecaggiano.it

74 ac - 150,000 bt

66 Caggiano is synonymous with Taurasi. Antonio, a surveyor by training, really has revolutionized the terroir, setting up the first visitable cellar and imposing his own inimitable style on Aglianico, a mixture of hard work in the vineyard and elegance in the bottle. He was a pioneer on this journey but now, luckily, he's no longer alone 99

PEOPLE - This, one of the wineries responsible for creating the Taurasi legend, has now celebrated its twentieth birthday. Born of the meeting between Antonio Caggiano and Luigi Moio, it was the first to use small wood, inventing a unique style and turning out wines that, two decades on, are now approaching perfection.

VINEYARDS - The two best known wines come from the historic vineyards just a few yards from the cellar and are named for them: Salae Domini, with vines over 30 years old, and Vigna Macchia dei Goti, planted at the start of the 1990s. Both stand at an altitude of 980 feet.

WINES - Back from a "gap year," the classic **Campi Taurasini Salae Domini 2011** (● aglianico; 15,000 bt) is very elegant and quaffable, with great wood-fruit symmetry. **Irpinia Aglianico Taurì 2013** (● 35,000 bt) is fresh and fruity. Moving on to the white, made with bought-in grapes fermented in steel vats, the classic **Fiagre 2013** (○ fiano, greco; 25,000 bt) is already well-balanced, tangy and ready to drink, with good mineral thrust. **Fiano di Avellino Bechar 2013** (○ 25,000 bt) and **Greco di Tufo Devon 2013** (○ 25,000 bt) are both enjoyable.

slow wine TAURASI VIGNA MACCHIA DEI GOTI 2010 (● 13,000 bt) This debutante wine confirms the cellar's style. Fine and elegant on the nose, with fruit supplemented by pleasant balsamic notes and a very fresh palate with velvety tannins.

FERTILIZERS organic-mineral, green manure	
PLANT PROTECTION chemical, copper and sulphur	
WEED CONTROL mechanical	
YEASTS selected	
GRAPES 25% bought in	
CERTIFICATION none	

TAURASI (AV)

Contrade di Taurasi

Via Municipio, 39
tel. 0827 74483
www.contradeditaurasi.it
info@cantinelonardo.it

12 ac - 20,000 bt   **10% discount**

66 Research and expectancy. These are the two words that sum up the work of this small family cellar, which picks out and emphasizes the very essence of the terroir 99

PEOPLE - Antonella Lonardo and her husband Flavio Castaldo oversee the cellar as a full-time job and have even chosen to live in the old center of Taurasi. Founder Sandro Lonardo still follows every phase in production carefully and, seeing the good work his successors are doing, has no qualms about the future of his family's Taurasi.

VINEYARDS - The vineyards are situated in the historic production zone inside the commune of Taurasi. Thanks to agronomist Giancarlo Moschetti and enologist Vincenzo Mercurio, the different morphological matrices of the single vineyards have been identified, and the selection of the two crus – Vigne d'Alto and Coste – has proved a huge success. All work is done by hand using organic methods.

WINES - **Taurasi 2009** (● 3,000 bt) is a perfect base wine with classic fruity tones of cherry and pepper, good acid thrust and gutsy tannins. Complex, well-crafted and splendid on the palate, **Taurasi Vigne D'Alto 2009** (● 1,300 bt) is made with grapes from a century-old *starzeto*-trained vineyard near the cellar. **Grecomusc' 2012** (○ roviello; 5,000 bt) is getting better and better; it has smoky, spicy tones and a well-rounded palate spliced with biting freshness. All in all, an essential, constantly improving range that we intend to follow carefully in the years ahead.

slow wine TAURASI COSTE 2009 (● 1,300 bt) Deep, expressive and enfolding, austere on the palate but already very enjoyable and elegant.

FERTILIZERS none	
PLANT PROTECTION copper and sulphur	
WEED CONTROL mechanical	
YEASTS native	
GRAPES 25% bought in	
CERTIFICATION organic	

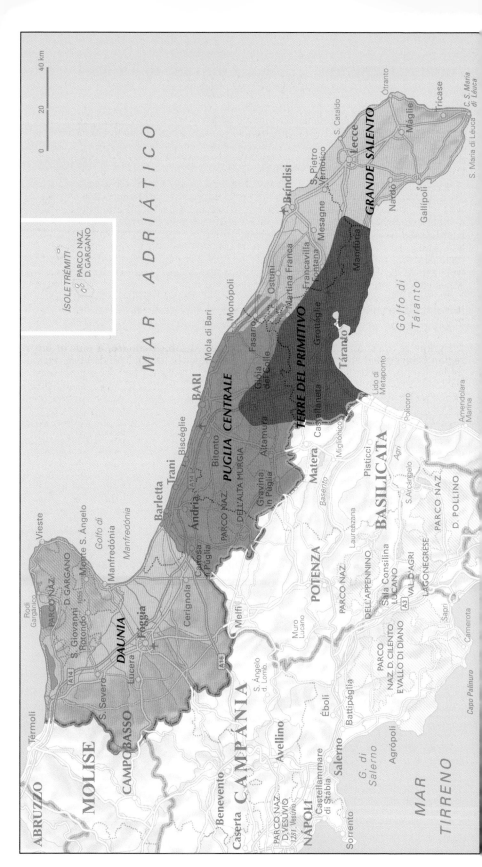

PUGLIA

The key fact this year is that, while the number of quality wines is increasing and that of table wines decreasing, the region is more and more in the pink – in the sense that, at long last, it's beginning to assert its vocation for rosé wine production. Generally speaking, quality is on the up in northern Puglia. Daunia and the central belt confirm all the great work carried out in recent years by the many producers keen to pursue quality and push the grape varieties, such as bombino bianco and uva di Troia, that best express the terroir's potential. Bombino bianco is meeting the expectations of winegrowers who have "liberated" it from the production of blending wine, hence from the journey to other areas of Italy, and elevated it to the role of a grape perfect for quality sparkling wines. Uva di Troia, in the meantime, is being vinified with growing expertise and skill and looks set to threaten the position of primitivo and negroamaro as symbols of the region. Having said that, the latter two grapes continue to offer great reds of increasingly well-defined identity and are exemplary ambassadors of their respective terroirs. White wines paid the price for a changeable growing year in which the harvest was brought a little too far forward, in some cases recklessly so. Hence the triumph of rosé wines.

It is now an established fact, at last acknowledged by producers themselves, that Puglia is one of the best Italian regions for this type of wine. From Daunia, with uva di Troia, through central Puglia, with bombino nero to Terre del Primitivo, with the grape of the same name, to Grande Salento, with negroamaro, a tour of the region brings great rosé wines to the fore. No longer banal and predictable, they perfectly encapsulate a tradition that goes way back in time. Their freshness, persistence, drinkability and "matchability" with food make these the wines to bank on for real market success. For anyone wishing to take a gamble or overcome one of the prejudices that surround the typology, namely its alleged insignificance, we suggest buying one of these rosés and storing it with care, as if it were a great red or white, and uncorking it a few years after its release. Try it and you'll be amazed how bottle-aging has allowed it to evolve to a degree you can't imagine. If it's true that one of the prerogatives of a great wine – besides sensory quality, sense of place and strong personality – is precisely its aging capacity, then we believe that some of the rosés we are talking about deserve the epithet "great." Producers deserve it, the terroir deserves it and so does the "wine of one night," to use the term coined by no less than Severino Garofano, who has loved and made fine rosé wine for well nigh 60 years.

ANDRIA (BA)

Giancarlo Ceci

Contrada Sant'Agostino
tel. 0883 565220
www.agrinatura.net
info@agrinatura.net

173 ac - 400,000 bt | 10% discount

66 Giancarlo Ceci is a man with his feet firmly on the ground. He's also a man with a "vision," thanks to which, after graduating in agriculture, he took over his family's farm and through conversion first to organics, then to biodynamics, has turned it into a model of efficient production – a model to imitate 99

PEOPLE - Antonio Pistillo takes care of the cellar, while Lorenzo Landi provides enological consultancy. The company constantly pursues lower impact on the environment and a 1-megawatt photovoltaic power plant guarantees energy self-sufficiency.

VINEYARDS - The farm, which affords a view of Castel del Monte, covers a huge area of 864 hectares, 70 of which are taken up by woodland, vital for natural equilibrium and biodiversity, and 70 by vineyards with bilateral spurred cordon-trained vines on well-drained and ventilated pebbly limestone soil.

WINES - The company style places the onus on the freshness and minerality of the wines, supported by stylish elegance. We were very impressed by **Moscato di Trani Dolce Rosalia 2013** (○ 2,000 bt) with its caressing aromas and sweetness braced by acid verve and great fleshiness. **Castel del Monte Bombino Bianco 2013** (○ 25,000 bt), with its field green freshness and zesty, harmonious palate, and the potent, complex **Castel del Monte Parco Marano 2012** (● uva di Troia; 25,000 bt) are both very good. The fruity, juicy **Castel del Monte Almagia 2013** (● uva di Troia, montepulciano; 13,000 bt) is without added sulphites.

slow wine CASTEL DEL MONTE FELICE CECI RIS. 2011 (● 7,000 bt) An excellent interpretation of a monovarietal uva di Troia with a well-developed, complex nose, silky tannins and massive, well-modulated structure.

FERTILIZERS	green manure
PLANT PROTECTION	copper and sulphur, organic
WEED CONTROL	mechanical
YEASTS	selected
GRAPES	100% estate-grown
CERTIFICATION	biodynamic

COPERTINO (LE)

Severino Garofano Vigneti e Cantine

Località Tenuta Monaci
tel. 0832 947512
www.garofano.aziendamonaci.com
vini@aziendamonaci.com

89 ac - 220,000 bt | 10% discount

PEOPLE - Renata and Stefano Garofano run the company with their customary courtesy, always present in the *masseria*, or farmhouse, that's also their place of work, always ready to promote the local as much as their own wines, if not more so. It's no coincidence that their father, Severino Garofano, made history in the Puglia wine world. He has now retired and we can imagine him sitting back at home admiring his children's work.

VINEYARDS - The company owns 40 acres of vineyard and rents another 50 in the countryside round Copertino, where the mainly negroamaro vines are high-trained. Antonio Protezione oversees the land, which he fertilizes with green field bean manure, reducing the use of plant protection products and chemicals to a bare minimum.

WINES - The negroamaro grape has treated the company to half a century of success and continues to be its principal grape. Waiting for the new vintages of I Censi, Simpotica and Eloquenzia, this year we greeted the release of the flagship **Le Braci 2007** Great Wine (● negroamaro; 10,000 bt), elegant for its color, ruby red with garnet highlights, and also for its broad suite of aromas, which range from fruit to undergrowth to leather with balsamic note, its magnificently structured palate and its refined, bright and breezy finish. Girofle 2013 Everyday Wine (⊙ negroamaro; 55,000 bt) is a typically Salento rosé: an attractive coppery onionskin in color, it offers a variegated bouquet with hints of red berries, thyme, oregano and myrtle, followed by a palate with chewy fresh fruit and a long balsamic finish.

FERTILIZERS	green manure
PLANT PROTECTION	copper and sulphur
WEED CONTROL	mechanical
YEASTS	selected
GRAPES	100% estate-grown
CERTIFICATION	none

GIOIA DEL COLLE (BA)

Polvanera

Strada Vicinale Lamie Marchesana, 601
tel. 080 758900
www.cantinepolvanera.com
info@cantinepolvanera.it

GRAVINA IN PUGLIA (BA)

Botromagno

Via Archimede, 22
tel. 080 3265865
www.botromagno.it
info@botromagno.it

173 ac - 250,000 bt

111 ac - 300,000 bt   `10% discount`

❝ Filippo Cassano didn't invent Primitivo di Gioia del Colle – you'd have to go back three centuries to find out who did – and he wasn't the first person to make it in the modern age either. But he was the one who gave the wine identity and *goût de terroir*, a merit that goes well beyond the market success he has achieved. No small feat! ❞

PEOPLE - Filippo is a simple but determined kind of guy who shoulders all the company responsibilities, from countryside to market. His young daughter Alessia is now starting to lend him a hand.

VINEYARDS - Close on 85 acres of vineyard have been planted on rocky terrain in the last two years, 25 of which around the cellar itself. Here the soil is unique, with a rocky stratum of a couple of feet from which the roots draw minerals. Then there are the vineyards out in the country at Acquaviva, whose 60-year-old bush-trained vines provide the grapes for the company's crus. Farming methods are certified organic and vineyard management is very attentive indeed.

WINES - All wines are fermented in steel vats for an inimitable style characterized by freshness and drinkability, despite occasionally high alcohol levels. Two stand out above the others: the land-rooted, fruity, spicy, mineral **Gioia del Colle Primitivo 17 2011** (● 20,000 bt) and **Gioia del Colle Primitivo 16 2011** (● 20,000 bt), which go head to head in a race to elegance and potency in which the outright winner is the consumer. Their "little brother" **Gioia del Colle Primitivo 14 2011** (● 80,000 bt) is little only because it comes from younger vineyards, but the well-gauged balsamic and mineral noes are unmistakable. All the other wines are well crafted: from **Rosato 2013** (☉ primitivo, aleatico, aglianico; 30,000 bt), redolent of Mediterranean scrub, to the refined, concentrated **Minutolo 2013** (○ 50,000 bt).

PEOPLE - This was a wine cooperative until 20 years ago, when lawyer turned quality wine producer Beniamino D'Agostino took it over and turned it into a modern cellar. Today Botromagno, run by D'Agostino with his brother Alberto in collaboration with the trusty Matteo De Rosa and enologist Goffredo Agostini, is an institution in the local area.

VINEYARDS - The vineyards are situated in the best growing areas round Gravina at an altitude of 1,300-2,000 feet. The soils are karstic and alluvial, clayey and pebbly, and the hillsides are steep. Drainage is good and the luscious surrounding vegetation gives the wines, especially the whites, unmistakable complexity, salinity and minerality. The farming methods adopted have received organic certification.

WINES - We were impressed by **Pier delle Vigne 2010** (● aglianico, montepulciano; 18,000 bt), wood-aged for two years: youthful and fresh-tasting and well-built, it has deep, delicately fruity aromas and velvety tannins. **Fiano B.D. XXX IV MCMLXIV 2013** (○ 6,000 bt) has the aromas typical of the grape: its bouquet is spacious and entrancing, its palate soft and nicely acidic with a long finish. **Gravina Poderi D'Agostino 2013** (○ greco, malvasia; 100,000 bt), which never disappoints, has blossomy aromas and sharp minerality. Made with the same grapes, **Gravina Poggio al Bosco 2013** (○ 2,200 bt) has the stuffing of a great white; vinified with native yeasts, it has good body and delicate flavor. **Rosé di Lulù 2013** (☉ uva di Troia; 1,800 bt) has an original fruity nose, while **Primitivo 2012** (● 36,000 bt) is well crafted.

FERTILIZERS none	**FERTILIZERS** manure pellets, natural manure
PLANT PROTECTION copper and sulphur	**PLANT PROTECTION** copper and sulphur
WEED CONTROL mechanical	**WEED CONTROL** mechanical
YEASTS selected	**YEASTS** selected
GRAPES 100% estate-grown	**GRAPES** 100% estate-grown
CERTIFICATION organic	**CERTIFICATION** organic

Agricole Vallone

Via XXV Luglio, 7
tel. 0832 308041
www.agricolevallone.it
info@agricolevallone.it

398 ac - 400,000 bt `10% discount`

❝ A historic winery that has stuck to tradition but also innovated a great deal by bringing in new blood ❞

PEOPLE - Francesco Vallone, 38, nephew of the owners, sisters Vittoria and Maria Teresa Vallone, is the new administrator. Giuseppe Malazzini, the sales manager, and Oronzo Lazzari, the agronomist are roughly the same age. The enologist for some years has been Graziana Grassini, who has kept the style and quality of production consistent. The general supervisor is the indefatigable Donato Lazzari.

VINEYARDS - Three vineyards are farmed very attentively using conventional systems. Tenuta Iore, at San Pancrazio Salentino, covers an area of 75 acres, including the Caragnuli cru, with bush-trained vines planted over 70 years ago. Tenuta Castel Serranova is a fortified *masseria*, or farmhouse, in the countryside near Carovigno, where some of the grapes are withered. Tenuta Flaminio, in Brindisi, has 224 acres of vines, constantly caressed by the wind, and is where the renovated wine cellar is situated.

WINES - Made with raisined grapes, **Graticciaia 2010** (● negroamaro; 12,000 bt) is fruity, balsamic, elegant and austere with fine tannins. Brindisi Rosato Vigna Flaminio 2013 `Everyday Wine` (☉ 18,000 bt) and **Brindisi Rosso Vigna Flaminio Ris. 2010** (● 6,000 bt) are both made with negroamaro e montepulciano grapes: the first is balsamic with floral notes, bright and very long; the second is decidedly land-rooted. **Vigna Castello 2010** (● 6,000 bt) and **Tenuta Serranova 2013** (○ fiano; 4,000 bt) come from the Serranova property. The first, a blend of the long neglected susumaniello grape and negroamaro, has soft fruit, balance and good acidity; the second is a fresh, tangy, floral white. **Salice Salentino Vereto Ris. 2010** (● 6,000 bt) is a refined Negroamaro.

FERTILIZERS green manure	
PLANT PROTECTION copper and sulphur	
WEED CONTROL chemical, mechanical	
YEASTS selected	
GRAPES 100% estate-grown	
CERTIFICATION none	

Alberto Longo

Contrada Padulecchia
S.P. Lucera-Pietramontecorvino, km 4
tel. 0881 539057
www.albertolongo.it
info@albertolongo.it

86 ac - 130,000 bt `10% discount`

PEOPLE - Alberto Longo has done everything on his own. After studying at the Bocconi University in Milan and becoming a successful manager, he answered the call of the land of his birth and decided to set up this winery. Today he can count upon the collaboration of a first-rate technical team consisting of general operations manager Michele Di Gregorio, trusty cellar man Sebastiano Matarazzo, and vine dresser Antonio Quaranta, as well as the external consultancy of enologist Graziana Grassini and agronomist Enzo Corazzina.

VINEYARDS - The vineyards are on relatively flat land and are divided into two main properties: Fattoria Cavalli, where the soil is more calcareous, and Masseria Celentano, where it's sandier. Both have good air circulation and sharp night-day temperature swings thanks to the proximity of the sea and the high peninsula. The vines are Guyot-trained and yields are generally rather low. Both native and international grapes are grown.

WINES - The production style veers towards modern wines, hence clean and well-extracted, with a well-judged use of small wood for the more important reds. We were highly impressed by **Cacc'e Mmitte di Lucera 2012** (● uva di Troia, montepulciano, bombino bianco; 60,000 bt) has a complex nose with balsamic notes and hints of aromatic herbs, a sappy palate and a long, clean finish. At its first release, the challenging **Montepeloso 2011** (● aglianico; 3,150 bt), has spicy notes and nice flesh. **Le Fossette 2013** (○ falanghina; 18,000 bt) is tangy with good supporting acidity. Also worthy of mention are **Capoposto 2012** (● negroamaro; 20.000 bt), with its chewy, harmonious palate, and the moreish Piacevole il **Donna Adele 2013** (☉ negroamaro; 10,000 bt).

FERTILIZERS organic-mineral	
PLANT PROTECTION copper and sulphur	
WEED CONTROL mechanical	
YEASTS selected	
GRAPES 100% estate-grown	
CERTIFICATION none	

LUCERA (FG)

Paolo Petrilli

Località Motta Caropresa
tel. 0881 523982
www.lamotticella.com
lamotticella@libero.it

27 ac - 25,000 bt

66 Paolo Petrilli is for quality without compromise and at all costs. His secret is total control and constant monitoring of the whole supply chain 99

PEOPLE - Paolo has always sought high quality and sustainability in his farming: first with tomatoes, then (since 2000) with wines, now with the pasta he makes with his own grains. He's helped by agronomist Filippo Giannone, enologist Andrea Boaretti and cellarman Giuseppe Sirena.

VINEYARDS - The vineyard is a single plot of 27 acres on a slight slope at an altitude of just under 980 feet, not far from Lucera. The very pale soil is mainly limestone and, thanks to the proximity of the Gargano peninsula, enjoys good night-day temperature swings. Zoning work has been completed and, despite Paolo's initial qualms, light tilling of the land has led to healthier, disease-resistant vines.

WINES - This was another "gap year" with the most important bottles being deferred to 2015. But, we repeat, for Paolo quality isn't a matter of compromise; the fact is that uva di Troia is a great grape that needs time to express its full potential. Nonetheless, we were able to take consolation in an excellent value-for-money wine, well worth buying: **Fortuita 2012** Everyday Wine (● sangiovese, montepulciano, uva di Troia, aglianico; 13,500 bt), which has a deep, complex nose with a rich, fleshy palate. We also treated ourselves to a second tasting of Cacc'e Mmitte di Lucera Agramante 2011, which is still on the market: the elegant nose is now enhanced by fantastic balsamic notes and the silky palate is still full and succulent.

MANDURIA (TA)

Morella

Via per Uggiano 147
tel. 099 9791482
www.morellavini.it
info@morellavini.it

43 ac - 23,000 bt

66 A cellar born of the love between two people, Lisa Gilbee and Gaetano Morella, in love with each other and also with the splendid bush-trained vines of the Manduria countryside 99

PEOPLE - Lisa has a strong character, great technical knowledge and unbridled passion for vines and wine. Hence her decision, years ago, first to settle in Manduria with her partner Gaetano, then to invest in the bush-trained vineyards she'd grown so fond of.

VINEYARDS - It's always a thrill to walk among the old bush-trained vines, some planted 80 years ago, which together with the more recently planted spurred-cordon trained ones, are tended with care by Lisa and Gaetano. There can be no doubt that they give wine nose-palate qualities from a different age. Recently another couple of acres of primitive were saved from explantation.

WINES - Tradition and technique fuse into wines of great backbone and personality. They evolve in the bottle in exemplary fashion and, if you're prepared to wait, offer a crescendo of emotions even years after bottling. The excellent **Primitivo Old Vines 2011** Great Wine (● 4,000 bt) is the fruit of a selection from the oldest bush-trained vines, which add elegance and interminable length. The two blends are very interesting, too: **Primitivo Malbek 2011** (● 7,000 bt) has good body, freshness and symmetry, while **Primitivo Negroamaro 2011** (● 3,500 bt) impresses with its extraordinary minerality. We closed our tasting with the two base wines: **Mezzanotte 2013** (● 5,000 bt), a refreshing, thirst quenching Primitivo, and **Mezzogiorno 2013** (○ 3,000 bt), a mineral Fiano with beautiful acidity.

FERTILIZERS none
PLANT PROTECTION copper and sulphur
WEED CONTROL mechanical
YEASTS selected
GRAPES 100% estate-grown
CERTIFICATION biodynamic

FERTILIZERS biodynamic preparations, green manure
PLANT PROTECTION copper and sulphur, organic
WEED CONTROL mechanical
YEASTS native
GRAPES 100% estate-grown
CERTIFICATION none

SALICE SALENTINO (LE)

Castello Monaci

Contrada Monaci
tel. 0831 665700
www.castellomonaci.it
castello.monaci@giv.it

SAN SEVERO (FG)

d'Aprì

Via Zannotti, 30
tel. 088 2227643
www.darapri.it
info@darapri.it

---

520 ac - 2,000,000 bt   **10% discount**

PEOPLE - This winery, owned by the Seracca Guerrieri and Memmo families, came into being in the early 20th century. In 1999, the major national Gruppo Italiano Vini acquired an interest and has since overseen production and sales. The vineyards, however, still belong to the families, and are managed directly by Vitantonio Seracca Guerrieri, who is also the company president. Supervising work in the vineyard is Sergio Leonardo.

VINEYARDS - The company's 520 hectares are subdivided into three distinct properties. The red grapes are cultivated on a large plot near the cellar at Salice Salentino; the white ones grow near the sea on sandy soil in the Tuturano countryside, in the province of Brindisi; and another 25-acre plot is to be found at Trepuzzi, inland in the province of Lecce.

WINES - The wines are modern and all delightful. **Artas 2012** (● primitivo; 10,000 bt), produced with grapes from an old bush-trained vineyard, is a red with a well-rounded, lingering palate. Kreos 2013 Everyday Wine (☉ negroamaro; 50,000 bt) is an agreeably fresh-tasting rosé characterized by bracing balsamic notes and concentrated fruit. **Salice Salentino Aiace Ris. 2011** (● negroamaro, malvasia; 8,000 bt) is fruity and robust, while **Negroamaro Maru 2013** (● 100,000 bt) is fresher and suppler, an easy drinker. Made with grapes from a vineyard planted 40 years ago next to the cellar, **Medos 2013** (● malvasia nera; 10,000 bt) gave a good account of itself. Standing out among the whites was the tangy, refreshing **Pietraluce 2013** (○ verdeca; 13,000 bt).

---

30 ac - 82,000 bt   **10% discount**

66 Now it's easy to gamble on bombino bianco grapes to produce Metodo Classico, but 30 years ago no one would have dared. No one, that is, except the people at this winery 99

PEOPLE - Thirty-five years ago, a deep passion for wine and the local area persuaded three friends-cum-partners Girolamo D'Amico, Louis Rapini and Ulrico Priore to invest in this 18th-century underground cellar in the old part of San Severo.

VINEYARDS - The high-trained vineyards are situated in the countryside near San Severo in a favorable microclimate that ensures protection from frost and ice and good air circulation, which helps to preserve the grapes from disease. The clay-limestone composition of the soil gives the slightly sloping terrain their typical yellow-gray color. The small walled vineyard which we saw come to life in the town of San Severo itself is now fully productive.

WINES - The Metodo Classico d'Aprì range combines craftsmanship and technical skill to achieve stylish, long perlages and nose-palate symmetry. The excellent **Brut Gran Cuvée XXI Secolo 2008** (○ bombino bianco, pinot nero, montepulciano; 8,500 bt) has a complex nose with mineral notes, a creamy palate and an enjoyable finish. **Pas Dosé** (○ bombino bianco, pinot nero; 15,000 bt) offers varietal notes, brightness and length. The silky, caressing **Brut** (○ bombino bianco, pinot nero; 39,000 bt) and **Brut Rosé** (☉ montepulciano, pinot nero; 16,500 bt), with its intriguing sweetness and crispness, are both very good.

slow wine **RISERVA NOBILE BRUT 2010** (○ 10,000 bt) Yet another brilliant demonstration of how to use the Metodo Classico with the bombino bianco grape. The nose is bright, very intense and complex, the palate is soft, tangy and very leisurely.

FERTILIZERS organic-mineral, manure pellets	FERTILIZERS none
PLANT PROTECTION chemical, copper and sulphur	PLANT PROTECTION copper and sulphur
WEED CONTROL mechanical	WEED CONTROL mechanical
YEASTS selected	YEASTS selected
GRAPES 10% bought in	GRAPES 100% estate-grown
CERTIFICATION converting to organics	CERTIFICATION none

Gianfranco Fino

Via Piave, 12
tel. 099 7773970
www.gianfrancofino.it
gianfrancofino64@libero.it

22 ac - 20,000 bt | **10% discount**

66 Just ten years have gone by since Gianfranco Fino embarked on his adventure in wine, yet he has succeeded in the brief space of time since, in becoming one of the best known, most respected Puglia producers in Italy and worldwide 99

PEOPLE - Gianfranco's wife Simona Natale has played a fundamental role in his professional career. While he attends to the vineyard and cellar, she oversees sales and public relations. It's the irrepressible Simona who best represents the company image.

VINEYARDS - Gianfranco's finest vineyards are the old bush-trained ones scattered round the Manduria countryside, all rescued from a state of semi-abandonment. His new one, in Contrada Li Reni, has started to yield its fruits. The viticultural approach is attentive and most operations, pruning in particular, are carried out by hand.

WINES - Gianfranco and Simona's wines have certainly helped to further enhance the image of Primitivo di Manduria. In fact, over the last ten years they have become ambassadors of "new" winemaking in Puglia. **Primitivo di Manduria Es 2012** Great Wine (● 15,000 bt) performed superbly once more: potent yet, at once, elegant, it can be enjoyed immediately. The company also presented an interesting new wine this year: **Primitivo di Manduria Dolce Naturale Es Più Sole 2012** (● 1,800 bt), which has well-concentrated fruit with notes of jam, suave spiciness and an excellent balance that make it a joy to drink.

FERTILIZERS natural manure
PLANT PROTECTION copper and sulphur
WEED CONTROL mechanical
YEASTS selected
GRAPES 100% estate-grown
CERTIFICATION none

Castel di Salve €

Frazione Depressa
Piazza Castello, 8
tel. 0833 771041
www.casteldisalve.com
info@casteldisalve.com

120 ac - 150,000 bt | **10% discount**

PEOPLE - Francesco Winspeare and Francesco Marra are in love with the land of their birth, the Salentine Peninsula. Their vineyards used to be scattered round the area, but in 1990 they joined them together to give life to this winery. The headquarters is at Depressa, a tiny village near Tricase, where they have restructured the old cellar to fit in with the local architecture. Their collaborators are enologist Andrea Boaretti and Filippo Giannone.

VINEYARDS - The vineyards are situated in three areas in different positions with different soils. Abate Bosci is at Monteroni, on the outskirts of Lecce, where the company has restructured an old farmhouse; Masseria Pisari is at Ugento, by the Ionian Sea; Masseria Bosco Belvedere is inland at Supersano. The second two are set in landscapes in which many typical Mediterranean tree and plant species grow.

WINES - The wines are all excellently crafted and reflect the company's original aim: namely to valorize native grape varieties with respect for the local tradition. **Santimedici Rosato 2013** (☉ negroamaro; 20,000 bt) is fruity, fresh and tangy. **Santimedici Rosso 2013** Everyday Wine (● negroamaro; 13,000 bt) offers intense aromas and soft, lingering, caressing tannins. The robust, leisurely **Armecolo 2011** (● negroamaro, malvasia nera; 20,000 bt) works well once again. **Priante 2011** (● negroamaro, montepulciano; 10,000 bt) displays commendable fruit-spice symmetry, good length and a delectable, slightly bitter finish. **Cento su Cento 2012** (● primitivo; 22,000 bt) is a pleasure to drink, and **Lama del Tenente 2012** (● primitivo, malvasia nera, montepulciano; 9,000 bt) is well-structured and complex.

FERTILIZERS manure pellets, green manure
PLANT PROTECTION copper and sulphur
WEED CONTROL mechanical
YEASTS selected
GRAPES 100% estate-grown
CERTIFICATION none

BASILICATA

Basilicata and Aglianico del Vulture: a region and a wine. The red aglianico grape accounts for 47% of total production and comes an easy first in the region over other varieties. It is, alas, an achievement that the creation of the new DOCG struggles to sustain, and the fact that it has the same name as the DOC doesn't help when it comes to media communication: that's our modest opinion anyway. Some of the limits we have pointed out in every edition of this guide so far are still on the table: namely the ongoing failure of producers to join together in a network, at least to defend concrete common interests. Indeed, the past year has only served to increase concerns about the divisions and misunderstandings that still spoil the agenda of one of the finest terroirs in the South. Fortunately, there are encouraging signs as well. The first, entirely unexpected, comes from the latest figures available. It's true that these date back to 2012, but they do mark a turnaround – at last – from the constant drop in production over the previous ten consecutive years. The output of 4,992,851 gallons restores regional viticulture almost to the levels recorded in 2008, though it's still a long way off the 7,925,161 gallons that constituted the average in the golden years. Production breaks down into 3,988,997 gallons of red wine, while white stayed constant at 1,003,853 gallons. The reorganization of the DOC has raised the production of "certified" wine to 1,056,680 gallons with an increase of 116%. IGT production is also up, by 106%, from 369,840,873 to 792,516,157 gallons. Overall production thus shows a record increase of 21.2%, double that of a decade ago. In short, the Basilicata region is producing less but better. From the point of view of flavor, reds are breaking free from the oppressive concentration and excessive use of wood that characterized vintages from 2001 to 2007, all to the advantage of balance, drinkability and food matching in the case of Aglianico. Sweet notes are increasingly marginal in both whites and reds. Speaking of whites, we would like to stress yet again the need to explore their potential in this volcanic, mountainous area with sharp night-to-day temperature swings. We are against the introduction of often caricatural international white wines and suggest regional producers bank on the moscato, malvasia and fiano grapes.

snails ◎↩

214 MUSTO CARMELITANO
215 CANTINE DEL NOTAIO

bottles ▮

214 BASILISCO

coins €

215 GRIFALCO

BARILE (PZ)

Basilisco

Via delle Cantine, 22
tel. 0972 771033
www.basiliscovini.it
basiliscovini@gmail.com

MASCHITO (PZ)

Musto Carmelitano

Via Nenni, 23
tel. 0972 33312
www.mustocarmelitano.it
info@mustocarmelitano.it

---

67 ac - 55,000 bt   **10% discount**

PEOPLE - "We're working for future generations," is a favorite phrase of Antonio Capaldo, owner of Basilisco and president of Feudi di San Gregorio. His viticultural philosophy is palpable at his winery where the completion of a new cellar heralds the birth of a "village of wine," which will include the reorganization of all the vineyards with an eye to the world market. The heart and soul of the project are sales manager Viviana Malafarina and production manager Pierpaolo Sirch.

VINEYARDS - An area of 66 acres of vineyard has been added since last year at an altitude of 1,600-1,900 feet. The oldest vines were planted about 45 years ago and are all ungrafted. The most recent aglianico plantings were made between 2001 and 2004. The soils are of volcanic origin and the viticulture practiced is certified organic.

WINES - **Sofia 2013** (○ fiano, traminer; 7,000 bt) is an interesting white but we believe it could do without its 5% of traminer grapes because the potential of fiano from Mount Vutures has yet to be explored and we are curious to see what it can do. The excellent, drinkable **Aglianico del Vulture Teodosio 2012** (● 30,000 bt), aged for about a year in second- and third-use barriques, is well-balanced, stylish and bright with nice acidity and flavor and well-amalgamated tannins. **Aglianico del Vulture Basilisco 2011** `Great Wine` (● 14,000 bt) matures for a year in new and second-use barrels and is impressively full-bodied, well-rounded and mineral. Its prospects for aging are excellent.

---

10 ac - 20,000 bt   **10% discount**

❝ Basilicata also has a young face, like those of sister and brother Elisabetta and Luigi, who defend the ancient vines of the Maschito area and produce wine placing the priority on environmental and biodiversity protection. They stand as an example in a region sometimes drawn to fashion and the appeal of hollow, faraway models ❞

PEOPLE - Elisabetta and Luigi Mosto and Sebastiano Fortunato, an enologist from the Irpinia district near Naples, have created a perfect symbiosis between clean farming and personality-packed, unaffected wines. Partly thanks to Elisabetta and Luigi's father Francesco and their uncle Luigi Carmelitano, the winery has grown by leaps and bounds since 2007.

VINEYARDS - The winery prides itself on its three vineyards: Maschito, at an altitude of around 1,950 feet; Pian del Moro, where the soil is hoed manually and the ungrafted vines date back 60-90 years; and Serra del Prete, where the vines are 45 years old.

WINES - The two outstanding versions of Aglianico del Vulture shouldn't distract attention from the quality of the three youngest wines. **Maschitano Bianco 2013** (○ moscato; 4,000 bt) has a fresh, intense nose and a typical lingering palate. **Maschitano Rosato 2013** (⊙ aglianico; 1,400 bt) impresses for its flavor and acidity. **Maschitano Rosso 2012** (● aglianico; 5,000) is pleasant and approachable. **Aglianico del Vulture Pian del Moro 2010** (● 4,000 bt), finally, made with grapes from the oldest vines in the vineyard of the same name passed the test with flying colors.

> **slow wine** AGLIANICO DEL VULTURE SERRA DEL PRETE **2011** (● 8,000 bt) Fermented in steel and cement vats, this wine has a full, nuanced nose, a lingering, justly tannic palate, and a delicious, drawn-out progression. Fairly priced, it's sure to become a classic.

FERTILIZERS natural manure
PLANT PROTECTION copper and sulphur
WEED CONTROL mechanical
YEASTS selected
GRAPES 100% estate-grown
CERTIFICATION organic

FERTILIZERS green manure
PLANT PROTECTION copper and sulphur
WEED CONTROL mechanical
YEASTS selected
GRAPES 100% estate-grown
CERTIFICATION converting to organics

Cantine del Notaio 🐌

Via Roma, 159
tel. 0972 723689
www.cantinedelnotaio.it
info@cantinedelnotaio.it

Grifalco €

Località Pian di Camera
tel. 0972 31002
www.grifalco.com
grifalcodellalucania@email.it

---

74 ac - 250,000 bt　　　　**10% discount**

❝ Gerardo Giuratrabocchetti is an untiring optimist, always busy raising the profile of every aspect of Aglianico and devoting attention to form as well as substance, namely to clean, eco-compatible viticulture, to the pursuit of clones and the still unexplored potential of this fantastic terroir ❞

PEOPLE - More and more wine lovers are coming to do the guided tour of the historic cellars, complete with caves, enjoying tastings and snapping souvenir photos. The spacious new cellar is now totally functional as well.

VINEYARDS - The vineyards cover an area of 74 acres, 49 of which given over to aglianico, the rest to moscato, malvasia and fiano. The oldest, which occupy about seven acres are over 100 years old and grow on volcanic soil in the best Vulture growing zones: Casano at Maschito, Pian dell'Altare at Ginestra, Le Querce at Barile, Cugno di Atella at Rionero in Vulture, and Piano del Duca at Ripacandida.

WINES - The fresh and quaffable L'Atto 2013 Everyday Wine (● 85,000 bt) is again elegant and clean with distinctive cherry, redcurrant and spicy notes. **Aglianico del Vulture Il Repertorio 2011** (● 20,000 bt) has hints of undergrowth and is sure to age well. **Aglianico del Vulture La Firma 2011** (● 20,000 bt) is complex and tangy. Produced with late-harvested grapes, **Aglianico del Vulture Il Sigillo 2010** (● 15,000 bt) may be a little too potent and burly, but also manages to be enjoyable with a soft, full palate. Also good is the aglianico rosé, **Rogito 2012** (◉ 25,000 bt), which is elegant and rounded with crispy cherries. The cellar also produces a Metodo Classico with aglianico, **Stipula Rosé 2010** (◉ 6,000 bt), which is fresh and enjoyable.

35 ac - 70,000 bt　　　　**10% discount**

PEOPLE - The winery founded by Tuscan Fabrizio Piccin is currently being developed and reorganized. Its wine is sold in Italy and overseas by reliable distributors under the watchful eye of Fabrizio's wife Cecilia Naldoni. Their son Lorenzo has completed his studies at the School of Enology in Alba and works with his father in the vineyards and in the cellar. It will be his job to run the new winery at Forenza, not far from Venosa, where they have bought 15 acres of land planted with old aglianico vines.

VINEYARDS - The underground high-tech cellar is in the Pian di Camera district, where the soil is volcanic. It is encircled by the youngest vineyard, planted ten ears ago, which covers an area of ten acres. The oldest parcels were bought in the upper part of the Vulture, at Rapolla, Ginestra and Maschito. The canes aren't cut in the traditional fashion as here they prefer their wines to be bright as opposed to soft.

WINES - Damaschito wasn't released in 2010, which was very rainy and produced grapes unsuited for a selection. After missing the 2008 vintage, **Aglianico del Vulture Bosco del Falco 2009** (● 6,000 bt) has spicy, fruity aromas of licorice and walnuts on the nose and a fresh, acid, vibrant palate. **Aglianico del Vulture Gricos 2012** (● 35,000 bt) releases a bouquet of hazelnuts and almonds followed by intense, lingering tannins on the palate. The new Forenza wine presented three well-crafted Aglianicos, Kamai, Arberesko and Siir, all with the typical characteristics of the grape and all ready to go on sale.

slow wine | AGLIANICO DEL VULTURE GRIFALCO 2012 (● 30,000 bt) A complex yet, at the same time, land-rooted wine with distinctive notes of hazelnut on the nose and a palate braced by vivacious brightness.

FERTILIZERS organic-mineral, natural manure, green manure
PLANT PROTECTION copper and sulphur
WEED CONTROL mechanical
YEASTS selected
GRAPES 25% bought in
CERTIFICATION biodynamic, organic

FERTILIZERS natural manure, green manure
PLANT PROTECTION copper and sulphur
WEED CONTROL mechanical
YEASTS native
GRAPES 100% estate-grown
CERTIFICATION organic

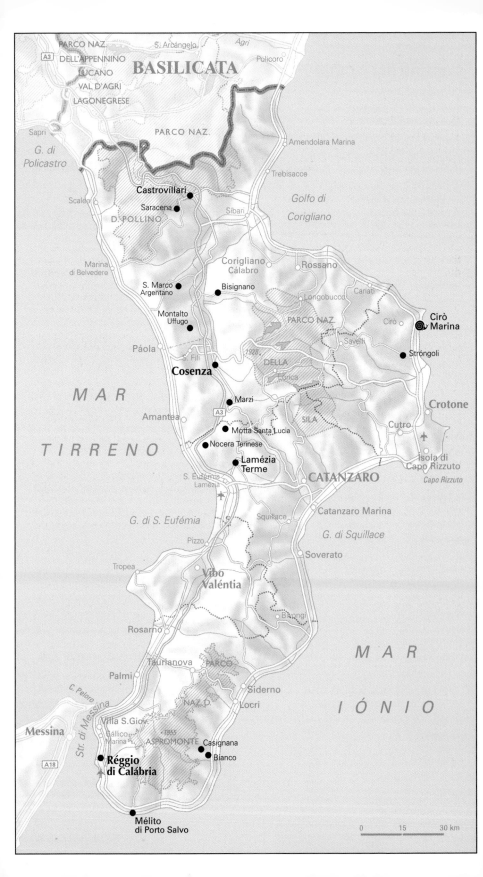

CALABRIA

The three main strengths of Calabrian wine over the last few years have been:

1) Cirò. Precisely at the moment in which the decision was taken, wrongly, to allow international grapes to enter the DOC, hitherto based solely on gaglioppo, we saw the reaction of young producers whose simple and precise interpretation of this typical distinctive variety offers a message of quality. A couple of historic wineries also refused to deviate from the straight and narrow.

2) Sweet wines. We refer not only to Moscato di Saracena and its interpreters, but also to wineries, especially in the Aspromonte mountains, that produce interesting passitos of great ancestral charm. This a sector that has failed to enjoy great fortune in Italy but has enormous potential and deserve to be exploited.

3) The relaunch of Magliocco in the province of Cosenza. Stylistic uncertainties aside, this wine is becoming more and more interesting every year, especially when producers bring out its freshnesss and flavor without the ridiculous pretense of producing bottles that are caricatures of other terroirs. This is something that is happening, alas, in many areas where sales have gone up recently. In 2013 the region produced 9,721,531 gallons of wine, an 8% drop with respect to the previous year but nonetheless in line with the average for the last six years. We believe the decrease was due most of all to the ungovernable conditions during a year that offered quality only in patches. Remember that Calabria is a highly variegated region in which the torrid heat of the Ionian coast and the cool mountain climate of the Pollino and the Sila mountains are only a 30-minute drive apart.

A very encouraging sign was the growth in the number of certified wines, from 18% to 41% in 2012 (the last year for which data are available). The figure marked an unprecedented quantum leap in quality, all the more so given the ongoing decrease in total wine production.

Moving on to the different typologies, white wine production increased from 16% to 31% in the same period, confirmation of an idea we have often expressed in this guide over the years: namely that cold, altitude and sharp temperature swings are essential conditions for interesting whites in Calabria, too. These three conditions do exist in the region, so what is now important is to insist with native grapes and avoid planting those bereft of either history or tradition.

Our overall judgment is positive and we are convinced that the region is bound to grow even more thanks to the conscientiousness of an increasing number of producers.

CIRÒ MARINA (KR)

Sergio Arcuri

Via Roma Vico III, 3
tel. 0962 31723
www.vinicirosergioarcuri.it
info@vinicirosergioarcuri.it

10 ac - 10,000 bt   `10% discount`

66 This small winery in the heart of the Cirò zone is at the forefront of the movement to defend the traditional values of the gaglioppo grape and Cirò the wine – which only needs to be respected to express itself to the full. This is what Sergio has been doing since he took over the cellar where his father Giuseppe taught him the ropes 99

PEOPLE - Here, save for recent organic certification, little or nothing has changed in the last 40 years. Following a tradition consolidated since the postwar years, the wine is fermented in cement vats and aged in the bottle.

VINEYARDS - Gaglioppo is the only bush-trained grape in the old 1945 vineyards, being high-trained in the new ones planted in 2005. On the red soil, rich in iron and minerals, behind the village, almost at sea level, it isn't hard to practice eco-compatible viticulture since the good air circulation keeps off molds. These are the conditions in which the "prince of Calabrian grapes" gives of its best.

WINES - Two typical, precise, immediately recognizable wines, the precious fruits of a small winery that we are following with great interest. The intriguingly copper-colored **Marinetto 2011** (⊙ gaglioppo; 3,500 bt) has notes of blossom and pink grapefruit on the nose, excellent fresh mouthfeel and a precise, clean finish. The superb Cirò Cl. Sup. Aris 2011 `Everyday Wine` (● 3,500 bt) is fermented in cement vats according to the tradition established by Giuseppe's father; it has elegant hints of rose and red berries and a pleasant, uncompromisingly dry attack. The palate is pacey and dynamic thanks to silky mellow tannins with slightly salty, earthy sensations leading into a long, lingering finish which leaves you wanting to start all over again.

FERTILIZERS green manure
PLANT PROTECTION copper and sulphur
WEED CONTROL mechanical
YEASTS native
GRAPES 100% estate-grown
CERTIFICATION organic

CIRÒ MARINA (KR)

'A Vita

S.S. 106, km 279,800
tel. 0962 31044
www.avitavini.it
avita.info@gmail.com

20 ac - 10,000 bt

66 Francesco de Franco is a living example of how it's possible to defend the coherence of a terroir by creating a movement and spreading the word without remaining in one's shell. It was he who kindled the hope of protecting the biodiversity of the Cirò area 99

PEOPLE - It's just ten years since Francesco set his project into motion by fitting out a small wine cellar under his family's store.

VINEYARDS - Sant'Anastasia, Muzzunetto, Frassà and Fego – these are the localities where the winery has its four vineyards, all on the clay and red sand typical of the Ionian coast, which receives winds from the sea and breezes from the Sila plateau. The whole operation has always adopted organic methods.

WINES - Thanks to a favorable growing year **Rosato 2013** (⊙ gaglioppo; 3,000 bt) is a minor masterpiece. Bronze in color, it is unconcentrated with a blossomy nose and citrusy notes of pink grapefruit; on the palate it is rich, savory, very long, precise and clean. Just as good is the scented, flavorsome, lingering **Cirò Rosso Cl. Sup. 'A Vita 2011** (● 8,000 bt).

`slow wine` **CIRÒ ROSSO CL. SUP. 'A VITA RIS. 2010** (● 6,000 bt) A red wine that ennobles the entire denomination: it has hints of soil and ripe cherry on the nose, a very rich palate with well-balanced tannins and a long, lingering finish.

FERTILIZERS green manure
PLANT PROTECTION copper and sulphur
WEED CONTROL mechanical
YEASTS native
GRAPES 100% estate-grown
CERTIFICATION organic

Librandi €

Contrada San Gennaro
S.S. 106
tel. 0962 31518
www.librandi.it
librandi@librandi.it

Luigi Viola

Via Roma, 18
tel. 0981 349099
www.cantineviola.it
info@cantineviola.it

---

642 ac - 2,500,000 bt `10% discount`

PEOPLE - The transition phase that began with the death of Antonio Librandi in 2013 isn't over yet, but the cellar, supervised by Antonio's brother Nicodemo, is still an institution for viticulture in Cirò. The new generation, in the person of Nicodemo's son Paolo, is playing an increasingly prominent role. What we like about Librandi is the determined but understated way in which it sticks to the traditional gaglioppo style.

VINEYARDS - The company's vineyards, 640 acres in all, are scattered between Cirò, Melissa and Strongoli. There are three main properties: Cirò Marina, where the cellar is surrounded by the plots belonging to the vinedressers; the spectacular Rosaneti estate where most of the vineyards are concentrated; and Melissa, a DOC that the company revived and relaunched in the mid 1990s. The vinedressers are supervised by company technicians.

WINES - The two whites are dry and bright: **Melissa Asylia 2013** (O greco; 60,000 bt) is fruity and floral on the nose, tangy and long on the palate, whereas **Efeso 2013** (O mantonico; 12,000 bt) is more ambitious, though we reckon they release it too soon. The wines are made with gaglioppo grapes are well crafted and enjoyable. **Cirò Rosso 2013** (● 300,000 bt) is fresh and rich in fruit with bracing flavor. **Magno Megonio 2012** (● magliocco; 30,000 bt) is leaner and more symmetrical than previous versions. **Gravello 2012** (● gaglioppo, cabernet sauvignon; 70,000 bt) is again soft and pleasurable with plenty of body and is sure to be a hit with nostalgic lovers of the native-international duo.

`slow wine` **CIRÒ ROSSO CL. DUCA SAN FELICE RIS. 2012** (● 120,000 bt) A red that, over the years, has become the flagship of the denomination. It has notes of citrus fruit and red berries with a long, enjoyable palate and gives of its best after five to six years.

7.5 ac - 10,000 bt

PEOPLE - A name, a wine and a legend: it was more than 20 years Luigi Viola that revived a practice, the art of raisining, once common in this village on Monte Pollino, promoting it among enthusiasts without in any way adulterating it. Today the company, where the grapes are still raisined using artisan methods, is run by Luigi's sons Alessandro, Claudio and Roberto with the collaboration of agronomist Luigi Ferraro and enologist Alessio Dorigo.

VINEYARDS - The new magliocco planting, which began producing three years ago, has allowed the company to supplement its sweet wine with reds. The vineyards in the Contrada Rinni, at an altitude of 350 meters, are certified organic. Sharp night-day temperature swings and the winds that blow down from the mountains and up from the sea add freshness and vigor to the grapes.

WINES - We liked the new version of **Rosso Viola 2012** (● magliocco dolce; 3,700 bt) more than the last on account of its fuller, riper fruit and its dynamic palate, which features mellow tannins and notable freshness. It will be interesting to see how this elegant, essential wine evolves.

`slow wine` **MOSCATO PASSITO DI SARACENA 2013** (O 4,000 bt) A certainty on the Calabrian wine scene made to a protocol tried and tested for 20 years. It's characterized by freshness and brightness, but also nice tanginess, which are superimposed to create great complexity in the glass: hence ripe orange, licorice, caramel, characteristic notes of moscato and echoes of Mediterranean scrub. The dry, clean finish is terrific.

FERTILIZERS green manure	**FERTILIZERS** manure pellets, natural manure, green manure
PLANT PROTECTION copper and sulphur	**PLANT PROTECTION** copper and sulphur
WEED CONTROL mechanical	**WEED CONTROL** mechanical
YEASTS selected	**YEASTS** native
GRAPES 100% estate-grown	**GRAPES** 100% estate-grown
CERTIFICATION organic	**CERTIFICATION** organic

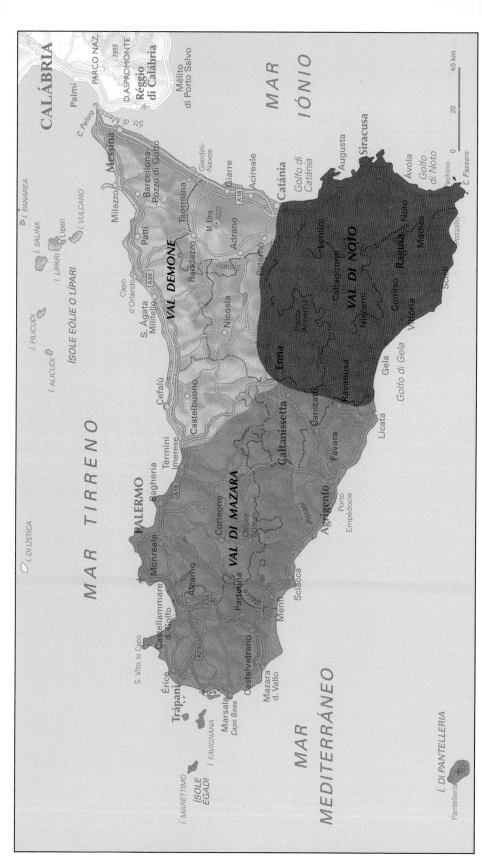

SICILY

Sicily is present and correct and always will be. Despite being the Italian region with most vineyards. Despite its 23 DOCs (whose protocols even allow for the "spumante" typology, and the newest of which, the Sicilia DOC, absorbs most of DO production on its own, thereby creating a gallimaufry of indistinct origin and sensory standardization). Despite its 12 "wine routes" (plus a regional federation), sometimes bereft of substance but invariably with their own organizations and offices. Despite all the various protection consortia. Despite the regional authority's efforts to airbrush the activities of Irvos, the Sicilian Regional Institute for Oil and Wine. Despite the ongoing attempt to stun Marsala and Sicilian passitos into an irreversible coma (as has already happened, at least in part, for Nero d'Avola). Despite, on occasion, Sicilian producers themselves, know-it-alls, who now believe in organics and respect for the vineyard and the soil, who are well-versed in the market and its dynamics. Despite climate change, peronospora and wine OCMs. Despite everything and despite everyone (trade insiders included), Sicily is present and correct. This emerges loud and clear from our tastings for this edition of the guide. The quality of Sicilian production is high and still growing. From the "Three Valleys" (Demone, Mazara and Noto) came richly nuanced, distinctly landrooted Catarrattos and Grillos, delicious Frappatos and compelling Cerasuolos, fruity Nero d'Avolas and Perricones, valid representatives of corners of the island brimming with history, stylish and deep Nerellos and Carricantes, and Passitos and Marsalas that are worthy witnesses and ambassadors of the sun and the passing of time. In 2013 wine production in Sicily, musts excluded, totaled 6.2 million hectoliters with an increase of 40% with respect to 2012. 2013, more than 2011 e 2012, was characterized by a mild, quite rainy winter, a cool, well-ventilated spring, and a not overhot summer with excellent night-day temperature swings. Climatic conditions were thus atypical but by no means unfavorable and, with due exceptions according to terroir, allowed the grapes to ripen gradually without stress. Everything seemed set for a good vintage, but during the harvest heavy rain damaged the quality of the grapes in some places. We recorded an increase in organics, natural production, respect for zones, coherent vinification, and increasingly less invasive cellar practices. It's our hope that this "new" conscientiousness will spread further and turn eventually into concrete action.

snails 🐌

223	VALDIBELLA
223	MARCO DE BARTOLI
225	FERRANDES
227	GRACI
229	GIROLAMO RUSSO
230	I VIGNERI
230	TENUTA DELLE TERRE NERE
231	FRANK CORNELISSEN
235	COS
235	ARIANNA OCCHIPINTI

bottles 🍾

227	MASSERIA SETTEPORTE
228	I CUSTODI DELLE VIGNE DELL'ETNA
228	PASSOPISCIARO
229	TENUTA DI CASTELLARO
233	GIANFRANCO DAINO
234	GULFI

coins €

224	CANTINE RALLO
234	POGGIO DI BORTOLONE

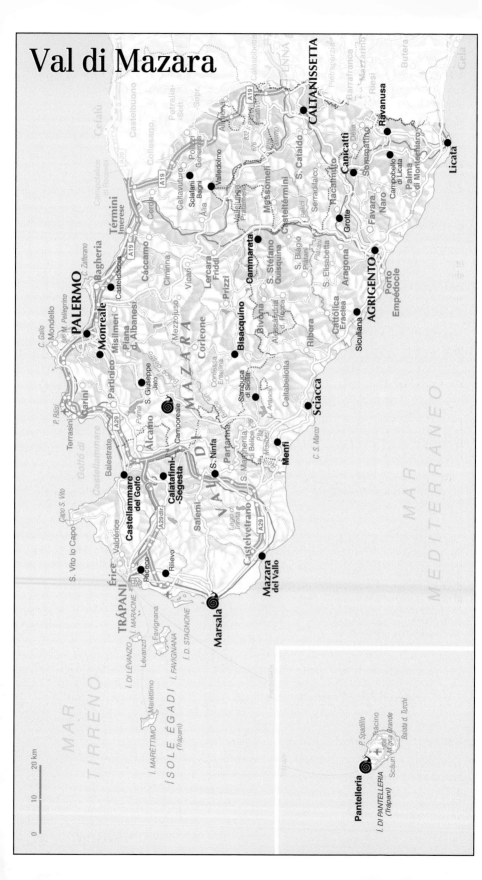

Valdibella

Via Belvedere, 91
tel. 0924 582021
www.valdibella.com
info@valdibella.com

103 ac - 95,000 bt | **10% discount**

66 If we were to explain the axiom of 'good, clean and fair' with a tangible example, we firmly believe that Valdibella would be a good one to choose 99

PEOPLE - Born of the insight of ten farmers in 1998, Valdibella is part of the Salesian-inspired "Jonathan" project in which members of the cooperative engage to help youngsters at the Itaca community to integrate in society. Mission accomplished!

VINEYARDS - The aim of the Valdibella project according to Massimiliano Solano is "To give back farmers the dignity of their job." Last year an ancient grain cultivar, known as *tumminia*, was reintroduced and new plantings of zibibbo, nerello mascalese and cappuccino have been added. The vineyards cover a vast area and are beautifully kept. The external consultants are Vincenzo Drago and Benoit De Coster, the cellarman is Pietro Vaccaro.

WINES - The number of wines made with native yeasts has increased and the range has expanded. From a ten-year-old vineyard, **Sicilia Acamante 2012** (● perricone; 6,600 bt) has enjoyable juiciness that captures and releases the properties of the grape: a wine to drink and discover. Black mulberry and grassy notes characterize Sicilia Kerasos 2013 Everyday Wine (● nero d'Avola; 30,000 bt) which, after a subtle, timid entry, develops unstoppably on the palate. In Sicilia Ariddu 2013 Everyday Wine (○ grillo; 6,000 bt), notes of mandarin, sage and chamomile flowers are followed up by a precise, well-defined palate. The tangy, dense **Sicilia Isolano 2013** (○ catarratto; 6,000 bt) will improve with age. **Sicilia Munir 2013** (○ catarratto; 20,000 bt) is varietal and bright and **Sicilia Memorii 2012** (○ catarratto, grillo; 1,300 bt) is a joy to drink.

FERTILIZERS	biodynamic preparations, green manure
PLANT PROTECTION	copper and sulphur
WEED CONTROL	mechanical
YEASTS	selected, native
GRAPES	100% estate-grown
CERTIFICATION	biodynamic

Marco De Bartoli

Contrada Fornaia Samperi, 292
tel. 0923 962093
www.marcodebartoli.com
info@marcodebartoli.com

42 ac - 90,000 bt

66 Albeit sticking to tradition, the style Renato De Bartoli has given his wines continues to begiule. He has achieved a mature identity without ignoring the lessons learned from his family 99

PEOPLE - In recent years, going back to Samperi without being able to say hello to the late Marco De Bartoli had become a heartbreaking experience. But today, thanks to his children Renato, Sebastiano and Giuseppina, it's one of the high points in our calendar.

VINEYARDS - The Samperi and Bukkuram vineyards are farmed with the awareness that these are places where good wine is born. Samperi in particular possesses special charm: situated in a very pretty hollow of alluvial origin, some parts of which are below sea level, it adds important sensory characteristics to the grapes that grow in it.

WINES - The range of wines presented was electrifying. The classy **M. Cl. Brut Nature Terzavia** (○ grillo; 11,000 bt) and **Cuvée Campagne di Samperi Terzavia** (○ grillo; 1,200 bt) tickle the palate with depth and delectability. The juicy, dynamic **Marsala Sup. Ris. 10 anni** (○ 6,000 bt) exudes freshness, fruitiness and well-calibrated oxidation. **Lucido 2013** (○ catarratto; 10,000 bt) and **Pietra Nera 2013** (○ zibibbo; 13,000 bt) are on a par.

slow wine **GRAPPOLI DEL GRILLO 2012** (○ 10,000 bt) An amalgam of the tufa substratum in the Samperi vineyard and aromas of iodine, seaweed and sea urchins – a wine of enormous appeal.

slow wine **VECCHIO SAMPERI VENTENNALE** (○ 6,000 bt) One of the best wines tasted this year: acidic, vibrant, never-ending … Enough hyperbole! Suffice it to say that the components are noble syntheses and testimonies to time past!

FERTILIZERS	none
PLANT PROTECTION	copper and sulphur
WEED CONTROL	mechanical
YEASTS	native
GRAPES	10% bought in
CERTIFICATION	none

Cantine Rallo €

Via Vincenzo Florio, 2
tel. 0923 721633
www.cantinerallo.it
info@cantinerallo.it

Planeta

Contrada Dispensa
tel. 091 327965
www.planeta.it
planeta@planeta.it

---

222 ac - 350,000 bt

897 ac - 2,254,000 bt

PEOPLE - The company has been owned by the Vesco family since 1920 and is run today by Andrea, who has geared it towards sustainability and the protection of biodiversity. The vineyards are in the Contrada Patti Piccolo between Alcamo and Camporeale, and the lovely 19th-century cellar is in Marsala. Since last year the consultant enologist has been Carlo Ferrini.

VINEYARDS - The organically certified vineyards are spread over almost 200 hectares in the Alcamo DOC zone. In accordance with the company's philosophy, numerous islands of natural biodiversity are protected between the vine rows, with consequent positive effects on the vines themselves. About 25 acres of bush-trained grillo grow in the Marsala countryside, while in Contrada Bugeber on the island of Pantelleria grow five acres of zibibbo.

WINES - **Sicilia Inzolia Evrò 2013** (○ 17,000 bt), fruity with notes of pear, is bright but also very soft and evolving towards citrus fruit. **Sicilia Grillo Bianco Maggiore 2013** (○ 64,000 bt) has a green-appley bouquet, bright freshness and concentration. **Sicilia Beleda 2013** (○ 5,000 bt), made with catarratto grapes, is well crafted with notes of grapefruit and broom, salty character, great structure and length. Sicilia Il Principe 2013 Everyday Wine (● 100,000 bt), made with a base of nero d'Avola, is simple and fruity with a touch of grassiness from the addition of a small percentage of merlot. **Sicilia Il Manto 2012** (● nero d'Avola; 28,000 bt), the company cru, is given a boost by wood and comes with good complexity and mellowing notes of aromatic herbs. **Rujari 2012** (● 10,000 bt) is a blend of nero d'Avola, merlot and cabernet sauvignon in which the salty notes of the native grape predominate.

PEOPLE - Anatomy of Restlessness. It's the title of a famous book by Bruce Chatwin but it also sums up the spirit with which Alessio, Santi and Francesca Planeta continue their pursuit of perfection across their island; from Menfi to Noto, from Vittoria to Etna to Capo Milazzo. Every year they get closer and closer.

VINEYARDS - Now, 20 years on from its foundation, the winery's properties are vast in terms of area and geographical distribution and various for conditions, altitudes, positions and soils. Hence about 900 hectares of vineyard, two R&D fields, 16 red grape varieties and 10 white and six wine cellars: Ulmo, Dispensa, Dorilli, Buonivini, Feudo di Mezzo and La Baronia. These are the facts and figures that sum up the immense commitment of Planeta.

WINES - A high-quality range. **Sicilia Cometa Fiano 2013** (○ 60,000 bt) is juicy, full-bodied and creamy. **Sicilia Chardonnay 2012** (○ 170,000 bt) is fruity and fleshy, elegant and leisurely with fresh-tasting, almost salty mouthfeel. **Etna Bianco 2013** (○ 23,000 bt) and **Sicilia Eruzione 1614 Carricante 2013** (○ 26,000 bt) are well-defined and well-crafted. Three distinctly land-rooted wines comes from the Dorilli estate: **Vittoria Frappato 2013** (● 14,000 bt), which is subtle and juicy, **Cerasuolo di Vittoria 2012** (● 83,000 bt), which is varietal and eminently quaffable, and Cerasuolo di Vittoria Cl. Dorilli 2012 Great Wine (● 16,000 bt), which is complex and full-bodied with hints of black mulberry, capers and spices, likely the best version ever. **Noto Nero d'Avola Santa Cecilia 2011** (● 67,000 bt) is juicy and salty.

FERTILIZERS natural manure
PLANT PROTECTION copper and sulphur
WEED CONTROL mechanical
YEASTS selected
GRAPES 100% estate-grown
CERTIFICATION organic

FERTILIZERS organic-mineral, green manure
PLANT PROTECTION chemical, copper and sulphur
WEED CONTROL mechanical
YEASTS selected
GRAPES 100% estate-grown
CERTIFICATION none

PANTELLERIA (TP)

Ferrandes

Contrada Tracino Kamma
Via del Fante, 8
tel. 0923 915475
www.passitodipantelleriaferrandes.com
dsferrandes@meditel.it

5 ac - 3,000 bt

66 Navigators of old knew that the sea can't be controlled, it can only be complied with. And it's like a navigator of old that Salvatore Ferrandes complies with the sea of time, prepared to cope with its changing conditions, particularly perilous on this strip of volcanic rock in the middle of the real sea 99

PEOPLE - Having put a very difficult growing year behind, Salvatore charmed us once again with his stories and, even more so, with his passito.

VINEYARDS - This time round we were lucky. After years of rain and wind, this year we were able to admire the beauty of the sunny plain of Mueggen, where the vines are traditionally trained in the hollows to shelter them from the wind. The soil is composed of very soft volcanic sand and this makes tending the vineyards very hard work. The cellar nearby is at last fully operational.

WINES - The 2007 is still on the market to enable Salvatore to have two versions: one "young," the other "less so."

slow wine **PASSITO DI PANTELLERIA 2009** (O 3,000 bt) After not a little resistance and perplexity – typical of a man in eternal pursuit of perfection – Salvatore has at last decided to release a new vintage, 2009, of which he produced 11 hectoliters in all. A beautiful amber yellow in color, it has a deep and sensual nose which already reveals tertiary aromas. It opens gradually with notes of incense that act as a connective tissue with a sequence of honey, dehydrated and dried fruit and, finally, raisins. A wine of great sweet-acid symmetry with an apparently more approachable character than previous versions.

FERTILIZERS manure pellets
PLANT PROTECTION copper and sulphur
WEED CONTROL mechanical
YEASTS native
GRAPES 100% estate-grown
CERTIFICATION organic

SCLAFANI BAGNI (PA)

Tasca d'Almerita

Contrada Regaleali
tel. 091 6459711
www.tascadalmerita.it
info@tascadalmerita.it

825 ac - 3,000,000 bt

PEOPLE - One of the brands that exports the name of Sicily worldwide. After beginning life in the province of Palermo, the winery's interests have expanded to embrace the whole of the island. Tasca now grows grapes on five estates, with its "heart" at Regaleali. Captaining the ship are Alberto and Giuseppe Tasca.

VINEYARDS - Convinced of the need to restore environmental sustainability, Tasca d'Almerita adheres to SOStain, a project coordinated by the Università Cattolica del Sacro Cuore (Catholic University of the Sacred Heart). On the historic estate of Regaleali, the beating heart of the winery, vines are trained in such a way as to reduce outside interventions. The winery also adheres to Viva, a project promoted by the Italian Ministry of the Environment, to ensure the total sustainability of the production chain right to the wine in the glass.

WINES - The concentrated **Dydime 2013** (O malvasia; 18,000 bt) offers the full suite of aromas of the variety without turning into caricature. **Sicilia Buonora 2013** (O carricante; 30,000 bt) is stylish and full of character with a compelling citrusy finish. **Contea di Scafani Nozze d'Oro 2012** (O inzolia, sauvignon; 47,000 bt) has nice acid texture and great fruit. **Contea di Sclafani Chardonnay Vigna San Francesco 2012** Great Wine (O 30,000 bt) is enthralling, succulent and deep, its buttery, citrusy notes fused masterfully with hints of vanilla, acidity and flavor to put it on a par with the best Chardonnays Northern Italy has to offer. **Sicilia Lamùri 2012** (● nero d'Avola; 180,000 bt) is varietal. Born in 1970, **Contea di Scafani Rosso del Conte 2010** (● nero d'Avola; 30,000 bt) is dynamic and recherché, a synthesis of four decades of history. The bright, breezy **Grillo Mozia 2013** (O 1,200 magnum) is made with grapes from the Whitaker estate.

FERTILIZERS organic-mineral
PLANT PROTECTION chemical, copper and sulphur
WEED CONTROL chemical, mechanical
YEASTS selected
GRAPES 20% bought in
CERTIFICATION none

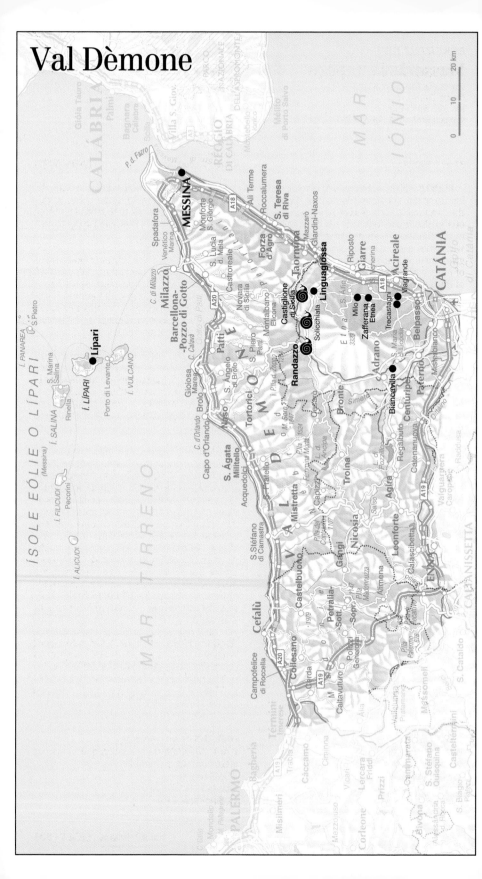

Val Dèmone

BIANCAVILLA (CT)

Masseria Setteporte

Contrada Setteporte
Piazza Trento, 2
tel. 335 5338152
masseriasetteporte@email.it

37 ac - 25,000 bt

PEOPLE - If the south side of Etna is coming up with new wine cellars every year, on the southeast side Masseria Setteporte is one of the most consolidated. It is situated in the Biancavilla district where the sun always shines on the vineyards. "This is our great fortune," says Piero Portale, a lawyer of unique charisma who has made the most of this enormous viticultural heritage.

VINEYARDS - We toured the vineyards with consultant agronomist Giovanni Marletta, who told us all about the favorable conditions of the area. The vines, over 30 acres of them, stretch as far as the eye can see in a succession of broad terraces. Most of them are high-trained for simplicity's sake and to optimize costs. The main grapes grown are nerello mascalese and cappuccino, and new plantings of carricante are planned for the future.

WINES - Sanguine and concentrated, yet, at the same time, stylish and elegant, Piero Portale's wines distill the essence of the South. The warm **Etna Rosso 2012** (● 10,000 bt) has a fresh, fruity bouquet with mineral notes, a good palate with youthful, tearaway but never invasive tannins, and massive body for a base wine. The cellar's minor masterpiece **Etna Bianco N'Ettaro 2013** (○ carricante, catarratto; 5,500 bt) is made with grapes from a two acre of vineyard cultivated with white grapes. This year it has noteworthy structure, a generous nose, and a relatively balanced palate with very salty mouthfeel.

> **slow wine** **ETNA ROSSO NERELLO MASCALESE 2012** (● 5,000 bt) Concentrated and complex on the nose, a wine that engulfs the palate in mellow tannins. A fully-rounded, memorable drink.

CASTIGLIONE DI SICILIA (CT)

Graci

Contrada Arcuria Passopisciaro
tel. 348 7016773
www.graci.eu
info@graci.eu

44 ac - 63,000 bt   **10% discount**

❝ Tenacity, passion and a desire to put themselves on the line: these are the qualities that have led Alberto Aiello Graci and his sister Elena to create a first-rate winery and practice healthy agriculture ❞

PEOPLE - A visit to the cellar is like making a journey through winemaking. It's situated in the hamlet of Passopisciaro and housed in an old building fit out with the most modern technological gizmos, but also enormous chestnut barrels and rudimentary 19th-century winemaking machinery.

VINEYARDS - Most of the vineyards are in the Contrada Arcuria, the others are in Contrada Feudo di Mezzo and Contrada Barbabecchi, the latter at an altitude of 3,200 feet. Alberto has insisted on bush-training even for the youngest planting, much of which still ungrafted.

WINES - "Simplification of the traditional vinification process by cutting out some of the various stages." This is the credo of Alberto, who reduces racking and clarification to a minimum to keep body intact and produce more expressive wines. **Etna Bianco Arcuria 2012** (○ carricante; 3,500 bt) is a concentrated, full-bodied wine from a rich vintage and shows good supporting acidity. **Etna Rosso Arcuria 2012** (● 10,000 bt), an unctuous wine with elegant fine tannins, starts with red berries which then evolve into balsamic tones. **Etna Bianco 2013** (○ catarratto, carricante; 15,500 bt) is attractively bright.

> **slow wine** **ETNA ROSSO 2012** (● 29,000 bt) A wine with the typical aromas of the terroir, lingering and tannic to just the right degree. Packed with character, it's also reasonably priced.

FERTILIZERS none
PLANT PROTECTION copper and sulphur
WEED CONTROL mechanical
YEASTS native
GRAPES 100% estate-grown
CERTIFICATION organic

FERTILIZERS natural manure
PLANT PROTECTION copper and sulphur
WEED CONTROL mechanical
YEASTS native
GRAPES 100% estate-grown
CERTIFICATION organic

I Custodi delle Vigne dell'Etna

Contrada Moganazzi
tel. 393 1898430
www.icustodi.it
info@icustodi.it

33 ac - 45,000 bt

PEOPLE - Mario Paoluzzi has big ideas for his company and he's putting them into practice with the innate spirit of enterprise he's displayed every since we first met him. "Winemaking in total autonomy" – it'a a fundamental principle for Custodi. Hence plans to restructure the cellar over the next few years. The heart of the estate is in Contrada Moganazzi di Castiglione.

VINEYARDS - The vineyards are in the most magical corners of Etna and are immediately recognizable by virtue of their painstakingly cared for appearance. Vines are bush-trained by hand, a winning formula for good winemaking and a *sine qua non* for the Vigneri consortium, of which Custodi is a member.

WINES - The fresh-tasting, fragrant **Etna Rosato Alnus 2013** (☉ 4,000 bt) is as chewy as a cherry in the mouth. The easy drinking, moreish **Etna Rosso Pistus 2012** (● 14,000 bt) is fruity and juicy with just the right tannins. **Vinujancu 2012** (○ riesling, chenin blanc, carricante; 1,300 bt), previously released under the Vigneri logo, this year comes under the protective wing of Custodi, who manage the vineyard in Contrada Nave; it's a blend that conjures up France more than Etna and will be well worth a second taste in a few years' time.

> **slow wine** **ANTE 2012** (○ carricante, grecanico, minnella; 4,200) Another year, another version of great character. It attacks the nose with fruit and blossom, which then give way to a light mineral note. On the plate it injects well-balanced acidity and bracing flavor.

FERTILIZERS natural manure
PLANT PROTECTION copper and sulphur
WEED CONTROL mechanical
YEASTS native
GRAPES 100% estate-grown
CERTIFICATION converting to organics

Passopisciaro

Frazione Passopisciaro
Contrada Guardiola
tel. 0578 267110
www.passopisciaro.com
info@passopisciaro.com

64 ac - 85,000 bt

PEOPLE - Andrea Franchetti began making wine in Tuscany (in the Val d'Orcia) and saw Etna as a terroir open to interpretation and needy of valorization. He began to invest there and 2000 saw the birth of Passopisciaro, a hilltop cellar surrounded by vineyards just outside the village of the same name near Castiglione. With the experience and knowhow accrued in Tuscany, Andrea has captured the essence of the new terroir, which he instills into very wine he makes.

VINEYARDS - A long walk through the vineyards guided by estate manager Vincenzo Lo Mauro showed us what a various wine company this is. The land round the cellar is characterized by dense plantings of some of Andrea's favorite native varieties such as petit verdot, cesanese and chardonnay. All the other contradas, from Chiappe Macine to Rampante, from Porcaria to Guardiola to Sciara Nuova, are all unique for typicality.

WINES - "The Etna universe in a glass" is the company's slogan. The limestone soil gives **Contrada C 2012** (● 3,500 bt) softness, making for a fruity, juicy, well-balanced wine. **Contrada G 2012** Great Wine (● 3,500 bt) is elegant on the nose with notes of mint and pomice stone. The full-bodied, well-structured **Contrada S 2012** (● 2,000 bt) releases mixed fruit and flint. **Contrada R 2012** (● 3,500 bt) interweaves fruity, mineral and earthy notes, then brings sweetness to the palate before unleashing an explosion of tannins. **Passopisciaro 2012** (● 45,000 bt) has notes of aromatic herbs. All the wines above are nerello mascalese monovarietals, unlike **Franchetti 2012** (● petit verdot, cesanese; 2,000 bt), which offers extraordinary aromatic complexity.

FERTILIZERS natural manure
PLANT PROTECTION copper and sulphur
WEED CONTROL mechanical
YEASTS selected
GRAPES 100% estate-grown
CERTIFICATION none

CASTIGLIONE DI SICILIA (CT)

Girolamo Russo ◎ⱼ

Frazione Passopisciaro
Via Regina Margherita, 78
tel. 328 3840247
www.girolamorusso.it
info@girolamorusso.it

37 ac - 50,000 bt `10% discount`

❝ Walking round Giuseppe Russo's estate we saw how just much care and attention he dedicates to his vineyards in the contradas of San Lorenzo, Feudo and Feudo di Mezzo. Hence wines with a great sense of place ❞

PEOPLE - Giuseppe Russo still lives in the house in which he was born at Passopisciaro, and underneath it is the small wine cellar where his fortunes began. At a certain point in his life he found himself looking after the vines his father Girolamo left him. Over the years he has grown increasingly conscious of his own potential and achieved outstanding results.

VINEYARDS - Some of the vines are bush-trained, others are wire-trained. They are situated at altitudes of 2,100 to 2,600 feet on the north slope of Etna among patches of broom and hazelnut groves, and are cultivated entirely with organic methods.

WINES - Taking part in a vertical tasting of San Lorenzo from the first year of production (2006) led by Giuseppe is like reliving his career so far. We were pleasantly surprised by the body, structure and turgor of the older vintages. The latest version of **Etna Rosso San Lorenzo 2012** (● 6,500 bt) explodes in a sequence of different fruity, mineral and balsamic notes; an exhibition of pure elegance on both nose and palate. The beautifully textured **Etna Rosso Feudo 2012** (● 6,000 bt) has ripe fruit and spicy notes with an enfolding palate, well-rounded body and long finish. Approachable and full of impact, **Etna Rosso 'A Rina 2012** (● 29,500 bt) drives straight to the heart with its aromas, fleshiness and pulp. **Etna Rosato 2013** (◉ 4,300 bt) is nicely refreshing.

LIPARI (ME)

Tenuta di Castellaro ▮

Via Caolino
tel. 035 233337
www.tenutadicastellaro.it
info@comarkspa.it

22 ac - 25,000 bt `10% discount`

PEOPLE - Novelties are the order of the day in the Aeolian Islands. Take Massimo Lentsch, owner of Tenuta di Castellaro, for example. After inaugurating his new cellar, built according to the principles of bio-architecture and environmental sustainability in June 2013, he then released two new labels: a Malvasia delle Lipari and a rosé. Not bad for such a young winery which, once again this year, proved one of the best on the regional scene.

VINEYARDS - If the cellar possesses an environmental value all of its own, the vineyards are so beautifully well kept, they might be likened to "heritage sites." Here Lipari's farming tradition reigns; the consultancy of Salvo Foti and members of his group does the rest. The bush-trained vines are very densely planted (4,500 per acre) and are held up by chestnut poles. The crus are named for the contradas where they grow: Cappero (where the malvasia grapes are grown), Castellaro, Maggiore, Lisca, Caolino and Gelso.

WINES - **Nero Ossidiana 2012** (● corinto, nero d'Avola; 6,500) is not subjected to temperature control, matures in second- and third-use barrels and is well aged in the bottle. The bouquet is rich with suggestions of mulberry and caper, the palate is succulent and very deep. **Rosa Caolino 2013** (◉ corinto, nero d'Avola; 4,000 bt) is interesting.

`slow wine` **BIANCO POMICE 2012** (○ malvasia, carricante; 11,000 bt) A white made with modern, but relatively non-interventionist techniques, without fining and with low sulfur. Hence a very direct, very fresh-tasting, acidy, flavorful wine with elegant aromas. Snappy and refined, it brims over with minerality.

FERTILIZERS natural manure	FERTILIZERS natural manure
PLANT PROTECTION copper and sulphur	PLANT PROTECTION copper and sulphur
WEED CONTROL mechanical	WEED CONTROL mechanical
YEASTS native	YEASTS native
GRAPES 100% estate-grown	GRAPES 100% estate-grown
CERTIFICATION organic	CERTIFICATION none

I Vigneri ☺

Largo Signore Pietà, 17
tel. 0933 982942
www.ivigneri.it
info@ivigneri.it

Tenuta delle Terre Nere ☺

Contrada Calderara
tel. 095 924002
www.tenutaterrenere.com
info@tenutaterrenere.com

4.5 ac - 7,000 bt

❝ 'The hard bit is not cultivating the wines, but cultivating the people to form a team.' Anyone who has the honor of meeting Salvo Foti has before them the creator and inspirer of the fortunes that Etna enology is currently enjoying ❞

PEOPLE - His determination has revived the antique splendors of the workers of Vigneri, an old association of expert vinedressers dating back to 1473 that now has eight member producers.

VINEYARDS - The century-old vines are a sight to behold! Each has its own distinctive form and contorts itself round its own chestnut pole. As Salvo has written in a book, "It's their way of opposing themselves to man who forces them, every year with the January moon, to shape what appear to be living sculptures." Maximum care is taken of the vines in every season. The old Bosco vineyard, hidden in a wood of holm oaks at an altitude of 4300 feet, is an enchanting place.

WINES - "The finest ingredient of a wine is the honesty of the person who produced it." With these words, the source of inspiration for all the work he has done over the last few years, Salvo uncorked the first bottle up for tasting, **Vigna di Milo 2012** (○ carricante; 1,200 bt), a monovarietal Carricante, calm and stylish on the nose, bright and tangy on the palate. The unusual **Vinudilice 2010** (◉ alicante, grecanico, minnella; 1,300 bt), a Metodo Classico made with red and white grapes, has an attractive color and strikingly floral, fruity and mineral notes with an impressive lively and lingering palate. **Etna Rosso I Vigneri 2012** (● 3,000 bt) made with grapes from the consortium's various producers, is a forthright, earthy wine that synthesises the cellar's teamwork.

---

69 ac - 180,000 bt | **10% discount**

❝ Thanks to the position of the vineyards, scattered round the various contradas of Etna, it's possible to grasp differences of terroir in every wine Marco De Grazia produces ❞

PEOPLE - If you happen to find yourself on Etna, be sure to stop off at Marco's place! With his experience of and love for the volcano, he's capable of transmitting a wealth of fascinating information. Thanks to his constant exploration and discovery of areas suitable for viticulture, he exploits the characteristics of this unique environment to the full.

VINEYARDS - Contrada Calderara, where the soil is rough and pebbly, gives wines density and body. Guardiola, where it's a blend of sand and volcanic ash, adds a considerable acid-tannic component. Santo Spirito offers elegance, Feudo di Mezzo softness and an abundance of aromas.

WINES - Marco sets out the facts: the year was hard to figure and still is, but will produce amazing results in the course of time. Mineral and razor-sharp, **Etna Rosso Guardiola 2012** (● 7,000 bt) conceals notes of flint. **Etna Rosso Santo Spirito 2012** (● 7,000 bt) is pervasive and elegant with well-rounded fruit and well-polished tannins. The dense, full-bodied **Etna Rosso Calderara 2012** (● 7,000 bt) is a wine that leads with fruit to embrace notes of spices and tobacco. **Etna Rosso Pre-fillossera Vigna Don Peppino 2012** (● 3,000 bt) attacks with sweet fruit and follows up with body and never-ending length. Last but not least, the mineral-packed **Etna Bianco Vigne Niche 2012** (○ 10.000 bt) is an essay in how to use the carricante grape.

> **slow wine** ETNA ROSSO FEUDO DI MEZZO 2012 (● 7,000 bt) Gentle and intoxicatingly aromatic, this was the wine we enjoyed the most for its sense of place, harmony and drinkability.

FERTILIZERS natural manure	**FERTILIZERS** natural manure, green manure
PLANT PROTECTION copper and sulphur	**PLANT PROTECTION** copper and sulphur
WEED CONTROL mechanical	**WEED CONTROL** mechanical
YEASTS native	**YEASTS** selected
GRAPES 100% estate-grown	**GRAPES** 30% bought in
CERTIFICATION none	**CERTIFICATION** organic

SOLICCHIATA (CT)

Frank Cornelissen

Via Nazionale, 297
tel. 0942 986315
www.frankcornelissen.it
info@frankcornelissen.it

VIAGRANDE (CT)

Benanti

Via Garibaldi, 361
tel. 095 7893438
www.vinicolabenanti.it
benanti@vinicolabenanti.it

44 ac - 45,000 bt

66 Frank Cornelissen is a master at the art of vinification and experimentation with different production methods, and has managed to identify the best places for wine production in the area. This year's results at last repay him for all the efforts he has made 99

PEOPLE - There's only one Frank Cornelissen! He knows Etna like the back of his hand, almost as if he had been born there. It's hard to imagine that he only left his native Belgium to come to live in the tiny hamlet of Solicchiata 14 years ago.

VINEYARDS - Always on the lookout for new places to explore, Frank likes to figure out which have the best characteristics to create wines of unique character. The highest vineyards, Tartaraci, Barbabecchi and Monte Dolce, are all outside the Etna DOC, but this has never been a problem for Frank, who has captured the essence and raised the profile even of lesser-known corners.

WINES - The bright, sappy **Rosato Susucaru 2013** (⊙ nerello mascalese, malvasia, moscatello, catarratto; 11,000 bt), is made the old-fashioned way with a blend of red and white grapes. It takes time and patience to appreciate all the complexity of **Munjebel 9 CS 2013** (● nerello mascalese; 1,600 bt), balsamic with notes of flint and liqueur cherries and depth of palate. **Munjebel 9 MC 2013** (● nerello mascalese; 1,600 bt) has notes of honey that recur in the mouth. The superbly complex **Magma 2012** (● nerello mascalese; 1.350 bt) is a web of sweet and sour notes in which licorice predominates.

slow wine MUNJEBEL **9 VA 2013** (● nerello mascalese; 1,600 bt) Officinal herbs and blackcurrants and brambles on the nose, astonishing structure and body on the palate. Buy it and drink it in a few years' time!

69 ac - 120,000 bt

PEOPLE - He's been described as the "Patriarch of Etna," Giuseppe Benanti, the man who, 20 years ago, brought the area to the world's attention through his wine. His sons Salvino and Antonio took over the reins of the cellar a few years ago and are now busy developing a major reorganization project.

VINEYARDS - The vineyards are scattered over the various sides of the volcano, a fact that is one of the cellar's strong points. Contrada Caselle, east of Milo, is the best zone for growing white grapes. In the contradas of Rovittello and Verzella, further north between Randazzo and Castiglione di Sicilia, there are other good parcels. More vineyards and the wine cellar itself are to the southeast on Monte Serra, and more still are situated at Viagrande, southeast of the cone, in the area of Santa Maria di Licodia.

WINES - Four years for the crus and two for the base wines: these are the house rules, established by the Benanti brothers and technician Enzo Calì (who has 12 years of experience at the company under his belt), as far as aging is concerned. The dual aim is to allow the nerello mascalese to give of its best and to mellow the carricante. The warm **Etna Bianco Bianco di Caselle 2012** (○ carricante; 35,000 bt) starts with notes of almond, which are followed by a snappy, nicely acid palate and a long finish. **Etna Rosso Rosso di Verzella 2012** (● 45,000 bt) amazes with the approachability of its aromas and is soft and mellow on the palate. **Etna Bianco Sup. Pietramarina 2010** Great Wine (○ 10,000 bt) is a complex Carricante with nuances of flint, a salty attack and extraordinary balance. Made with grapes from the north side of the volcano, **Etna Rosso Rovittello 2010** (● 10,000 bt) brings out ripening fruit, which then gives way to balsamic tones.

FERTILIZERS none	FERTILIZERS none
PLANT PROTECTION copper and sulphur	PLANT PROTECTION copper and sulphur
WEED CONTROL mechanical	WEED CONTROL mechanical
YEASTS native	YEASTS selected
GRAPES 100% estate-grown	GRAPES 35% bought in
CERTIFICATION organic	CERTIFICATION none

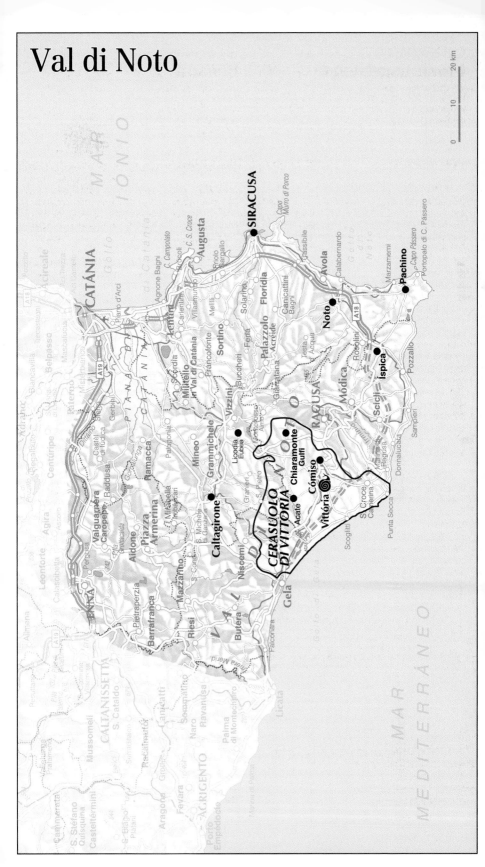

Val di Noto

CALTAGIRONE (CT)

Gianfranco Daino

Via Croce del Vicario, 115
tel. 0933 58226 - 335 5243345
www.vinidaino.it
info@vinidaino.it

CALTAGIRONE (CT)

Judeka

Contrada San Mauro sotto SP39/II Km 3,8
tel. 09331895310
www.judeka.com
info@judeka.com

7.5 ac - 13,000 bt   **10% discount**

PEOPLE - It isn't easy to start a wine company from scratch the way Gianfranco Daino has done. The sacrifices have been enormous but we have to admit that the results achieved have been staggering, at least as far as the sensory qualities of the wines and the beauty of the vineyards are concerned. It's a very young winery and we've followed it right from its impressive debut.

VINEYARDS - Sicily is an island of huge contrasts where natural beauty alternates, alas, with human interventions that have a deleterious effect on the environment. Here, instead, all is harmony with a single eight-acre surrounded by the Bosco di San Pietro Nature Reserve, home to secular cork trees. The vines are densely planted (4,500 plants per acre) and are trained in the same style as Salvo Foti's I Vigneri: namely using the bush system with one chestnut pole per vine. The viticulture adopted is certified organic and a forklift truck is used for some operations.

WINES - We'd like the extremely high quality of the only wine produced by this small winery to receive more acknowledgment in Italy and abroad, because reds like this truly are hard to find. All due credit therefore to Gianfranco Daino first and foremost, and to the great Catania enologist Salvo Foti, whose contribution has been vital.

> **slow wine** **SUBER 2012** (● nero d'Avola, frappato, alicante; 13,000 bt) Is aged in barriques and second-use tonneaux, The bouquet is a triumph of black berries, of mulberry in particular, and complex notes redolent of caper and Mediterranean scrubland, hence oregano and rosemary. The palate is fleshy with perfect harmony between acidity and alcohol.

---

37 ac - 700,000 bt

PEOPLE - The protagonists of this adventure are single-minded people. Not even the difficulties they encountered before opening the cellar, in December 2013, could stop them. It wasn't easy to engage in a new, albeit exciting field like viticulture. Nonetheless, Valentina Nicodemo, her husband Maurizio Nicolosi, and her brother Cesare have managed to set up an enterprise that combines quantity and quality. They count upon the collaboration of enologist Nicola Centonze.

VINEYARDS - The owners hail from the village of Ramacca and they chose the Caltagirone area because it's part of the Cerasuolo di Vittoria DOCG. The cellar covers an area of 13,000 square feet built according to criteria of ecocompatibility: hence low impact on the environment, minimum energy consumption, photovoltaic panels, a solar power plant, and a sewage treatment plant. The soils are characterized by red earth and clay and the vines are Guyot-trained.

WINES - The cellar is on the border of the Cerasuolo zone, where frappato is also known as "nero capitano". It markets a number of different lines of wine. We tasted the so-called "terroir prestige" labels. **Vittoria Frappato 2013** (● 40,000 bt) is wrapped in red berries, which make an enjoyable encore on the palate in a long, flavorsome finish. **Cerasuolo di Vittoria 2013** (● 75,000 bt) is juicy and elegant with perfect palate-nose symmetry and a soft but steely tannic texture. **Vittoria Nero d'Avola 2013** (● 20,000 bt) is fruity and enfolding with perfect tannins. **Insolia 2013** (○ 25.000 bt) impressed us with the symmetry between its aromas and freshness.

FERTILIZERS natural manure
PLANT PROTECTION copper and sulphur
WEED CONTROL mechanical
YEASTS native
GRAPES 100% estate-grown
CERTIFICATION organic

FERTILIZERS natural manure, green manure, humus
PLANT PROTECTION copper and sulphur
WEED CONTROL mechanical
YEASTS selected
GRAPES 50% bought in
CERTIFICATION converting to organics

Gulfi

Contrada Patrìa
tel. 0932 921654
www.gulfi.it
info@gulfi.it

Poggio di Bortolone €

Frazione Roccazzo
Contrada Bortolone, 19
tel. 0932 921161
www.poggiodibortolone.it
info@poggiodibortolone.it

172 ac - 250,000 bt · **10% discount**

37 ac - 70,000 bt · **10% discount**

PEOPLE - An enterprise born of Lombard businessman Vito Catania's desire to develop the winemaking concern his family had been carrying forward for three generations. The result is a gorgeous winery in the Chiaromonte countryside, complete with a beautifully appointed inn and a restaurant. The intention has always been to practice eco-friendly viticulture, hence the decision to hire Salvo Foti as consultant enologist right from the outset.

VINEYARDS - The decision to use Salvo Foti translates into bush-trained vines and non-invasive vinification techniques. The criterion is resolutely applied both in the vineyards in Val Canziria in the heart of the Cerasuolo classic zone, where the cellar is situated, the even more favorable growing districts near Pachino, and in a number of parcels on Etna.

WINES - The wines submitted for tasting this year were generally good again. But in an area renowned for its red wines, we prefer to shine the spotlight on two whites. One is our Slow Wine, the other, **Valcanzjria 2013** (O chardonnay, carricante; 20,000 bt) has notes of exotic fruit accompanied by compellingly tangy flavor. As authentic and terroir-based as ever, **Cerasuolo di Vittoria Cl. 2013** (● 20,000 bt) is attractively juicy with perfect nose-palate symmetry. The nero d'Avola cru we liked the most is **NeroSanLorè 2010** (● 7,000 bt) has embracing aromas of ripe red berries with a long, snappy finish. **NeroMaccarj 2010** (● 7,000 bt) is a decent wine, and **RossoJbleo 2013** (● 34,000 bt) is well-crafted and varietal.

> **slow wine** CARJCANTI 2012 (O carricante; 18,000 bt) A very complex wine with hints of chalk and hazelnut, and a palate with a nice acidy finish that promises to develop well. We tasted the 2006 at the company and it was simply stupendous.

PEOPLE - This grape farm as it is today was inaugurated in the 1970s, but it actually goes back more than two centuries. The name Poggio di Bortolone (*poggio* means hillock in Italian) refers to the old hilltop farmhouse. Pierluigi Cosenza, a jack of all trades but a trained agronomist first and foremost, carries forward the family business with a mixture of tradition and innovation.

VINEYARDS - The farm owns about 150 acres of land, growing grapes on 40 of them, partly in the hills and partly in a valley between two rivers, and olives and cereals on the rest. It was one of the first to take part in the revival of Cerasuolo production and, besides nero d'Avola and frappato, grows some international grapes and, to save them from extinction, a few plants of the old grosso nero variety.

WINES - The star of the show this year is Cerasuolo di Vittoria Cl. Contessa Costanza 2011 Everyday Wine (● 5,000), a blend of equal parts of nero d'Avola and frappato, has a bouquet of red berries braced by a note of flint, an almost fleshy palate and a pleasingly tannic finish. We were also impressed by **Cerasuolo di Vittoria Cl. Poggio di Bortolone 2011** (● 15,000 bt), fresh-tasting with just the right acidity. The terroir-based monovarietal **Frappato 2013** (● 10,000 bt) is fruity and mineral with symmetrical aromas. The excellent **Addamanera 2012** (● syrah, cabernet; 12,000 bt) has all the characteristics of the grape varieties. The same grapes provide the base for **Pigi 2012** (● 2,500 bt) and add softness to the palate. **Petit Verdò 2013** (● petit verdot; 4,500 bt) is intriguing.

FERTILIZERS manure pellets, green manure
PLANT PROTECTION copper and sulphur
WEED CONTROL mechanical
YEASTS selected
GRAPES 100% estate-grown
CERTIFICATION organic

FERTILIZERS mineral, natural manure
PLANT PROTECTION copper and sulphur
WEED CONTROL mechanical
YEASTS native
GRAPES 100% estate-grown
CERTIFICATION none

Cos

S.P. 3 Acate-Chiaramonte, Km. 14,500
tel. 0932 876145
www.cosvittoria.it
info@cosvittoria.it

89 ac - 200,000 bt

 66 Giusto Occhipinti and Titta Cilia: pioneers, dreamers and, above all, great winemakers who over the years have treated us to very great wines with non-interventionist farming and enology 99

PEOPLE - The two, architects by profession, began out of pure passion then went far beyond their initial intentions. The winery they set up in now one of the most admired in all Sicily, not for its albeit significant production figures, but for the quality of its wines, acknowledged in Italy and abroad. The enologist is Jacques Mell.

VINEYARDS - The vineyards are situated in the Bastonaca and Fontane contradas, between Acate and Vittoria, on limestone and sandy soils in which strata of clay and tufa alternate. For some years now, the company has been oriented towards biodynamic agriculture and is energetically self-sufficient. The wines are aged mainly in fiber glass-lined cement vats, though terracotta jars are used for the Pithos and wood barrels for some wines.

WINES - Frappato 2013 (● 2,000 bt) starred as always: light and elegant, it expresses the juiciness, aroma and depth of the grape to perfection. **Pithos Rosso 2012** (● nero d'Avola, frappato; 22,000 bt) is supplemented by minerality and grassy notes. **Maldafrica 2011** (● 10,000 bt) is a Bordeaux blend that combines good structure with textbook tannins. Elegance and attractive softness characterize **Contrada 2008** (● nero d'Avola; 4,000 bt). **Ramì 2012** (○ inzolia, grecanico; 22,000 bt) is tangy and mineral.

> **slow wine** CERASUOLO DI VITTORIA CL. 2011 (● 76,000 bt) This hugely impressive cask-aged red promises to give even greater satisfaction in the future.

FERTILIZERS biodynamic preparations
PLANT PROTECTION copper and sulphur
WEED CONTROL mechanical
YEASTS native
GRAPES 100% estate-grown
CERTIFICATION organic

Arianna Occhipinti

Contrada Bombolieri
SP 68 Vittoria-Pedalino, km 3,3
tel. 333 6360316 - 0932 1865519
www.agricolaocchipinti.it
info@agricolaocchipinti.it

54 ac - 120,000 bt

 66 A sincere bond with the land, respect for nature and technical know how are the bases of a Arianna's winemaking philosophy 99

PEOPLE - Exactly ten years after setting out in Contrada Fossa di Lupo, Arianna Occhipinti shifted the winery's headquarters to within a stone's throw of the new, functional cellar in Contrada Bombolieri. "Natural Woman," as she is nicknamed, still follows the production change firsthand with the stalwart collaboration of Nicola Massa, who tends to hospitality and communication.

VINEYARDS - In the vineyards that surround the cellar, the existing 17 acres of nero d'Avola and frappato were recently supplemented with nine of frappato in a landscape characterized by fruit trees and aromatic herbs. The other half of the vineyards includes the historic core of Fossa di Lupo and a property planted over half a century ago in the Pettineo district.

WINES - SP 68 2013 (● frappato, nero d'Avola; 55,000 bt) is to all intents and purposes a Cerasuolo, a red with a distinctive sense of place, fruity, tannic and enjoyably long. In **Siccagno 2011** (● nero d'Avola; 12,000 bt) the ripe berry aromas and sweetness supplement a lively saline note. Less bright than usual, in our view, but still good, the monovarietal **Il Frappato 2012** (● 22,000 bt) is made with grapes from the oldest wines. The white **SP 68 2013** (○ moscato, albanello; 24,000 bt) combines the typical notes of the grape with just the right degree of acidity and a follow-up of freshness.

FERTILIZERS green manure
PLANT PROTECTION copper and sulphur
WEED CONTROL mechanical
YEASTS native
GRAPES 100% estate-grown
CERTIFICATION organic

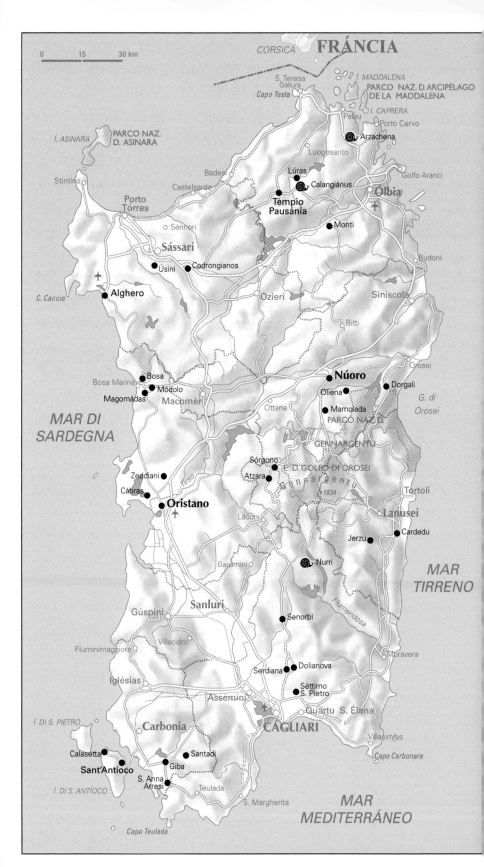

SARDINIA

Contrary to popular belief, Sardinia means more than just sea. Sure, it has a coastline of incomparable beauty, but this constitutes only a small part of what the island has to offer. Landscapes that stretch from the hills to the mountains and tumble down into the sea and soaring peaks like Tacchi di Jerzu or Monte Limbàra testify to its huge climatic, geographical and geological complexity. All these elements, combined with the island's deep historical and cultural roots, offer a snapshot of what Sardinia really is. Or at least of what wine in Sardinia really is. Over the last few years our tastings have evidenced a constant improvement in the quality of wines produced. Just a pity the region fails to communicate the results it achieves adequately and to promote its wines effectively outsidebeyond its boundaries. We hope we can do our bit by highlighting the specificities and peculiarities of a place in many respects still waiting to be discovered.

In the north of the island, Gallura achieves flattering results with its main grape variety, vermentino, 2013 proving one of the best vintages so far this century. The torbato and cagnulari grapes, typical of Alghero and Usini respectively, give rise to enjoyable, personality-packed selections.

Much to their credit, producers in central Sardinia continue to come up with wonderful Vernaccia di Oristano (despite ongoing economic problems) and Malvasia di Bosa. We were also impressed by new deep versions of Cannonau della Barbagia (especially in the Oliena, Mamoiada and Dorgali zones) and the wines from the teeny-weeny Mandrolisai denomination (made with muristellu, cannonau and monica grapes).

In the south, the star of Carignano del Sulcis continues to shine by virtue of objectively high average quality and, this year, of an increase in production.

snails 🐌

62 ORLANDO TONDINI
63 GIUSEPPE SEDILESU
64 PANEVINO

bottles 🍾

62 CAPICHERA

ARZACHENA (OT)

Capichera

S.S. Arzachena-Sant'Antonio, km 4
tel. 078 980612
www.capichera.it
info@capichera.it

CALANGIANUS (OT)

Orlando Tondini

Località San Leonardo
tel. 079 661359
www.cantinatondini.it
cantinatondini@tiscali.it

---

124 ac - 250,000 bt

PEOPLE - In the 1970s the Ragnedda decided to convert their pasture land to viticulture. In 1980 youngsters Mario and Fabrizio Ragnedda, now respectively sales manager and vineyard and cellar manager, took over the reins of the winery and, followed by their other brothers, produced their first bottle in 1981. Success arrived after a decade and the winery became the standard bearer of Sardinian Vermentino worldwide, a role it still plays to this day, and deservedly so.

VINEYARDS - The vineyards, Guyot-trained or spurred cordon-trained or bush-trained, are situated in the Arzachena countryside. They are split into two main plots: one near Tomba dei Giganti, an archeological site popular with tourists, which produces the grapes for Capichera, the other, which produces the grapes for Vigna 'ngena, near the cellar. On either side of the vineyards are vines growing in the granite rock.

WINES - All the wines submitted for tasting this year were top-notch, with vermentino playing a central role. **Capichera 2012** Great Wine (O vermentino; 6,000 bt) is complex and elegant, taut, mineral and floral – a masterpiece. Following suit is the monumental **Santigaini 2010** (O vermentino; 1,500 bt), which is chalky, granitic and very, very typical. More approachable but very elegant nonetheless is **Vermentino di Gallura Vigna 'ngena 2013** (O 50,000 bt), whose finish is redolent of flint. We also enjoyed the smoky and spicy **Vendemmia Tardiva 2012** (O 20,000 bt) and **Lintòri 2013** (O vermentino; 40,000 bt). Worthy of mention among the reds is the heavyweight **Mantenghja 2009** (● carignano, cannonau, syrah; 3,500 bt), with its notes of red berries and Mediterranean scrub.

62 ac - 100,000 bt

66 A great wine is made with great grapes. In the cellar you can ruin all the work you've done in the vineyard.' These words, spoken by Orlando Tondini, give some idea of the care he and his collaborators devote to their farming 99

PEOPLE - Orlando's four children help him manage the vineyards and one of them, Antonio, is the winery's enologist.

VINEYARDS - The vineyards, which were planted over 20 years ago, are situated between Luras and Calangianus at an altitude between 950 and 1,300 feet in one of the best growing areas for the vermentino grape. The soils are a breakdown of granitic rock and constant winds ensure sharp night-day temperature swings. The vines are upwards-trained and Guyot-pruned. Yields never exceed 4 tons per acre.

WINES - Terroir and typicality: these are the words that come to mind tasting the range of wines presented. **Vermentino di Gallura Sup. Karagnanj 2013** (O 80,000 bt), named for Caragnani, the Gallura version of Calangianus, is chalky, full-bodied and rich with a finish of dried fruit and Mediterranean maquis. We also enjoyed **Lajcheddu 2010** (O moscato; 3,000 0.375 lt bt), a sweet bright and breezy Moscato redolent of tea, gentian, and tobacco. Interesting too are **Taroni 2012** (● cannonau, nebbiolo, sangiovese, carignano, cagnulari; 5,000 bt), with notes of red berries and officinal herbs, and the mineral, spicy **Siddaju 2011** (● nebbiolo, cannonau, sangiovese, carignano, cagnulari; 3,000 bt). The new entry, **Vermentino di Gallura Sup. Katala 2013** (O 5,000 bt), is made with late-harvest grapes.

FERTILIZERS organic-mineral, green manure
PLANT PROTECTION chemical, copper and sulphur
WEED CONTROL chemical, mechanical
YEASTS native
GRAPES 5% bought in
CERTIFICATION none

FERTILIZERS organic-mineral, manure pellets
PLANT PROTECTION chemical, copper and sulphur
WEED CONTROL mechanical
YEASTS selected
GRAPES 100% estate-grown
CERTIFICATION none

Giuseppe Sedilesu

Via Vittorio Emanuele II, 64
tel. 0784 56791
www.giuseppesedilesu.com
giuseppesedilesu@tiscali.it

42 ac - 100,000 bt   **10% discount**

66 Nowadays, speaking about Mamoiada, you evoke not only the Mamuthones, the village's typical Carnival masques, but also Cannonau. Much of the credit for this must go to the Sedilesu family who, over the years, have made a name for their mountain Cannonaus 99

PEOPLE - Francesco farms the vineyards and oversees the cellar, Salvatore sees to the sales and administrative side of the business, and their brother-in-law Emilio Mulargiu looks after hospitality.

VINEYARDS - The vineyards are all bush-trained with vines planted 60-100 years ago at an altitude of 1,800-2,600 feet. The soils are a breakdown of granitic rock and, given the steepness of the slopes and consequent difficulty in using machines in some parts of the vineyards, are sometimes worked with ox-drawn plows. Worth mentioning is that two great wines are made with granazza di Mamoiada, a grape now on the verge of extinction.

WINES - The three new wines of the year are fascinating from the taste point of view. **Cannonau di Sardegna Gràssia Ris. 2011** (● 10,000 bt) has sumptuous stuffing, fantastic depth and a spicy finish: **Cannonau di Sardegna Giuseppe Sedilesu Ris. 2010** (● 12,000 bt) is rich and fleshy, while Cannonau di Sardegna Sartiu 2009 Everyday Wine (● 16,000) is drinkable and dynamic with a tangy aftertaste. Further demonstrations of quality came from the well-structured **Cannonau di Sardegna Rosato Erèssia 2012** (⊙ 5,000 bt) and the two wines made with granazza di Mamoiada: **Perda Pintà 2012** (○ 4,000 bt) is very mineral and sets off residual sweetness with great brightness and **Perda Pintà sulle Bucce 2011** (○ 600 bt) an extraordinary sipping wine.

FERTILIZERS biodynamic preparations, green manure	
PLANT PROTECTION copper and sulphur	
WEED CONTROL mechanical	
YEASTS native	
GRAPES 30% bought in	
CERTIFICATION organic	

Panevino

Via Trento, 61
tel. 348 8241060
mancagfranco@tiscali.it

15 ac - 14,000 bt

66 I ask the vineyard's permission to express its soul.' These words sum up the rapport that exists between Gianfranco and his vineyards, which he sees as living entities to be treated with respect and according to their specific needs 99

PEOPLE - Gianfranco Manca made his first steps in the vineyard under the guidance of his grandfather and took it from there in a shuffle of experiments, amusement and enjoyment. He doesn't like being pigeon-holed or catalogued and he shuns cliché. He speaks of his work as "leisure" and he's currently engaged firsthand in defending his vines from an unscrupulous, invasive wind power plant that threatens to gobble up a lot of farming land in the area.

VINEYARDS - The vineyards are situated at an altitude of 1,300-2,200 feet on unique, mostly shale terrains, some of which very steep. They are bush-trained and are a bulwark of increasingly rare biodiversity.

WINES - "I've attended courses that taught me what not to do with wine. In my bottles I like to tell something different. Every time it's like painting a picture in a different color according to my mood and my rapport with nature." Zero sulphites, zero filtrations, zero interventions – but, nonetheless, clean wines, indeed "clean precisely for this reason." We tasted three wines from the last harvest. **Panevin... en rose 2013** (⊙ ciliegiolo, montepulciano, barbera; 2.000 bt) is high on acidity and a joy to drink. **Pikade 2013** (● monica, carignano; 6,000 bt) is succulent and complex. **Su Ki No Nau 2013** (● 6,000 bt) is a truly unique expression of the cannonau grape, very rich and highly scented, at once elegant and potent.

FERTILIZERS biodynamic preparations, green manure	
PLANT PROTECTION copper and sulphur	
WEED CONTROL mechanical	
YEASTS native	
GRAPES 100% estate-grown	
CERTIFICATION organic	

INDEX of wineries

INDEX of places

OTHER RECOMMENDED PRODUCERS

Besides the 328 wineries reviewed here, we also recommend the following, all awarded with the coin or bottle symbols

Abruzzo and Molise

🍾 Cirelli *Atri (Te)*

€ Angelucci
Castiglione a Casauria (Pe)

€ Tenuta I Fauri *Chieti*

€ Costantini *Città Sant'Angelo (Pe)*

🍾 Dino Illuminati *Controguerra (Te)*

€ Tiberio *Cugnoli (Pe)*

🍾 Nicodemi *Notaresco (Te)*

€ Citra *Ortona (Ch)*

€ Cantina Frentana *Rocca San Giovanni (Ch)*

🍾 Masciarelli *San Martino sulla Marrucina (Ch)*

🍾 Feudo Antico *Tollo (Ch)*

€ Cantine Salvatore *Ururi (Cb)*

€ Italo Pietrantonj *Vittorito (Aq)*

Alto Adige

🍾 Ignaz Niedrist *Appiano/Eppan (Bz)*

🍾 Stroblhof *Appiano/Eppan (Bz)*

€ Glögglhof - Franz Gojer *Bolzano/ Bozen*

🍾 Waldgries - Christian Plattner
Bolzano/Bozen

🍾 Hartmann Donà
Cermes/Tscherms (Bz)

€ Cantina Valle Isarco *Chiusa/ Klausen (Bz)*

🍾 Tiefenbrunner - Castel Turmhof
Cortaccia/Kurtatsch (Bz)

€ H. Lun *Egna/Neumarkt (Bz)*

🍾 Cantina Nals Margreid
Nalles/Nals (Bz)

🍾 Falkenstein - Franz Pratzner
Naturno/Naturns (Bz)

🍾 Abbazia di Novacella
Varna/Vahrn (Bz)

🍾 Köfererhof - Günther
Kerschbaumer *Varna/Vahrn (Bz)*

🍾 Strasserhof - Hannes Baumgartner
Varna/Vahrn (Bz)

Campania

€ Fattoria Ciabrelli
Castelvenere (Bn)

🍾 Rocca del Principe *Lapio (Av)*

🍾 Quintodecimo
Mirabella Eclano (Av)

🍾 Salvatore Molettieri *Montemarano (Av)*

€ Antico Castello *San Mango sul Calore (Av)*

🍾 Ciro Picariello *Summonte (Av)*

🍾 Guido Marsella *Summonte (Av)*

€ Fontanavecchia *Torrecuso (Bn)*

€ Benito Ferrara *Tufo (Av)*

€ Torricino *Tufo (Av)*

🍾 Nanni Copè *Vitulazio (Ce)*

Emilia-Romagna

- Gianfranco Paltrinieri *Bomporto (Mo)*
- Costa Archi *Castel Bolognese (Ra)*
- € Casa Benna *Castell'Arquato (Pc)*
- € Cantina San Biagio Vecchio *Faenza (Ra)*
- Gallegati *Faenza (Ra)*
- € Tenuta Pertinello *Galeata (Fc)*
- € Baraccone *Ponte dell'Olio (Pc)*
- € Manaresi - Podere Bellavista *Zola Predosa (Bo)*

Friuli Venezia Giulia

- € Mulino delle Tolle *Bagnaria Arsa (Ud)*
- Villa Russiz *Capriva del Friuli (Go)*
- € Bortolusso *Carlino (Ud)*
- Colle Duga *Cormons (Go)*
- € Francesco Vosca *Cormons (Go)*
- Franco Toros *Cormons (Go)*
- € Maurizio Buzzinelli *Cormons (Go)*
- € Valentino Butussi *Corno di Rosazzo (Ud)*
- € Visintini *Corno di Rosazzo (Ud)*
- € Vigneti Le Monde *Prata di Pordenone (Pn)*
- € Ermacora *Premariacco (Ud)*
- Petrussa *Prepotto (Ud)*
- € Pizzulin *Prepotto (Ud)*
- € Castelvecchio *Sagrado (Go)*
- € Gradis'ciutta *San Floriano del Collio (Go)*
- Lis Neris *San Lorenzo Isontino (Go)*
- € Quinta della Luna *San Quirino (Pn)*

Lazio

- € Tenuta La Pazzaglia *Castiglione in Teverina (Vt)*
- De Sanctis *Frascati (Rm)*
- € Occhipinti *Gradoli (Vt)*
- € Donato Giangirolami *Latina*
- € Proietti *Olevano Romano (Rm)*

Liguria

- € Luigi Bianchi Carenzo *Diano San Pietro (Im)*
- Terre Bianche *Dolceacqua (Im)*
- VisAmoris *Imperia*
- Campogrande *Riomaggiore (Sp)*
- Possa *Riomaggiore (Sp)*
- Maccario Dringenberg *San Biagio della Cima (Im)*
- € Sancio *Spotorno (Sv)*

Lombardy

- Bosio *Corte Franca (Bs)*
- Guido Berlucchi & C. *Corte Franca (Bs)*
- Bellavista *Erbusco (Bs)*
- Ca' del Bosco *Erbusco (Bs)*
- Mamete Prevostini *Mese (So)*
- € Marangona *Pozzolengo (Bs)*

Marche

- € Tenuta Spinelli *Castignano (AP)*
- € Fiorano *Cossignano (Ap)*
- € Brunori *Jesi (An)*
- € Vicari *Morro d'Alba (An)*
- € San Filippo *Offida (Ap)*

Piedmont

- Albino Rocca *Barbaresco (Cn)*
- € Cascina Roccalini *Barbaresco (Cn)*
- € Giuseppe Cortese *Barbaresco (Cn)*

- Marchesi di Grésy *Barbaresco (Cn)*
- € Produttori del Barbaresco
  Barbaresco (Cn)
- Luciano Sandrone *Barolo (Cn)*
- € Ascheri *Bra (Cn)*
- Michele Chiarlo
  Calamandrana (At)
- Matteo Correggia *Canale (Cn)*
- Monchiero Carbone *Canale (Cn)*
- € Paolo Avezza *Canelli (At)*
- Luigi Tacchino
  Castelletto d'Orba (Al)
- Azelia *Castiglione Falletto (Cn)*
- Bricco Rocche - Bricco Asili
  Castiglione Falletto (Cn)
- Paolo Scavino
  Castiglione Falletto (Cn)
- € La Casaccia *Cella Monte (Al)*
- € Renzo Castella *Diano d'Alba (Cn)*
- Quinto Chionetti *Dogliani (Cn)*
- Giovanni Battista Gillardi
  Farigliano (Cn)
- Mario Marengo *La Morra (Cn)*
- € Borgo Maragliano *Loazzolo (At)*
- Giuseppe Mascarello e Figlio
  Monchiero (Cn)
- Domenico Clerico *Monforte d'Alba (Cn)*
- Giacomo Conterno *Monforte d'Alba (Cn)*
- € Giovanni Almondo
  Montà d'Alba (Cn)
- Bruno Giacosa *Neive (Cn)*
- € Erede di Armando Chiappone
  Nizza Monferrato (At)
- Luigi Pira *Serralunga d'Alba (Cn)*
- Massolino *Serralunga d'Alba (Cn)*
- € Rizzi *Treiso (Cn)*

Puglia

- € Sergio Botrugno *Brindisi (Br)*
- € Antica Enotria *Cerignola (Fg)*
- € Michele Biancardi *Cerignola (Fg)*
- L'Astore Masseria *Cutrofiano (Le)*
- Plantamura *Gioia del Colle (Ba)*
- € Alessandro Bonsegna *Nardò (Le)*
- Francesco Candido
  San Donaci (Br)
- € Cantina Ariano *San Severo (Fg)*
- € Casa Primis *Stornarella (Fg)*
- € Vetrere *Taranto*

Sardinia

- Fradiles *Atzara (Nu)*
- Giovanni Battista Columbu
  Bosa (Ot)
- Depperu *Luras (Ot)*
- € Cantina del Vermentino
  Monti (Ot)
- € Cantina Tani *Monti (Ss)*
- Agricola Punica *Santadi (Ci)*
- Cantina Santadi *Santadi (Ci)*
- Argiolas *Serdiana (Ca)*
- € Pala *Serdiana (Ca)*

Sicily

- € Cantine Valenti *Castiglione di Sicilia (Ct)*
- Barraco *Marsala (Tp)*
- Palari *Messina*
- € Centopassi *San Giuseppe Jato (Pa)*
- € Castellucci Miano *Valledolmo (Pa)*

Tuscany

- Tenuta dell'Ornellaia *Bolgheri (Li)*
- € Migliarina e Montozzi *Bucine (Ar)*
- Ca' Marcanda *Castagneto Carducci (Li)*

- Grattamacco
  Castagneto Carducci (Li)
- € Tenuta di Bibbiano *Castellina in Chianti (Si)*
- € Villa Pomona
  Castellina in Chianti (Si)
- Castell'in Villa *Castelnuovo Berardenga (Si)*
- € Castellinuzza e Piuca *Greve in Chianti (Fi)*
- € Casteldelpiano
  Licciana Nardi (Ms)
- € Fabbrica di San Martino *Lucca*
- Brunelli Le Chiuse di Sotto
  Montalcino (Si)
- € Caprili *Montalcino (Si)*
- € Fornacina *Montalcino (Si)*
- Talenti *Montalcino (Si)*
- Tenuta Le Potazzine
  Montalcino (Si)
- € Terre Nere *Montalcino (Si)*
- Contucci *Montepulciano (Si)*
- € Palazzo Vecchio
  Montepulciano (Si)
- € La Parrina *Orbetello (Gr)*
- € Santa Lucia *Orbetello (Gr)*
- € Fattoria San Donato *San Gimignano (Si)*
- € Fontaleoni *San Gimignano (Si)*
- € Il Colombaio di Santa Chiara *San Gimignano (Si)*
- € Russo *Suvereto (Li)*
- € Paterna
  Terranuova Bracciolini (Ar)

Trentino

- Tenuta San Leonardo *Avio (Tn)*
- € Bellaveder *Faedo (Tn)*

- € Rudi Vindimian *Lavis (Tn)*
- € Nicola Balter *Rovereto (Tn)*
- € Endrizzi
  San Michele all'Adige (Tn)

Umbria

- € Zanchi *Amelia (Tr)*
- € Di Filippo *Cannara (Pg)*
- Fratelli Pardi *Montefalco (Pg)*
- Romanelli *Montefalco (Pg)*

Veneto

- Vignalta *Arquà Petrarca (Pd)*
- Il Filò Delle Vigne *Baone (Pd)*
- € Il Mottolo *Baone (Pd)*
- Vignale di Cecilia *Baone (Pd)*
- € Costadoro *Bardolino (Vr)*
- € Bele Casel
  Caerano di San Marco (Tv)
- € Andreola *Farra di Soligo (Tv)*
- Allegrini *Fumane (Vr)*
- Monte Santoccio - Nicola Ferrari
  Fumane (Vr)
- € Vini Cris *Lonigo (Vi)*
- € Domenico Cavazza *Montebello Vicentino (Vi)*
- € Pegoraro *Mossano (Vi)*
- € Cantina Valpolicella Negrar
  Negrar (Vr)
- Giuseppe Quintarelli *Negrar (Vr)*
- € Albino Piona
  Sommacampagna (Vr)
- Cavalchina *Sommacampagna (Vr)*
- Ruggeri *Valdobbiadene (Tv)*
- € Frozza *Vidor (Tv)*
- Piovene Porto Godi *Villaga (Vi)*
- € Monteforche *Vò (Pd)*